The Tree and
the Canoe

Lee Boo of Belau: A Prince in London, by Daniel J. Peacock, 1987.
   Out of print.
Nuclear Playground, by Stewart Firth, 1987.
France and the South Pacific: A Contemporary History, by Stephen
   Henningham, 1992.
Cargo Cult: Strange Stories of Desire from Melanesia and Beyond,
   by Lamont Lindstrom, 1993.

The Tree and the Canoe

History and Ethnogeography of Tanna

JOËL BONNEMAISON

Translated and adapted by JOSÉE PÉNOT-DEMETRY

South Sea Books
Center for Pacific Islands Studies
School of Hawaiian, Asian & Pacific Studies
University of Hawaii

University of Hawaii Press, Honolulu

Originally published as *La dernière île*. © 1986 ARLEA/ORSTOM, Paris
English translation published by University of Hawaii Press 1994

Printed in the United States of America

99 98 97 96 95 94   5 4 3 2 1

Library of Congress Cataloging-in-Publication Data

Bonnemaison, Joël, 1940–
  [Dernière île. English]
  The tree and the canoe : history and ethnogeography of Tanna / Joël
Bonnemaison ; translated and adapted by Josée Pénot-Demetry.
      p.   cm. — (South Sea books)
  Includes bibliographical references (p.   ) and index.
  ISBN 0–8248–1525–4 (acid-free paper)
    1. Tanna (Vanuatuan people)—History.   2. Tanna (Vanuatuan
people)—Government relations.   3. Tanna (Vanuatuan people)—
Cultural assimilation.   4. Human geography—Vanuatu.   5. Vanuatu—
Discovery and exploration.   6. Vanuatu—History.   7. Vanuatu—
Social life and customs.   I. Pénot-Demetry, Josée.   II. Title.
III. Series.
DU760.B6713   1994
995.95—dc20   94–14319
                                                    CIP

ORSTOM Publication of this volume was supported in part by ORSTOM and the
French Ministry of Foreign Affairs.

Line drawings by Georges Kihm

Cartography by Manoa Mapworks, Inc., Honolulu, Hawaii

University of Hawaii Press books are printed on acid-free paper and meet
the guidelines for permanence and durability of the Council on Library
Resources

Designed by Kenneth Miyamoto

Editor's Note

Joël Bonnemaison's *The Tree and the Canoe* is the fifth title in the South Sea Books series published by the Center for Pacific Islands Studies, University of Hawaii, in association with the University of Hawaii Press. While the series is designed for the general reader with interests in the Pacific, this volume will also command the attention of a wide range of social scientists and historians.

The book is about the people and the Island of Tanna, one of the eighty-some islands that make up the Melanesian nation of Vanuatu in the southwestern Pacific. The archipelago was among the earliest to be discovered by Europeans, when the Spaniard Pedro Fernandes de Quiros came upon its shores in 1606. Over a century and a half were to elapse, however, before the islands were charted and called the New Hebrides by none other than Captain James Cook, the titan of all the European explorers.

The subsequent colonial history of the archipelago has been unique, troubled, and among the most fascinating in the region. The New Hebrides became a pawn in the European power struggle over the partitioning of the Pacific, and the islands were the last to experience formal colonial rule. An even three centuries after Quiros, in 1906, Britain and France jointly established the Anglo-French Condominium of the New Hebrides, the most bizarre colonial administration in the entire history of the Pacific. At its best, the arrangement was awkward, and in the end, it complicated the process of decolonization. Of all the Pacific nations that have achieved unfettered political independence, this was the last to regain its sovereignty: a new nation was born from chaos when the New Hebrides became Vanuatu in 1980.

A French cultural geographer, Bonnemaison has had extensive experience in the South Pacific. Between 1968 and 1981, he lived and worked in New Caledonia and Vanuatu. Bonnemaison now resides in Paris where he is a researcher with ORSTOM (Scientific Research Institute for Development in Cooperation). The work at hand is a translation and revised version of his *La dernière île,* a book based in part on his doctoral dissertation and first published by ARLEA-ORSTOM in 1986.

As this work makes clear, island societies are necessarily different from those of continents. As part of this difference and perhaps more than others, contemporary Pacific societies cannot be understood from the vantage point of any single academic discipline. Appropriately, Bonnemaison views his topic through multiple lenses, and he writes as an anthropologist, geographer, and historian. Moreover, and with the collaboration of his translator Josée Pénot-Demetry and the series' manuscript editor, Linley Chapman, Bonnemaison's work reads like a good piece of literature. A good story well told.

Bonnemaison anchors Tanna in the sea of Vanuatu's larger history. His analysis of the ethos of Tanna society is an eloquent exposition that raises questions about the fundamental nature of island societies in general. In Tanna, culture, society, and identity are rooted in the land, divisions of the land, and features of the landscape. Notions about time and space are about an eternal ordering of things that gives meaning to both past and present. These notions evoke comparisons with the Dreamtime of Australia's Aborigines.

One of the major themes of Bonnemaison's narrative is found in other analyses of contemporary Melanesian societies—the power or resilience of custom or (more commonly in the anthropological literature) *kastom.* The path or road of custom represented local autonomy, and in the face of external forces for change that threatened obliteration, the Tannese fought back by a reexamination, a reinvention, and a return to custom that has provided them with the strength to endure. The story of Tanna involves the well-known John Frum millenarian movement and has much to say about the problems of modern nation-building in the Pacific, especially Melanesia. Bonnemaison also suggests that certain elements of Tannese society and history may provide lessons for humankind's exploitation of and relationship with that ever-shrinking larger island, the planet Earth.

The Tree and the Canoe is complemented and enhanced by the most recent volume in the South Sea Books series, anthropologist Lamont Lindstrom's *Cargo Cult,* which draws heavily on Lindstrom's own research on Tanna.

ROBERT C. KISTE

Contents

Illustrations

ix

Following page   *182*

Kastom people in their village, southwest Tanna
Jonson Kowia
Tannese youngster with panpipe
Sand play
Tom Yopat in his yam garden
Yam mound with stakes
Toka dancers
Children watching *nao* dancers
Nao dance
Toka dancers selecting pigs
A yam *niel*
A dancing place decorated for a *niel*
Pigs and kava at a *niel*
Kiel and Noklam Niko
Niluan

Following page   *314*

Kastom supporters at Tanna's last Bastille Day celebration
Two irreconcilable viewpoints
John Frum drill, Ipeukel, 15 February 1978
Practicing the US military drill
The American flag floating over Ipeukel
Tom Mweles
Leaders of the John Frum movement
Willy Kuai
Two wise men
In the land of the "black crosses"

Translator's Note

A Study in Cultural Sustainability

> Geography . . . is about how human beings have created "homes" or "worlds" out of nature.
>
> YI-FU TUAN, *Morality and Imagination*

In this slightly revised version of geographer Joël Bonnemaison's *La dernière île,* the author writes about an Oceanic society whose cultural history is one of resoluteness and vitality—resolution and adventure—and, above all, unabated resilience. As a process of adaptation to change through continuity, resilience neither forgoes the past unnecessarily nor rejects established values. It allows for the melding of change and tradition and—in the specific case of Tanna, an island in southern Vanuatu—for the interplay of conquest and autonomy. How Tanna's inhabitants have shaped, enhanced, and managed this process of cultural sustainability is the subject of this book, which can also be read as an investigation into the nature of geographical consciousness.

The Tannese perceive space as a formidable constraint. Yet space and territory also provide them with the means of enriching their lives on many levels. To cope with insularity and separateness, Tanna's inhabitants have integrated the reverse concept of a barrier-free space into their spirituality. Furthermore, their sense of space explicitly anchors their identity and directly affects their daily existence. In Bonnemaison's words, a Tannese villager believes that his territory is "a live person, a political figure, a mediating agent between himself and the cosmos, and the link in a chain that connects him with his allies through the spatial dimension and with his ancestors through time" (1987, 72).

Not only is the Islanders' metaphysical, indeed mystical, traditional worldview rooted in the boundless, timeless "Great Space" of the island's origins, but the Great Space itself is a metaphor for the "inner space" of the mind. The Tannese seem to move easily in that environment, which seamlessly merges into their perception of outer space. Also mediated by space is their collective and personal identity as defined by Tanna's great myths, which delineate a geography of creation and, as the island's history progressed, have combined influences from the world at large. In the light of Tannese mythology, space is present before the inception of linear time, territory precedes the social order, and the social order finds its meaning in territory. Finally, Tannese customs and the traditional way of life *(kastom)* are affected by, and in turn directly affect, the island's spatial attributes. Warfare in particular epitomizes the mediating role of territory. In this respect, mysticism did not prevent or interfere with wars on the island. The proponents of Tannese *kastom* were never passive, politically naive mystics; they fought and survived.

The island of Tanna is not only associated with warfare as such, but more specifically with conflict—the dialectical processes that permeate Melanesian thought. In Tanna, these processes found a multifarious expression through history and mythology, as the reader will discover. The first part of this book is an overview of contact in the archipelago and its aftermath as outsiders fought for the inhabitants' souls and for labor, land, and other resources. In the second part, Tannese myths and traditional lifeways intertwine a number of major dialectical themes such as the Islanders' rootedness and mobility. The third and final part chronicles Tanna's tumultuous recent history. Throughout the book, great mythical and historical heroes emerge—some archetypal, and others entirely unique to the island.

In terms of its approach, this study stands as an example of the new French school of ethnogeography. The latter may be defined as the analysis of the interaction between a society and its spatial representations and interpretations. Thus the ethnogeographer endeavors to see through the eyes of the "other" and to investigate a vision of time and space other than that of his or her own society. Equally mindful of process and outcome, Bonnemaison acknowledges what he calls the Islanders' "search for meaning."

Here is a timeless story of tradition and change, conquest and autonomy, which the author tells in a voice that is both objective and personal. Particularly relevant for our time is that this story took place on an island where inhabitants, although faced with severe environmental and sociopolitical constraints and limitations, empowered themselves with a bold strategy of conservation. "Global citizens" are now becoming aware of limitations which they understand but cannot control. In this light, the experience and store of knowledge of Tanna Islanders provide a creative, compelling lesson in stewardship.

In many ways, a translation is an anthropological exercise—a process of re-creation from one language to another, a transfer of information from one culture to another. My field of study was *La dernière île*. Several people assisted in this endeavor. Jane Philibert reviewed the manuscript, and I am grateful for her suggestions; I also received helpful comments from Darrell Tryon. In Honolulu, Jane Eckelman's cartographic mastery and cordial cooperation were appreciated. Special thanks are due to Linley Chapman for her interest in this project and skillful and cheerful help.

During the journey of bringing this work to completion, Renée Heyum's loyal friendship and discerning advice encouraged me, and my husband Nicholas Demetry's own creative process, together with his wisdom and sense of humor, was invaluable.

Preface to the English Edition

Three centuries after the first landings of white navigators on the shores of Oceania, a Pacific island community was still brandishing the shield of *kastom* and claiming the right to live according to its own myths and beliefs. While everywhere in the Pacific newly independent states were in the process of modeling their structures on those of the western world, the island of Tanna dared to be shockingly different. The young Republic of Vanuatu had to send its police to master the situation. Unknown to the rest of the world, this violent, forced integration into modernity represented the last episode of a thought-provoking story marked by wars and tragedies.

Of all Pacific islands, Tanna is perhaps the most singular. Subjected to the strong-arm proselytism of missionaries and to the violence of nineteenth-century adventurers in the sandalwood and labor trades, summoned to abandon their culture, Tanna's pagans decided to initiate a philosophical counter-inquiry of their own. One pagan boarded a trade steamer at the turn of the century and went incognito to the "white world," which was then held as a model. On his return after several years, the man from Tanna advised his fellow Islanders to resist westernization with the following message: "White people themselves do not believe in what missionaries are saying."

Most Tannese adopted a position of cultural dissidence, which their descendants have maintained to this day. The adventure of Tanna's pagans illustrates the thrust of westernization onto traditional societies and the ensuing clash of cultures. From the Islanders' choice stems the modern history of Tanna, its cultural vitality, the budding of an astonishing millenarian movement called the cult of John Frum, and the final revolt at the time of independence.

For social scientists, writing represents a way to repay the debt owed to the community of which they were guests. Yet writing is all the more difficult as the theme is still a personal one. As an ORSTOM[1] cultural geographer whose purpose was to make a land tenure survey, I lived in Tanna—first in Imanaka, then in Loanatom, and finally in Lamlu— between 1978 and 1980, alternating with stays in Port Vila. On this island, vegetation is not as oppressive as in the northern part of the archipelago. Landscapes are open and tree ferns make up most of the thinned-out bush, which is interspersed with savanna woodlands and extensive grassland. Shaded grassy trails and hedges surrounding inland gardens under cultivation may give visitors the feeling of contemplating a grove in a temperate country. Along with the prevailing light and colors, harmonious landscapes evoke what has been called an "Austral Mediterranean land." Tanna is beautiful and fertile. Its relief, its dimensions, and even its volcano are consistently human sized. The Melanesian people that put down roots here created a vigorous, egalitarian society of peasants who like to question and challenge. Tanna is also an enchanted space—a space scattered with stones that carry magic powers, and immersed in the great origin myths of the Melanesian cosmogony.

What fascinated me most during my stays in Tanna was the quasi-magical word *kastom, kastom blong yumi* in local pidgin or Bislama— "our traditional Melanesian way of life." My purpose was not to judge or even analyze but to understand sympathetically and, as far as possible, to see through the Islanders' eyes. Yet can one really see through the eyes of others, especially when dealing with a people whose situation and culture are so distant from one's own? Generations of anthropologists, geographers, and historians have attempted it, some on this very island. Did they ever succeed? Have I?

The understanding of landscapes comes only through communion. In a brilliant article, *"Le paysage comme connivence,"* geographer Gilles Sautter wrote that "[f]rom a personal and cultural standpoint, to look at a landscape is to look at oneself to some extent" (1979, 41). The same concept applies to societies. In the human sciences, any genuine research based on fieldwork has an emotional, and therefore subjective, component. Researchers are more likely to perceive the truth of others when that truth is closer to their own or when it touches them personally. Besides, Tanna is such a strong island that it influences all who live there and commit themselves to it.

Through living with Islanders who followed *kastom* and wrapped the term in a mystique of its own, I had the feeling, be it right or wrong, that my commitment to them kept growing. It is not so much their "discourse" that interested me most, nor even the underlying ideology, but their world of representation, sensations, imagination, and dreams. I attempted to enter the mental universe of Tanna's inhabitants; I tried to understand the passions of this population, which sometimes led it to surprising attitudes, at least as far as western standards are concerned. I pushed my commitment to the limit. Step by step, I reached a state where measuring, counting, investigating, and asking questions looked increasingly derisive and even made me ill at ease.

To live with these people, join in their daily routines, walk on their trails for hours, drink kava (made from a plant whose chewed roots bring intoxication) with them, know every one of them, and live in this warm and complex society as one of its members—all this was enough for me. In such a perspective, I felt less like a scientist or a researcher. I lost the taste for being so, although I did not become an "indigenous" person or an "inhabitant." I was in this ambiguous and increasingly uncomfortable position when my research came to a forced stop: my situation necessitated my return to France and, further, clashes on the island were escalating into warfare. It would have been difficult to stay without openly choosing one side or the other. This book reflects that feeling of ambiguity to some extent. In its tone as well as its contents, it is at once a personal testimony and a scientific endeavor.[2]

In the final analysis, I believe that one can understand the restless people who live on the island only if one acknowledges the epic dimension at the heart of their worldview, and only if one shares, in one way or another, their sense of destiny, that is, the belief that the questions these people have been asking are also relevant to Europeans and Westerners. For, even though the message from Tanna is conveyed through images and metaphors that may be surprising, it tells us much about the meaning of human destiny and the "dialogue" of cultures. That message shows, if need be, that there is neither cultural "superiority" of one people over another, nor a basic heterogeneity among cultures. There are only uneven political balances of force and unequal historical situations that may temporarily prevent these cultures from communicating. The differences among peoples enrich the rainbow of cultures. In this text, I have tried to gather the various elements that can illuminate the truth of the people of Tanna.

Acknowledgments

I thank the Islanders who welcomed us, Martine and me, without stinting their hospitality and generosity: Noklam Assol, Noklam Posen, Noklam Niko (or Sip), Kooman, Yopat, Nako, Yalulu, Ya'uto, Pierre Yamak, Mikael Kapalu, Romain Nako, Maurice-Niluan, and Iolu Abbil, all of whom gave continuous support to my work.

I still think of the elderly *kastom* leader Niluan who received me so congenially in his village of Loanatom. He opened up the alleys of *kastom* to me and made me understand its depth and beauty. One evening, he aimed his gun at his heart and, with eyes closed, pulled the trigger. Turning down all food that would sustain his life, he died two months later. Life had become unbearable to him now that it no longer offered the meaningfulness and enchantment of traditional culture. When Niluan, weary of frequent quarrels, felt that *kastom* was leaving the land of Tanna and that his fellow villagers seemed to be breaking away from it, he decided to go as well, bequeathing us a message that lives on.

I also remember Alexis Yolou. We were friends. In the Islanders' memory, his death represents both the mark of deep sorrow and the sign of a tragic destiny.

The staffs of the French and British residencies in Port Vila generally extended a fine welcome. Special thanks are offered to Gérard Fabre, who was in charge of political matters for the French Residency in the early 1970s, and to Keith Woodward, his British counterpart. Their discernment and the interest they showed for the Melanesian civilization helped lift some of the obstacles and suspicions that Condominium status created in ample measure at the time.

Without being able to name each one individually—how can one make a list of the people met over a ten-year period?—I wish to thank all others, Europeans and Melanesians alike, settlers, missionaries, physicians, civil servants, teachers, inhabitants, met for a moment in time, on a bush trail, or while drinking kava over the space of an evening, all those who came in contact and showed interest in this work.

I salute my colleagues Monty Lindstrom and Julia Wilkinson, whom I met in the White Sands area of Tanna where they were carrying out fieldwork and whose works are remarkable, as well as Ron Adams, Ron Bastin, Ron Brunton, and Jeremy MacClancy, whose research also led them to Tanna, in remembrance of our friendly discussions in Canberra and Vila. This island left a profound mark on all of us.[1]

Among my fellow researchers in Vanuatu, I am indebted to Jean-Michel Charpentier (1979, 1982*a*, 1982*b*) for his ethnolinguistic work; Jean-Marc Philibert (1976, 1981) for his work on modernity in a suburban village on Efate; Margaret Rodman (1981, 1984) and William Rodman (1973) (Ambae); Robert Tonkinson (1968, 1982*a*, 1982*b*) (Ambrym); Darrell Tryon (1976, 1987); and my ORSTOM colleagues, Pierre Cabalion (1984*a*, 1984*b*) (Erromango and Pentecost), Bernard Vienne (1984) (Banks), and Annie Walter (in press) (Pentecost). Their works illuminated my research, even if they dealt with other islands, and their friendship and pleasant welcome sustained me. This book is preceded by Jean Guiart's pioneering work published in 1956: *Un siècle et demi de contacts culturels à Tanna (Nouvelles-Hébrides)*.

I also wish to thank Kirk Huffman, honorary director of the Vanuatu Cultural Center in Vila, who kindly lent me several photographs for this book.

In the course of my research work, a number of people provided help, in particular as they allowed me access to administrative or personal archives. On the French side, they included René Gauger and Jean-Jacques Robert, resident commissioners, as well as André Pouillet and Roger Payen, district agents in Tanna. Thanks to Jean Massias, I was able to gain access to the French archives of the Joint Naval Commission and to more recent documents. Maurice Tostain let me read his unpublished translation of de Leza's journal and Quiros's letters from Spanish to French. Thanks to the friendship of Father du Rumain, Monseigneur Julliard, and Monseigneur Lambert, I was able to use the archives of the Catholic mission in Vila. Many others, such as Gérard Leymang, offered spontaneous and informal help. I am grateful to all and keep them in my thoughts.

I extend my greetings to private surveyor Hubert Goron, who traveled from the island of Santo to Tanna to map traditional territories and *kastom* places with me. We had long wished to carry out a land survey of this type and had often discussed it beforehand.

Special thanks are due to Robert Kiste whose long-standing interest and support have allowed this book to be published.

Lastly, Josée Pénot-Demetry not only translated the text but also collaborated on it. She asked many questions, challenging me to be more precise in my thinking; she added comments and made numerous suggestions. *The Tree and the Canoe* is her work too. I warmly thank her for fully joining the cultural fight of the people of Tanna. The ultimate wish of the island's inhabitants, in particular that of John Frum partisans, was for their message to be known in the rest of the world—particularly in Big Land, the America of English speakers, which the Islanders also call *hammer iken* or "hammer country," another metaphor for the "country of technology." Thanks to Josée's deep sympathy, her work and talent, the dream of the Tannese is perhaps a step closer to realization, or at least acknowledgment.

Conventions

Language

The author transcribed vernacular words as he heard them in the field and as Tanna's Melanesians themselves write their own language. The translator did not modify that original spelling.

Lynch (1977, 1978) delineated three major linguistic areas: that of the northern and north-central part of the island, which includes the related dialects of North Tanna, White Sands, and Lenakel; that of south-central Tanna, comprising the related dialects of Nivhaal, Imreang, and Nivai; and the area south of Mt Tukosmera and Mt Melen, from Green Point to Port Resolution, where the Kwamera language is spoken (see map 4). Bislama is used as the lingua franca.

All words quoted in vernacular languages originate from the neighboring dialects of the western part of the island (Lenakel) and Middle Bush. When a term in another island dialect is introduced, its origin is stated. The vowel *u* is pronounced *oo* as in "shoe," *e* is pronounced as in "bet," and *g* is pronounced as in "glass"; occasionally, *g* is hardly distinguishable from *k*.

Unless otherwise noted, quotations originally in the English language appear as such in the text; all other quotations were translated from the French.

Maps

The maps in this book show several places that bear the same name because, according to the Tannese, two places may hold the same power and the same identity but be located in different territories. For example, Towermul (see map 7) is an evil spirit with two legs—one on each side of the island—and a heart—or a head—at Lepmol. Similarly, a modern-day village may be at a distance from a dancing place by the same name, as is the case, among others, of Yaneumwakel.

Only permanent streams are indicated on the maps. The location of Danket, based on data provided by local informants, is approximate.

PART ONE

THE INVADED ARCHIPELAGO

[I]t is much to be lamented that the voyages of Europeans cannot be performed without being fatal to the nations whom they visit.

FORSTER, *A Voyage Round the World . . .*

1 On the Path to Myth: Quiros's Great Voyage

> One should not judge the inhabitants of these regions in rela-
> tion to our own needs, our concerns, our greed, and our
> assessment of the value of things; they should be seen as men
> who endeavor to live with the least amount of toil, unlike us
> in our exhausting search for the superfluous.
>
> PEDRO-FERNANDEZ DE QUIROS,
> Eighth Petition to the King of Spain

The Spanish Saga

The Austral Land[1] was still a complete enigma after Magellan's journey from 1519 to 1521. According to Indian traditions, several islands to
the southwest of the American continent were the outposts of a larger
continent. In the course of a great westward voyage led by Tupac
Yupanki, the Incas were said to have discovered fabulous islands from
which they brought back black-skinned slaves and gold (Descola 1954).
The Spaniards, reinterpreting the Bible, thought this was the Land of
Ophir, the Old Testament source of King Solomon's gold.

Alvaro de Mendaña, a young man of twenty-five and nephew of the
viceroy of Peru, was sent to the Land of Ophir as leader of a new expedition. After eighty days at sea, Mendaña's fleet reached a group of islands
thenceforth called King Solomon's Islands. Rapport with the inhabitants,
who were unimaginatively called "Indians," rapidly turned sour; arquebuses answered the flights of arrows. New islands had been discovered,
but neither a continent nor gold. Yet numerous and pugnacious "dark
brown Indians" had been found: the first European image of Melanesia
became that of fierce "cannibalistic" warriors.

Although such results were not very encouraging, Mendaña organized a second expedition. Like many others, he thought that the discovery of the Solomon Islands presaged the great continent of the antipodes.
In 1595 he departed again. The certainty that Terra Australis existed was
such that the vessels took entire families to settle it. Beaglehole portrays
Mendaña as follows: "His bearing on the two voyages which he commands shows him to have been rather an idealist than a skilled navigator.
Yet, if he was no seaman, neither was he of the company of the great
adventurers, ruthless and unswerving in determination, the conquistadors who have carved out the Spanish empire in the West: there was in

3

him a gentleness and humanity, a feeling for the rights even of savages
and heathen" (1968, 42). The expedition reached the Santa Cruz Islands
southeast of the Solomons, but had a disastrous outcome. Decimated by
disease and besieged by Islanders who attacked them, the Spaniards were
not able to fulfill their dream of colonization. Many among them—
including Mendaña—died.

The pilot was a Portuguese who served Spain after the two crowns
merged—Pedro-Fernandez de Quiros, who was to provide the detailed
story of the expedition. Quiros's personality can only be understood in
the context of the extraordinary saga of Spanish endeavor in the southern
Pacific at the end of the sixteenth century. He experienced Mendaña's
failure, but showed brilliant navigational skills during the ordeal. Both
he and Mendaña were men marked by the spirit of the Catholic Counter-
Reformation.

Knights and Indians

After time-consuming canvassing in Lima and Madrid and a pilgrim-
age to Rome where he won the Pope's confidence, Quiros received a new
commission and the means to carry it out. On 21 December 1605, the
expedition left the port of Callao, Peru, with great ceremony. There were
three vessels in the fleet: the *San Pedro y San Pablo,* a sixty-ton ship, the
San Pedrico, a forty-ton vessel, and a smaller ship, *Los Tres Reyes de
Mayos,* which was a *zabra,* a small two-masted frigate. The crew of sailors and soldiers included about two hundred men, as well as six Francis-
cans and four nursing brothers from the order of St. John of God. Luis
Vaez de Torres, an experienced seaman, was second in command. The
expedition was under the patronage of Our Lady of Loreto and carried a
piece of the True Cross which Quiros had brought back from Rome.

"On that day," wrote the expedition pilot Gonzales de Leza, "with
our desire and our will to serve God, to spread our Catholic faith, and to
extend the royal crown of our lord the king, everything seemed easy
to us."[2]

Quiros's purpose was to go back to the Santa Cruz Islands, then
move on to the supposed shores of the "Austral Continent" and sail westward toward the Moluccas, thereby undertaking a circumnavigation that
would repeat the century-old exploit of Magellan by a more southerly
route.

In the instructions that he read aloud on the day of departure, Quiros
established a very strict moral code. Crew members were forbidden to
swear, blaspheme, fight, and play cards, dice, or games of chance; the
Salve Regina (Hail Mary) had to be recited while kneeling on deck every
evening. More significant still were Quiros's recommendations regarding

the expected behavior vis-à-vis Islanders. "Let it be noted very especially that the natives are to be loved as sons and feared as deadly enemies" (Munilla in Kelly 1966, 144–145). In other words, love and, just as much, mistrust. The Spaniards did affirm the evangelical dimension of their trip, but they knew that "contact" would be dangerous. One should "love" these natives, but with weapons in hand and "at a distance."

Quiros's other instructions were very detailed and indicated he had some experience in the matter, as de Leza wrote in his journal. The "Indians" deserved to be respected in all circumstances. Firearms were not to be used against them except in dire extremity, and then only to restrain, not destroy them. At anchor, the watch would be kept night and day. Quiros recommended guarding the buoys attached to the anchors because the "Indians" coveted them. The "natives" were to be received on board in small numbers and under armed surveillance. On land, it was forbidden to disperse, wander any distance away, or leave one's weapons unattended. One should try not to be encircled or surrounded, never turn one's back and, if need be, step back in orderly and gradual fashion. Quiros warned his men not to be alarmed by the natives' cries. He instructed the sailors to shoot either blank cartridges or skyward on first contact in order to intimidate them, then to seek their friendship. Lastly, should the situation turn sour, Quiros recommended holding the *cacique* 'leader' and keeping him hostage as long as necessary.

The voyage began on a calm sea where the monotony seemed endless. After fifty-two days at sea when only low-lying, inhospitable islands had been seen from afar, the expedition at last came across the first inhabited land. It was the Polynesian island of Hao in the Tuamotu archipelago (Quiros was to name it The Conversion of San Pablo). "Being close to the land, we saw people on the beach and our joy then doubled." The welcome was warm and friendly. The sailors who had gone ashore on the first boat were grasped in the midst of the surf, pressed from all sides, and kissed. "The one who appeared to be their leader took a green palm leaf and gave it to one of us as a token of peace, with a forceful demonstration of friendship, crossing his hands and never growing tired of holding our men in his arms," wrote de Leza (10 Feb 1606). Surrounded by their women and children, the Islanders, of their own accord, put their weapons down on the beach. The Spaniards in the first boat did likewise. After gorging themselves on coconuts, they gave away in exchange their shirts, their knives, everything they owned. The visitors were then invited to go inland to visit houses and eat their fill.

However, with neither anchorage for the vessels nor drinking water, the expedition could not linger and set out again on the evening of the second day, leaving both seamen and Islanders saddened by the departure. "All during the night, our men never ceased to talk about what they

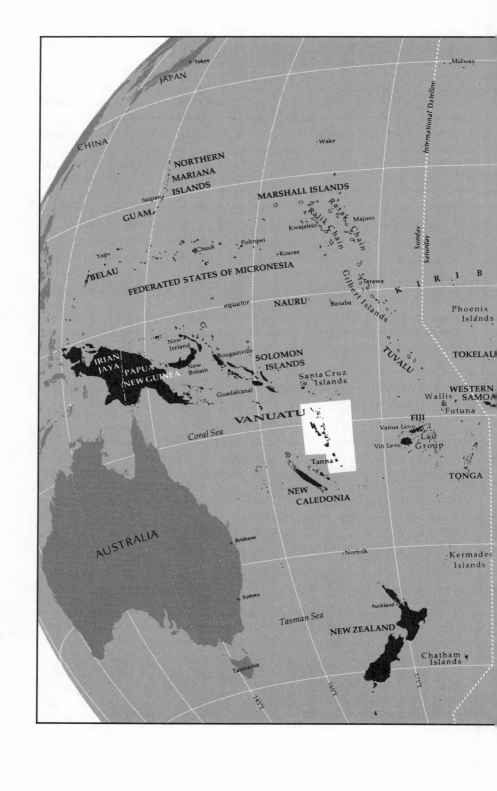

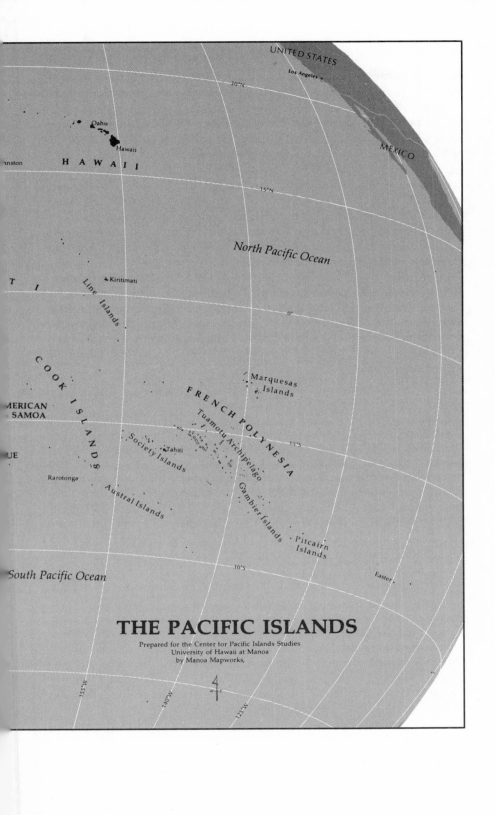

UNITED STATES

Los Angeles

30°N

MEXICO

Oahu

Hawaii

H A W A I I

nston

15°N

North Pacific Ocean

Kiritimati

T

Line Islands

0°

C
O
O
K

Marquesas
Islands

FRENCH POLYNESIA

MERICAN
SAMOA

15°S

I
S
L
A
N
D
S

Tuamotu Archipelago

Society Islands

Tahiti

Gambier Islands

Pitcairn
Islands

UE

Rarotonga

Austral Islands

30°S

South Pacific Ocean

Easter

THE PACIFIC ISLANDS

Prepared for the Center for Pacific Islands Studies
University of Hawaii at Manoa
by Manoa Mapworks,

135°W

120°W

105°W

had seen, being grateful to God for having them discover those islands
with the sea in their midst[3] and meet people of such pleasant disposition"
(11 Feb 1606).

At last, on 2 March, the *Los Tres Reyes* lookout announced new
land. The small island, low-lying and covered with coconut trees, would
be later identified as Rakahanga in the northern Cook Islands. There
again, numerous canoes moved close to the fleet. "The sight of us and of
our ships quite astonished them. In return, we were astounded to see men
who were so well proportioned and pleasant and we deplored their living
on such remote lands without having received the light of baptism." The
Spaniards admired the large Polynesian double outrigger canoes with
their woven sails. These canoes could be twenty meters long, two meters
wide, and hold nearly sixty people.

The long voyage continued westward. On board, brawls occurred,
and there was a desperate shortage of water. At the beginning of April
the precursory signs of land appeared. Finally, on 7 April, the outline of a
high island made up of two mountains was seen against the horizon. It
received the name Our Lady of Loreto. The Spaniards had reached the
Melanesian world. They were in fact cruising around the island of
Taumako, in the Santa Cruz archipelago.

Here the welcome was quite different: the Islanders showed neither
enthusiasm nor amazement, only great wariness. They had obviously
received the news of the events that had occurred eleven years earlier during Mendaña's expedition in the neighboring islands. When the first
boats approached, the men grouped on the beach were armed; they had
hidden wives and children and put their most precious goods in a safe
place. Astonishingly, at first contact they motioned the Spaniards not to
be afraid and not to threaten them with their arquebuses. "We were very
glad we had found such a pleasant people," de Leza noted (10 April
1606). "We noticed they were well-built, bearded, and very intelligent.
. . . Their leader has a loud voice and through gestures told us to keep
calm, adding that there was water and that he would give us some." This
leader, by the name of Tumai, cleverly intervened between his people and
the foreigners to prevent any clash. He tried his best to satisfy all the
white men's requests while constantly watching their slightest moves.
Perhaps he feared an attempt at colonization and at a settlement by force
as had been the case in Santa Cruz. According to Munilla, Tumai asked
Quiros how long the foreigners intended to stay on his island. When
Quiros indicated that they would not stay beyond five days, the Melanesian chief seemed extremely satisfied. In fact the fleet stayed at Taumako
for eight days, and Tumai became anxious when he realized that the
announced time of departure had not been respected.

The Spaniards' sojourn on Taumako was darkened in the end by

Quiros's order to capture several Islanders. On the eve of departure, without the knowledge of the rest of the population, Torres seized four men, who had to be chained because of their stiff resistance. Two of them successfully escaped during the night. The Spaniards were certain they were acting in the best interest of those they had abducted, because they were going to give the prisoners a higher level of civilization and the light of Christian baptism. Besides, they thought they could learn the island language from the abducted Islanders and use them as guides, interpreters, and ambassadors.

Quiros noted some of Chief Tumai's characteristics:

Tumai is a man of reason, of handsome stature, with a thin nose, long and wooly beard and hair, and, in his own way, a serious demeanor. He came to see us on board and I asked him questions: first I showed him his island, the sea, our ships, and our men, then I indicated all the points on the horizon and made other signs to ask whether he had already seen ships and men like ours. To this, he answered no.

I asked him if he knew anything about other lands, close or remote, peopled or not; as soon as he understood me, he quoted the names of over seventy islands and of a mainland he called Manicolo.[4] As to myself, Sire, I wrote down everything with the help of the compass to know their location: they are situated to the SE, SSE, W and NE of his island respectively. To make me understand that there were small and large islands, he made smaller or larger circles. To speak of the mainland, he opened his arms wide without closing them, to show it was beyond his comprehension. To indicate their remoteness, he showed the sun's trajectory from the Orient to the Occident, placed his head on one of his hands, closed his eyes, and counted the nights of sleep during the trip on his fingers. Likewise, he told me whether their residents were white, black, indian or mulatto, whether they were of mixed race, and whether they were friends or foes. He added that on some islands, human flesh was eaten and to make me understand this, he pretended to bite his arm while showing aversion to that people. Thus all his mimicry was understood. I had him repeat all of this so many times that he became somewhat weary. As he wished to go, I gave him a few objects and he took leave by giving me a kiss of peace on the cheek, followed by other marks of friendship. (Quiros, report of 1609, in Tostain)

De Leza and his companions shared Quiros's sentiment about Tumai: "Telling about the good qualities of this chief would be endless, for never in a barbarian had one found the common sense this one had" (12 April 1606).

The evocation of a neighboring "mainland" interested the Spaniards most. As their vessels headed south, they encountered many islands: first Tikopia[5] and eventually the Banks Islands in northern Vanuatu.

Gaua, which Torres called Santa Maria, was the first island where the Spaniards attempted contact again. After the vessels appeared, a throng filled the beach within a few hours. The men who had been sent to search for an anchorage dared not disembark from their boat in the presence of such a crowd. Showing neither fear nor aggressiveness, the Islanders swam toward the flagship. Two of the swimmers were raised on board.

> Their beard and hair were cut, which pleased them immensely, then they were clothed, given hats and other trinkets such as bells, and led back to land by the same men who had brought them. . . . Then a large number of men and women jumped into the water with presents for us: bananas and other fruit, which are plentiful on their island; they also gave us a large-sized pig. Their friendliness was such that they dared come aboard with their children in their arms: they were showing them to us and our men were taking them in their arms and kissing them, to their great joy. . . . We stayed at anchor for about four hours and saw a countless number of residents. One should note that no one from the other tribe dared go to this [area]; indeed the island was divided in half and under the rule of two chiefs. Each [inhabitant] has boundaries that he cannot cross. (29 April 1606)

The flagship sailed around the island the following day. People were gathered in each cove, motioning the navigators to go to them. The Spaniards were considerably impressed with so warm a welcome; however, they feared that, should they disembark, they could not master the situation. In contrast with Taumako, the local people had apparently no knowledge of Westerners. As de Leza noted, a strict territorial division seemed to prevail. Each group occupied a cove or part of a beach, but could not go beyond an invisible boundary. They were calling the navigators toward their own territory and were greatly annoyed to see the visitors go away to meet other groups.

To the south of Gaua, the horizon was scattered with new islands. On the next day, a great range of mountains appeared in the distance and the ever-hopeful expedition steered that way. On the evening of 30 April, de Leza wrote in his journal: "The entire land we are seeing is wide and very high, it can only be the mainland, God willing."

On the first day of May 1606, the vessels sailed into a large bay,[6] which was named Bay of St. Philip and St. James. According to de Leza, "it is of very wide extent and pleasant to see: all the fleets in the world could go into it without the least concern. . . . Because of such splendor, our general decided to anchor there" (1 May 1606).

Quiros did not doubt that he had found the great antipodean continent, and the largest and richest land ever discovered by the Spaniards. All accounts emphasize its beauty.

One could see a vast forested plain and, farther on, powerful moun-

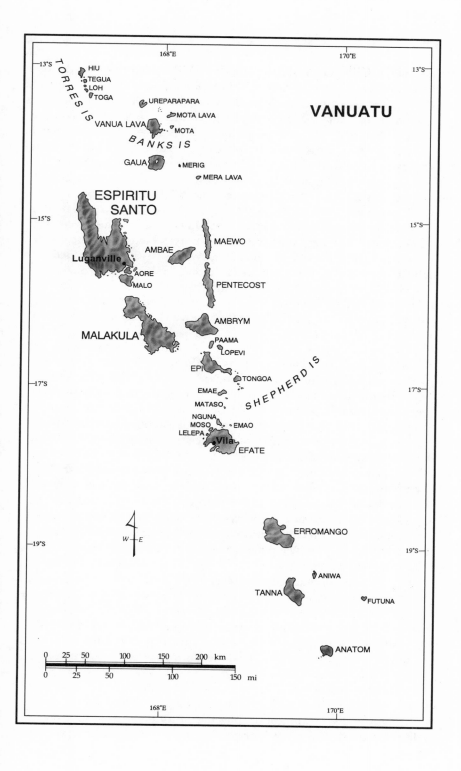

VANUATU

13°S — 13°S

TORRES IS

HIU
TEGUA
LOH
TOGA

UREPARAPARA

MOTA LAVA

VANUA LAVA
MOTA

BANKS IS

GAUA
MERIG

MERA LAVA

ESPIRITU
SANTO

15°S — 15°S

MAEWO

AMBAE

Luganville
AORE
MALO

PENTECOST

AMBRYM

MALAKULA
PAAMA
LOPEVI

EPI
TONGOA
SHEPHERD IS

17°S — 17°S
EMAE
MATASO

NGUNA
MOSO
EMAO
LELEPA
Vila
EFATE

W — E

ERROMANGO

19°S — 19°S

ANIWA

TANNA
FUTUNA

ANATOM

0   25   50   100   150   200   km

0   25   50   100   150   mi

168°E   170°E

tain spurs. In the center of this plain flowed a braided river, "wider than the Guadalquivir River in Seville."[7] The climate, cool at that season and pleasant, appealed to the Spaniards. On land, the leaves of numerous coconut palms were waving, and songs of many bird species could be heard. "There is no region as beautiful as this in America and very few in Europe," wrote Quiros. Already, however, a growing number of islanders was flocking to the beach. The Spaniards were to dislike the inhabitants as much as they were to delight in the country. It seemed that the die was cast in the first moments of contact. A boat was put into the water. It moved close to shore in order to look for an anchorage but could not find one, so deep was the bay. On land, armed men were waiting along with children, probably "to mislead us better as to their actual intentions," wrote the old friar Munilla, ever distrustful of "heathens" (in Kelly 1966, 185). A few yards from shore, from either side of the surf, Spaniards and "Indians" eyed one another. The first impression was unfavorable in both camps. Shortly thereafter, the boat backed up while arrows flew at it. Arquebuses were shot skyward; at the noise, the people on the beach fled for cover.

Thinking it more advisable to land in force, the Spaniards first looked for a harbor where anchors could reach bottom. Three days elapsed. During that time, on the beaches, hundreds of men did not take their eyes off them. However, no outrigger canoe ever went out to the fleet as had been the case in the Polynesian atolls. At night, the beach was lit by many fires and reverberated to the noise of chants and dances, mingled with the sound of instruments such as "horns, drums, and something that sounded like sleigh bells" (3 May 1606).[8]

A fairly satisfactory anchorage was eventually found in the bay's eastern corner, in a spot that Quiros was to name El Puerto de Vera Cruz, at the mouth of a small river with clear water that was called El Salvador.[9] During the next two days, both sides came in contact several times. Again, Spanish craft followed the shoreline. The "Indians" moved closer. The seamen threw a red taffeta shirt to a man who appeared to be a *cacique*. Undecided, he did not know what to do with it, so two unarmed Spaniards jumped ashore and helped him put the shirt on. Everything went smoothly from then on. The two sailors, grasped by vigorous arms, were kissed and plied with fruit and bunches of bananas. In sign language the Spaniards asked the "Indians" to lay down their weapons, which they did without any difficulty. Some Islanders then fetched pigs to give to the strangers; the word *poes* 'pig' was the first that the Spaniards learned.

Suddenly arquebuses were shot from the ships to recall the crew members involved in a careless adventure on land. They went back but, to the natives' dismay, forgot the pigs meant for them. Undoubtedly, the right opportunity was missed for good that day. The next few days were spent exploring the shoreline by boat. A landing was out of the question. De Leza wrote that "the residents rushing to the beaches to see us were so numerous that they covered the ground. The mountains themselves were inhabited" (8 May 1606).

The Confrontation

This first face-to-face meeting, a wavering encounter, became tragic on 9 May. On that day, Quiros decided to take symbolic possession of the land and, to that end, sent Torres ashore at the head of seventy armed men. An energetic and tough Galician, Torres thought he had to show his strength to be respected by the Islanders.

When the Spaniards disembarked from their boats, the hundreds of surrounding "Indians" did not oppose their landing. The two sides observed one another tensely but also with much curiosity. Once on the beach, the sailors set up a large cross and cut branches nearby in order to build a temporary shelter, which was then covered with canvas. Groups of warriors, visibly worried, drew nearer in close ranks while many others, brandishing their bows, hid in the surrounding bush. Torres's men were anxious—the drumming as well as the cries, warlike dances, and agressive gestures on the part of the Melanesians made them nervous. Eventually, three men walked toward the Spaniards, obviously wishing to negotiate. One was tall and the apparent chief. Next to him were two other men, "elderly and grizzled," de Leza said. A few yards from the Spaniards, the delegation stopped and hesitated. Torres went to meet them and motioned them to move still closer. A dialogue began by way of gestures. To the Spaniards' astonishment the three men drew a line on the sand, indicating that it could not be crossed by the seamen, then signaled that they would lay their weapons on the ground if their opposites did likewise. Torres refused. Later he was to write in his report to the king that such insolence on the part of the "Indians" was unacceptable. Confrontation became inevitable.

As the warriors' threatening circle tightened around the Spaniards, Torres motioned the "Indians" to leave. Behind him, sailors and soldiers were now aiming at the "savages," who started to retreat slowly while dancing and shouting. An arrow had yet to fly when Torres signaled his men to shoot. "Their audacity was too great," de Leza wrote by way of explanation. One "Indian" was killed, a few others were wounded and crawled toward shelter. Neither the chief nor his advisors were hit. The Spaniards did not seek a massacre but wanted to demonstrate their strength: most of them fired into the air. At point-blank range the Melanesians' losses would otherwise have been very heavy. Yet this first casualty put an end to Quiros's hopes for peaceful conquest.

Deafened by the detonations, the "savages" retreated into the bush in confusion. By way of a warning, the dead warrior's body was hung by one foot from a tree; it looked like a lugubrious and symbolic flag near the cross raised by the Spaniards. Quiros had heard the gunshots from the flagship and, in a commotion, sent a boat. The order was for Torres's party to go back on board. It was unfortunately too late as groups of "Indians" reappeared and shot with their bows at the soldiers, who retaliated with their arquebuses. Munilla wrote that the chief who had appeared at the beginning of the drama walked alone toward the Spaniards while a great silence fell on the beach. He asked to retrieve the corpse hanging from the branches. The Spaniards agreed but warned him with much gesturing that the man's fate would be that of all who did not show them respect. After removing the body, the chief and two of his companions saw for themselves that the man was dead then took him back "in great distress" (Munilla in Kelly 1966, 212). Everything was over, it was thought, but suddenly renewed shouting erupted. A delegation approached once again and asked to negotiate with signs of peace. When Torres, surrounded by a few of his men, advanced in turn, some warriors jumped out of the bushes. The fighting, now generalized, rekindled. On both sides, violence had prevailed. The "Indian" chief was killed, other "Indians" were wounded; most warriors fled. Only blood remained on the sand.

Abandoning the bodies of their victims, the Spaniards destroyed the shelter where they had intended to spend the night and went back on board. The news of the confrontation overwhelmed Quiros. In the eyes of the navigators, the magical charm which had hung over this land was broken forever. They were hardly proud of their "victory." In his diary, Munilla noted that "our men . . . regretted having to do this because by this time their blood was up. But they obeyed their general" (in Kelly 1966, 213).

After that fateful day, the beaches of the "Great Bay" were empty and not a single "Indian" reappeared. Every day, the Spaniards disembarked and walked inland; the people fled ahead of them. Convinced that they now had to deal with enemies, the Spaniards no longer restrained themselves from taking the property of the "Indians." In any case they had to take on fresh supplies of water and wood, and they had lost any opportunity of getting fresh food unless they stole it. De Leza participated in one of these raids on 10 May. Half a league from the coast, the Spaniards discovered a beautiful village abundant with fruit trees; apparently it had just been abandoned. Numerous animals ran around: pigs, hens, and roosters "similar to those in Spain." Protected by reed fences, the low-lying huts were filled with yams of all sizes, methodically lined up on wooden trays as a protection against damp. Some yams were bulky: "There was a yam root so large that one man alone could not manage it"

(Munilla in Kelly 1966, 213). On the ground lay dishes of carved wood and numerous pots. The Spaniards helped themselves to these goods; as one of them noted, apparently without irony, "nobody was there to prevent us from doing so" (10 May 1606).[10]

The New Jerusalem

Quiros was living in a dream. This land was less reality than fantasy; it haunted him but he was in no hurry to explore it. Such behavior did not escape the notice of his men who increasingly considered their general to be half insane and mistrusted his orders. Their attitude was to contribute to the expedition's final outcome.

On the eve of Pentecost, Quiros met with officers and men of God. His purpose was to set up a town council for the "New Jerusalem" that he intended to build. A new order was also created on that day, the "Knights of the Holy Spirit," to which all expedition members were to belong without exception, and which was to be called on to colonize the "Austral Land" and to evangelize and "protect" the "Indians." The order's symbol was a cross in blue taffeta sewn on every man's chest—with the size of the cross in proportion to the knight's hierarchical position. This last idea was not well received, particularly by the Franciscan brothers who saw "unreasonableness and vanity" in it. Quiros insisted. On the beach, the Spaniards built a temporary chapel with trunks and branches; banana leaves covered the inner walls. On 14 May, at dawn, all expedition members were ashore. In de Leza's words:

> On Pentecost day, army officers disembarked with their men and set up posts on paths and other spots where the enemy might appear. Then our general went ashore with a seven-span-long cross which had been made according to his order. . . . As soon as they landed, our chaplain and the other friars came to welcome them; shoeless, they received the cross and, singing hymns and in deep contemplation, transported it to the church. There the general took it and with tears in his eyes placed it on the altar. The infantry fired all their arquebuses and the flag-bearers lowered their banners. (14 May 1606)

In a long speech, Quiros asserted that he was taking possession of this land and all those between it and the South Pole in the name of Pope Clement VIII and the King of Spain, Philip III. This land was baptized "Terra Austrialis del Espiritu Santo and this for ever."[11]

Shortly after Mass, Quiros named the major officials and advisors to the new city. Thirty-four posts were assigned and the officeholders sworn in. On the same day, two black slaves who were working on board as kitchen helpers were freed and made knights of the new Order of the

Holy Spirit. Munilla sarcastically noted that "[i]t was a marvellous thing to see such diversity of knights, for truly nothing like it has ever been seen since the world began, because here there were sailor-knights, grummet-knights, ship's page-knights, mulatto-knights and negro-knights and indian-knights and knights who were knights-knights"[12] (in Kelly 1966, 223). Pedro, the last prisoner from Taumako, also became a knight.[13]

Last Contact

The Spaniards went on more forays. On 17 May, Torres led a group far inland. They climbed a very steep slope up to the plateau now bearing the name of Cape Quiros, above the present village of Matantas. The vastly forested region seemed completely uninhabited. Upon hearing chants and seeing smoke, some men climbed to the top of tall trees to gain a vantage point. Soon they found a path, then a village which they invaded. Taken by surprise, the residents had not had the time to hide their belongings. The new "knights of the Holy Spirit" drove out about fifty tethered pigs, then several women and children who had taken refuge in the dark recesses of huts. De Leza wrote wistfully that "we had captured several women—beautiful in the extreme—whom we released, because our general did not want even one woman aboard our ships" (17 May 1606).

The Spaniards went back, taking with them fifteen handsome pigs—the largest they had found—and three young boys, the eldest of whom was less than eight. But the "Indians" had returned and were now on their heels, attacking them in force. Three hundred opponents kept harassing the Spanish column. "We fought with great merit on that day," wrote de Leza. One sailor was wounded by stones thrown at him, and the Spaniards encountered considerable difficulty on the steep slope going down to the beach. When, exhausted, they finally reached the Spanish camp, their pursuers ceased to attack them.

In all these expeditions, Pedro, the Taumako captive and recently appointed "knight of the Holy Spirit," joined the navigators' cause and actively participated in their undertakings. He did not seem to appreciate the people of Big Bay whom he perceived as total strangers. To the Spaniards who were beginning to understand him, Pedro confided that he did not hail from Taumako but from "Chikayana" (actually Sikaiana in the Solomon Islands). A captive of chief Tumai, he had become his servant. This was probably why he had not tried to run away from the Spaniards.

There was now open warfare between navigators and Melanesians. On 19 May, during a fishing trip on the river of Matantas (El Salvador), soldiers were ambushed a few yards from shore and could only get away after shooting. Quiros, watching from the ship, had a naval gun fired in order to extricate his men. The previous evening, "great earthquakes" had occurred; in de Leza's words, "we felt them on board as if our ships were smashing onto a reef."

Corpus Christi was celebrated on Sunday 25 May with great pomp; a formal mass and a procession took place under the protection of naval guns. Clothed in silk and with bells tied to their feet, the crew danced and sang to the sound of flutes, drums, and guitars until late in the afternoon. All were very moved. Weariness and homesickness were starting to affect the members of the expedition. That very night, on board, Quiros met his officers and told them of his intention to leave the Bay of St. Philip and St. James the next day and continue exploration to the south. His vision of long-lasting colonization had vanished in the face of the hostility of the "Indians."

Quiros's decision was welcomed by most expedition members, who were tired of going further inland day after day in order to find food on increasingly dangerous forays. Yet, furious to have been led into what looked like a blind alley, some officers were seen talking violently to their general. The Knight of Prado criticized Quiros: "You would give us so much gold and silver that we could not carry it, and the pearls should be measured by hatfuls. . . . We have found only the black devils with poisoned arrows; what has become of the riches? . . . All your affairs are imaginary and have gone off in the winds" (in Spate 1979, 137).

Quiros had no reaction, seemingly overcome by a nervous breakdown. On the following day the departure was postponed because of fish poisoning.[14] This enforced rest meant that all crew members had to stay on board, in what looked "like the hospital of a town touched by the plague" (30 May 1606).

Meanwhile, the Melanesians, who had continuously watched the visitors' whereabouts, became bolder and, step by step, took possession of the shoreline. On the morning of 31 May, while the Spaniards were recovering, a group of about three hundred armed men appeared on the beach and invited the seamen to join them. Was it a peace overture? Quiros was certain that the behavior of the "Indians" stemmed from their worry about the three boys who had disappeared. He sent a boat with the children; a second launch followed, under the command of Torres himself. When they saw Torres, whom they had identified as the foreigners' war leader, the Melanesians moved into their fighting positions. Under Torres's order, a gun was fired skyward in order to clear the beach. Then the Spaniard went ashore and invited the "Indians" to approach. None accepted, and an odd dialogue was initiated at a distance.

The oldest boy was crying and calling to his father who hesitated, then moved closer. Separated by a few yards, father and son started talking. The man asked about the fate of the other two children; eventually the oldest captive pointed them out, next to their guards. The boy's father also enquired about the way they were treated and seemed reassured. After the child told him that they would be liberated for a price of pigs and hens, the man walked away, motioning that he intended to return.

Two hours later, the Spaniards, who were back on their ships, saw several Melanesians tie a pig on the beach. A sailor jumped into the water and brought the animal back. An animated discussion followed: Quiros wanted to keep the children whatever the price offered, but his men were thinking of the length of the voyage to come and wished to take advantage of the situation to lay in provisions. Quiros's answer to the captive children who were beginning to cry was: "Silence, child! You know not what you ask. Greater benefits than the sight of and dealings with heathen parents and friends await you!" (in Markham 1904, 14: 276–277).

The next morning, the Melanesians offered two other pigs and, in exchange, the sailors tied one male and one female goat on the beach. First intrigued, then amused by these unknown animals, the Islanders considered themselves shortchanged by the exchange. After much calling and shouting, the crowd forced the Spaniards to recover the unwanted animals.

According to Quiros's account, the two youngest children were returned on the day of departure. The eldest sailed back to Mexico along with Pedro, the man from the Solomons. The two captives were baptized on the return voyage when a strong storm endangered the ship, with Quiros as their godfather—for a brief time only, as they died shortly after their arrival in the New World. In one of his letters, Quiros evoked at length the child he had adopted, being certain that he had acted for the boy's good. "All that knew him loved him as he was very docile and pleasant. Like Pedro, he said the four prayers and crossed himself with obvious joy. . . . He would tell us of a great river near his village, adding that in his country there are numerous warlike tribes that are enemies of one another but do not eat human flesh. . . . As he was a child and in poor health, we were not able to find out everything we wanted to know from him" (Quiros report, 1609).

On 8 June, after thirty-six days spent in Big Bay, the Spaniards sailed away forever. They wanted to continue to the southwest, but encountered a heavy sea and strong contrary winds. Two vessels sailed back to the bay during the night, in constant danger of being driven ashore, while the *San Pedro y San Pablo,* under Quiros's command, made leeway without sighting the anchorage. In the morning, Quiros's crew realized that they had been driven out beyond the bay, out of sight of land. The flagship's return voyage to Mexico took a very long time, and some officers, such as Iturbe, did not accept that the exploration was over. Quiros said he was sick and did not leave the berth in his cabin. The *San Pedro y San Pablo* reached the port of Acapulco, Mexico, on 23 November 1606.[15]

Torres waited in the bay for fifteen days while searching for possible traces of a wreck along the shoreline. Then, considering that he had been wrongfully abandoned, he opened the sealed orders delivered by the viceroy in case of disappearance of the flagship. The orders stipulated that they should search for a southern route to India. Torres decided not to question these orders. He was to write in his report to the king that, in spite of the inclination of the majority, he did so "for my temper was different from that of Captain Pedro-Fernandez de Quiros" (in Spate 1979, 139).

Torres sailed down the west coast of Espiritu Santo to the latitude of twenty-one degrees south. As no more land was in sight, he began his return voyage. It is not known whether he landed in or saw the real Australia, yet his discovery of the strait to which his name has been given represented a giant step in geographical knowledge.[16] Torres eventually reached Manila on 22 May 1607, one year after leaving the Big Bay of Espiritu Santo (Hilder 1976).

A Garden of Eden

Having set out in search of a utopian land, Quiros journeyed back convinced of its existence. According to him, the land he had discovered was indeed Terra Australis Incognita, and in his eyes it was adorned with fabulous characteristics and riches. However, the Spaniards had not been able to gain the trust of the "Indians," and therefore the expedition was not entirely successful.

Quiros himself was responsible for this failure. He had given his orders from afar, from his own bed, leaving the task of "making contact" to Torres who, though not a bloodthirsty man, attached more importance to the safety of his own men than to anything else. A surprise attack by determined "Indians" could have eliminated all soldiers and sailors ashore. This fear of close combat explains why the Spaniards had always kept the "Indians" at a distance, avoiding any genuine exchange and not hesitating to shoot when they moved closer.

Everything in the Melanesians' attitude baffled the Spaniards, who had a hierarchy, while the Melanesians seemed to have none. Each community—as in Gaua—had its own territory but no specific leader. At times, a spokesman with no great authority would walk toward the visitors and then go back to his people to discuss what to do. Each warrior acted on his own; some were friendly, others belligerent. Around the

Spaniards, groups danced and gestured, each group seeking to establish contact with the navigators for itself. Further, the boundary that the people of Big Bay drew on the sand was the very symbol of mutual misunderstanding. The Melanesians were thereby marking their sovereignty; the Spaniards saw only arrogance.

Had trust been created in the first phase of contact, it could only have been precarious. After several months of sailing, the navigators had an urgent need for fresh supplies, but their demands were too heavy, given the resources of small fragmented societies whose food surpluses were strictly rationed to human and ritual needs. Inversely, what the Spaniards could offer held no interest for the Melanesians, who did not understand the advantages of iron and were indifferent to colorful clothes since they lived naked. Likewise, no Spanish goat was worth a local pig to the Islanders. In the absence of transactions that would satisfy both sides, the Spaniards, convinced of their superiority, helped themselves in good conscience—believing they were in a bountiful garden. In fact, they had landed in May, right after the great harvest of yams, which were then stored on trays; that month also represented the beginning of the great ritual cycles of food exchange among allies and the time for sacrificing the best pigs.

Quiros gave a pious image of the residents of the "Land of the Holy Spirit": they were heathens who were waiting for the light of Christian salvation to attain civilization. But one of his knights, Prado, only saw insolent "black devils" (in Kelly 1966, 87). In a restrained style, Torres made no value judgment and regretted having to open fire on them. He wrote: "The natives did not at any time wish to make peace with us and though we frequently conversed together and I made them presents, never with their goodwill did I set foot on shore" (in Kelly 1966, 87). De Leza spoke of the "Indians" with astonishment and some objectivity, without despising them. Finally Munilla, the old Franciscan friar, was moved by the dances and the drums but assumed that "[t]hese black [people] must spend all their time dancing" and come together for "orgies" (in Kelly 1966, 229).

The Spaniards' accounts shed some light on Melanesian society and its landscapes. The navigators were struck by the absence of large villages and the apparent lack of social organization: "No organised settlement was to be seen. All the villages and dwellings were isolated, we might say, twenty dwellings here, and ten there, in one part only were fifty found. The whole country was in this way covered with settlements, the inhabitants being exceedingly numerous because, in the limited part we did see,[17] there must have been more than two thousand huts disposed thus" (Munilla in Kelly 1966, 229). In his petition to King Philip

III, Quiros, for his part, painted a picture that was as idyllic as it was detailed and interesting:

> This unknown region represents one-fourth of the globe and could contain twice as many kingdoms and provinces as Your Majesty owns today. And all this without having to fear neighbors such as the Turks, the Moors, and other nations that are accustomed to harass and attack others.[18] . . . The nations peopling this region are many: the color of some is pale, others are brown, mulatto- or indian-like, or else of mixed blood. . . . All these indifferences [sic] reveal their commerce and their communication. . . . They seem to have neither defense works nor ramparts, no organized army, and neither king nor laws. They are simple peoples divided into rival factions. Their weapons are usually poisonless bows and arrows, clubs, sticks, spears, and casting weapons made of wood. These men cover their private parts, they are clean and joyful, they can reason and are grateful, as I have experienced it myself. . . . They will be easy to pacify, indoctrinate, and satisfy.
>
> Their houses are built of wood and roofed with palms. They use clay vessels, . . . make flutes and drums. . . . Their crops are carefully tended and fenced in. They make much use of mother-of-pearl shells which they turn into wood chisels, fishhooks, and many types of neckwear. These islanders own well-made boats that can go from one island to the next. An outstanding characteristic is that they know how to castrate pigs and turn roosters into capons. . . .
>
> The easiness and attractiveness of life in this region[19] obviously correspond to the qualities of the well-cultivated, cool, and pleasant earth: it is black, firm, and may be used to make bricks, tiles, and other items. . . . The harbor of the True Cross can hold over one thousand ships. There are many villages in the vicinity: during the day, plumes of smoke are rising as far as the eye can see, and at night fires can be seen. . . .
>
> Here the sky seems mild and nature well-ordered. (Quiros report, 1609)

The documents of the Quiros expedition were kept secret for an entire century. The Spanish Crown, on the verge of exhaustion, refused any new expansion and devoted itself to its own empire. Off the shipping routes, the land of the Holy Spirit fell out of favor in a generally mercantile age. Yet the myth of the great continent of the Southern Hemisphere continued to be of interest.

2 Happy "Savages"?

> [W]e sat down in their domestic circles with
> that harmony which befits the members of one
> great family.
>
> FORSTER, *A Voyage Round the World . . .*

In the eighteenth century, the French and the English tackled the last geographical enigma of the South Seas. Times had changed. The issue was no longer to propagate the faith of the Catholic Counter-Reformation, or even to find new sources of supplies for trading purposes, but to extend the range of scientific knowledge. The Age of Enlightenment and the theory of the "noble savage" were the philosophical underpinnings of such endeavors. The need to expand the empire and plant the flag in new lands was there as well, but the spirit and justification of discovery involved more than mere annexation.

Louis-Antoine de Bougainville

In eighteenth-century Europe, there was no thought or philosophy that did not have a geographical component; understanding the world implied knowing about other cultures. The lands beyond the tropical seas were no longer considered to be peopled by "pagans" but, without disparaging connotation, by "savages." According to Jean-Jacques Rousseau, savages knew the secret of happiness and "natural virtues."

In this context, some intellectuals played a major part, such as the French mathematician Maupertuis and the president of the Dijon *Parlement,*[1] Charles de Brosses, whose chronicles entitled *History of the Voyages to Austral Lands* were published in 1756. For de Brosses, the distinction of settling the question of Terra Australis Incognita once and for all was the prerogative of the French nation as a whole, not of one individual or one trading company. The discovery of new lands would allow for the foundation of more sophisticated societies built by generations of young settlers whose new towns would bring renewed vitality and power to the older European nations. Colonization was a source of glory and wealth because it implied the strengthening of trade and the betterment of scientific knowledge. Indeed, colonization was the most thorough manifestation of the idea of nation-state.

English geographers understood these ideas well. John Callender translated the work of de Brosses and concluded that the Pacific had to be explored so as not to leave it to the French (Dunmore 1978). Callender wrote:

> It is very certain that the discovery of *Terra Australis Incognita* is considered by many wise and knowing people, as a kind of philosopher's stone, perpetual motion, or, in plain *English,* as a chimera, fit only to take up the empty brains of wild projectors. Yet there seems to be no sufficient reason, why such as are competent judges of the matter in dispute, should decide, peremptorily, that there is no such country: or, if there be, that it is not worth the finding. These sort of hasty conclusions are extremely fatal to science in general and to the art of navigation in particular. (In Beaglehole 1968, 191)

Another geographer, Dalrymple, found the Spanish manuscript of the account of Torres's voyage in Madras. Dalrymple upheld and confirmed Quiros's ideas on the existence of the southern continent and, on the basis of a theory of sea currents and Pacific winds, concluded that it was located in the yet unexplored ocean at about latitude fifty degrees south. There, finally, British colonization could freely expand while avoiding the disappointments that American colonies had created for the motherland. In this climate of intellectual, philosophical, and geographical curiosity and excitement, new imperial dreams were born among the French and the British.

Louis-Antoine de Bougainville was the hero of the French saga, whom Beaglehole praised as follows: "In that age of classicism and politeness, none was more classically polite than he; but he had also greater qualities—talent, a warm heart, a generous energy, enterprise, a faith in the capacities of his countrymen which defeat could not diminish" (1968, 214). In the race with the British, Bougainville was to encounter James Cook, an old adversary. Their confrontation had begun in Canada when the Frenchman, a young officer in the marine infantry, served as Montcalm's aide de camp in Quebec opposite General Wolf's English troops. Cook was then pilot of the landing barges.

After the Franco-Canadian defeat, Bougainville, bitterly contemplating the loss of Quebec, looked outside France for an outlet. In the empty Malouines (Falkland Islands), which were assumed to be the keystone of the Pacific route through Cape Horn, Bougainville attempted to steal a march on the British by setting up a French colony with families of Acadians who had been expelled from their country. The project consisted of

recreating another little Canada in the South Atlantic. He invested his
personal savings and all his energy in it. "Seeing that the north was closed
to us, I thought of the means to give back to my homeland in the austral
hemisphere that which she no longer had in the boreal hemisphere"
(Bougainville in Dunmore 1978, 64). But forsaken by the Duke of Choi-
seul, a government secretary who was his sponsor, Bougainville had to
yield to Spanish demands.

On the return voyage Bougainville suggested taking another turn
around the world. Taking his inspiration from the ideas of President de
Brosses, of whom he was a disciple, Bougainville wished to reach the
East Indies through the South Seas and search for the austral continent.

The Great Cyclades

The expedition left the port of Nantes in November 1766, with the
knowledge that English vessels had moved ahead of it in a similar circumnavigation. Three hundred men were aboard the frigate *La Boudeuse*
and the store ship *L'Etoile;* there was also a woman disguised as a man,
the companion of one of the expedition scientists, Mr de Commerson.
Once in the Pacific, Bougainville followed the eighteenth parallel. The
French discovered the Tuamotu atolls; in Tahiti and the Society Islands,
their vessels were warmly welcomed. There, amazed by the free mores
and under the spell of the women's beauty, they saw the geographical
manifestation of the myth of the "noble savage" living in a free and natural society. "New Cythera" (as Bougainville was to call it) or "the Republic of Utopia" (according to the expedition botanist de Commerson)
entered the European imagination. De Commerson wrote later that in
New Cythera he had found "the state of natural man, born essentially
virtuous, with no prejudice, and who follows, without suspicion or guilt,
the gentle impulses of his instinct, an instinct always reliable because it
has yet to degenerate into reason"[2] (in Bougainville 1966, 392).

What came next was harder. The long quest for the great southern
land went on, in the midst of deprivations and scurvy, and on a violent
sea. Bougainville was on Quiros's tracks and continuously assessed his
route in relation to that of the Spanish navigator. On 22 May 1768, at
last, four islands appeared: an isolated volcanic cone, the Star Peak
(Mere Lava today), and a group of three islands which Bougainville was
to name Aurora (Maewo), Pentecost, and Lepers Island (Ambae or
Aoba). The expedition went ashore on Ambae for a brief time. "High
and steep, forested all around," that island inspired Bougainville much
less than New Cythera. The French wanted to land essentially to take on
new supplies of wood, drinking water, and fresh food. At the sight of a

small cove-shaped beach on the northwest shore of the island, boats were launched.

While drums reverberated on the mountain side, the rocky coastline became filled with a multitude of brown-skinned men, all of whom were armed. Coincidentally, it seems that the Melanesians of Ambae were preparing to confront a local group of enemies when the French appeared! Mistrust and perplexity were obvious on both sides. Eventually the sailors went ashore, gave away brightly colored cloth, and started cutting wood with the spontaneous help of some of the "savages." Bougainville also went ashore. Declaring that the island was taken over by the Crown of France, he buried a title engraved on an oakwood plate under a tree. As in Big Bay when the Spaniards built their shelters, the gesture displeased the Islanders. Tension started to build up around the French sailors. Ill at ease, the men at work, surrounded by a growing crowd, hurried their task to completion and pushed their boats off. Their departure acted like a signal. Instantly a cloud of arrows and stones reached the navigators, who shot back with their muskets. Once again, the "savages" had chosen the moment of re-embarking to attack, perhaps for tactical reasons. When returning to their boats, the whites were exposed since they were no longer lined up with their guns pointed at the beach.

This shooting ended the brief Ambae interlude. Nevertheless, Bougainville brought back some information:

> These islanders are small, ugly, poorly proportioned and most are eaten away by leprosy.[3] . . . On their arms, they wear a large bracelet-like ring made of what I believe is ivory and, around their neck, plates of tortoise-shell, which animal is common on their shores as they gave us to understand.[4] . . . The place where we landed was very small. Twenty steps from the coast one finds the foot of a mountain whose slope, although very steep, is entirely wooded. One sees many roads throughout the woods, and spaces enclosed by three-foot-high fences. Are these entrenchments or simply the boundaries of various properties? The only huts we saw were five or six small ones into which we could go only by creeping on the ground. We were, however, surrounded by a numerous people. (1966, 245–246)

Bougainville exerted his moderating influence during the scuffle on the beach. In his eyes, the forces were too conspicuously unequal for the French to go on fighting or attempt a landing in force. They might as well search for a more propitious and welcoming place, which they did by sailing to the southwest. The fleet reached the place described by Quiros, and Bougainville realized that the fabled southern continent did not exist; he gave the islands the name Archipelago of the Great Cyclades.

While returning to France a little later, Bougainville came across Carteret's English vessel in the Atlantic Ocean, obviously sailing back from an identical trip. The officers greeted one another with courtesy and merely talked about winds and the morale of their men.

James Cook

Three years later, and with the same purpose, James Cook sailed to the waters of the Archipelago of the Great Cyclades. There were fifteen scientists on board his vessels, *Resolution* and *Adventure,* including the German botanist Johann Forster, Forster's son Georg, and the Swede Anders Sparrman. This international team of scientists and astronomers gave a definitely scientific aura to Captain Cook's second voyage in the Pacific. A genuine "geographic" field study, the expedition allowed for long-term contact between Melanesians and Europeans for the first time. All were able to go beyond a threshold of mistrust and misunderstanding.

This second expedition sailed from west to east. Cook's mission was to get as close as possible to the South Pole, to settle the issue of unknown lands in the Southern Hemisphere. Were any land to be discovered, the order was to take it over in the name of the British Crown and keep its location secret.

In July 1774, the weather foggy and rainy, the navigators saw the first islands in the archipelago: Ambae, Maewo, and Pentecost. Numerous inhabitants thronged the shoreline to watch the British vessels. Local outrigger canoes, few and small-sized, were not comparable in terms of size, beauty, and efficiency to the canoes used by Polynesians or the people of Santa Cruz discovered by the Spaniards. Cook then sailed toward the southern tip of the island of Malakula where he discovered the great bay that became Port Sandwich (from the name of the Earl of Sandwich, First Lord of Admiralty, who was his superior at the time). There, Cook decided to go ashore.

A large group of people, nearly five hundred men, greeted the navigators. Cautiously, women and children looked on from afar. From both shoreline and inland areas, all groups from the southern tip of Malakula headed to the vessels as the news of the visitors' arrival spread. One word was on everybody's lips: *tomar* 'ancestors' in the Port Sandwich dialects. Aboard the canoes moving in the direction of the landing boats, men were waving green leaves and filling up their hands with sea water, which they would splash on their faces. The English did likewise. Cook was the first to go ashore with a green branch in his hand. He then received a small pig and a few coconuts.

The sight of Malakula's Melanesians never ceased to amaze the British, who until then had known only Polynesian shores. The visitors described Melanesian Islanders as small-sized men, with brown or black skin, and curly and wooly hair. Their faces and chests were painted black and orange and they were practically naked except for a belt made of bark that held a penis sheath directed upward. "Most other nations invent some kind of covering, from motives of shame; but here a roll of cloth continually fastened to the belt, rather displays than conceals, and is the very opposite of modesty"[5] (Forster 1777, 206).

Indeed, the *nambas* was their only piece of "clothing"; it held the male organ up toward the belt and adorned it in red colors, thereby underlining and magnifying it. In Cook's words, "they weare a cord or belt round their waist, just under the short ribs, and over the middle of [the] belly, this is tied so tight, that they look as if they had two bellies, the one above and the other below the belt" (in Beaglehole 1961, 466).

In spite of the Melanesians' basically friendly attitude, the British were disappointed. They were not able to leave the shoreline and move around freely. Furthermore, there were few fresh supplies and no drinking water. On the other hand, the cloth, medals, and nails proposed as gifts by the navigators did not appeal to the Islanders, who seemed dissatisfied by the terms of exchange. Although still cordial, the Melanesians soon ended the gift-giving. Two days after his arrival at Port Sandwich, Cook decided to leave earlier than anticipated.

One remark by Forster is noteworthy: the numerous but small and rudimentary outrigger canoes could only hold four or five persons. As for Cook, on leaving the island he wrote: "The Mallicolocans [*sic*] are quite a different nation to any we have yet met with, and speak a different language" (in Beaglehole 1961, 467). He left Malakula disappointed but happy that no incident had occurred, noting that Bougainville was less "fortunate" at Lepers Island.

In a hurry to reach the southern tip of the archipelago and perhaps make a greater discovery there, Cook did not land on any of the islands he sighted on the way, showing no concern for his reserves of wood and even water, which had hardly been replenished on Malakula. Cook's companions, enthralled by their first landing, eagerly wished for renewed contact with the Melanesians. "The company of savages, and an opportunity of contemplating their manners, dwellings and plantations, were at present, in our estimation, desirable objects," Forster wrote (1777, 246). Unfortunately, the second landing was not as smooth. In a large bay in the southeast of Erromango Island, two boats headed for land; but the sailors saw a crowd of armed men and hesitated to land. Cook set foot on the island anyway and insisted on initiating an exchange. Rapidly surrounded on all sides, with stones and arrows raining down upon them, the English sailors opened fire in order to disengage themselves. This task was made harder by the fact that "not half our musquets would go of[f] otherwise many more (of these poor people) must have fallen," Cook stated (in Beaglehole 1961, 479).

This time, Cook had done no better than Bougainville. He gave up. In the distance, to the south, there was another large island toward which the vessels headed. "Several fires appeared upon the island at night, one of which blazed up from time to time like the flame of a volcano," noted Forster (1777, 259). Cook would call it "Tanna" which in the local dialects simply means "the land."[6]

First Perspective on Tanna

The ships anchored in the bay on the southeast side of the island, subsequently called Port Resolution (map 3). A crowd of men had gathered, watching in utter silence. Hesitantly, a few canoes finally moved closer; from one of them, a man threw a few coconuts toward the crew. Cook himself went down into a boat and presented some colored cloth. Then, abandoning restraint, all the "savages" rushed to the ships. "[T]heir behavior was insole[n]t and daring; their [sic] was nothing within their reach they were not for carrying off" (Cook in Beaglehole 1961, 482), in particular the flag at the launch's bow, the rudder, and the floating buoys above the anchors. A total of seventeen outrigger canoes holding at least two hundred Melanesians surrounded the English vessels. Overwhelmed, the seamen first fired into the air, then used their naval gun, which caused a generalized dive and the retreat of the "savages." Consequently, the Islanders' attitude was mixed. Some were friendly, like the elderly man who made several trips between the vessels and the shore to bring coconuts and a yam. Others were very excited and did not stop "shouting and jeering." Still others were openly hostile.

In the afternoon, Cook went ashore with a heavy detachment of armed men. Facing him, he wrote, were about nine hundred armed Islanders split into two compact groups. In the middle, in an empty space, lay a present of bananas and yams. A path led to it, indicated by four reeds set between the offering and the beach. The elderly man they had seen earlier was vigorously motioning them to move closer and take the food. Mistrustful, Cook requested, but to no avail, that the Melanesians step back and lay down their weapons. The elderly man supported the visitors' request but, as mentioned by Cook, "as little regard was paid to [the old man] as us." The group on the right seemed more aggressive than the group on the left, to which the elderly man belonged. Cook made his men shoot over the heads of the group on the right, but "in an instant they recovered themselves and began to display their weapons, one fellow shewed us his back side in such a manner that it was not necessary to have an interpreter to explain his meaning" (see Beaglehole

1961, 485). There was gunfire once more, and the ships even contributed some cannonballs. This made no difference and although all became quiet again, both sides held onto their weapons.

The English learned the elderly man's name, Paowang. Visibly the master of the place, he was offering them hospitality. He allowed them to cut wood and also to fill two casks of water in a pond nearby, but warned them not to touch coconut trees. Cook, by then highly agitated, ordered his men to re-embark. There was a second expedition in the afternoon. Paowang gave a small pig to the detachment leader and went aboard for a visit. He returned an ax which the wood-cutting party had left behind, then asked to be allowed to take his leave. "We thought we might explain this behaviour as a kind of ceremony, and that they did not think it civil to leave their guests alone in their own country. This circumstance would imply, that they have ideas of propriety and decency, which we would hardly have expected among an uncivilized people," noted Forster (1777, 284). The English were discovering the tactfulness of the Melanesians.

Little by little, each side sized up the other and more stable relations were established. Another positive note: their curiosity once gone, the men from neighboring areas did not reappear and sailors and scientists could move around more freely among Port Resolution residents. Every day boats would take men to shore for water and wood-cutting chores. Naturalists would go and collect plants, pushing farther inland as mutual trust improved.

Yet the visitors were never able to explore the southern tip of Port Resolution Bay. Chants often emanated from that site, which was off limits to them during their whole stay. Further, the English were not free to move too far toward areas that belonged to different and perhaps antagonistic groups. The Islanders unhesitatingly told the visitors that beyond a certain limit they were at risk of "being eaten."

Although the Melanesians had to deal with the invasion of their domestic life by strangers full of curiosity, their reserve disappeared fairly quickly. At the end of their stay, increasingly relaxed meetings took place on the trails and especially near the huts. The visitors exchanged their names with the Melanesians they met, learned words, and saw women and children approach them without reticence. Paowang behaved as an ambassador but did not appear to have any particular authority. One day, Cook and his companions wanted to get closer to a volcano which intrigued them with its intermittent din and thick columns of smoke. Leaving the shoreline territory, they walked north toward the mountain. A man stopped them at a path junction. Cook wrote that "the attitude we found him in and the ferosity which appear'd in his looks and his beheavour after, led us to think he meant to defend the path he stood in" (in Beaglehole 1961, 492). When Cook decided to go on, the Melanesian guide whom he had recruited ran away. Shortly afterward, the small group met about thirty armed men, extremely anxious, who again prevented them from going farther. Wishing to avoid quarrels and knowing they could not find their way by themselves, the English retraced their steps. A moderate and subtle observer, Cook commented:

> [T]hus we found these people civil and good natured when not prompted by jealousy to a contrary conduct,[7] a conduct one cannot blame them for when one considers the light in which they must look upon us in, its impossible for them to know our real design, we enter their ports . . . , we land . . . and meintain the footing we . . . got by the superiority of our fire arms, in what other light can they than at first look upon us but as invaders of their country. (In Beaglehole 1961, 493)

Except for such incidents, the sojourn of the English in Port Resolution was pleasant, without excessive heat or coolness. The "savages" asked their visitors several times how long they would stay. When told that ten days would be the limit, the Islanders seemed satisfied.

On the last days preceding their departure, the British sailors felled a large tree in order to replace the tiller on one of their vessels. Paowang was the first to worry. Cook offered him cloth and a dog, in vain. Very quickly part of the population—in particular, allied groups from farther away—crystallized their opposition to the visitors around this event. The next day Cook had to use a screen of soldiers to protect the work team in charge of taking the tree out. While sailors were loading the trunk on the boats, a group of men walked to them, wanting to know where the wood was headed. An English sentinel drew a boundary on the sand, asking the Melanesians to stay beyond it. As the soldier was threatening one of the "savages" with his weapon, the latter wielded his bow, according to witnesses. The sentinel shot point-blank. Removed by two of his kin to shelter, the wounded Islander soon expired; in a moment the beach was empty. Eventually, the ship's surgeon, who had been sent for, arrived to certify the death. At the time of the incident, Forster was alone on the hill, collecting plant samples. Lost in contemplation of the bocage-like scenery, he shuddered on hearing the shot and hurried to the seashore. On the way he met Sparrman. Worried, he and Sparrman saw several men flee when they drew near. "At last, when we stepped out of the wood, we beheld two natives seated on the grass, holding one of their brethren dead in their arms. They pointed to a wound in his side, which had been made by a musket-ball, and with a most affecting look they told us 'he is killed' " (Forster 1777, 351).

Cook put the sentry in irons but his commanding officer undertook his defense with the reminder that, according to orders, "the least threat was to be punished with immediate death" (Forster 1777, 353). Following this incident, the navigators deemed it advisable to leave without delay and raised anchor during the night of 20 August.

The voyage continued to the south where the positions of Erronam (Futuna) and Anatom (Aneityum) were plotted. Realizing the archipelago ended with Anatom Island, Cook did not call anywhere and sailed back northward while taking time to make the first map of the archipelago. He tried to find an anchorage in the Great Bay of St. Philip and St. James but encountered the same navigational problems as Quiros. A considerable crowd had gathered on the beach at Big Bay. Eventually, two small outrigger canoes under sail moved with the greatest caution toward the English vessels. The seamen threw ropes to which they had attached ship's nails as presents, and a gesture-based dialogue ensued. "[They gave] us the names of such parts of the country as we pointed to, but we could not obtain from them the name of the island," Cook noted (in Beaglehole 1961, 515). These men, darker skinned than those of Tanna, robust and their heads covered with feathers, did not understand any of the Polynesian-language words used in Tanna or Malakula. They fled hurriedly when two boats that had been sent to reconnoiter the bay moved closer to their canoes. This was to be the last contact between Cook and the archipelago's inhabitants.

Leaving this vast landscape, Forster wrote in indirect homage to the Spanish navigator, "Quiros had great reason to extol the beauty and fertility of this country; it is indeed to appearance, one of the finest in the world" (1777, 373). This impression was confirmed by Cook. "The sides of the mountains were checkered with plantations and every vally watered by a stream of water. . . . These together with the many fires we have seen by night and smokes by day make it highly probable the country is well inhabited and very fertile" (in Beaglehole 1961, 517–518).

After sailing around the island, the vessels headed for New Zealand. The outcome of the voyage was a survey of the geographical location of all islands in the group—and, for the first time, genuine interaction with Melanesians on Tanna and Malakula. Cook was to conclude: "I think we have obtained a right to name them and shall for the future distinguish them under the name of the *New Hebrides*" (in Beaglehole 1961, 521).

The name remained. Perhaps that is to be regretted· it is not necessarily an improvement on "the Great Cyclades."

Harmony

Cook and his companions noted the low technological level of this society frozen in the stone age, but underlined its high degree of social courtesy and cultural harmony. Serenity and intelligence are the hallmarks of the portraits they made of their hosts. The image of peaceful happiness is uniformly present. In Forster's words, "we sat down in their domestic circles with that harmony which befits the members of one great family" (1777, 350). The discoverers from the end of the eighteenth century were curious about a civilization other than their own and did not project on it—not yet at least—their own instinct of superiority and their will to evangelize. As for the Melanesians, once the first visual shock had subsided, they greeted the visitors with courtesy and pleasantness, provided their territorial sovereignty was respected.

On the eve of departure, Forster, alone, climbed the hill that overlooks the Port Resolution plain to the north. There, on the Yenkahi range, he watched a man who was singing while planting yams. The month was August; the gardens had been harvested, and there remained only banana trees. Already the early work of clearing and planting for the following year had begun. Cut off by hedges of banana trees and wild cane, yam gardens covered practically the whole side of the hill. "The numerous smokes which ascended from every grove on the hill, revived the pleasing impressions of domestic life; nay my thoughts naturally turned upon friendship and national felicity" (Forster 1777, 348).

To bring the land into cultivation, the Islanders used two types of ax: one of black sharpened stone, the other a "hatchet, to which a broken shell was fastened instead of a blade" (Forster 1777, 313). In spite of these mediocre tools, agricultural practices seemed judicious and expeditious. Cook described the clearing method as follows: tree branches were felled with an ax and the roots brought to light through digging. Fire would then destroy the tree while leaving the blackened stumps standing.

The economy of these Islanders seemed essentially land based. Unlike the northern residents of the archipelago, they did not know netfishing techniques although they did use rudimentary outrigger canoes and were seen fishing on the reef with a bow or a spear. "I believe . . . that the sea contributes but little towards their subsistance; whether it is because the coast does not abound with fish or that they are bad fishers I know not," wrote Cook (in Beaglehole 1961, 502–503). On the other hand, each subsistence garden looked to the navigators like a work of art, carefully tended on a grass-free soil, and whose hedges gave it a bocage-like appearance. Forster noted the presence of odoriferous and decorative plants aesthetically arranged: "[T]he plantations . . . were more delightfully situated than any we had hitherto seen" (1777, 313). Thus, the first image of Tanna's traditional Melanesian landscape appeared in the descriptions by Cook and his companions. Spaces where gardens were contiguous made up cultivated islets in the midst of thinned-out bush. As for villages, they were dispersed in groups of a few low-lying huts. The Islanders seemed to enjoy a rural, quiet happiness which delighted eighteenth-century Europeans.

The philosophers' image of the "noble savage" was not far away. Forster noted the natural courtesy of the voyagers' hosts:

> The civility of the natives was, upon the whole, very conspicuous towards us. If they met us in a narrow path, they always stepped aside into the bushes and grasses in order to make way for us. If they happened to know our names, they pronounced them with a smile, which could be extremely well understood as a salutation; or, if they had not seen us before, they commonly enquired our names in order to know us again. (1777, 341–342)

A Leaderless Society?

The apparent lack of social organization puzzled the British navigators just as it had the Spaniards. Cook stated that one day he asked Paowang whether there was a chief on the island or, to use his own words, a "king" whose authority was the same as that of the Polynesian *ariki*. Port Resolution people understood the latter word. Paowang's answer was positive, and Cook and his companions were led to a small village to see a man named Yogai, who "was very old but had a merry open countenance" (in Beaglehole 1961, 496). Nothing distinguished this chief from other Islanders, either in his way of life or his attitude. His only distinctive style of dress was a belt made of tapa bark with black and red stripes.[8] Apparently he did not own any particular riches and his hut was not unusual. That laughter-filled old man was indeed an odd chief or king, but Cook took this apparent powerlessness in stride. "We know . . . very little of their government. They seem to have chiefs amongst them . . . but these . . . seemed to have very little authority over the rest of the people. . . . [I]n our neighbourhood, . . . if there had been such a [chief], we certainly should some how or a nother [*sic*] have known it" (in Beaglehole 1961, 507–508). Further, "it had been remarked that one of these kings had not authority enough to order one of the people up into [a] cocoa nutt tree to bring him down some nutts, altho he spoke to several, and was at last obliged to go himself; and by way of revenge as it was thought, left not a nutt on the tree, took what he wanted himself and gave the rest to some of our people" (in Beaglehole 1961, 497).

To conclude, as a people of peasants and pig breeders, these "savages" appeared happily ensconced in a simple society divided into autonomous territorial groups. It was a society without a state, seemingly made up of "equal" men.

A Sort of Dialogue

The Port Resolution people spoke or understood three languages: their own, that of their neighbors north of the volcano area, and a language with Polynesian sounds very similar to the language spoken in the Tongan archipelago, which the English navigators themselves knew to some extent (see map 4). The last offered a means of relative communication. It was also spoken on the two small neighboring islands visible offshore, Aniwa and Erronan (or Futuna). Yet the known universe of the Port Resolution people was limited. In Cook's words, "the people of these islands are a distinct nation of themselves. Mallicolo, Apee & c^a were names intirely unknown to them, they even knew nothing of Sandwich island which is much the nearer; I took no little pains to know how far their geographical knowledge extended and did not find that it exceeded the limits of their horizon" (in Beaglehole 1961, 504).

By comparison, groups of navigators from Santa Cruz could name seventy islands very remote from theirs and sail to Fiji, the Solomon Islands, and the northern New Hebrides. Thus, the Tannese were looking inland much more than toward the horizon. There was one exception, however: some kind of contact, more remote, seemed to exist between Tanna and the Loyalty Islands. Forster made an interesting comment on the topic. After he had climbed a hill with a Port Resolution man, the latter showed him the outline of Anatom Island to the south, then "the native pointed a little to the north of it (Anattom), where he said another island was situated, which he called Eetònga. This circumstance strengthens the conjecture which I ventured before, that there is some connection or intercourse between Tanna and the Friendly Islands. The name of Eetònga has a great familiarity with that of Tonga-Tabboo" (Forster 1777, 310).

All writers noted the Islanders' taste for body ornamentation. The Tannese liked to set hawk feathers in their hair and adorn themselves with bracelets made of carved coconut on which they stuck sweet-smelling plants. By way of necklaces, they frequently wore tortoiseshell or green jade pieces pierced in the middle.[9] Finally, the complicated hairstyles of males—smoothed down, surrounded by sticks and pulled back —did not appear elsewhere in the archipelago.

What about the women? Their lot shocked the visitors. The major part of daily chores was their responsibility. Cook observed that of women "they make pack-horses. I have seen a woman carrying a large bundle on her back, or a child on her back and a bundle under her arm and a fellow struting before her with nothing but a club, or a spear or some such like thing in his hand" (Beaglehole 1961, 504–505). The porterage task allocated to women created an equivocal situation. Forster, the walker and botanist, used to take a young sailor along with him to carry his sample bag. Tannese males assumed he was a woman and, quite straightforwardly, tried to tempt him into the bush several times. Faced with such insistence, the English believed it was a manifestation of homosexual customs—until the "savages" realized their mistake and stopped their "sexual harassment."

The navigators estimated the population of the whole island to be twenty thousand inhabitants, in no way indicating overpopulation. Permanent worry about the residents of other territories, which led to a war-like ambience in the vicinity of these neighbors, contrasted with the peacefulness of domestic life within the area visited by the British. Forster made a comment about "the manufacture of arms, upon which they now spend more time than on any other" (1777, 362). Apparently the Tannese never parted with their weapons. Forster added that "the people seem to live dispersed in small villages, consisting of a few families; and their constant custom of going armed is a certain sign that they formerly had, and probably still have, wars with neighbouring islanders, or quarrels amongst themselves" (1777, 359).

The visitors wondered about the apparent lack of religious forms: "[I]n their general behaviour we did not take notice of the least religious act, nor of any thing that could be construed into superstition" (Forster 1777, 363). The only mysterious spot was the eastern tip of the bay, off limits to the navigators, where a "solemn song" could be heard every morning. They thought a place of worship was hidden there, but were not able to solve the mystery. In fact, the eastern point of Port Resolution Bay was a taboo area carrying magical powers (see chapter 11).

"These people seem to have as few arts as most I have seen, besides knowing how to cultivate the ground they have few others worth mentioning" (Cook in Beaglehole 1961, 506). There was indeed no weaving, nor pottery-making, nor even artistic creations such as ritual masks or statues. In a few specific areas, however, the Tannese demonstrated their creativity and were even close to perfection. The British were struck notably by the beauty of their songs and that of the sound of reed flutes which the visitors deemed superior, in terms of harmony, to everything they had heard on the other islands.

In the dialogue that took place, the Melanesians put themselves on an equal footing with the visitors. Never did they help whites who were working or carrying loads; they would just watch—in a silence that was difficult to interpret. Similarly, they kept a close watch on the visitors' moves and explorations. All incidents with Europeans at the time of first contact stemmed from the nonobservance of territorial law. The Big Bay incident occurred because the Spaniards did not want to confine themselves to the boundaries drawn on the beach; that at Ambae because

Bougainville "buried" something in the island soil; and that on the eve of Cook's departure because a tree was felled and a soldier drew a boundary line in front of a Melanesian. This very sharp sense of territorial sovereignty appeared as a common characteristic to all "discovered" peoples in the archipelago. Masters of the land, the Islanders did not allow the whites to draw boundaries or to give them orders. Conversely, whenever they went aboard, they would respect the visitors' rules scrupulously. Cook was wise enough to abide by his hosts' regulations. As he said himself, "[never] did we touch any part of their property, not even wood and water without first having obtained their consent" (in Beaglehole 1961, 501). From this mutual respect was born an unusual relationship that departed from cultural standards on both sides. It did not develop in the context of the generous welcoming rituals of Melanesians—and neither did it demonstrate the Westerners' preoccupation with conquest and domination. Hardly ever would this type of relationship, equal and novel, re-occur.

Ancestors or "Spirits from the Bottom of the Sea"?

It is now generally acknowledged that the Melanesians mistook the first white navigators for their own ancestors. According to Codrington, the traditional Melanesian view of the world is that of a sea scattered with islands and capped by the sky: the universe amounts to the lands of which men are aware. Farther out, the sky plunges into the sea, tightly sealing the horizon, beyond which there is nothing more than "spirits." A sacred world under the sea is the home of deceased forebears. In other words, space is stratified vertically, not areally. The appearance of huge vessels hailing from the horizon line and maneuvered by unknown white-skinned individuals represented a difficult problem for the Melanesians. "[T]hey were indeed quite sure that they [the navigators] did not [come from any country in the world], but must have been made out at sea, because they knew that no men in the world had such vessels. In the same way they were sure that the voyagers were not men; if they were they would be black. What were they then? They were ghosts, and being ghosts, of necessity those of men who had lived in the world" (Codrington 1891, 11).

As far as the Melanesians were concerned, these spirits could only be those of their ancestors, or their heroes, coming back to strike a new alliance. One may understand the emotion that overwhelmed the Islanders on the beaches where the vessels cast anchor. These men had been elected to receive the bounty from beyond, they had become the chosen ones of the supernatural world. In the belief they would partake of a fabulous potlatch[10] with their forebears, they readied themselves to present these traveling spirits with all their goods and receive in exchange superior and sacred gifts. Therefore, on most islands where first contact occurred, the immediate welcome was delirious. Inhabitants went to the beach in a great state of excitement. What looked like war dances were in fact welcome dances; as for cries and chants, they were greeting signals. In most cases, however, the navigators misunderstood the Islanders' behavior and reacted as if they were being threatened.

The visitors' attitude of guardedness was incomprehensible to the Melanesians. In the latter's eyes, the individuals from the ships did not behave at all like ancestors; their glances, their faces were not necessarily friendly; they were turning down exchanges, and they had unknown and terrifying weapons. Their presents of cloth or medals were worthless. In brief, although these newcomers were not ordinary, they assuredly were not the expected ones. As a result, mistrust returned, and the beings who had come from the horizon's edge were seen by the Tannese as *yarimus enao neta'i* 'spirits from the bottom of the seas'. The visitors had nothing in common with ancestor spirits, or thus with men. In fact, the initial misunderstanding was short-lived. But which attitude to adopt?

The English enjoyed a peaceful stay on the island thanks to Paowang's welcome, even though neighboring groups were aggressive, even "arrogant," as both Spaniards and Britons observed. But the euphoria of the first moments was short-lived. The Tannese no longer entertained illusions about their visitors' status, and the great curiosity of the early days abated. Personal relations between the navigators and their hosts improved, however, as days went by. The visitors had the same traits as other men. They were hungry, hot, and thirsty; they walked and were tired; they were not able to understand the Islanders' local language. However the navigators were not entirely men. Neither were they ancestors. They were a strange sort of being—naive yet dangerous. Therefore, nothing more was expected from these visitors than that they depart.

It is meaningful that on Santo, Malakula, and Tanna, the Melanesians' first gesture was to present their visitors with a small pig, a gift that was never repeated subsequently. In Melanesia, the pig is a sacred animal. It is offered, it is shared with allies in exchange for gifts of equivalent value. With this first offering, Islanders symbolically initiated a cycle of ritual exchange which was misunderstood and, in their eyes, turned down. Once they realized their error, they definitely kept their gifts of value: these are not shared with wandering spirits, with *yarimus*. This is why the British could obtain neither the fat and shiny pigs scavenging near the huts during the day, nor even the poultry. The Melanesians refused to let these strange beings enter their world and kept to themselves, while accommodating the visitors with minor gifts. For seamen who, for several months, had been eating salted meats and heavy navy biscuits, such rejection was probably painful. Cook and his companions were heroic enough not to be antagonized by it. Forster, for instance, showed an Islander how to use an ax and wanted to trade it for a pig, but "they were deaf to this proposal, and never sold us a single hog during our stay" (1777, 337).

Not only did the Melanesians conceal some sacred sites and fringes of their territories, but they also concealed the essential parts of their society, dances, and rituals. They kept *kastom* to themselves—in other words, their "powers," key beliefs, and prestigious foods. Yet Forster was probably right when he wrote that "they who had been used to see in every stranger a base and treacherous enemy, now learnt from us to think more nobly of their fellow-creatures. . . . In a few days they began to feel a pleasure in our conversation, and a new disinterested sentiment, of more than earthly mould, even friendship, filled their heart" (1777, 350).

The navigators left Tanna with fine memories. About this community, which had welcomed them without ever revealing itself, they concluded that it was a "natural" and simple society without hierarchical organization or real knowledge of commerce.

3 Wild Contact

> If you want to know about the British Empire, listen to me.
> The British Empire is the product of the sweat and blood
> and tears, not shed but only suffered, of the poor beasts
> that have suffered as I have suffered. And it isn't only the
> British Empire. The French and the German and the Dutch
> and the miserable white man's empire everywhere, where
> the white man has been driven out by his instinct for land
> and space.
>
> ROBERT FLETCHER,
> *Isles of Illusion*

For half a century after Captain Cook's expedition, only whalers
ploughed the seas of the archipelago, and they avoided calling there as
much as possible because of the inhabitants' reputation for "ferocity" and
cannibalism.

For the Melanesians, the respite lasted until the discovery of sandalwood in 1825.

The Sandalwood Rush

In the early nineteenth century, the Pacific islands became attractive
to commercial interests when bêche-de-mer and sandalwood, two products much in demand on the Chinese market, were discovered in the
area. The bêche-de-mer, a sea slug whose name derives from the Portuguese *bicho do mar,* grows on sandy atoll bottoms or in the recesses of
fringing reefs. According to the Chinese, this food had aphrodisiac qualities. They had been buying it for three centuries from Malay, Filipino, or
Portuguese intermediaries who imported it from the Indo-Pacific world.
Between 1820 and 1850, bêche-de-mer collecting in Oceania took place
mostly in the Fiji Islands where more than thirty Australian ships participated in the trade (Ward 1972).

Sandalwood cutting in the New Hebrides was on a quite different
scale. Yet again, the issue was to offset the trade deficit with China. The
Chinese would buy unlimited quantities of sandalwood to be used for
ancestor worship, while the Australian colonies were great importers of
tea, which they bought almost entirely from China. Therefore the trade
in bêche-de-mer and sandalwood in particular served to lessen Australia's
trade imbalance. Since sandalwood prices, although unstable, could

yield substantial profits, the quest for sandalwood became one of the reasons for stepping up the exploration of the Pacific islands (Shineberg 1967).

The sandalwood trade peaked in the years 1846 and 1847. It facilitated the diffusion of the Pidgin English language Bislama[1] over the entire geographical area plied by sandalwood ships. Concurrently, Anatom (Anelgohat Bay), Erromango (Dillon's Bay), and Tanna (Port Resolution) became trading centers. Between August 1841 and August 1851, there were nearly 150 expeditions, each punctuated by various calls at, and reconnoiterings of, islands yet undiscovered by Westerners. Forty ships a year called at Anatom, according to Shineberg (1967).

Indifference toward European goods vanished when Melanesians realized they could benefit from having scissors, knives, axes, saws, and fishhooks. Once those needs were satisfied, demand was high for brightly colored cloth and blankets—in other words, items of adornment acquired for aesthetic purposes and which could also be exchanged with neighboring groups. Tobacco use became widespread after 1848: all ship's logs show it as the major exchange item. For the tobacco, the Melanesians finally agreed to cut sandalwood themselves and bring it to the ships. This new passion for a consumer product that was cheap and easy to transport gratified the traders. "Traders sold tobacco for Pacific islanders to smoke in order that the Chinese might burn sandalwood in order that Australians might drink tea" (Shineberg 1967, 151). An ideal exchange, completed to the greater satisfaction of ship owners and businessmen!

For Westerners to succeed it was necessary to appeal to the Islanders' goodwill through the seduction of commerce. The Anglican Bishop Selwyn, scarcely an admirer of merchant adventurers, repeated comments made in confidence by the sandalwood trader Paddon in 1841: "By kindness and fair dealing I have traded with these people for many years. They have cut many thousand feet of sandal-wood for me, and brought it on board my schooner. I never cheated them, I never treated them badly—we thoroughly understand each other" (Armstrong 1900, 7).

The thirty-five years of sandalwood traffic (1830–1865) were characterized by massacres of Melanesians on Erromango and Efate (Shineberg 1967). Among sandalwood traders, the clumsiest paid for their mistakes with their lives or with financial failure whereas those who succeeded were accepted not as a result of force but of trust. Paddon lived all his life with a Tannese woman by whom he had four children.[2]

Early witnesses such as Codrington were struck by the speed with which iron tools came into daily use. Coastal groups in direct contact with sandalwood traders drew great advantage from the new business as they transferred European goods to more remote inland communities. Likewise, the thousands of axes and knives and the hundreds of guns that traders sold in Tanna spread to other islands beyond the sandalwood trade. The political position of groups in contact with Westerners was strengthened, which explains why coastal residents were interested in seeing a European on their beach, in other words, a beachcomber: he might be an assured source of supplies.

Guns played an essential part in the trade although they were introduced later, around 1850. For warlike societies like those of Tanna and Erromango, owning and trading firearms was the Islanders' highest goal and, in the latter phases of the trade, guns inevitably appeared in all transactions.

The Labor Trade

Once the sandalwood had been depleted, most station owners considered other activities. They attempted to develop commercial undertakings such as gathering and dressing bêche-de-mer, preparing copra, and, on Anatom and Santo, provisioning whaling ships. Another form of exploitation soon appeared, bringing more violent trauma. Relying on the structures set up by sandalwood traders, it used the same individuals and the same channels, and was bound to grow with unmatched efficiency. It was no longer sandalwood that was carried to Australia, but men. For the worked-out sandalwood sources, speculators were substituting labor sources. This activity was called "blackbirding."

Robert Towns became the first trader to organize the migration of Melanesian labor. A cautious capitalist, he was probably the only businessman who had actually made a fortune in spite of the pitfalls of sandalwood trading. His new goal was to grow cotton on the Townsville property he had just acquired on the banks of the river Logan in northern Queensland. Towns's strategy was based on the fact that the American Civil War prevented the Confederate States from selling their cotton. The first labor shipment called at Brisbane on 18 August 1863, with sixty-seven men aboard, mostly from Tanna, Anatom, and the Loyalty Islands. Ross Lewin, the recruiting skipper, was a former sandalwood trader who had worked on Towns's behalf.

In Australia, numerous voices spoke against "the slave traffic" for humanitarian reasons, but also out of concern for ethnic preservation—to no avail, as the venture grew and became profitable. Even the fall of cotton prices after 1870 did not dampen demand since the production of sugarcane, a speculative substitute, required even more labor.

Given the liberal philosophy of the time and the development of colonial capitalism, the authorities were prepared to let private initiatives grow despite strong dissenting opinion from part of the public. Between 1863 and 1904—when the traffic was abolished—Queensland imported 60,819 Kanaka,[3] at least half of whom were originally from the Solomon Islands and the New Hebrides. British planters who settled in the Fiji Islands between 1864 and 1911 imported close to 20,000. The French did likewise for their mines in New Caledonia and, to a lesser extent, so did the Germans in Samoa. Overall, the number of displaced individuals reached nearly 100,000 (Parnaby 1972).

The height of the labor trade was reached in the 1880s. Twenty-eight Australian ships were then actively involved in recruiting workers in Melanesia—especially in the New Hebrides and the Solomon Islands, regarded as the best providers. The people in these areas were used to working with Western entrepreneurs and appeared stronger and psychologically better prepared. For example, in the single year 1867, eighteen recruiting vessels followed one another to Efate. They "removed" 250 men, mostly young, out of a total population of 3000 to 4000 inhabitants (Parnaby 1972, 130). The moral and social impact of blackbirding on island life was disastrous.

Rather than banning this traffic, the authorities attempted to "moralize" it by putting it as much as possible into a detailed legal framework. Blackbirding, more or less controlled, continued until 1904 when it was finally banned by the Australian federal government; the mechanization of cane cultivation had made human labor less vital. Still, the traffic grew until 1911 in Fiji, until 1913 in Samoa, and persisted in New Caledonia, although on a lesser scale (about a hundred men a year). The recruiters had simply traded flags.

The last Kanaka men were repatriated from Australia starting in 1906. Those who had been in Queensland for twenty years were allowed to stay: 1700 made that choice (MacClancy 1980, 60), in other words, 15 to 20 percent of the labor force employed on the cane fields, a figure of some magnitude. These Melanesians created small communities in Maryborough and Mackay, keeping the memory of their original ties and places alive.[4]

A Roving Disposition

Melanesians were ambivalent about blackbirding. In spite of dubious recruiting methods and inhuman travel conditions, what would be a totally different life on Queensland plantations appealed to many. After their return, a number of them volunteered to go back, which persuaded many youths to follow suit. Along with their wish to make a long trip and see the outside world, there was also the constantly reinforced need to acquire European goods, which Melanesian society could no longer do without. The Islanders did not always fight off recruiters, the most skillful of whom avoided kidnapping and violence. When the British historian Morrell stated the arguments of the missionaries and the Australian humanitarian party against labor traffic, he noted: "The weak spot in the case was the roving disposition of the islanders" (1966, 174).

In the early phase of the trade, ships' captains could not make the Islanders understand the real nature of the commitment involved. Therefore, they preferred to recruit in the areas where residents had the experience of wage labor, in particular the southern islands and Efate. However, as demand increased, they had to go farther; blackbirding soon affected the whole archipelago. Kidnapping became common. The first victims were men navigating from one island to another, fishing along the coastline or boarding the vessels in full confidence in order to barter. This was one reason, Codrington believed, why interisland connections by outrigger canoe disappeared. Sea travel had become dangerous.

A Vanishing People?

The missionaries rightly noted that recruiting depleted the islands' vitality and threatened the survival of the Melanesian people. Numerous coastal villages nearly lost their entire adult male population, especially those on heavily populated small islands near Espiritu Santo and Malakula. Children, women, and elderly men were the only ones left. Besides, the labor traffic coincided with the diffusion of epidemics caused by new viruses introduced by Westerners, which affected groups where only the most vulnerable members remained. Together with increasing mortality, the lower fertility rate associated with the outmigration of young men painted a thoroughly disastrous demographic picture.

Futuna had 900 residents in 1871 and only 238 in 1905. Anatom had approximately 4000 inhabitants in 1848, for a relatively high density of 40 per square kilometer. In 1875, there were only 1488 Islanders, 680 in 1895, and 186 in 1940. The population of Anatom decreased by a ratio of twenty to one—the most dramatic case of population decrease known in Vanuatu (Rallu 1991). Elsewhere in the islands, tuberculosis, smallpox, bronchitis, and dysentery decimated whole groups. Between diseases and recruiting, Loltong Bay, in the northwestern part of the Raga region on Pentecost Island, saw its population vanish entirely. A similar situation prevailed on Efate, the Torres Islands, and on the southern and eastern shores of Espiritu Santo. It was thought at the time that Melanesian ethnic groups would not survive. Hence the title of a survey completed by the group's first ethnologist, Arthur Deacon: *Malekula: A*

Vanishing People in the New Hebrides (1934). For the group as a whole, the population did decrease by an estimated 50 percent. In a few specific islands it decreased by 80 percent (McArthur and Yaxley 1967).

On their return, the Kanaka migrant workers found a country quite different from the one they had left. Many in their families had passed away or were in ill health. *Kastom* was in disarray and, with it, the basic tenets of traditional life. More than any form of cultural or political trauma, depopulation had delivered a fatal blow to the islands. Abandoning their villages, mountain people began to move down to the deserted shoreline while Christian missions gathered survivors of extinct groups around a bay or an accessible anchorage. Ancient territories were not forgotten, but they were abandoned or settled by others, thereby imprinting into island space the origins of a land-tenure conflict that would become an impasse.

The Kanaka could either go back to the forms and concepts of traditional life or adopt the way of life introduced by Westerners. Generally, their choice depended on the situation they found upon their return. In the case of coastal groups, the uprooting induced by demographic change could only lead them into relinquishing traditional society. The ancient link between *kastom* places and people had been severed, and escape seemed the only option: either into Christianity and the protective shelter of missions, or else by means of the cash economy which was then taking shape in the group on the basis of copra production. Some Kanaka became traders and copra makers on behalf of European companies. With the experience they acquired, these individuals played a part, often a decisive one, in the process of westernization. In the coming new society, they were likely to take over the important social roles of middlemen and leaders that older chiefs, either vanished or weakened, could no longer play.

Conversely, some Kanaka—who had rediscovered the traditional spaces and society of their islands—resumed *kastom* practices and even reactivated them through their new experience and riches. Among mountain groups that had remained in place, grade ceremonies[5] brought genuine renewal as well as the expanded use of material goods, both modern and traditional. Migrants wanted to make up for lost time and, further, local society wished to grant them the status and rank corresponding to their new stature. The migrants' return from a long journey was celebrated according to traditional rituals; the cargoes of useful or prestigious objects they brought back blended into the local culture. However, this was only the case in the islands and regions where Melanesian society had maintained its demographic stability and its territorial range, such as Pentecost, Ambae, and Tanna.

After the blackbirding phase, Melanesian society was weakened, deeply altered, and divided in cultural terms. A wedge had been driven between the groups remaining faithful to the traditional social organization and those stepping into the new "modernity."

Lawless Times in the Group

Recruiters needed secure centers where they could call and provision themselves. Some even transferred the Queensland plantation system to the very spots where labor was obtained. In the Fiji Islands, for example, bêche-de-mer trading agencies originally operated by beachcombers were turned into plantations. The same process soon reached the New Hebrides through the stations operated by sandalwood traders and blackbirders.

The first plantations were set up on the two islands most involved with Westerners, Tanna and Efate. In October 1867, the recruiter Ross Lewin became the first Westerner to purchase land from the Tannese; at Lenakel Bay, he planted cotton, corn, and coconut trees. In May 1868, another recruiter settled in the north of Efate Island at Eyema Bay (Port Havannah). Tanna's Lenakel station operated from 1867 to 1875 and Efate's Port Havannah station until 1880. Besides being farming centers, they were the focal points of the labor traffic. They became ports of call and *entrepôts* for the two or three scores of recruiting ships continuously moving through the archipelago. Further to the south, whaling stations were also set up on Anatom and Erromango.

A few adventurous traders lived in a rudimentary way on beaches, purchasing bêche-de-mer or coconuts from Islanders and sun- or smoke-drying the coconuts to make copra. In exchange, they distributed tobacco and trade goods; a stick of tobacco for ten nuts was the standard. The term *copra maker* was introduced to describe them. Melanesians accepted these new traders fairly well but kept a close watch on their moves and their activities. Copra makers were an odd group, according to a contemporary witness: "This career only tempts former sailors, half-castes, [men] who have lost their social position, and adventurers who have encountered all dangers and all diseases. . . . Some are wrecks from decent families—at least one can guess it—because no one knows for sure who they are or where they come from" (Imhaus 1890).

A trader's life was dangerous (Thompson 1981). In four years (1882–1886), thirteen isolated traders or copra makers were murdered in the group (Imhaus 1890). Yet the small-scale business went on, year after year, as though it was the only possible form of European presence. Eventually, in early 1880, a new colonial center grew up in southern Efate around Vila Bay. Several Europeans purchased property from the inhabitants of the present village of Erakor. These settlers included two

Swedish seamen, Rodin and Petersen, a sailor from New Brunswick, MacLeod, who had just moved from Tanna—too dangerous—and finally a Frenchman and a German working as associates, Chevillard and Zoeppfel. Each of their plots extended over several hundred hectares (Scarr 1967).

"Where Interests Are, Dominion Should Be"

The French seldom appeared in the group until the early 1880s. From 1870 onward, a few seamen had been left on the beaches by Noumea-based ships recruiting for the New Caledonia mines. Making a living from small-scale trading and often working with recruiters were beachcombers or copra makers such as Mathieu Ferray on Ambae, Fortuné La Chaise on Malo, and François Rossi on Ambrym. They seem to have been the first there.[6]

When, in 1853, Admiral Febvrier Despointes took possession of "New Caledonia and Dependencies," this term was left purposely vague. By 1875, New Caledonian settlers were openly claiming the New Hebrides as logical dependencies of New Caledonia. A campaign was launched to that effect in Noumea, orchestrated by a key figure of the colonization project, John Higginson. Pressure groups in Paris, notably those of the French Colonial Union, simultaneously called on the government to support French settlers in this respect. In 1885, John Higginson wrote to the Ministry of Foreign Affairs in France: "Without the New Hebrides, our New Caledonia colony would be weakened and lose most of its value; its independence and its future entirely depend on the possession of this Archipelago which is its necessary complement."[7]

Higginson's personality was unusual. Born in Great Britain, he was a Protestant of modest Irish upbringing. After emigrating to Australia, he reached New Caledonia in 1859 to work with Paddon—a key figure of the sandalwood trade, who by then had settled on Nou Island near Noumea. Higginson made a quick fortune and early on sided with New Caledonia's cause. He was naturalized as a French citizen in 1879. Higginson was able to acquire early stakes in the mines and founded the firm Société Le Nickel in 1876 (O'Reilly 1957, 99–103).

Higginson was interested in recruiting labor originating from the New Hebrides for his company, and accordingly Société Le Nickel began to use the services of local recruiters or beachcombers. He came to realize that Britain, pushed by its Australian colony, was preparing to annex the group. To Higginson, a portent of this was the missionary hold—Presbyterian to the south and Anglican to the north—and the rise of the first settlements.

On a trip to France, Higginson met Gambetta and Jules Ferry who granted him *carte blanche:* "The [French] government cannot do anything [about the current situation]. Act, we will help you" (Higginson 1926, 5). On his return he created the Caledonian Company of the New Hebrides. Higginson was to write later that "our goal was to do on a large scale what the English had heretofore been doing on a small scale—that is, to succeed through successive land purchases in putting into the hands of the French and therefore of France the ownership of the whole archipelago" (Scarr 1967, 182–183). Higginson's philosophy was condensed in a single phrase: "Where interests are, dominion should be."[8] The issue, then, was to build economic stakes bigger than those of the British so that annexing the New Hebrides would be a natural consequence.

"Buy the Archipelago"

To fulfill his purpose, Higginson created a company whose goal was simply to buy the archipelago from Melanesians—and from British settlers whom he knew were in trouble. He hoped to facilitate, first, the settling of French colonists in the New Hebrides and, second, the importing into New Caledonia of local labor from the New Hebrides.

In Father O'Reilly's words: "New Caledonians [felt] they [were] setting up a kind of East India Company, but a Company without a charter and without privilege, monopoly, war ship, or soldiers" (1957, 100). In October 1882, Higginson and his friends left for the New Hebrides with close to FF100,000 (US$19,300) in trade goods. Lieutenant-Commander Marin d'Arbel, officially "on leave," went on the trip as representative of the Noumea government. In this capacity, he was to make sure that land transactions would be managed correctly—and purchase a few strategic places that might be useful in securing possession.

After a few months, the company created by Higginson claimed over 700,000 hectares constituting the best land in the group. Early sellers were Efate's British plantation owners such as Higginson's friend Donald MacLeod, who parted with all the land he owned at Port Havannah and became the company's local manager. Robert Glissan alone stayed on his land at Undine Bay but, as Scarr noted, he "was isolated among a sea of tricolours" (1967, 183). This was indeed the case as nearly 150,000 hectares claimed by British settlers were transferred to Compagnie Calédonienne, the Caledonian Company. Still other very large properties were "bought" directly from Melanesians by the company's agents, notably 92,000 hectares on the island of Efate alone. At Boufa, over 10,000 hectares were transferred by the leader of the Eratap people, Kalmat, for "a box of dynamite, a box of primers and fuses, thirteen rolls of various pieces of cloth, one hundred kilograms of tobacco, a large matchbox, six dozen pipes, and two axes, for a total value of FF1190 [US$230], to which one must add FF130 [US$25] in cash" (LTO).

On the same day—note the speed of the transaction—and for amounts just as absurdly low of FF1229 and FF1400 (US$237 and US$270), nine-tenths of which were paid in trade goods, 22,000 neighboring hectares were purchased from two other Melanesian partners. A huge estate was pieced together, representing nearly half of the island in one undivided section east of Port Vila.

All such transactions make it plain that equal rates were not granted to Melanesians and Britons. The Land Tenure Office holds some information on this matter, for instance regarding the first piece of land, named Exema, in the northern part of the island. In 1867, Donald MacLeod acquired this 1200-acre plot for £15 (US$73), paid in merchandise, from an Islander who had returned from Queensland. Three years later he resold it to J. Hebblewhite for £130 (US$633). MacLeod then repurchased the plot for £475 (US$2312), eventually selling it to Higginson for FF125,000 (US$24,130). This final transaction scarcely compares with the FF3000 (US$579) that were given for the 40,000 hectares acquired from Melanesians in eastern Efate, even though the Exema property was a plantation already developed and operating. One hectare yielded FF263 (US$50.77) to Donald MacLeod (obviously a businessman with vision) as against FF0.07 (US$0.01) to Melanesians from eastern Efate.

The Caledonian Company soon extended its purchasing drive to the remainder of the archipelago. In 1882, many areas became virtual French holdings, such as most of the coastal plains best suited to settlement on the large islands of Espiritu Santo, Malakula, and Epi, along with the best harbors in the group, for example, Port Sandwich on Malakula. So did the Yasur volcano region on Tanna where sulfur could be mined, the Blackbeach area to the northwest of that island, and the Vanua Lava solfataras. On this immense estate, the tenure of which Higginson claimed officially, the Caledonian Company immediately endeavored to introduce French settlers. Homesteads of 25–50 hectares were given "free" to newcomers provided they agreed to develop them (Davillé 1895).

From 1883 to 1904, nearly one hundred emigrants took advantage of the opportunities granted by the French Colonization Agency, which dealt with the Caledonian Company. To manage exports from the group, Higginson set up a permanent sea link with Noumea. He started monthly mail service in 1886. In that year, the Caledonian Company could claim the virtual ownership of 780,000 hectares of land in an archipelago whose estimated area was 1,467,000 hectares—over half of it and nearly all of its better land. Higginson had been overambitious, however, and the company, poorly managed and too centralized, slid toward bankruptcy. Given the potential political impact of the venture, France stepped in in due time. In 1894, the Société Française des Nouvelles-Hébrides took over the Caledonian Company's assets.

French Settlers

On their arrival in the New Hebrides, French settlers soon realized that nothing was ready for them. Plots were hidden in the bush, and labor to clear them was scarce. With little money to invest, most newcomers became financially dependent on Noumea trading firms. An impartial observer described the situation: "Settlers who are under the weight of debts owed to Noumea trading firms (Ballande, Barrau and so forth) are now starting to liberate themselves from their oppressors' yoke. One may hardly describe otherwise the tyranny imposed by these lenders from New Caledonia! Once he is in their hands, the settler is obliged to accept all supplies that the creditor may wish to send him—or else return the borrowed funds immediately."[9]

The ambiguous nature of colonization in the New Hebrides was entirely apparent in this initial phase. Although the venture started poorly, the result on some islands was an unquestionable effort at agricultural development. In 1894, Efate had thirty-four farms with French legal status and a European population of 119 individuals, with the majority concentrated around Vila, between Tagabe and the Mele Plain (Brunet 1908). A small hotel was located alongside the harbor, next to the stores and offices of the large Noumea trading firms and their Australian competitor Burns Philp. The two largest plantations were one to the east, Franceville, belonging to Chevillard—whose German associate, Zoeppfel, had been killed in 1882 while on a recruiting trip to Santo—and one on the Mele Plain to the west, Framnais, belonging to Petersen-Stuart.

As of 1 January 1894, there were 122 settlers and 84 members of their families in the group. Among settlers, 81 were French, 33 British; of the latter, most were copra makers, in other words, traders rather than plantation owners (Davillé 1895, 121). Overall, the French plantations employed 700 Melanesian workers including 60 on the Franceville property alone. Two steamers, respectively owned by the Société Française des Nouvelles-Hébrides and the Australian New Hebrides Company, called once a month at Vila, the archipelago's new focal point of colonization. In fact, the colonization game was already over and the Condominium in place. The French held the land, the British dominated commerce, and English-speaking missionaries were in charge of souls. Vila was bilingual and fully cosmopolitan. Among a dozen nationalities, there was a fluctuating population of Scandinavian and German sailors tempted by adventure, some Portuguese, Spaniards, Swiss, Belgians, and so forth, while creoles from La Réunion accounted for nearly half of the French settlers. A handful of American adventurers tried their luck as traders in the islands. Additionally, settlers of Anglo-Australian origin operated about ten farms.

An Australian journalist visiting Vila in the early part of the twentieth century wrote:

> In 1878, there was not a single Frenchman in these islands. Nowadays one can hardly hear anything but French on the street. Unquestionably French are the planters and shopkeepers, slim and dark-haired, with big mustaches, and their wives and daughters, pale but elegantly dressed; the bottles of light Bordeaux set on tables and the window frames show no relation to pints of beer and English window sashes.[10]

Locally, the great man of the era was Chevillard. An Austrian count, journeying through the Pacific Ocean with his young bride, on his own yacht, for a honeymoon that lasted eight years(!), described Chevillard as a cultured and refined man who lived in a spacious stone house.

> Joyful and outspoken despite the mystery that surrounded him, a lover of good meals, and a man who enjoyed life like all his fellow citizens, he seemed very wise. Somewhat of a sultan as well, he had a small harem that he recruited on Lepers Island (Ambae). . . . The Frenchman grows coffee, coconuts for their copra, and banana trees whose fruits are shipped to Australia. His very productive plantations look like a fancy garden. Coconut trees are aligned in wide alleys as in a park designed by Lenôtre. Cacao trees are grouped in grovelike fashion and coffee plants growing in the shade of trees make pleasant bushes. (de Tolna 1903, 199)

According to various sources, it seems that Chevillard was of royalist persuasion, and for that reason on bad terms with the Republican government and its representatives. He had been a "youth of fine social status" who had left France following a brawl. Father O'Reilly described him "as one of the most interesting and contrasted personalities of the [New] Hebrides" (1957, 40).

From Vila, French settlement spread to other islands in the group. Three centers were set up in the 1890s, on Epi (Ringdove), Malakula (Port Sandwich), and primarily Espiritu Santo (Segond Channel). The Société Française des Nouvelles-Hébrides—which was soon to go bankrupt itself—acted as a real estate company, creating successive colonization fronts.

Meanwhile, where was Melanesian society? Apparently, it was sunk in a state of deep trauma. Self-assured and convinced they were the bearers of "civilization," the new settlers were behaving as the masters of the archipelago. Armed with their title deeds, they were the manifestation of a balance of forces that had totally swung over to white power. The door opened by sandalwood traders and early beachcombers had led to a situation of domination whose thrust was reaching one island after another, unchecked even by the laws of a distant metropolis. The archipelago still had no laws, but it had masters.

Yet, was the serene world of Melanesian society irreparably doomed after its sudden collapse? To what—to whom—was this people going to turn since even its magic was ineffective in the face of new diseases and Westerners' weapons? The foreigners' religion was there, a diversion or a solution, mostly the means to get closer, perhaps, to the knowledge and the secrets of these new masters. Soon the "wild" islands began to listen to the missionary message.

4 The Gospel and the Kingdom

> By the aid of a spy-glass, we noticed some persons
> walking in front of [an iron house], dressed in long
> priestly robes. In this we recognized at once the mark
> of the beast. . . . A new enemy has entered the field.
> The battle is no longer to be fought with Paganism
> alone, but with Paganism and Popery combined.
>
> Letter from JOHN GEDDIE, 1848

In the years 1800 to 1910, characterized by historians as "the great century of Protestant missionary expansion," capitalism—which was linked with Protestant philosophy—buttressed the diffusion of religious symbols and values. Missionary societies created by private Christian groups grew in numbers and collected funds. The evangelical aspect was allied with a will to work on the social, educational, medical, and scientific levels.

The evangelization of the New Hebrides began with the London Missionary Society. In Polynesia, the society had obtained promising results. One of its most dynamic leaders, John Williams, reached Melanesia and the southern islands of the New Hebrides in 1839. His first contact with Tanna encouraged him to some extent, and there he left three Polynesian teachers, or catechists, in charge of preaching the Scriptures and paving the way for the coming of European missionaries. The next day as he disembarked unarmed in Dillon's Bay on Erromango, Williams was killed along with one of his companions.

John Williams's martyrdom prompted numerous vocations. As John Campbell, another member of the London Missionary Society, wrote, "for the reputation of Mr Williams, and for the purposes of history, he died in the proper manner, at the proper place, and at the proper time" (Daws 1980, 67). In the New Hebrides, henceforth depicted in edifying missionary literature as a wild and dangerous land, the missionaries symbolized the unarmed flag of "civilization." Williams's demise ennobled their undertakings by granting them the epic grandeur of a struggle between good and evil.

Shortly after Williams's death, the ship *Camden* took to Tanna two Scottish missionaries of the London Missionary Society, Thomas Nisbet and George Turner, and their wives (Howe 1984, 293). Literally besieged, they lived for seven months on the coast at Port Resolution while the group that had accepted them was involved in a violent war against a northern group. Eventually the two couples had to escape in the middle of the night in a boat. Shortly thereafter, a dysentery epidemic, which was attributed to their presence, decimated the Port Resolution group.

A few Samoan teachers also landed on Tanna, Futuna, and Anatom. The teachers on Futuna were killed by the Islanders; those on Tanna succumbed to a large-scale smallpox epidemic in 1853. Accused by the Melanesians of being responsible for the epidemic, the last teacher was saved by a passing copra maker's boat. The London Missionary Society abandoned the idea of posting missionaries in Melanesia.

Such a retreat allowed other religious organizations to take up Williams's torch. John Geddie, a Presbyterian missionary, moved to Anatom in 1848, followed by John Inglis in 1852. Geddie, who had emigrated to Canada, was answerable to the Secession Church of New Scotland while Inglis, an emigrant to New Zealand, belonged to the Reformed Presbyterian Church of Scotland. A few years later, other ministers from Australian or Canadian congregations joined the ranks of Presbyterian missionaries. In 1879, eleven of them, originally from Scotland, Australia, New Zealand, and Canada, were to be found throughout the islands of the central and southern parts of the archipelago. They met every year for a synod and set up a quasi-autonomous Presbyterian Church.

Most of these early missionaries, of middle-class or modest origin, were from small towns in Scotland. John Paton, the best known and most representative among them, belonged to a family of eleven children from Dumfries in the Lowlands (Parsonson 1956). These men were courageous and sincere but with little schooling beyond their theological and medical studies. They were often narrow-minded and enclosed their missions within the inflexible limits which they had imposed upon themselves. Further, their sectarian views meant that they were not inclined to take tolerant views of the society and the culture they would find—nor of the other Christian religions competing with theirs.

"[W]e recognized at once the mark of the beast. . . . A new enemy has entered the field," wrote John Geddie in 1848 when from his boat he saw with some bitterness a few Catholic missionaries pacing up and down the shore of Anatom Island. Fortunately for Geddie's mental health, the priests soon departed; they had taken refuge on Anatom while waiting to go back to New Caledonia. Although they were neighbors, the representatives of the two rival churches met only once within a two-year period, and Geddie described the meeting as courteous but cold. On the other hand, the French missionaries were on good terms with the traders at the sandalwood station, especially Paddon, whom Geddie hated (R. Miller 1975).

With its greater fundamentalism, the Reformed Presbyterian Church of Scotland was different from other Calvinist churches. It rejected the distinction between spiritual and temporal which Christian churches generally acknowledge, and it did not believe in civil power or in a society not based on Christian principles (Adams 1984). At the beginning of the nineteenth century, this hard-line religious attitude had led the Reformed Church of Scotland to acknowledge neither the government nor the official church. The dream of a "Christian nation" or, more precisely, of a theocracy seemed easier to develop in a new country than in Europe.

The Presbyterian Model

John Geddie was the first minister to achieve success. In 1859, after eleven years of missionary presence, the island of Anatom was thoroughly Christianized and paganism had apparently been eradicated. To reach his goal, Geddie had learned the language: after six weeks he was said to be able to deliver his first sermon before the people of Anatom (Parsonson 1956, 111). Thereafter he worked intensively at teaching the people to read and write. He translated the New Testament and numerous hymns into the local language. Having mastered the problem of communication, Geddie gathered around him a group of about one hundred Anatom Islanders who came to live next to the mission. They dressed in the European way, learned to read the Scriptures, and participated in church services. These catechumens who had banned all ancient laws and customs linked with traditional society were, for the most part, Melanesians accustomed to Europeans and European culture, such as laborers, former sailors and, subsequently, Kanaka who had returned from Queensland. The Christian village was called a *skul,*[1] a school that taught the teachers-to-be, who were then expected to diffuse the missionary word to the rest of the island.

Conflict with traditional chiefs was inevitable. According to Geddie, the sandalwood station managed by Paddon gave moral support to the "pagan party." In his diary, Geddie accused Paddon of having homicidal intentions and of setting the Islanders against him. Ancient rifts were resurfacing between the Christian party gathered around coastal stations and the pagan party, more at ease in the inland spaces of the island. No compromise could be expected, although the missionary presence did prevent resort to open warfare. In the course of this conflict, which went on for three years, the pagans set fire to Geddie's house and church. The balance of forces rapidly swung to the Christians' side after Paddon left the island, depriving the pagans of their most reliable support. Further, London Missionary Society vessels visited the island regularly, buttressing the general opinion that the Christian party benefited from outside help. The pagan party had only magic, which was no longer effective.

In October 1853, the island of Anatom had one church and fifteen Samoan teachers. Six years later, sixty local teachers were in charge of fifty-six bush schools—one per village or hamlet—and eleven large churches, including the main one at Anelgohat which could hold twelve hundred people (Parsonson 1956). There was not a single avowed "pagan" on the island. In less than twelve years, Geddie to the south and Inglis to the north had won their battle: paganism had been conquered and a "biblical nation" was being shaped. *Kastom* as a whole was relegated to the sphere of Satan (see chapter 13).

Missionaries endeavored to build a new social order. The church became the real center of each village, and the teacher its political leader. What was taught was Bible reading, religious hymns, and the commandments of the new moral order. While "local courts" made up of eager Christians judged recalcitrants, a local "police" enforced court decisions; fines and jail terms were converted to forced labor on roads, or service for the mission and Christian communities. By creating a private police and a legal system, the Presbyterian mission was, in its opinion, filling the void caused by the destruction of the traditional order. Next, the pastors prompted Islanders to start coconut plantations for trade purposes. They also levied a tribute which was paid in arrowroot—a plant originating from America whose flour, once manufactured and dried, was sold in Europe to benefit the missions.

With such "redeeming Christian work," part of which filled the mission coffers, the new communities seemed at last to be built on the desired principles—simplicity, work, and virtue. For the converts who, within a few years, had gone from a traditional society to Calvinist Christianity, the transition had been brief and radical.

On a visit to Anatom in 1869, Agnes Watt, the young wife of the missionary William Watt, described the missionary dream as it was finally being fulfilled:

> The Mission Station here is quite a model, nothing trifling or flimsy like, and all very clean. There is a Church, a Training Institution, and a dwelling house with many appendages such as carpenter's shop, smith's shop, store-room, etc. . . . In the morning we were awakened by the church bell ringing the people to school, which all attend from six to seven, before going to their plantations. The Bible is the sole book. It is a real national Scriptural education the natives here receive. There are schools all over the island, within ten minutes' walk of each home, and these are presided over by native teachers. These teachers are of great

value, and, I may say, give their labor free, for they only receive £1 per annum [US$4.87] for their services. The natives are well behaved; in each house family worship is held morning and evening. (1896, 66–67)

Agnes Watt underlined the part played by the bell in Christian villages. It was the very symbol of the new order, imparting a rhythm to the hours of prayer, heralding when to eat, go to bed, and get up in the morning. Along with "Christian time," the missionary discipline also shaped a Christian space that emphasized a village-based organization and novel house styles.

"Missionary kingdoms" following this model incorporated all facets of the converts' social life. With no choice but to accept Presbyterianism, decimated by a kind of slow death that went on well after the 1860 epidemic, the people of Anatom fell into a deep lethargy noted by all visitors. More than a century later, in the 1970s, almost half the population changed religions and converted to Catholicism. Given local patience, one may assume that the island was never really unanimous about the forced acceptance of the Presbyterian order.

The Shelling of Tanna

In 1860, a measles epidemic carried by a sandalwood ship struck down the inhabitants of the southern islands, particularly the people living around the Anelgohat anchorage on Anatom Island. According to mission sources, 1100 out of 3560 Islanders died within a few weeks. Depopulation did not stop. Anatom never recovered from that epidemic (see chapter 3). In Tanna and particularly in Erromango, also struck down by disease, missionaries probably believed "they were racing against death"; the entire population they were converting was expiring in their arms.

Yet the death that fell on the islands also strengthened pagan resistance. The missionary Gordon and his wife were murdered on Erromango. On Tanna, John Paton had to flee Port Resolution at night and find shelter southward, with his colleague Mathieson. Soon the two pastors took advantage of a recruiting ship passing through and left the island. Christianization was marking time: the Anatom mission was ruined, and Erromango and Tanna had killed or expelled their missionaries.

John Paton went back to Tanna in 1865, but this time the small mission boat was escorted by an armored ship of the British Navy, HMS *Curaçoa*. The man of God wanted to get even with the majority pagan party that had forced his ignominious flight. Paton had convinced Wiseman, captain of the *Curaçoa*, that the people of Tanna needed to be taught a lesson after twenty years of "murders, misdeeds, and arrogance" vis-à-vis the mission. Heavy gunfire filled the bay, followed by the landing of 170 British sailors who set fire to villages, canoes, and plantations in the area. Several casualties occurred among the Tannese when a shell exploded a few days later (Adams 1984; Howe 1984).

The very next day, Paton had the terrorized Islanders sign a letter of his own invention by which he received their promise to respect the missionaries' rule of law as well as that of the representatives of Queen Victoria and the British Navy. The document, signed by Port Resolution people and in Paton's handwriting, concluded:

> Formerly we had been guilty of so many murders that we feared men-of-war could come and punish us; we all thought and said they durst not try, and so we delighted in our bad conduct. Then we had no idea of the multitude of fighting men in a man-of-war, and of her awful power to destroy us and our lands; but now we have seen it, and our hearts have failed us. We are all weak and crying for fear. The great inland chief, Quantengan, who came to help us fight the man-of-war, was cut down by one of [its] chiefs [officers], and many more are hurt, and we know not how many are shot and dead. Our canoes, our houses, and our lands are laid waste by [its] fighting men. We never saw anything like this and plead with the chief of the man-of-war not to punish us any more, but to go and leave us, and truly we will obey his word. Tell him to inform your good Queen Victoria that we will kill no more of her people but in future be good, and learn to obey the word of Jehovah. (Adams 1984, 159)

Unquestionably this event had a profound impact on the Australian public. Geddie himself publicly deplored the shelling, stating that it was "one of the most humiliating events in the history of modern missions" (Parsonson 1956, 122). The Sydney paper *The Empire* published a sarcastic article that painted Paton as a "sacerdotal hypocrite." As for Wiseman, he was disowned by his own military authorities. The attack on Tanna represented the first occurrence in a fairly long time of a European ship shelling a community because of its refusal to convert to Christianity. It was believed that Paton had acted primarily out of revenge, and all the arguments that he put forth subsequently did not erase that belief.

The shelling of the island had contradictory effects. While it reinforced the rejection of evangelization within Tanna, it also forced the Tannese to wonder about and deeply question the island's ability to resist. Violent acts against Christians did stop. However, the Islanders who supported the mission became circumspect and advised Paton against his return. Two years later, a missionary couple, the Nielsons, received a hostile reception on the island: "When Mr Neilson presented himself, the Tannese vigorously opposed his landing, and threw the timber for his house back into the sea as quickly as it was put ashore. . . .

They gave as a reason, that they were angry because HMS *Curaçoa* had bombarded them" (Watt 1896, 50). Eventually the Nielsons were accepted, thanks to Geddie's influence. Settling to the south of Port Resolution, they spent fourteen years on the island without converting a single Islander. Thoroughly discouraged, the couple left in 1882.

In 1869, the Watts landed in the southeast of the island, at Kwamera, and received just as poor a welcome. When William Watt suggested that he and his wife settle there with a teacher from Anatom, the Islanders did not dare to refuse. Before Watt could preach, however, they advised him to wait for them to end their war with their neighbors. A number of missionaries were soon to share the disenchanted opinion expressed by Agnes Watt in a letter of 1871: "The truth is, it is traders, not missionaries, that the Tannese want" (1896, 127).

A new wave of epidemics complicated matters. Islanders did not know how to interpret the missionaries' presence: were they allies who could protect them from the harsh new diseases or, on the contrary, were they the propagators of such scourges? Owing equally to local wars and the memory of the shelling, Presbyterian missionaries on Tanna did not get positive results until the turn of the century. Conversions were insecure before then and there was no Christian party next to the mission stations. "The Tannese have opposed the gospel till they have become a proverb and a byword, and have by their waywardness sorely tried our faith," sighed Agnes Watt (1896, 284).

The proof is that, after fifty years of effort, the mission in 1882 included only a few assistants from Anatom and less than ten local catechumens. On the whole island, hardly one hundred individuals attended the Sunday service and then, more out of curiosity than conviction. Apparently, one full generation needed to pass before the memory of the British vessels and the unfair death that had come from the sky dimmed.

A "Christian Nation"

In 1870, Presbyterian missionaries began to expand the range of evangelization to include the islands at the center and north center of the archipelago. Only Tanna and, to a lesser extent, Erromango represented the breakwater-like pagan resistance. The missionary effort moved up to Malakula and Santo after 1880. Agnes Watt, who had journeyed to these two islands on the *Dayspring,* noted in 1887 that "[t]hese northern islanders seem much less savage and heathenish than those down south. . . . No one could feel nervous among such quiet, docile people. . . . [A]t each settlement we were more and more pleased with our reception" (1896, 278–279).

Thanks to Paton's fund drive and propaganda, the Presbyterian mission was then rich and famous. His book *John G. Paton, Missionary to the New Hebrides: An Autobiography* was a best-seller in England and Australia, and a special illustrated reprint was published to enlighten the youth of these two countries. The funds collected by Paton soon gave the Presbyterian mission an air of opulence that could not fail to impress converts. Not only did ministers benefit from good wages and regular vacations in Australia or New Zealand with their wives and children but upon their arrival in the islands a team of lay assistants would build a comfortable house for them. There was also a specially chartered boat, the *Dayspring,* which made regular calls at each missionary center.

Apart from Tanna, the mission's achievements became truly impressive by 1890. A new generation of missionaries replaced the preceding one, which had been personified by such men as Geddie, Watt, and Inglis. As Guiart emphasized, these early missionaries had spread the Gospel, come what may (1956*b*). A life of trials in nearly complete solitude had influenced them in favor of moderation. Some of their efforts did not go unnoticed; for instance, the memory of Agnes Watt, who died in 1894, is still alive in Tanna. She is famous for the beautiful songs she wrote in the local language. On her grave these simple words are inscribed: "She loved the people of Tanna" (Father Monnier, pers comm). By contrast, the new generation of missionaries moved into conquered territory and behaved triumphantly. The Presbyterian dream of a biblical nation could unfold at last without any contrary force to contest its power in the islands.

In 1900, in this archipelago of approximately sixty thousand residents, there were 26 Presbyterian missionaries and their families, along with about 10 lay technical personnel (4 physicians, several educators, and nurses). An impressive total, to which one should add 313 local teachers who, under the control of missionaries, managed as many Bible schools and religious districts spread over Anatom, Santo, and Ambrym (Picanon 1902).

Presbyterian missionary activity reached such a level of power that on Tanna itself the Christian party won the battle, if not the war: the once active pagan resistance became passive. Two militants of the second generation of missionaries, the reverends Nicholson—also a physician—at Lenakel and MacMillan at White Sands, took over the island. They endeavored to enclose Tanna in a totalitarian theocracy and limit outside contacts as much as possible.

Parsonson, historian of the Presbyterian mission, wrote that missionaries "were men who could not think about Christianity outside the context of their own society. . . . Wherever it was successfully preached, it produced a deplorable imitation of the Scottish Christian, dressed in European cast-off clothing, delivering Puritan clichés and following Presbyterian Sunday rituals with the utmost exactness" (1956, 124).

The Condominium's British District Agent Wilkes discovered Tanna in 1910 at a time when the Christian party was imposing its rule. He expressed his dismay in a letter to the British Resident:

> [There existed] ample evidence of a "forcible feeding" with theological pabulum and of a "mailed fist" type of evangelization that I have nowhere else in the Pacific been privileged to see, while to such an extent has the fanaticism . . . of an imperfectly comprehended faith been carried by the Deacons of this island [Anatom] that the wearing of coconut armlets, the decking of the head with flowers by young women and girls, the cooking of food on Sundays, and the singing of purely innocent secular songs, have been denominated "offences" and totally proscribed as "heathenish" and "works of the devil." (30 Sept 1913, in Scarr 1967, 245)

Over this self-contained and increasingly powerful religious world, the French had little hold. Settlers in particular found it increasingly difficult to recruit labor, and violent controversies broke out. In a newspaper for settlers, *Le Courrier des Nouvelles-Hébrides: Pro Patria,* one could read: "The time has come when the negrophile hypocrisy of Presbyterianism has to yield to wider and more humanitarian ideas. It is not through dull propaganda that a people becomes civilized, on the contrary it is by getting the widest possible view of its rights" (Benoist 1972, 21). From another periodical, *Le Néo-Hébridais* of March 1910, here are a few quotations selected at random: "Presbyterians are the mere tool of English policy in the New Hebrides as well as its stronghold. . . . They have created small states where they are absolute masters. They take the place of the authorities, dispensing justice, handing out fines, levying taxes, and so forth." On a similar note but with more restraint, a French officer commented:

> It is sad to compare the outer aspect of our Catholic missions and that of English missions. With rare exceptions, ours have mediocre huts, theirs are tidy dwellings built by carpenters from Australia who bring in all needed materials, with sheds for one or two boats. . . . Nearly all [Presbyterian missionaries] are middle-aged men who have been in this country for a long time and whose previous jobs as carpenters, mechanics, and the like prepared them for this life of colonization; they receive a nice salary of 4 to 5000 francs [US$772 to US$965], plus 1000 [US$193] if they are married, and 10 pounds [US$49] upon the birth of every child. This money allows them first to enjoy a level of comfort that our Marist fathers do not know and second to encourage the natives, since the Hebrideans are ready to embrace the religion and consequently the nationality which is the most generous. And for the natives, Presbyterian means Englishman and Catholic equals Frenchman.[2]

To some extent, the Presbyterian ministry played for. the British camp the part played on the French side by the Société Française des

Nouvelles-Hébrides. While the ministry annexed souls and built political kingdoms, the company grabbed land and attempted to construct a world of colonial plantations. The two institutions emerged simultaneously, but their divergent purposes were to have unwieldy political implications for the Condominium partners later on.

The Presbyterian mission was evangelizing a land deemed in Europe to be one of the most dangerous—a land of "degraded human beings" as John Paton said charitably. Such endeavor, however, gradually lost favor in the religious English-speaking world. In the twentieth century, missionaries were less numerous and not as wealthy. But the "Presbyterian nation" was already deep-rooted. Melanesian ministers took over by the end of World War I and in 1948, in agreement with the mother churches of Scotland and Nova Scotia which had supplied the largest number of European missionaries, the synod proclaimed the independence of the Presbyterian Church of the New Hebrides. Reverend Graham Miller, the first moderator of that church, was to write in his book *Live,* "a self-governing church is the preparation for a self-governing nation" (n.d., 125). For the new ministers and teachers, another fight remained, that of political independence. The religious dream was again a secular dream. Had it ever ceased being so?

The Anglican System

The Anglicans expanded their Melanesian ministry shortly after John Williams's martyrdom. Melanesia, within the New Zealand diocese, was Bishop George Selwyn's sphere of action. The Anglican Church had no specific social goals and its attitude vis-à-vis local customs was not systematically hostile. The missionaries themselves were different. Selwyn, Patteson, and Codrington, who were members of the Anglican High Church, belonged to the aristocracy or the upper class and were more highly educated than their Presbyterian colleagues. As far as evangelizing and dealing with other civilizations were concerned, their ideas were then considered liberal or "progressive."

Besides, Selwyn was convinced that no Westerner could live permanently north of Erromango Island, so intense were the heat and humidity. He thought it fruitless to plan a system of missionary stations in those islands. For him, the solution lay in evangelizing Melanesians out of their milieu, in other words, educating them in temperate countries, then sending them home so they could in turn diffuse Christianity and lay the foundation of a local church. There were cultural reasons involved apart from the climate-related arguments, in particular the large number of island languages.

Selwyn focused his effort on a complete educational system which for the most part would take place in New Zealand. Locally, the task of European missionaries was limited to recruiting students and visiting local Christian communities on a regular basis. The Anglicans had a broad pedagogical purpose. "Two firm and unalterable rules the Bishop laid down for the work. 1. That he would never interfere with any Christianization already undertaken by any religious body or sect whatever; so that he would never bring before the Islanders the great stumbling-block of divisions among Christians who should be as brethren. 2. That in taking to them the religion of Englishmen he would in no way force upon them English methods and ways of life, except in so far as they are part of morality and godliness" (Armstrong 1900, 9). In the liberal view of Selwyn and his assistants, the issue was to evangelize without destroying. The practices of traditional society were to be respected when they did not conflict with Christian moral values.

Selwyn's other rule was never to compete on religious grounds with another missionary church. He abandoned the southern islands of the New Hebrides to the Presbyterians while the Isle of Pines, south of New Caledonia, went to the Catholics who were there first. Later, in 1881, the archipelago was divided up among Presbyterians and Anglicans and the amicable arrangement was respected by both parties. To prosper, the system advocated by Selwyn had to rely on large-scale financial means to allow for the purchase of a medium-tonnage ship, the intake and maintenance of students in an overseas school, and the running of island-based schools. Thanks to donations from England, Australia, and New Zealand, the necessary financial support never fell short. Purchased in 1853, a seventy-ton ship, the *Southern Cross,* served the mission on a full-time basis.

Half a century later, the gamble had succeeded. By 1900, the Melanesian diocese of the Anglican Church had 9 missionary priests, including 2 Melanesians, and 420 permanently employed teachers. The total Anglican community was estimated at twelve thousand baptized and catechized Christians in the Solomon Islands and northern New Hebrides (Armstrong 1900).

The Evangelization of Mota, Banks Islands

In 1861, the diocese of Melanesia was freed from its links with New Zealand and Patteson became its first bishop. A great figure of the Anglican mission with a talent for languages, Patteson like Selwyn had an excellent rapport with people. The real growth of evangelization took place in the northern islands of the group. Every year, about fifty young people from the Solomon Islands and the New Hebrides journeyed aboard the *Southern Cross* to the Auckland theological school. Most turned out to be gifted students and quick learners. They could not adjust to the climate, however. The theology school was therefore transferred to Norfolk in 1871, to what became St. Barnabas College.

In the early years of missionary development, the Banks Islands were seemingly the most open to evangelization. Patteson decided to settle on Mota Island to manage the first regional school that would be open all year long. But he encountered the hostility of Mota's traditional leaders, and that of an entire society whose "idols and superstitions" he was denouncing. Patteson reached the same conclusion as Geddie: Christianity was not compatible with pagan Melanesian society. *Kastom* had to be "cleansed."

The new Christians in Patteson's diocese soon abandoned their traditional practices and, in the ministers' opinion, asserted themselves as a model of Christian edification. Mota became for the Anglicans what Anatom was to the Presbyterian Church; indeed, it moved toward Christianity on an identical path. As a first step, a Christian party made up of zealous and radical converts established itself around the mission school. These men lived under a genuine messianic spell, perhaps not unlike the first Christians in Rome. They spent their days waiting for prayers, the return of the missionary ship, or any sign that could be interpreted in religious terms. However, their aversion and contempt for everything related to their own ancestral beliefs and customs went beyond the wishes of the missionaries themselves. What concerned the priests was the converts' complete renunciation of their traditional way of life which, despite its "original impurity," supplied an adequate social structure.

> At Mota, for example, the people were giving up fighting, were losing faith in their old charms and contrivances for compassing the death of their enemies, and would soon be at peace throughout the whole island. Then, unless their whole social and domestic life were changed, and a new character infused into them, they would become entirely idle, talk infinite scandal, and indulge in unlimited gluttony; so that, while professing to believe Christianity, their whole life would be in entire opposition to it. The practical object now, and the most difficult, was to teach them to become industrious, honest, persevering, tidy, clean, and careful with children. How was it to be done? (Armstrong 1900, 62–63)

In other words, the issue was to turn these new Christians into individuals who would be in step with the moral standards of Victorian England.

By 1871, victory seemed complete for *skul* proponents. Grades and secret societies[3]—the two traditional ways to gain power—officially ceased to exist. A coral stone church was consecrated and, in July 1871, ninety-seven children were baptized in a collective ceremony. On Mota, which had become Christian of its own accord, the growth of George Sarawai's village—he was the leader of the island's Christian party— paralleled the abandonment of the surrounding pagan hamlets. There was a "flood of baptisms," and one hundred fifty adults slept by the church at night in order to be immediately on hand for services and sermons the next morning. Sarawai, already master of the island, was ordained deacon. Mota's Christians then undertook to evangelize other islands. With its focus and roots on Mota, the Anglican mission, although sometimes concerned about the political scope of its success, could now draw on the local human resources that were needed for its continuing development.

An unforeseen tragedy occurred in 1871. Bishop Patteson was killed at Nukapu in the Santa Cruz Islands after he had gone ashore alone. Wrapped in mats, his body was sent back to the mission boat in a canoe: five wounds were visible and, in a coconut palm leaf placed on the chest, five knots had been made. The symbol was clear. Patteson was paying for the disappearance of five men whom blackbirders had abducted a few days earlier.

Spontaneous Evangelization?

George Sarawai was ordained a priest in 1873. With 184 students, the Norfolk school was so successful that the mission had to turn down potential candidates. A network of Bible schools had been set up on most shores of the group's northeastern islands, and Anglican projects were being carried out throughout the northern part of the islands. Yet a serious issue remained to be solved, which was not the resistance from a pagan party that was then everywhere in retreat—except perhaps on Ambae—but island depopulation caused by intensive labor recruiting. Christian villages located near accessible anchorages, therefore more exposed to recruiting, were gradually losing their male population. Codrington devoted most of his time to warning people against the labor trade, yet, as related by Armstrong, "[t]hey agreed, but fell away under the temptation of the traders' axes and knives, with the further hope of obtaining a gun" (1900, 142–143).

John, George Selwyn's son, was ordained bishop of the Melanesian Church in 1877, replacing Patteson. Christianization was moving forward very rapidly in the Banks Islands. On Mota, the majority of the population attended at least one of the five church services held daily; on the other islands, twelve missionary teachers were proving their competence. Satisfied with this self-generating system, Selwyn endeavored to use his political influence to limit blackbirding and impose tighter control over recruiting ships and labor conditions on the plantations.

The great expansion of the Anglican Church that took place at the end of the nineteenth century ran concurrently with Presbyterian expansion in the southern and central parts of the archipelago. Sharing the islands between them, these two churches were then at the height of their missionary drive. After being away for six years, Codrington went back to Melanesia and was struck by the changes that had occurred. He referred to his stay in the islands as a "triumphant journey." The diffusion of Christianity had indeed been incredibly fast, eating away, nearly everywhere, the system of traditional political hierarchy based on grades. Anglican missionaries generally acknowledged the disappearance of the grade system as a sign of moral progress. Armstrong recounted that in 1894 the highest graded man in the Torres Islands, Tequalqual, asked to be baptized. The missionary requested that he first relinquish his grade. Along with his kin, Tequalqual erased the path he had followed in the course of his life: over the next few days, he killed fewer pigs of decreasing value and ate at more common hearths. On reaching the lowest level of the hierarchy, the chief stated that he was "free" and was then baptized. The grade system was abandoned in the Torres Islands.

Some inland population groups on the largest and hilliest islands such as Ambae, Maewo, and Gaua were immune to evangelization,[4] however, and concurrently the wave of rapid conversions remained fragile. Many teachers "lapsed" periodically; they would quietly board a recruiting boat on its way to Queensland, or compromise themselves in local cases by using the power acquired at the mission for their own benefit. Mota itself, the focal point and cradle of the mission, went through periods of laxity that missionaries found difficult to interpret. Whereas the Christianity of the Melanesian Church was a triumph everywhere else, in 1898 the missionary Cullwich exposed the surprising reawakening of *kastom* and secret society rites on the island. This led him, on his own authority, to close a district school. As Armstrong wrote, "Mota was now well visited by traders, who supplied the people with tobacco, &c., and the Mission ship was no longer looked forward to as it used to be" (1900, 345). Like Anatom, the model island had gone into a sort of cultural lethargy which has not entirely disappeared today; it was as if, somehow, the formidable millenarian expectation induced by the missionary discourse had left a huge vacuum upon its collapse. Severe depopulation struck Mota, and the departures of Islanders for Queensland were more numerous than elsewhere.

The number of European traders and settlers in the group started to increase in the 1880s. The arrival of Catholic missionaries on islands that the Melanesian mission considered its territories was perceived as a threat, and a decision was made to establish a form of permanent presence.

Consequently, the Banks, most of East Ambae, North Pentecost, and Maewo organized themselves into independent mission-structured districts operating in close cooperation with the British administration. The Melanesian Church shaped a sort of autonomous "nation" with the mores and language of Britain. It was a natural choice, one which puts the history of the Condominium in its true light. When New Caledonian settlers launched themselves into large-scale land purchases after 1882, they thought they could annex the islands on behalf of France. By that time, however, the Melanesian population was under the influence of the Anglican and Presbyterian churches, both cultural and political manifestations of the English-speaking world.

5 Catholic Peasant Missionaries and Marginal Churches

> The pagans are in no doubt. They realize full well that, when they become Christians, the real source of their vitality dries up; namely, their pagan feasts. The pagan village appears to be brimming with life: the Christian village seems dead. Are we not too severe?
>
> FATHER EDOUARD LOUBIÈRE, 1905

In a letter dated 20 March 1884 to Father Colomb, head of the Marist mission, John Higginson requested that Catholic missionaries be sent to the New Hebrides, confidentially promising the support of his company: "The presence of your missionaries in the archipelago would be for me a guarantee that Presbyterian missionaries would not, because of their intrigues, hold an exclusive ascendancy over the natives and therefore could not thwart the annexation of the New Hebrides by France. . . . It is now up to you to help me turn these islands into a French territory despite all the blunders of the mother country."[1]

Although so directly called upon, the Catholic ministry did not actually receive much support from Higginson's company, with the exception of a few gifts of land to set up stations and a grant upon the arrival of each missionary. Besides, the Catholic mission became increasingly less willing to play the political role expected of it and refused to transform itself into the docile tool of the French administration and the Compagnie Calédonienne. Yet the sending of French Catholic missionaries was perceived as a political gesture in the local context of the late 1880s. The Catholic Church was the *franis skul* in Bislama—in other words, the church of the French and the settlers' cultural reference point.

French Marist missionaries, to whom the Holy See had given the task of evangelizing the Pacific Islands, knew they would face difficult circumstances. From New Caledonia, a veteran missionary wrote to his brother:

> Far be it from me to blame our Superiors, who want very much to start work again in the New Hebrides. But what pains me is the thought that we're going there accompanied by the military and at the behest of political agitators. I'm convinced that the Protestants will shout from the roof-

67

tops that our presence was imposed by force, with the backing of gun-
boats. I'm convinced too that before long we'll be at loggerheads with
the Company, whose purpose is clear anyway: they just want to make
use of us as an advance guard in places they're finding it difficult to get
into. God help us! (Father Montrouzier in Monnier n.d.*b*, 12)

On their arrival in the islands, Marist missionaries met with hardship. Not only were they the very last to get to the archipelago, but also
they were poor. In their favor, however, was the fact that all or nearly
all were from peasant families. Many originated from the poverty-
stricken regions of the Massif Central or Brittany and embodied qualities
which were to be of value to them in the field, namely sobriety and tena-
ciousness.

The French priests also affirmed an optimistic general philosophy.
Catholic theology stated that man is the fruit of divine creation and is
able through his own spiritual growth to reach "universal truths." This
approach meant that particles of truth existed in all civilizations, even the
least Christian ones. The doctrine of an already saved individual reflecting some of God's splendor within his natural state contrasted with
Calvinist doctrine that saw man as a fallen being who could only be
saved through a complete break with himself. In its pastoral practice, the
Catholic Church granted the faithful considerable moral freedom, provided they observed the general commandments of the church, especially
with regard to the sacraments.

Nevertheless, beyond an open global perspective that often led Catholic missionaries to look for signs of implicit faith amidst local beliefs,
the Marists had hardly any real political strategy. How could they outline
one without the material means to implement it? They had neither ship,
nor money, nor "party" on their side, and survival was foremost in their
minds wherever they landed. Overshadowed by their Anglican and Presbyterian rivals, the Marist fathers were reduced to a type of missionary
presence based on the practice of poverty, a poverty that would not have
displeased more modern theologians. Such penury, the great distinctive
sign of the French clergy, was a genuine handicap in the early years, however. Poverty also implied a kind of humility, if only by necessity. At the
turn of the century, given the official policy of "separation of church from
state," the Catholic mission was no longer granted any aid from the
French colonial administration.[2]

An English witness who was personally indifferent to religious matters wrote these words about French priests in the New Hebrides:

The Catholic missionary lives a very different life to his John Knoxian
brother. He gets £30 a year all told [US$146]. He generally lives in a
grass hut and feeds on native food until he has made his plantation and

made it pay. [Catholic missionaries] encourage the natives in all their old customs, and have much more influence—despite their poverty—with their flock than do the Presbyterians. They are the only people here who know anything about the folk-lore and old customs of the natives. (Fletcher 1986, 203–204)

Survival

On 20 January 1887, a few Marist missionaries, along with assistants from New Caledonia, disembarked from a French trading vessel on Efate (Mele Bay), Malakula (Banam Bay), and Santo (Port Olry). Nothing was known about the number of local residents and their state of mind, nor about the healthiness of these places. The priests were left on the beach with a few boxes and trunks. Later, *La Dives,* a French Navy sloop, brought in the lumber that was used to build their first house. The Presbyterian mission immediately sent pastors to the very spots where the Marists were established. Father Deniau gave an account of the beginnings of the two Marists on Malakula:

> Unfortunately, the Protestant ministers, jealous of [the Marists'] achievements, settled at their door, so to speak. And instead of staying at their own posts to work at civilizing the poor natives, as they say, they came to show islanders an example of the darkest jealousy, turn them away from the fathers with despicable slander against France and Catholic priests, and attract them with the use of disreputable means. (Letter, 11 Sept 1887, CMA)

A different viewpoint obviously prevailed on the Presbyterian side. In 1888, Agnes Watt and her husband accompanied a nephew, Reverend Legatt, who was settling at Aulua near the Marist site on the east coast of Malakula. She was pleasantly surprised; in one of her letters she reported the following statement by local Melanesians:

> "Man Malakula he no like French missionary, he no got boat, he no got wife, he no got piccanniny, he no got nothing."[3] Their joy was great when they saw that T. W. L. [Reverend Legatt] had got all three, or rather all four. They gave him a good site for his house, plenty of good land, with fruit and other trees on it, beside a nice little stream of fresh water. For two weeks the missionaries and their able assistants wrought late and early, first clearing the land, and then house-building. . . . we left them very comfortably settled. (Watt 1896, 274–275)

The two Catholic missionaries, Father François-Xavier Gaudet and his companion, Father Joseph Lambotin, did not have the material resources to compete and chose not to stay. Alone, Father Gaudet headed to the northern part of the island and the nearby islets, which were

densely populated—and fiercely hostile to missionaries. In a wild race
with the Presbyterian missionaries who seemed to be on his tracks, he
settled on the islet of Rano, then left because, in his words, "it was a city
of cannibals." He moved to the nearby islet of Wala where he built a hut
with boards from a shipwreck. He wrote that he was scared night and
day and avoided ambushes that pagans would lay for him by keeping his
gun within reach at all times. In 1891, exhausted, Father Gaudet asked
to be relieved of his mission: "I started the hare, but I do not have the
strength to run after it," he wrote to his bishop (in Monnier n.d.*b*, 25).

The Mele mission was hardly more successful, and any expectation
regarding Efate was soon relinquished. *"C'est le boulevard du protestantisme,"*[4] Father Pionnier concluded with some bitterness in a letter to his
bishop.[5] Through the force of circumstances, the thrust of the mission
moved to the buffer zone between the Anglican northern realm and the
Presbyterian southern domain.

These early years were survival years for Catholic missionaries. They
found themselves practically without support, far from Noumea, and
with no real links with Melanesian society. First and foremost they had
to fulfill their needs, which meant reclaiming land, building, and planting—in other words, working like settlers.

Father Lambotin told how Father Gaudet landed on Malakula:

> Upon landing with his box, the father . . . starts building a temporary
> shelter for the night; then he takes an ax and begins clearing land. The
> settler clergy of the Middle Ages have survived to this day. . . . Kanaks
> come crowding in to see the missionary, look at his trunk, and check
> whether he has any tobacco or brandy. Indeed many among them have
> lived in Noumea and Brisbane. Then they sit on the ground and smoke a
> pipe while watching the father work. (1891)

"Poor mission of the New Hebrides"—Father Pionnier wrote in a letter dated 1896, at a time when Anglican and Presbyterian Churches were
blossoming—"twenty-five of our missionaries went through the New
Hebrides and we have less than twenty Christians."

On Malakula and Santo, evangelization scarcely showed any sign of
hope. Catholics preached to deaf ears.

In 1898, the first two missionary nuns of the Marist mission arrived
in the New Hebrides; their number increased later. The nuns played an
essential role. In addition to the domestic life of the stations, they were in
charge of education and health care. Thanks to them, Catholic missions
began to be of genuine service to Melanesian communities. Besides, by
entering the world of women and making converts, the nuns were working on the weak link of traditional pagan society: they offered Melanesian women an alternative to subordination. The largest Marist stations

were not supplied with these teams for at least another two decades, however.

The "Dialogue"

The history of the Catholic mission everywhere, but especially in northern Malakula, is characterized by its rivalry with the already established Presbyterians. With their high density of population, the northern islets (Wala, Rano, Atchin, Vao) were much disputed stakes. Hostile, or at best wholly indifferent to the missionaries' message, local pagan groups were strongly committed to their customs, such as grade ceremonies, exchange cycles, and traditional wars, some of which seemed quite ruthless. The specter of anthropophagy was frequently alluded to in their letters by missionaries posted on the northern Malakula islets—which they described as places of hardship and violence where elders were buried before they died (Monnier n.d.*b*, 30). Father Jean-Baptiste Jamond landed in Vao in 1900, two years after the death by food poisoning of Father Jean-André Vidil.[6] Quite aware of the Islanders' feelings about him, he wrote in his diary: "These people do not want to be converted. . . . They are just not interested. You have only to live with them for a week to realize that. What [is one] to do? I pray a great deal, sowing my Ave Marias in every corner of Vao, . . . often at night, I say the rosary." Father Jamond's experience led him to conclude: "We must be loved by the people, otherwise we can do nothing. I think that, here in Vao, I have done what I could for that" (Monnier n.d.*b*, 34, 35).

On the small island of Wala, where Father Casimir Salomon landed in 1898, replacing Gaudet, the enemy had a different face. Shortly after Salomon's arrival, Reverend Crombie, a missionary physician, and his wife settled next to him. The Islanders sold the Presbyterians and the Catholic two small contiguous plots on haunted ground where human victims had been dismembered in the past. Knowing that no one could live there without dying, the Islanders wanted to test the European missionaries' power. Besides wandering souls, the two rivals had to endure a difficult closeness.

Father Salomon's unpublished diary is filled with anecdotes regarding his relationship with Dr Crombie, whom he called "the minister of error"! Although the two men could see one another daily from their respective houses, they communicated by means of letters carried by Melanesian messengers. Among other things, Father Salomon took Reverend Crombie to task for exercising political authority over the island, and that such authority rested on the *Pegasus*, a British warship that was then plying the archipelago's waters. At one time, the two missionaries acted out a scene of epic proportions. The starting point was a medal of the Blessed Virgin that Father Salomon had given to a Wala man. Later, the man told the father, who was asking him why he was not wearing it, that Reverend Crombie had accused him of witchcraft and torn it from him. Furious, Father Salomon ran to his rival and launched into a lively theological discussion on the beach. Many Melanesian spectators attended the controversy, which took place in Bislama. When they ran out of arguments, the two servants of the Lord calmed down and Father Salomon was then told that in fact the man from Wala had only traded his medal for a cigar. Realizing that they had both been deceived, the two missionaries parted without saying a word and did not make peace.

In the early part of the twentieth century, copra makers favored the North Malakula islets because of their large populations and the presence of coconut groves. There were eight copra makers located between Norsup and the tip of Vao. Melanesians from the area received their European supplies from them and therefore did not expect anything of that sort from the missionaries. Reverend Crombie did extend some medical services to the Wala people. As far as the other missionary was concerned, the people appreciated little besides his house, which was built on stilts. Father Salomon reminisced about this in the following anecdote: "Tonight Malter Asso says to me: 'Father, when you die, we shall miss you very much.' In the belief this was a flattering compliment, I answer with pride: 'Another good priest will come to you.' Malter Asso then clarifies his thinking: 'We shall not miss you, we shall only miss your tobacco and not going up to your veranda in the evening.' "

For a long time, neither the Presbyterian nor the Catholic had much luck with their respective ministries. A Christian party eventually grew up around Reverend Crombie and a nucleus of a dozen Efate-born teachers who had organized a network of supporters. In response, the pagans went to the Marist father for help, which he eagerly gave them. In one case, the Christian party had set fire to the houses of Presbyterian converts who had reverted to *kastom* on the nearby islet of Rano. The intervention of the Catholic priest led to another fight. In his diary, Father Salomon told how he shouted at the teachers:

"Where have you seen in the Gospel that one should burn down the houses of those who abandon the *Skul*?" A teacher answered, "We burn houses on Efate, we shall burn them here." Rev. Crombie wrote to his rival: "Can you please tell me on whose authority you went to see my Rano teachers and threatened them yesterday? . . . You are trying to ruin my missionary work among the natives. The two houses were burned down with the consent of natives who had renounced their atheism."

The Presbyterian pastor was taking charge of the "modern" fringe of that society, whereas Father Salomon was propped up as the defender of *kastom.* The French priest fondly described many pagan ritual ceremonies, notably the *maki* (a local system of grade hierarchy). On Wala, the traditionalist party often took advantage of Father Salomon's presence to continue practicing its ancestral rites. The inhabitants also tried to gain his goodwill so as to protect themselves against possible reprisals by European ships. Because of the retaliation campaign of a French ship, *La Dives,* following a copra maker's murder in 1905, Atchin people fled to the main island of Malakula in a panic and hid in the forest for several days; according to Father Salomon, there were about seventy related deaths.[7] Father Salomon had a fierce argument on the subject with Captain Barbin of *La Dives,* who refused to believe that the cost of his act had been the loss of so many human lives.

The terror caused by warships was a major influence on the islanders' psyche. "The current generation has lost the fearlessness of the one before it," wrote Father Salomon in 1906. Residents of the coastal islets felt powerless in the face of gunfire, and this was undoubtedly one of the reasons for their ambiguous attitude vis-à-vis Christianity. Theirs was not a deliberate choice of the Christian religion, as in the Banks or the northeast islands; the balance of forces left them no other choice. The majority selected Catholicism probably because it was less threatening with respect to their customs. Yet the few conversions that occurred were long in the making.

Bishop Victor Douceré's 1920 census enumerated forty-two baptized individuals in the North Malakula islets after more than thirty years of missionary presence! This unimpressive score was far behind those of the competing religious movements of the time. However, the Catholic missionaries expected much of baptism. "Baptism is bestowed after some probing; if we were to become less strict, we would have a larger number of members, but as a matter of form, like the Protestants" (Douceré 1934). In their own words, the Marist fathers accused the Protestants of baptizing *à la lance d'arrosage* 'with a water hose'.

In 1930, the Catholic mission started to grow. For the most part, converts were adults who, as children, had been taught by the first priests. For a long time, the Marists baptized some of the dying and endeavored to educate, within their own system, the children entrusted to them. They were aiming at a long-term commitment and were not intervening in local affairs or acting directly within Melanesian society.

Christian Groups on Pentecost

In 1898, Father Emmanuel Rougier, a missionary in Fiji,[8] told the Marist mission in the New Hebrides that several New Hebrideans had converted to Catholicism during their stay on European plantations. Then on the verge of being repatriated, these Pentecost and Ambrym-born Kanaka wished to set up Christian communities on their home islands upon their return.

Two Marist missionaries, Jean-Baptiste Jamond and Jean-Baptiste Suas, went to Pentecost Island with Emmanuel Rougier in April 1898. They bought coastline plots that were large enough to accommodate the new converts. In May, the first stations were set up in Melsisi, Namaram, Loltong, and Wanour. The converts numbered seventy individuals, forty of whom settled on a small plain at the mouth of the Melsisi River. These small Christian groups were very active and stirred much curiosity on the part of neighboring pagan communities.

Describing the Wanour mission in south Pentecost on 8 August 1898, Father Jamond noted in a tone that recalls the letter Agnes Watt wrote on her return from Anatom twenty-nine years earlier:

> The catechist Lino, whose fervor and zeal are admirable, has founded a small school which fifteen children attend. The ringing of the bell regulates all village activities: getting up, praying, going to class, and so forth. Two or three times a week, Lino meets with those adults who are eager to learn about Christian religion: he can already account for a hundred individuals who recite the rosary, have obtained their medal,[9] and have asked for baptism. On Sundays, the group is larger; three hundred people attend catechism in the morning, at noon, and in the evening.

The catechists helping the Catholic missionaries played the same role as the teachers within Protestant churches. Demonstrating a similar zeal, they were impatient when faced with the pagans' reluctance.

The Christian party and its leaders went very far in their proselytizing zeal. As a missionary in Melsisi, Father Suas was often at issue with Stephano, the catechist of the village of Ilamre. In the missionary's words, the latter had a "brain eaten up with conceit." One day, the catechist wrote a letter to Father Suas, who quoted it in his diary: "You, the priests, we know that you are paid, but there is nothing for us, the catechists. We only have work and hardship before the next life. Yet we bear with it. . . . If only we were allowed to live according to the custom we had in the past. . . . Our Father [Jamond] was good then, but in the priest we have today, we only see a severe figure who despises us! We are going to organize a meeting between Catholics, Protestants, and pagans. I salute you . . . from afar."

The priest opposed his catechist on all levels:

> Suas designated catechists for the pagan villages. Stephano refused, pretending that seven catechists had already been killed or poisoned. For their safety, the catechists were to go only into their own villages. Suas took Stephano to task for his behavior vis-à-vis Protestants. He [Stephano] had gone too far. He had pulled out crosses from the graves!

Calling Suas a heretic, Stephano would have liked to wage war against recalcitrant pagan chiefs. Suas could not be away without Stephano immediately calling out his warriors. "Priests do not know anything about war," Stephano used to say. "War is the business of catechists." (in Monnier n.d.*b*, 66)

Stephano wanted to set up a local church and was close to creating a schism on Pentecost Island. Although this type of conflict often prevailed on the island, the diffusion of Catholicism proceeded swiftly, especially among coastal groups in Loltong, Melsisi, and Namaram. At the end of the nineteenth century, however, a series of epidemics decimated the coastal villages where the Christians had regrouped. The new diseases—dysentery and tuberculosis, in particular—greatly weakened enthusiastic leanings toward Catholicism and strengthened the hostile stand of the pagan party. All missions, wherever they were, experienced this type of scenario. The expansion of the mission came to a sudden stop, and hope of a rapid and generalized conversion, in the Banks style, evaporated. Pentecost was split into two areas: the coastline, or *ila* country, continued to belong to the Christian party, while the interior, or *kut* country, stayed under the domination of *kastom* and the pagan party. This state of affairs endured practically until World War II.

In central Pentecost, several full-fledged civil wars broke out between Christians and pagans. The most frequent cause for these wars was the disregard shown for ritual prohibitions that had been imposed by traditional chiefs. Some of the wives of polygamous chiefs fled to the coastal stations where missionaries took them under their protection.

Friction between pagans and Christians, often in the same village, indicated that one of the parties had to win if some unity was to be reestablished in the region. For example, a violent war took place in Tansip, a village in central Pentecost, because of the bell whose symbolism and noise bothered the pagans—the local group was split into two factions. The last episode occurred in 1939 when Father Guillaume, a missionary posted in Melsisi, was accused of stirring up violence by supplying cartridges to his supporters on the coast. Acting on his own authority, British District Agent Adam arrested Father Guillaume and his Christian warriors and closed the Melsisi Catholic mission following the Franco-British disaster at Dunkirk, in Europe. Adam was to authorize its re-opening after French citizens living in the Pacific area rallied to the London-based Free French movement. International events affected, sometimes unexpectedly, islands that were at the other end of the world.[10]

In Namaram, another priest, Jean-Baptiste Suas, a Breton, fired nearly every night at the *kut*, the inland inhabitants, who used to shoot at his house after nightfall. Father Suas was known in the region as an outstanding marksman, which perhaps was a positive influence on the rate of conversion.[11] Despite these multiple incidents, inland Pentecost was being gradually Christianized. Most pagan groups of the *kut* region relaxed their resistance after the end of World War II, for two major reasons. Father Louis Guillaume's successors, notably Fathers Louis Julliard (who would become a bishop) and René du Rumain, were on good terms with pagan groups, whose customs they respected and whose kava they enjoyed. Besides, the *kut,* like the *ila,* belonged to the same cultural world and were linked by numerous marriage alliances. The religious homogeneity of central Pentecost as a whole remained an overriding necessity for both sides if they wanted to maintain their traditional bonds and allow their communities to survive in peace. It is in keeping with the goal of regional unity that the last pagans converted to Christianity; yet many did so while only paying lip service to the idea.

A Belated Development

For a long time, the Catholic ministry was richer in men than money. In 1914, although it had twenty-eight priests, two coadjutor brothers, and about ten nuns from the Third Order of Mary, the ministry did not own any boat or have the minimum cash flow necessary to support itself (Douceré 1934). To move about, the priests would use canoes, or whaleboats for the more fortunate among them. Three priests and two nuns were shipwrecked and died at sea.

Each Catholic station became involved in an agricultural experiment of greater or lesser extent. A large vegetable garden provided food for school children and, on the developing coconut plantations, copra was sold to local traders. Forced to live off the land, the mission did rather poorly. Letters from the missionaries attest to the fact that their material circumstances were a serious concern: "Like everywhere else, we lack resources. At times I dream of completing our living quarters, but for this I need one thousand francs [US$193] and I am penniless right now" (letter from Father Suas, Ambae, 1898). From Ambrym (Olal), the same missionary wrote this about the eighty-nine children in his school: "We have to take care of all these children, boys and girls. They have to be taught as well as clothed and fed and we cannot rely on their parents in any way. . . . I am wondering how I can manage to support such a group when we ourselves have barely enough to survive!" (letter, 1899)

By necessity, most priests had turned into farmers and planters once again. "Here, amazingly, the natives buy yams and bananas from me. The world is upside down. Ordinarily they would sell the Whites these staples. [Nowadays] they prefer to cultivate copra—it is less fatiguing— and purchase their daily food with the money. What they enjoy is to sit, smoke their pipe, and prepare their mind-destroying [sic] *kava* to get inebriated and sleep in total drunkenness" (letter from Father Suas, Ambae, July 1911).

This state of affairs improved considerably when, in 1927, Bishop Douceré purchased a small motor boat, the *St. Joseph,* which allowed for regular calls at the various missionary stations. The boat soon became the savior of Catholic groups.

The steady growth of the Catholic mission only began in 1930, at a time when the development of Presbyterian and Anglican churches was at a standstill. The regions that converted to Catholicism were the ones that had remained pagan longest, and hence were the most attached to *kastom.* In 1931, there were 3000 baptized Catholics, and 7828 in 1965. According to the 1979 census, the number of Catholics in the group was 16,502, or 14.8 percent of the total population. In 1987, the centennial year of the Catholic Church in the New Hebrides–Vanuatu, Catholics numbered 19,322 and there were more than 5100 students in Catholic schools (Monnier n.d.*b,* 144).

Marginal Churches

Early in the twentieth century, new Christian churches made their appearance in the New Hebrides. Although they could not counteract the influence of the major churches, they gave the Islanders a political and religious alternative that had some weight locally. Among these, one of the oldest and most important was the Seventh Day Adventist Church (SDA). In 1917, its first missionary, Reverend Stewart, went to Atchin, one of the North Malakula islets, where his arrival compounded an already complex religious situation.

From the outset, Adventism had a great impact on the Melanesians. Because of its American origin, the SDA church was outside the French or British sphere of colonial influence, and the relative simplicity of its doctrine, in addition to its material wealth, corresponded rather well with the Melanesians' concept of a "good religion." The Adventist ministry progressed mostly at the expense of existing churches rather than within traditional pagan circles. On Ambrym, Ambae, Malakula, Tanna, and Tongoa, some Christian groups—Presbyterian especially—moved *en bloc* to the new religion, which immediately caused the Presbyterian hierarchy to protest vigorously, to no avail. In Tanna especially, things went quite far, as the men of the Presbyterian party burned the houses of those who had embraced the new faith and, besides, had sold land to the SDA mission. The story was greatly magnified at the time (1934). Father Bochu wrote in one of his letters:

> Several months ago, a Presbyterian decided to go over to the Adventist side. He was then told to clear out, because the plot where he was living

belonged to the Presbyterian mission. As he turned a deaf ear to this
request, one day his hut burned as if by chance; but foul play was never
established.

To guarantee its *monopoly over Tanna* and prevent any form of
competition, the Presbyterian Mission has purchased (?) a large number
of plots that it leases to the natives from whom it has bought (or
extorted) them. Naturally these are the best plots, the best docking
spots. We who live in the bush are not able to have even a small shed on
the shoreline to protect our goods against the rain, since the Presbyterian
Mission has even bought the sea! (Monnier n.d.*a*, 17)

The "Seven Day" doctrine, as it is called in the group, is the result of
a religious reform movement which took place within the Baptist Church
in the United States. It preaches a fervent millenarianism based on the
belief that Christ is soon to return to earth. It also expounds principles of
strict hygiene. Adventists abstain from meat, alcohol, tobacco, and coffee, eat unscaled fish, and drink chocolate. This diet gave them the label
of *man kakai grass* 'those who eat grass' in Bislama. Such a doctrine
replaced some interdicts by others, which fitted in well with traditional
ways. More deeply, it is probable that the millenarianism offered by the
SDA church and the announcement of the impending Second Advent fulfilled genuine expectations in a Melanesian society already imprinted by
Christian beliefs. By 1950, the wealthy SDA church was making use of
three ships calling at the various Adventist mission stations and groups in
the New Hebrides. Very rapidly, it also set up clinics and hospitals; the
Aore hospital is the headquarters of the whole SDA community.

The "Seven Days" have probably done more than any other group to
eradicate *kastom* and the foundations of the traditional way of life. In
their sanitary, impeccably clean villages, modern concrete houses are
ordered around a central lawn. The mission is still backed by its American sister churches and continues to prosper, thanks to a tithe that represents one tenth of its followers' salaries and a similar percentage of all
sales of local goods. The Adventists' moral strictness, coupled with a
strong business flair, helps explain their plentiful economic achievements
and distinct role in contemporary commerce.

Millenarianism, strong solidarity, religious fundamentalism, and a
capitalistic viewpoint are widespread characteristics of the smaller marginal churches. Following the Church of Christ and the Apostolic
Church, the Assembly of God is the latest to date. It originated in the
United States and reached Vanuatu through Fijian pastors in the early
1970s. Wealthy, practicing an aggressive form of proselytism—its
preachers hold loudspeakers and are backed by bands with electric guitars—this church has become popular in Vila and Luganville. Its efforts
in Tanna have met with more difficulties, especially among traditional

communities that remain very mistrustful. Vis-à-vis the three major denominations in the group, the Assembly of God is playing today the part that the Seventh Day Adventist Church played between 1920 and 1950. It is recruiting on the margins of the more established Christian churches, the Anglican and Presbyterian churches in particular, notably among young people who find its modern "American image" appealing.

New Religious Identities

The Melanesians took full advantage of existing missionary structures and actively participated in their growth. Soon they secured leadership positions within Christian groups, often demonstrating an eagerness at proselytizing that worried European missionaries themselves. Concurrently, the archipelago's Melanesian space was reshaped according to the new religious sociology. As far as the Melanesians were concerned, to embrace a faith meant first and foremost to accept a school that could provide the key to the Westerners' store of knowledge. For a long time, school teaching was left entirely in the hands of Christian missions. By adopting a religious creed, the Melanesians also chose a foreign language for educational purposes—English for the Protestants, French for the Catholics—and thereby a system of political alliance that established them within a certain vision and a specific European culture.[12]

The French administration was late in acknowledging the minority situation of its own language and, from 1958, endeavored to develop a large scale public educational system for French speakers. This policy was only a partial success because there was not enough time to allow for the development of a sizable elite.

By providing educational and medical services as well as a modicum of communications between islands, the missions shaped the framework within which new regional communities were forged and organized. As Christian churches shared the archipelago's space and population, they created specific identities as well as political groupings. Thus, the place of origin ceased to be the sole basic reference; the religious community became the source of a "modern identity."

In some cases, ancient links were completely severed because of conflicting religious influences, such as the traditional marriage alliances between Maskelyne Islanders, who had converted to Presbyterianism, and residents of the Lamap region (Port Sandwich), who had converted to Catholicism (Charpentier 1982a). In reverse, new links were created among groups belonging to the same denomination. For example, central Pentecost (Melsisi) residents and inhabitants of the island's southeastern (Barrier Bay) and northern (Loltong) areas are Catholics today and therefore allied, whereas formerly there was no connection among them. Similarly, some inland villagers living above Port Vato on the island of Ambrym, a twenty-minute walk from shore, had never been able to see the ocean because of their long-standing feud with groups in control of the coastline. By imposing an alliance on all new converts, the Presbyterian mission dispelled the ostracism (Speiser 1913).

The European missionaries' religious divisiveness was a boon to Melanesian society which, thanks to it, was able to break out of the traditional political division of space into little sealed-off territories, while at the same time establishing new, perhaps even more rigid, frontiers between the newly created groups. Social space was rebuilt on the basis of new wider networks of alliance. The Melanesians thereby achieved an ambivalent first step toward unity. That phase anticipated a more general one which could only take place at a political level, in other words, the independence of the archipelago and the building of a nation.

The "White Road"

The Melanesians' attitude vis-à-vis Christian missions was not unanimous, as we have seen. In some islands, such as the Banks, conversion was virtually spontaneous. Other Islanders refused to become converted for one or two generations, and sometimes longer, as was the case in Tanna, North Malakula, and some areas of central Santo and Pentecost.

The first to be converted were generally the coastal groups which had had the closest contacts with the European world and its material civilization. The change was all the more rapid because the Melanesians themselves took it in hand. Some island communities actually decided to become "Christian" even before the arrival of white missionaries. Evangelization in such cases was essentially the work of Kanaka back from Queensland. In the Banks, notably, Christianization was a response to an inner drive, somehow as if the missionary word had been expected by a society already questioning its own certainties and searching for a new path.

The prevalent religious feeling was at first millenarian. Not only did the new communities anticipate the return of Christ, but they expected their status and material well-being to change deeply. To be Christian also meant to follow the Westerners' way, opt for an alliance with them, and eventually become their equals. The choice of a religion included an essential secular component.

In a society in disarray, the Melanesians adhered to the faith of Westerners partly because they longed for a new alliance whereby a "modern" society would be built. In this perspective, Christianity and its distinctive churches became the subject of renewed competition among local groups and new leaders.

6 *"Gone with the Wind"*

[T]he Anglo-French entente. And what humbug . . . it is!

ROBERT FLETCHER,
Isles of Illusion

Was Annexation Necessary?

Higginson's maneuver and its aftermath, uncontrolled French colonization, had created a diplomatic standstill between the imperialistic interests of France and Britain. The two metropolitan nations reserved their judgment about becoming definitively involved in such faraway lands—unlike public opinion in Australia and New Caledonia.

In Australia, a strong campaign led by the Presbyterian missionary John Paton was stirring public feelings. Meetings and newspaper articles were prompting the British government to annex the archipelago unilaterally so as not to leave it to the French. At a meeting held in Melbourne in 1877, Paton claimed that it was a moral imperative for Britain to take possession since, he stated, "French civilization means the natives' extermination" (Deschanel 1888, 299). In addition to these humanitarian motives, there was another argument: French presence was "polluting" Oceania's shores by unloading its "garbage of convicts" there. A member of the Legislative Assembly of Victoria used this phrase as he stigmatized the French presence in New Caledonia and the New Hebrides. He was referring to the possibility that the *libérés,* French convicts who had been liberated but were legally unable to enter metropolitan France,[1] might be transferred to the New Hebrides (Deschanel 1888).

Delegations of Australian pastors, retailers, and representatives asked Lord Derby, at the Foreign Office, to act immediately. Derby's inertia on the matter led them to contact Victorian Premier James Service to demand that all Pacific islands that were not currently under the domination of a European power be annexed. Australian colonies had already adopted a geopolitical approach different from that of Britain: they wished to set up a protectorate over the islands on the western, or Australian, side of the Pacific.

The Earl of Derby wondered why Australians wanted to have their own colonies: "It is hardly too much to say that they consider the whole Southern Pacific theirs *de jure:* the French possession of New Caledonia they regard as an act of robbery committed on them" (letter, 29 June 1883 in Crowley 1980, 3:131). Such was their intention, however. The major Australian political circles felt threatened by the French presence in the New Hebrides and New Caledonia and by the German presence in New Guinea, and they were pushing for direct intervention. Following a meeting held in Ballarat (Victoria), an Australian daily newspaper wrote that "the islands of the Western Pacific have been brought into prominence, and made of commercial, political and strategic value by the energy and enterprise of British subjects in Australia and New Zealand; . . . their occupation by Australians is essential to Australasian unity" (Crowley 1980, 3:171). Australian and New Zealand colonies had the feeling they were staking their political destiny on the issue. Yet, in their own fight for power, neither France nor Britain wished to go too far and compromise relations that they deemed friendly, especially with respect to Germany's rise in Europe.

Queensland's proclamation of a protectorate over New Guinea on 14 April 1883 intensified the tension stirred by the New Hebridean stakes. The issue is reflected in the text of the following coded telegram that New Caledonia's Governor Pallu sent to Paris on 30 June 1883:

> The five Australian provinces, plus Tasmania and New Zealand, wired England on 11 June to annex New Hebrides. I fear repeat New Guinea coup.[2] Great agitation in Australia and New Caledonia. Act immediately so that London stops Australian move. I am even preventing by force Australian gang without mandate to annex New Hebrides, but this situation cannot go on. I request urgent instructions. Should I let Australia continue? Should I undertake annexation myself? Answer Sydney by 4 July. (FRA)

Paris and London tried to calm the patriotic zeal of their militant colonies. The long-term interests of France and Britain were more convergent than antagonistic; neither metropolitan nation wished to hurry the search for a solution, which had to stem from a general policy agreement on the whole of the Pacific. In 1885, Britain offered to trade the New Hebrides for Rapa Island in Polynesia provided France did not turn the archipelago into a dumping-ground for liberated convicts from the New Caledonia penal colony. France turned down the proposed exchange, but received an identical refusal when it proposed to take over the archipelago in exchange for closing the Caledonian penal colony and territorial compensations in the Leeward Islands and Newfoundland. The status quo continued whether the two powers liked it or not, and the shuttling to and fro of proposals and counterproposals already prefigured what future Condominium relations would be.

The Joint Naval Commission

Locally, the situation was hardly better. The list of incidents between settlers or copra makers and Melanesians was lengthening, and everyone deemed it necessary to set up a higher authority in the archipelago. In particular, the destruction of Caledonian Company stations at Port Sandwich and on Ambrym and the murder of their representatives had caused feeling to run high in New Caledonia (O'Reilly 1957). France took new measures: in May 1886, two contingents of marine troops landed at Port Sandwich (Malakula) and Port Havannah (Efate) respectively. The move stirred great expectations in New Caledonia where the *Conseil régional*[3] immediately telegraphed Paris: "We request that troops be maintained in the New Hebrides and that annexation be carried out immediately and unconditionally." Conversely, vigorous protestations were raised in Australia, notably from the premier of the colony of Victoria. The French contingents left within a few months (Deschanel 1888).

As a historian noted, "the French government hurried to retract the idea of annexing the archipelago, as the Caledonians had hoped and the Australians had feared it would, and proposed to the British government that they jointly implement a system of surveillance or policing to safeguard the security of all Europeans established in the New Hebrides" (Russier 1905, 194). The negotiations led to a general agreement on 16 November 1887 that solved the old issue of the Leeward Islands and instituted a Joint Naval Commission for the New Hebrides; it was made up of naval officers from the two nations, with the chairmanship alternating.

The Naval Commission was a makeshift organization that de facto institutionalized the Condominium, as it was already being called. Rivalry went on, "more intense than ever" (Deschanel 1888, 348). In 1888, the British installed an official representative with the title of consul, then removed him following French protests. When French settlers in Port Vila attempted to organize the township of "Franceville" with Chevillard as mayor, the Joint Naval Commission, under British pressure, refused to acknowledge them.[4]

Centrifugal forces were shaping the archipelago. Settlers, wherever they were, tended to set up small kingdoms, while missions organized Christian communities that were fully autonomous. Left to themselves, Europeans were imitating the Melanesian model: the society they were in the process of creating was already threatened with fragmentation and dominated by conflicting forces. In the field, Naval Commission officers faced issues that were not easy to solve. As a rule, these officers were not to step out of their strictly defined role of maintaining order—a police task they tackled with little enthusiasm. Besides, they had no real power to deal with the multiple local conflicts. In addition, most French settlers had been brought in by the semi-official Société Française des Nouvelles-Hébrides but were complaining about the lack of legal protection. More seriously, the estates the settlers were claiming had been neither surveyed nor officially recognized.

To sum up, navy officers from the two nations had been called on to enforce an order whose rules and regulations no one had defined. At the same time, Melanesians who opposed the takeover of their lands were becoming increasingly active, as demonstrated by the continuing incidents and murders.

The Cycle of Violence

Until 1888 when military control began, not a single year went by without several murders taking place in some part of the group. Commander Bigaut even wondered why there were not more: "I think the situation is fairly good as far as the Europeans' safety is concerned. Isolated incidents do not mean much, especially when one knows the Europeans who live in this country: generally [these] men are very violent and too forceful; they pay for their recklessness with their lives" (letter, 20 May 1890, JNCA). Faced with the European invasion, Melanesians attempted to negotiate and take advantage of the situation much more than to initiate violence, which was likely to trigger reprisals. Most murders were single acts of personal retaliation whenever the rules of Melanesian society had been challenged. In this context, Westerners as such were not especially threatened since Melanesians who had perpetrated acts contradicting customary laws could also be killed. However, there were some cases when one white man paid for offenses committed by another.

In the later case of the murder of the British copra maker Bridges and his five children, the reprisal expedition that followed was a failure. Fifty policemen and ninety sailors from the two Western powers were sent to search for the murderers but were routed by an ambush that killed seven and wounded two among them, including an Australian lieutenant. "The expedition in question was a deplorable fiasco," wrote the French settler Gabriel Frouin, as he reviewed the facts in a November 1916 issue of the newspaper *Le Néo-Hébridais*.

Other crimes were committed for ritual motives and according to the logic of magical thinking, for instance, the 1861 massacre of the Presbyterian missionaries who were thought to be responsible for epidemics on Erromango. Another ritual crime was performed in 1923 against the copra maker Clapcott at Tasmalum in southern Santo, because he was accused of appropriating for his own benefit the cargo brought in by commercial ships.[5] Taboo breaking or offenses against sacred powers were frequently interpreted as the cause for epidemics. At Nangire, on Ambae's north shore, people told me that their forebears had killed and "eaten" a young French copra maker because he had lit his pipe at a *tabu fire* within the sacred area of the *nakamal*.[6] He had done no other wrong but, as for any Ambae man breaching a taboo, the penalty was death. As a result of this murder, a warship shelled the area. The cannonballs were lost in the bush; when a patrol went ashore to search for the culprits, the murderer came to meet the sailors who were trying to find their way. He offered them bananas and coconuts, and showed them a spring of running water. The Islander told them that the others had fled because they were frightened but having nothing to blame himself for—which was true according to his own standards—he had not hesitated to come and meet them. Happy to see a helpful individual on this steep unknown coast, the French sailors became friends with him and, before leaving, gave him some tobacco.

The reprisal policy initiated by the Joint Naval Commission consisted of "shelling the coconut trees," as sailors used to say. Sometimes they refused to intervene, for example, after the murder of the British settler Trumble on Epi in 1905, and after the massacre of the eight crew members of a recruiting ship from New Caledonia, the *Petrel,* on Maewo in 1904. In those two cases, the officers of the Naval Commission judged that the "natives" had acted in self-defense. The French Commander Lecomte made perceptive remarks about the situation in which he and his men were involved:

> Although the Commission does endeavor to protect Europeans in a useful albeit insufficient way, it can do nothing on behalf of the natives who are often preyed upon by the Whites. Neither one nor the other [command] has sufficient means to implement an effective protection policy. Therefore one should acknowledge the fact that, except in the case of attacks by natives against Whites, there are neither uniform laws nor genuine protection. (Letter from the sloop *Scorff,* 23 May 1896, JNCA)

The Anglo-French Condominium

Neither of the two remote metropolitan powers was overly concerned about the situation. Each thought that free competition between their respective citizens would eventually push the archipelago into its own sphere of political influence. The imbroglio was growing, however, and the two European powers resumed negotiations in 1904, with the Condominium status being officially recognized in 1906. The deed was signed more for reasons of international diplomacy than for political purposes concerning the group itself.

Indeed a third power was becoming increasingly visible in the Pacific Islands in the early years of the twentieth century. Already present in Western Samoa and New Guinea, Germany was looking in the direction of the New Hebrides. In 1903, the Germans protested against the establishment of French settlers on the western shore of Epi and at Port Sandwich (Malakula) because one of their trading firms laid claim to these areas. The rapid intervention of Germany seemed likely to settle the Anglo-French issue by sending both away empty-handed. The threat promoted solidarity between London and Paris and hastened their agreement.

On 20 October 1906, the archipelago was granted a "joint" Anglo-French administrative organization, with the two nations stating their "co-sovereignty" over an "indivisible" territory. A Joint Court was to settle land tenure disputes and set up a legal system acknowledged by both tutelary powers.

Thanks to the Condominium, the New Hebrides avoided territorial division. Each power was sovereign with respect to its own citizens, who were acknowledged to have equal rights regarding residency and ownership. Both powers committed themselves to act jointly, in particular to maintain order and in matters of general policy. Foreign nationals from third powers had to choose either French or British status: about forty settlers of Scandinavian, German, Spanish, Portuguese, Chinese, and multiethnic origin lived in the archipelago at the turn of the century.[7]

There were two "governors," called resident commissioners, one French and the other British; district agents or *délégués* represented them in the various islands of the archipelago. The local police, or *milice,* was divided into two equal sections. Supported by local taxes, the joint condominium administration supplied common services: mail, telegraph and telephone, public works, coast guards, customs, and financial services, to which agriculture, veterinary services, mines, and land survey were added later. In other words, there were two national administrations, each under its resident commissioner, in addition to the so-called joint administration.

Melanesians did not have the right to obtain either citizenship. Like their territory, they were considered "subjects" and placed under "joint influence."

The most important part of the Anglo-French agreement dealt with the creation of a Joint Court whose primary task was to register the lands that had been purchased during the previous period. In homage to the nationality of the first European discoverer, the king of Spain was asked to designate the Joint Court president. A French judge and a British judge assisted the Spanish president, while the public prosecutor[8] was assumed to be neutral and therefore was Belgian. In the event of a disagreement between the judges, the president had the casting vote. The court soon became the symbol of all contradictions and delays of the Condominium. Fletcher, who was the court interpreter for some time, had to use four languages: Spanish for the president, French and English for the judges, and finally Bislama for the Melanesian inhabitants; in one of his letters, he stated that he was "nearly dead" at the end of the day!

In order to meet the settlers' demands, over 700,000 hectares of hypothetical land had to be surveyed and registered in an archipelago that no one really controlled. The task was close to being surrealistic and the Count of Buena Esperanza, the first president of the Joint Court, was overly optimistic when, upon his arrival in Noumea in August 1926, he stated: "I came here for the registration and I shall do it" (Grignon-Dumoulin 1928). In such matters, the presumption was on the side of the Europeans who wanted to register their land holdings. The Melanesian contestants, if any, were the ones who had to show proof. As a result, most rulings validated the purchases of the pre-Condominium era, occasionally reducing them through the creation of "native reserves" when it was discovered that a village was inadvertently located on the lands being claimed.[9]

The first judgment granting a land title was not delivered until 1929 and registration proceeded thereafter with a considerable lack of speed. In 1972, 317 cases, or one third of the initial number, remained to be heard by the court. Among the 600 judgments that had been delivered, there were 57 in which the Joint Court questioned the grounds for the European claim and did not grant the land title being requested. In 1980, on the eve of independence, numerous judgments were still pending. In total, 240,000 hectares (20 percent of the area of the group) were registered by the Joint Court, including 150,000 to the benefit of European settlers (Van Trease 1984). These only ever occupied a small part of it, about one-fourth or one-fifth.

Alienated Lands

Europeans bought land according to the standards of their own society. In 1886, the commander of the sloop *La Dives* made the comment that "the Kanak who sells his land does not realize he is being dispossessed. He only sells the right to purchase coconuts and other products of that land" (JNCA). About this issue another French officer, C. Liume, wrote the following letter in 1898:

> Some unscrupulous settlers extend their properties indefinitely without marking boundaries or, for a deceptively low price, buy properties from natives that these have no right to sell. In the early times of colonization,

some settlers obtained huge tracts of land . . . ; as long as [these settlers] did not show possession by clearing or cultivating, the natives did not understand the nature of the contract binding them to the purchasers, and in order to have a few more trade goods, they would go on with such sales whose scope they did not discern. Now, every year, parts of these lands are developed and the native residents are evicted. Next they go to the warship. . . . But [we] cannot do anything. They tell us, "Whom can we ask, if you reject us? Every day we are robbed, dispossessed of lands that our tribes have lived on from the earliest times and that we could not sell, even if we wanted to, since they are necessary for our livelihood." In some cases, the Kanaks do not want to acknowledge the validity of the contracts into which they have entered: settlers become the object of interference that would quickly degenerate into hostilities if the warships did not intervene. (JNCA)

In other words, the Melanesians who, as far as they were concerned, had only given hospitality to specific settlers, could not accept that land be resold without their even being consulted. For example, upon the death of Bernier, the Santo representative of the Société Française des Nouvelles-Hébrides, who had personally bought a property named Luganville, the former sellers asked the new manager of the company to pay once again or vacate the place. "These natives claim the right to take back the land they have sold to Bernier because they have learned of [his] death, which occurred a few months ago" (letter from Captain Gadaud, 1892, JNCA).

Even in cases when the agreement between the European buyer and the Melanesians was made in good faith, there was complete misunderstanding. Many Melanesian communities wanted a trader on their territory, to benefit from his goods and according to their own criteria, that is, as a guest. As a general rule, however, the areas that had been cultivated in the course of the initial phase of European expansion were not contested. The Melanesians believed the ground belonged to *kastom* but respected the fruits of a settler's labor, provided he lived on the land and gave them help.

The best-known land dispute is probably that of the Plantations Réunies des Nouvelles-Hébrides (PRNH, Associated Plantations of the New Hebrides) in northern Malakula. In 1925, a European landed in Norsup with a team of 30 Indochinese coolies to clear the 10,000 hectares which the Société Française des Nouvelles-Hébrides had "granted" his company. He found that the shore was populated by Melanesians from the village of Tautu and that the entire holding was sprinkled with cultivated areas and dwellings. As the Melanesians were becoming more antagonistic, the presence of a French warship was requested—a necessary precaution since each side was readying its weapons. "If the security of any of us is jeopardized, we will turn your huts into a bonfire," threatened the PRNH manager (FRA). Three years later, in 1928, a judgment of the Joint Court created a 237-hectare reserve (5 hectares per adult resident) at the site of the village of Tautu. Yet the conflict was not over. "These people never cease to spy on us and to protest," wrote the plantation manager (FRA). Several incidents occurred. Further, the Islanders did not agree to work on the plantation, considering it a usurped territory. Thanks to an Indochinese labor force numbering 421 individuals in 1930, the land was cleared, but only to the extent of 1200 hectares out of the 10,000 envisioned.

The PRNH repeatedly offered to come to an understanding with Tautu residents. In exchange for any new clearing, the company would clear and plant, without charge, an equivalent area that would then be given to the villagers. The answer was always negative. The Melanesians were not trying to "make a deal"; they only wished to recover their territories.

The Arrival of the Coolies

It was not believed that white people could perform physical work in a hot tropical climate like that of the New Hebrides. This very idea had been the Australians' justification for blackbirding. Yet, although the physical work on the plantations depended on the Melanesians' cooperation, they demonstrated neither taste nor disposition for this type of activity.

In one of his first letters, written in 1912, Fletcher, then a supervisor at a Santo plantation, showed no surprise about it: "The planters complain bitterly that the niggers won't come and work for them. Why should they? They have all they want, and, like me, they hate unnecessary work. They are enticed away by every species of trickery, often by actual violence, and then the gold-greedy white man wonders that they don't toil for twelve hours in the broiling sun with one meal of rice willingly and heartily in order that 'master' become rich" (1986, 50).

From 1890 onward, settlers used the services of professional recruiters. These men on their schooners were carrying out an undertaking nearly identical to that of Australian recruiters for Queensland, but did not meet with the same rate of success. Fletcher had a close view of their activities: "Concerning this recruiting, the place teems with yarns. It is only in certain islands that the natives will work, and from these they are recruited. Every planter keeps a schooner and goes round to try and get niggers to work for him. They are signed on for three years, and then shipped back again. . . . Needless to say . . . laws are set at defiance, openly by the French, secretly by most Britons" (1986, 30). After the setting up of the Condominium in 1906, larger numbers of settlers pushed up the demand:

> We all cry out that we no longer have a labor force. . . . Each mail boat brings new settlers who obviously need to find workers. When there were twenty or thirty employers, demand could be fulfilled [easily]. Now that there are twice as many, the task is much more difficult! The most remote corners [of the group] receive visits: where one or two ships used to call every year, there are now seven, eight or even more, and the law of supply and demand applies in these wild islands just as much as in the civilized world. (Henri Milliard in *Le Néo-Hébridais*, no. 4, Feb 1920)

At the turn of the century, every land concession was managed by two associates, especially when it was somewhat isolated: one associate was in charge of work on the land, the other went on recruiting trips on a schooner. Because Melanesians were hesitant to sign up for three years, even though they were promised a happy life, they started being offered shorter-term contracts (Bedford 1973). Between repatriating and recruiting trips, settlers had to endure endless shuttling through the islands—which did not solve the labor issue.

The pressure from settlers and trading houses eventually led the French administration to introduce indentured labor recruited in Indochina. From 1921 to 1940, 21,922 Indochinese workers—who were called coolies—arrived in the New Hebrides. Most came from the over-populated provinces of Tonkin where the trading firm Ballande was in charge of recruiting and transporting them to the New Hebrides. The Tonkinese left for five years at the end of which they had to be repatriated, unless they signed another contract. There were women among them, in a ratio of one to six approximately. Given repatriations and contract renewals, the inflow was continuous; the Tonkinese population reached 5396 residents in 1929, including 1200 women and 1000 children. Thereafter, it decreased and stabilized around 1200 individuals and a labor force of 500 persons.

This work force is credited with the development of the largest properties in the islands, in particular 1200 hectares at Norsup in northern Malakula. The French community as a whole heralded the coming of the first Tonkinese workers as the dawn of a new era: "We must remember this blessed year, which represents a decisive shift in the history of the New Hebrides, because it granted us a steady supply of labor."[10] "One could say, it is a blood transfusion from the great French colony of the Far East to the New Hebridean archipelago," according to the *Revue du Pacifique* dated September 1924. However, the Vietnamese labor force was costly and therefore primarily used by capital-intensive development companies. Settlers had to pay hiring and transportation costs, and monthly wages of 160 francs per employee. Most small settlers could not afford the expense; by comparison, the average salary of a Melanesian worker was then 20 to 30 francs per month (Bonnemaison 1986*b*).

After obtaining the status of independent workers in 1945, the Tonkinese organized themselves in teams of twenty to thirty workers and negotiated full-fledged contracts with the planters, who generally granted them 40 to 50 percent of proceeds in addition to room and board. They set up unions and became increasingly assertive and business-wise partners. Subsequently, many went to urban areas, working for themselves as shopkeepers or tradesmen in Vila and monopolizing the first taxi-driver jobs. Others started vegetable farming near town. The Vietnamese community evolved on its own, beyond the settlers' control. The last contingents to volunteer for repatriation left in 1963 after direct negotiation with the government of North Vietnam. A small community of 397 individuals elected to stay, its size remaining stable thereafter.

"Gone with the Wind"

Agricultural colonization was primarily a French endeavor which focused on the central part of the archipelago, away from the most populated islands, both in the north (Banks Islands, Ambae, north Pentecost) and the south (Tanna). Besides, access to those islands was made difficult by the hostile influence of Anglican missionaries to the north and Presbyterian missionaries to the south. Only traders and copra makers were tolerated in those areas; they made up a floating group of Europeans, mostly British.

In the early part of the twentieth century, the island of Epi became a major colonization center. The *Messageries Maritimes* steamer called there once a month. On the paths linking the plantations, settlers' wives and daughters, dressed in white and carrying umbrellas, would take carriage rides, projecting fleeting *Gone with the Wind*–style images onto a background of cotton fields, coconut groves, and Oceanian shores. Colonization was expanding along identical lines in places such as the Segond Channel on Santo, the island of Aore (which was totally under colonial influence), and large parts of Malo. In 1917, Santo settlers, most of whom were French, numbered eighty (as against twenty in 1906), in addition to about twenty others on the neighboring islands of Aore and Malo.

Between 1910 and 1930, some settlers became prosperous. Plantations kept on growing and the market prices of coffee and copra brought hefty profits. In 1929, there were sixty-nine French plantations and sixteen British plantations throughout the archipelago, representing an expatriate population of about one thousand individuals (Geslin 1948). Luganville had become the second colonization center in the group and, on the coastal plain of eastern Malakula, a string of plantations was being developed from Norsup to Lamap (Port Sandwich). The arrival of the Tonkinese workers allowed for a considerable expansion of French properties in terms of planted areas—these reached nearly twenty-six thousand hectares in 1930. Obviously, colonial society was at its peak in the 1920s (Bonnemaison 1986*b*).

The crash of 1929 and the subsequent economic crisis had a profound impact on the New Hebrides from 1931 onward. Market prices fell—so did the settlers' prosperity. The workers could no longer be paid and many returned to Tonkin. Remote plantations were abandoned while the pioneer generation, then disappearing, was only partially replaced. Yet some large firms that had emerged during the phase of prosperity kept on growing. They were managing agricultural areas of several thousand hectares and benefited from a cash flow quite unlike that of the early settlers. The human scale had been the hallmark of early settlement: it was replaced by large-scale, more impersonal structures. Along with a stronger administrative presence, such an evolution showed that the archipelago was on the verge of moving into a colonial phase more in step with the rules of the genre. But this process of "standardization" never went very far in the New Hebrides.

European colonization did not actually fail from an economic standpoint, but the dreams of prosperity slowly eroded. The speculative, fragile plantation economy suffered from the islands' remoteness from international markets, high shipping costs, and the hardships of interisland transportation. The same constraints affect the economic life of the group today.

Vila

From the early days, Vila had become the group's major colonization center. Unquestionably, the "Condominium's capital" owed its title to the presence of trading firms and the two resident commissioners. At the turn of the century, this odd capital was splintered into small farming stations[11] linked by grassy paths barely laid out. Two "national" areas were already being delineated: to the west, the French with their Residency, the Roman Catholic bishop's quarters, the Catholic school opened in 1900 at Anabrou and, farther away, the plantation of the Société Française des Nouvelles-Hébrides; to the east, across from the British Residency on Iririki islet, the British administrative offices, the Anglo-Australian trading firms of Burns Philp and Kerr Brothers, and the future headquarters and church of the Presbyterians. At the center of this configuration, at a symbolically higher elevation than the two national residencies, were the luxurious buildings of the Joint Court and the residence of its president, the Count of Buena Esperanza.

Urban planning and technical services were not initiated until 1920. Each Vila resident lived on his plot, using hurricane lamps, in a wooden house with surrounding veranda. Rain water ran down a brightly-painted tin roof into the essential *caisse à eau* 'water tank'. To get about there were horses; in 1925, a joint ruling finally banned galloping in the streets. Two small hotels in operation since the turn of the century, the Rolland—later to become the famous Hotel Rossi—and the Jullien, stayed open until late at night, especially when ships were calling. There the small world of recruiters, Vila planters, and their visitors met to play cards and drink heavily: champagne on great occasions, absinthe or gin otherwise. Scuffles were many. On his arrival in the New Hebrides in 1912, Fletcher wrote, perhaps overstating the facts, "I had two nights in the hotel at Vila, and it was enough. My room was an outhouse, and I shared it with the most awful collection of creeping things. The hotel was full of the most fearsome collection of beach-combers, ex-convicts, etc., who drank and fought all day and all night" (1986, 25–26).

Vila and Santo became genuinely urban with the advent of World War II. Hitherto neglected by the various administrations, their infrastructure (street network, bridges, water system, and so forth) came rapidly into being thanks to the establishment of American military camps. Yet the picturesque era of bygone days probably had some charm! Here are Fletcher's comments on the matter, from 1913:

> Vila is beautiful—really beautiful. . . . The bush has been largely cleared all round the town—which makes an enormous difference. . . . Then it is all grass covered. Again, there is a bay which is a very pearl. Also it is healthy—fever being practically wiped out owing to the bush-clearing. Also there are two doctors and a hospital and fresh milk and fresh meat and ice; so altogether I am feeling happy. (1986, 71)

He changed his opinion a little later: "The people here are nearly all impossible. The place is merely a seething pit of racial hatred, and every man, English and French alike, has his own pet grievance against some other fool" (1986, 76).

An Out-of-Joint Administration

From the outset, the Condominium was the object of intense criticism, both in Australia and New Caledonia, insofar as "the New Hebrides' destiny [was] to be French," according to the concluding words of a book by Bouge (1906). The irreverent newspaper for French settlers,

Le Néo-Hébridais, called it the *machindominium* 'whatsitdominium' and kept the better part of its sarcastic comments for the Joint Court: "This heterogeneous court made up of Spaniards, French, British, and Dutch is comical to the utmost degree" (July 1913). As he was greeting a new French Resident Commissioner to Vila, Lucien Colardeau, who presided over the welcome banquet, said: "We had brought our magnificent colony, fully organized, to the mother country: she did not want it. . . . For lack of something better and by reason of our ineffectual diplomacy, we were led into this constitution in disarray, this political monstrosity, this undertaking struck with death and sterility. I mean the Anglo-French Condominium" (*Le Néo-Hébridais,* Dec 1913).

Nobody ever imagined, on either the French or the British side, that the situation would last until the year 1980. By its very nature, which precluded any action unless both resident commissioners gave their agreement, the Condominium government was condemned to inertia. Apart from the unwieldy internal administrative machinery, a legal organization was created which bore no relation to what really went on in the islands. Settlers ruling over their plantations, traders, copra makers, and recruiters evaded without too much difficulty the edicts of the joint administration, notably with respect to selling alcohol. To the Melanesians, the power of *capmen*—the name they gave to civil servants with their gold caps—represented a remote and external reality. The Condominium authority was much more an "out-of-joint authority" than a joint one. French administrators managed settlers while English administrators, for the most part, relied on British missionaries in the field. With the Condominium, the archipelago did have laws but was minimally governed and always at the mercy of multiple "masters" who had created their own fiefdoms.

In a letter addressed to his superiors in 1950, the British Resident Commissioner defined the policy of his administration: "We . . . (as British Administration) work very closely with the Missions—and it pays! . . . You would be surprised by how well the natives here have responded to the fact that Pandemonium[12] conditions have led to their progressing along natural . . . lines without any high administrative planning or detailed supervision which of course would *jointly* be impossible" (Philibert 1982, 75).

At least, few illusions were harbored about "joint administration" prospects. In perpetual confrontation, the two powers were involved in a sterile mimetic rivalry that left little room for common action.

The Independence Crisis

The relative political equilibrium of the Condominium was shattered in the early 1970s by the appearance on the scene of a Melanesian nationalist political party called the New Hebrides National Party, which later became the Vanua'aku Pati.[13] This party wanted to establish Melanesian independence quickly. It was supported by the Presbyterian and Anglican churches; its main leaders were young pastors or students who had just graduated from the universities in Fiji and Papua New Guinea.

The purpose of the Vanua'aku Pati was to build a unified nation. To reach this goal, the party deemed it necessary to set up a centralized state based on a strong political organization. Some Melanesian groups had increasing reservations about this strategy, which to them seemed overly intrusive if not totalitarian. The political aims of the Vanua'aku Pati and the nature of the party that was to implement them worried Roman Catholics, "francophones," small settlers, multiethnic persons, and members of small "anglophone" churches—such as the Church of Christ—who felt ill at ease vis-à-vis the two main churches.

Very quickly, each of these minority groups set up its own political movement within the scope of the territory it controlled. All these groups subsequently coalesced within a heterogeneous alliance whose unifying principle was its opposition to the Vanua'aku Pati. While the anglophone nationalist party supported centralization, the minority movements favored a federalist structure. In contrast to the party's nationalist, Third-World stand, they chose a "moderate" platform in which the word *Kastom*—instead of *Nation*—progressively became the dominant theme. The minority groups also favored a slow and progressive move toward independence and a more conciliatory attitude regarding the rights of expatriates, whose investments they deemed necessary to the country's economy.[14]

Soon the nationalists and the moderates asserted their differences. The British supported the Vanua'aku Pati, while the French, wishing to delay an independence they deemed hasty, picked the moderates. The Condominium was ending in the same way it had begun—in rivalry and increasingly less cordial misunderstandings.

The issue of independence for the New Hebrides became a complex matter. In effect, the two powers pulled in opposite directions, colonial society tried to delay or control independence, and the Melanesians disagreed on the characteristics of the forthcoming post-Condominium state, both in terms of authority and organization. To some extent, the majority anglophone Protestants—representing about 70 percent of the population—opposed the francophone minorities,[15] who included the Catholics and the customary and neocustomary groups on Espiritu Santo and Tanna. What had seemed like a dormant past resurfaced, and the context of ancient Melanesian warfare, with its rivalries and systems of alliance, became an astonishing reality again. Some groups, mostly on Santo and Tanna, thought about setting up their own independent nations.

The moderate alliance adopted the name of Tan Union federation, the word *tan* meaning "land" in the Melanesian languages. By focusing on land, the moderate groups intended to go back to the roots of their culture. "Sons of the earth," they were also *"kastom's* heirs." Hence, they opposed Christian nationalist groups which they accused of "betraying *kastom.*" In response, Vanua'aku Pati nationalists criticized moderate groups for "betraying" independence. Given the complicated history of the Condominium and the Islanders' steadfast positions, reconciliation was not to be.

According to Tannese mythology, supreme powers are rooted around Yasur. The volcanic peak is approximately three hundred meters high and overlooks a plain of ashes and a swampy lake: both give this part of the island a distinctive, moonlike appearance.

"Cannibal feast on the island of Tanna" by Charles Gordon Fraser, 1891 (2m by 1m). The artist recorded the scene—an exchange ritual between two allied groups in Yenkahi near Yasur—with a wealth of ethnographic details. Although relatively rare, cannibalism was practiced in designated places following wars or great events. Fraser completed the work in Australia. A copy of the painting is at the Vanuatu Cultural Center in Vila; the original was auctioned at Christie's of London in 1988. (Courtesy of Christie's, London)

Tanna's food exchange festival
(niel), as observed by Boudier
in 1890. Banana stalks, artis-
tically braided, tumble down
from a banyan tree while,
at the center of the dancing
place, slaughtered pigs are
aligned for the gift-giving to
follow. (Engraved by Maynard
for Hagen's Voyage aux Nouvelles-Hébrides et aux îles
Salomon in Le Tour du
Monde)

Traditional Tannese hairstyle, photographed by F. de Tolna during his world tour in the 1890s. To achieve this elaborate style, worn during rituals, each lock of hair had to be meticulously wrapped around thin bamboo sticks. (From de Tolna's *Chez les cannibales*)

The renaissance of *kastom* has seen the return of traditional hairstyles. *Toka* ritual participant, Enfitana, 1977.

A man from Tanna wearing a *nambas*. The leather belt was a trade item. (From de Tolna's *Chez les cannibales*)

Father Jean Pionnier (1841–1929), one of the first Marist missionaries in the New Hebrides. He landed on Mele in 1887; the islet was still pagan, the only such area in Efate. Pionnier described Efate as *le boulevard du protestantisme* 'the preserve of Protestantism'. (From Monnier's One Hundred Years of Mission: The Catholic Church in the New Hebrides–Vanuatu 1887–1987)

Originally from Britanny, Father Jean-Baptiste Suas (1865–1933) reached Oceania in 1892. He clung to the Pentecost and Ambae coastal missions, in constant warfare with the "bush people." For the most part, the large-scale wave of conversions in these islands at the turn of the century (1900–1910) was the result of his efforts. A prolific letter writer, Father Suas published several ethnographic articles in the journal *Anthropos* (Vienna). (From Monnier's One Hundred Years of Mission: The Catholic Church in the New Hebrides–Vanuatu 1887–1987)

PART TWO

TANNA: STONES WITHIN CANOES

European custom is like a bird that has settled, that has flown to our shore just now. But our *kastom* has been here, like a banyan tree, since the world broke open. It was here at the start.

BONG OF BUNLAP, south Pentecost

7 Isle of Resilience

> An island is the absolute by definition, the break in all
> linkages . . .
>
> MICHEL TOURNIER,
> *"Entretien avec D. Bougnaux et A. Clavel"*

An island is defined by its shore. It is first and foremost a break and a dive into the ocean, a dive that can be idyllic or dramatic. "An island is linked only to the harmony that predates it," Tournier also has written (1979, 15).[1] Indeed, an island refers to the original oneness; it can only exist with the feeling that a larger oneness ties it with the rest of the world. Presumably, were it not so, no one could live on an island.

The clichés that circulate in Europe about Pacific Islanders portray carefree and idle individuals. Yet, in truth, Islanders have the awareness of the "break in all linkages" noted by Tournier. At the deepest level of their consciousness, there is anxiety in genuinely insular populations. Their territory is but a shore: behind them, hilly inland areas, which are often insufficient and, in some cases, uninhabitable or dangerous; before them, an endless horizon and a bottomless liquid abyss. In such places of complete solitude, Islanders perpetually are made aware of the original breaking point. That intense feeling explains the importance of network-style relationships to island communities. Their space is a sea, but their sea is a road. To establish linkages means to survive. Traditional journeys by canoe between the islands of Oceania were more numerous and frequent in the past than they are today; it seems that there has always been, in the midst of island cultures, the reaffirmed need for an "exit" carrying the expectation of a more intense link and alliance with the rest of the world.

Pacific Islanders expect—and even welcome—the influence of the outside world. Any new cultural item is taken in and tested before being merged into a larger synthesis whereby old custom and new culture are mixed and soon become indistinguishable. In part, this attitude may explain why, for instance, a large majority of Oceania's populations— except in Tanna and some other islands—adopted Christianity relatively

105

rapidly in the course of the missionary venture of the nineteenth century, or at least made an attempt.

In any case, such deliberate acceptance of the influence of the outside world does not imply that traditional island life is rejected. Insular patriotisms are among the strongest: the sole wish of those who leave their island—even the most remote—is often to return. Fundamentally, Islanders have a dual expectation; they wish to enjoy the serenity of their environment or even their seclusion while, at least periodically, being able to elude the syndrome of confinement, be it spatial or cultural. They can only achieve this by sustaining their links with the outside world.

Modern communications by sea or air, a recent factor, only affect a few large islands, indeed a few "capital" towns within island networks. In most cases, Pacific islands are not as well connected now as they were in the past; they have increasingly become scattered fragments of space searching for linkages across the open sea.

Tanna

Tanna, a medium-sized island (561 sq km), is one of the most populated in Vanuatu with 15,715 residents—or 28 residents per square kilometer—in 1979 and more than 20,000 at the end of the 1980s. Because of the high birth rate (32 per thousand per year), relative overpopulation has become an issue; so have land shortages, notably in coastal areas such as Lenakel on the west coast and White Sands on the east coast.

For the most part, the population is scattered in small groups of houses along grassy trails in the bush or a wooded landscape dominated by coconut groves on the coast and tree ferns in the inland hills. Houses are also found near the dirt or coral roads that circle the island and cross it in one spot. Formerly long and low-lying, most houses are now built on the European model although still with plant material; the roof, made of leaves and ribs of coconut palms, rests on screens of split cane. New materials such as corrugated iron and cement blocks are now being used, initially in the vicinity of trails suitable for vehicles. Few in number and primarily located near the coast, villages were created at the turn of the century under the influence of Christian missionaries.

Near each small group of huts or houses is a dancing place, *nakamal* in Bislama or *yimwayim* in the language of Tanna's west coast. This site is devoted to sacred and ritual or convivial events; it is a fairly extensive clearing (2000 to 3000 sq m) with bare soil, usually shaded by ancient banyan trees, and located at some distance, although not too far, from the hamlets.

Every day, men meet here at nightfall to drink kava together. This beverage extracted from an Oceanic plant of the pepper family, *Piper*

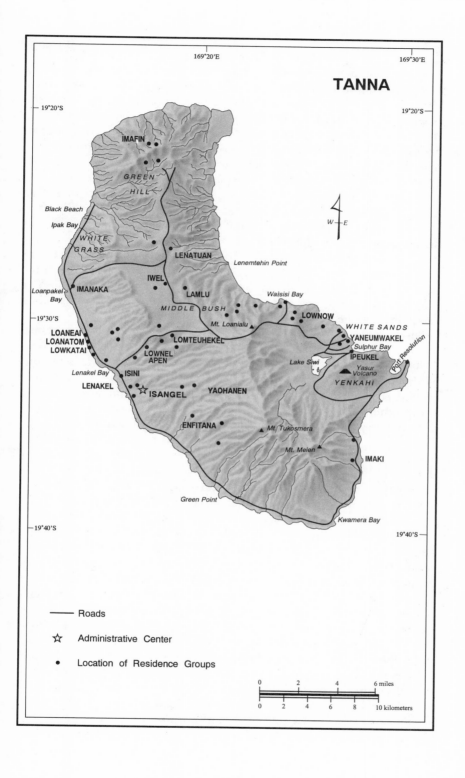

TANNA

169°20'E   169°30'E

19°20'S   19°20'S

IMAFIN

GREEN HILL

Black Beach

Ipak Bay

WHITE GRASS

LENATUAN

Lenemtehin Point

IWEL

Loanpakel Bay

IMANAKA

LAMLU

MIDDLE BUSH

Waisisi Bay

LOWNOW

Mt. Loanialu

WHITE SANDS

19°30'S

LOANEAI
LOANATOM
LOWKATAI

LOMTEUHEKEL

YANEUMWAKEL
Sulphur Bay

IPEUKEL

LOWNEL
APEN

Lake Siwi

Yasur Volcano

Port Resolution

Lenakel Bay

ISINI

YENKAHI

LENAKEL

☆ ISANGEL

YAOHANEN

ENFITANA

Mt. Tukosmera

Mt. Melen

IMAKI

Green Point

Kwamera Bay

19°40'S   19°40'S

—— Roads

☆ Administrative Center

● Location of Residence Groups

0   2   4   6 miles

0   2   4   6   8   10 kilometers

methysticum, plays an essential role in Tannese culture: the island is kava's kingdom. Most adult men drink kava daily. The youngest men chew the green roots, obtaining a liquid which each man drinks in turn, respectful of precedence. Kava is a nonaddictive drug, but its mind-altering effects can be strong, in which case one is plunged into silent drunkenness (see Brunton 1989, Lebot and Cabalion 1986, Lindstrom 1987). The sharing of kava in fellowship unites the men who drink it together on the dancing place while simultaneously tying these men to their ancestors' spirits. The individuals who meet daily make up the core of a local group, a "canoe" or *niko* as it is called on the island, which itself is often linked to a larger "canoe" made up of several patrilocal clans sharing the same territory and mythical heritage.

The landscapes of Tanna differ from those of the northern part of the group. With their extended vistas, they often allow one to view the entire island. At the center of Tanna, a rolling plateau called Middle Bush is scattered with clearings and hills whose summits are frequently bare, especially on the plateau's northern edge. Middle Bush abuts on an extensive volcanic chain to the south, either in subsidence at White Sands, or raised, with Mt Melen and Mt Tukosmera reaching 1047 and 1084 meters, respectively. The active Yasur volcano is located next to the White Sands basin and scatters endless ashes over it. Within the crater, regular eruptions occur approximately every fifteen minutes, spouting brown smoke that sometimes carries incandescent lava rocks over a powdery and grey ash plain, the Siwi. This small inland desert, devoid of villages, people, and vegetation, is characterized by the smell of sulfur. Footprints and the tracks of car tires are visible on the ground. Despite its dramatic appearance, Yasur's reputation is that of a volcano which presents no real danger to island residents—at least, until now. One village, Ipeukel, is located at the foot of the crater, on Sulphur Bay.

The island economy may be outlined in simple terms. A visitor is immediately struck by the beauty and multiplicity of traditional food gardens with their yam and taro root crops. The gardens have evolved on brown humus soils which are continuously renewed and fertilized by volcanic ash. Unless there is a hurricane or severe drought, these gardens provide subsistence food in varied and sufficient quantities for large surpluses to be exchanged among local groups in the course of alliance rituals. Modern resources that would allow for cash earnings are conspicuously absent, however. Therefore Tanna is both rich and poor. From the standpoint of a traditional way of life, the island population lives in abundance to some extent, yet it is a modern "proletariat" when considered in the context of an imported socioeconomic framework—abundance here and scarcity there. The Tannese are aware of their remoteness from today's consumer world, a world to which they barely have access. They involve themselves all the more in production and traditional ritual exchanges. Devoid of cash, the Islanders are rich in pigs, kava, and giant tubers, which they trade off with pomp and ostentation from one ceremony to the next. Poor in relation to the outside world, they endeavor to remain rich in their own context, in order to be generous among themselves.

A Place of Beginnings

The Tannese assert themselves as masters of the sacred power of *kastom*, and as an elected people. The impressive pride of Tanna's inhabitants underlines both their language and the island's cultural memory, which is carefully maintained by an array of chants, dances, metaphors, and myths.

Tanna's myths illustrate a worldview just as much as they bear the island's cultural memory. They deliver the secrets of a "black history," which is the deep-rooted counterpart of the history lived and told by "white" actors. Following the birth of the world, Tannese myths give an understanding of the emergence of space first, then men, women, and finally the island's society (chapters 8 and 9). Tannese history is revealed through diachronic myths embedded within one another. Under various forms, myths carry on their narrative until the time of contact with Westerners; they even cast light on more recent events. Images, myths, and metaphors are continuously transformed within this tradition in perpetual renewal.

Tanna's history is dominated by religious and political factors, nearly inseparable as these usually are. The Islanders have always been unruly: they have never really accepted any type of centralized authority, and they speak three major languages. Revolting against the hold of the Protestant missionaries' religious power, showing thereafter their independent streak vis-à-vis colonial authorities, Tanna's population—or at least part of it—also rebelled against the emerging state whose center was located on another island. This intense awareness of independence was first sparked by a cultural "rebellion," which made the entire island stand up against the Presbyterian mission's theocratic authority at the turn of the century. It was an unusual, even idiosyncratic, event in Oceania: Tanna's pagans "deconverted" the first island Christians and won them over to their cause. They were thereby affirming the primacy of *kastom*, in other words, their culture, over any other vision of the world.

Tannese pagans built a new conceptual system, half-traditional, halfmodern, which probably had more appeal and explanatory power than the "orthodox" biblical teachings offered by missionaries. Pagan "darkness" prevailed over the "enlightenment" of the West. To understand this

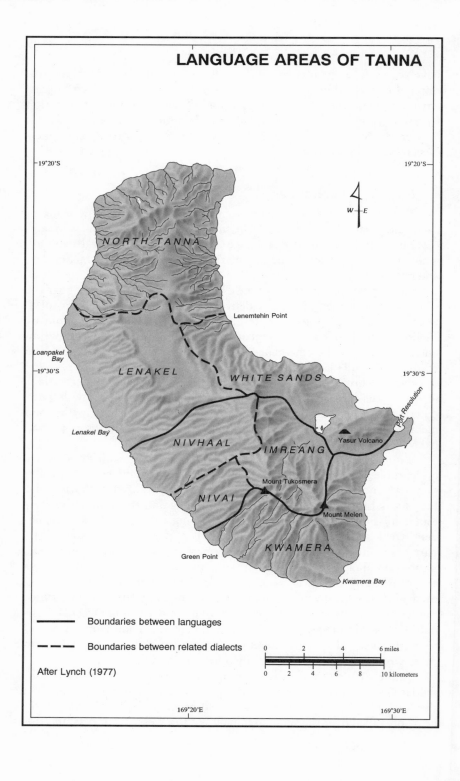

LANGUAGE AREAS OF TANNA

19°20'S

19°20'S

W — E

NORTH TANNA

Lenemtehin Point

Loanpakel Bay

19°30'S

LENAKEL

WHITE SANDS

19°30'S

Port Resolution

Lenakel Bay

Yasur Volcano

NIVHAAL

IMREANG

Mount Tukosmera

NIVAI

Mount Melen

KWAMERA

Green Point

Kwamera Bay

————— Boundaries between languages

– – – – – Boundaries between related dialects

After Lynch (1977)

0		2		4		6 miles

0	2	4	6	8	10 kilometers

169°20'E

169°30'E

victory, one needs to examine how the Islanders perceive, internalize, and account for the dual concepts of space and time. A number of origin myths illustrating these concepts anchor the distinct perspective of the Tannese, which they have maintained to this day. Without it, Tanna's history would be incomprehensible—or simply banal and even meaningless.

From the earliest to the most recent, the various rebellions in Tanna only find their meaning in light of the island's history and mythology, and in the very terms which the Tannese use to remember and refer to them. In this perspective, what can be expected from a foreign researcher is less an analysis than an understanding of the Islanders' message. For the people of Tanna are "unique," as Agnes Watt noted in one of her letters. Possibly the only Islanders within Oceania to assert that their view of the world was superior to that of Westerners, they reflected on the issues and sent emissaries to the world of whites in order to make better sense of it (chapter 13).

The Tannese fought and did not lose. They held out against a full-fledged cultural war that was perhaps more abominable than a mere war, because the very soul of their people was threatened. They won that war, even though they may doubt it at times—rather rarely, in fact.

Within this tradition of passionate resistance lies a mystery. Why did this island, peopled with a few thousand inhabitants, continue fighting in the name of its *kastom?* Why a struggle of such epic magnitude—a struggle whose true nature is cultural? And why does Tanna's history appeal so compellingly to Westerners who harbor the dream of progress but also all the misgivings that challenge that dream?

Perhaps Tanna held onto a vision that was more encompassing than that of other islands. In the eyes of its inhabitants, Tanna represents the original island, an island of foundation, a place of beginnings, a space entirely permeated with pagan spirituality. This magical space enchanted by gods and heroes, this founding place and center of the universe, imparted strength and continuity to Tannese culture. Rooted in a strong sense of place, the Tannese worldview gave rise to a remarkable capacity to resist. Tanna did not give in; the island started over again, even as it was believed to be overpowered; it lived through several cultural births, re-inventing its *kastom* and finding it anew, but never abandoning it. Thus, Tanna was able to re-create itself—along different and identical lines. The concept of resilience best characterizes Tannese history and culture.

A Nostalgia for *Kastom*

When confronted with the political and religious world of Westerners, Tanna's people revived their myths of creation. They felt nostalgic about their origins and, turning militant, built a political force. Their intent was to return to the equality of the "original" island community, or at least to their idealized image of it. Yet what was the "genuine" message of *kastom?* Countless meetings were organized to unveil that message. On the ancient dancing places, in the shade of banyan trees, the island's "elders," the wise men and the big men, sat down in a circle for convoluted discussions that lasted for months. These "living memories" delved into the chants, narratives, and myths of *kastom,* meticulously searching the lessons of the past in order to find new messages for the confrontations of the age. An entire population became the ethnologist of its own tradition and, in the process of going back to the island's origins, found its identity anew.

What came out of the quest was, in fact, a "new *kastom*"—partly rediscovered and partly re-created. Tanna's rebels justified their political discourse with it. In that discourse, they were longing for another society, for a reversal of the order of the contemporary world. Simultaneously, they were favoring tradition and cultural preservation and demonstrating an intense eagerness for power. *Kastom* represented a dual choice in favor of tradition on the one hand, and political and social change on the other. The apparent inconsistency did not weaken the customary movement. Rather, it made it particularly inspiring and even dangerously subversive; nor did its opponents misunderstand it.

8 Enchanted Space

> These cosmic hierophanes . . . clothe a
> discourse of much depth.
>
> GEORGES DUMÉZIL

> Imagination is more important than knowl-
> edge.
>
> ALBERT EINSTEIN

The linguist and ethno-historian Georges Dumézil calls hierophanes all
worldly manifestations of the sacred. For *homo religiosus,* water, land,
sky, fire, a volcano, a mountain, or a rock are not simply natural elements but hierophanes, because they reveal the sacred dimension of the
world. In Tanna, space itself is a live hierophane, and therefore the best
way to learn a myth in the island is to walk with "one who knows"—one
of the big men of *kastom*—through the space associated with the mythical hero, from place to place and from stone to stone. The mythical road
unveils a world which refers to an era outside of time. Yet it is an era
which no Tannese questions, because places and stones are there to cor-
roborate the story. The proof of Tanna's temporal myths is geographical:
one may challenge a man's words, but who can question the genuine tan-
gibility of a place and the magic associated with it?

Chants, dances, myths—recent and ancient—are anchored in a network of sacred sites that make up the great "book" of Tanna's *kastom*.
Remembered and inscribed in a "geography of creation" are the names of
individuals, groups, and "canoes," along with their essential deeds and
powers. Within a lattice of places, each myth generates a magical, symbolic territory that in turn gives the myth a tangible reality that makes it
familiar and always present. On the island, there is hardly any mountain,
spring, or large rock that does not refer to a myth. Between space and
mythology, places and culture, the symbiosis is complete.

Rooted in a sort of Tannese Dreamtime,[1] the island's great origin
myths explain the world through the saga of places. In Tanna, space is
harmony. It predates humans and—since it has a beginning but no end—
it exists out of time: here, Dreamtime turns into "Dreamspace."

Organized in a temporal lineage, the island's myths suggest a diachronic vision of the shaping of the universe. Mythological time does not

mirror reality: one cannot date the events that have occurred therein. Indeed, the actual genealogy that could be used is so short—registered names hardly go beyond any Islander's grandfather—that going back in time is impossible. According to the wise men of *kastom,* the Dream-space of the mythical circumstances of creation dates back to five or six generations at most. Besides, time is an indeterminate factor which exists only through space.

Myths indicate great logical continuity and are replete with topographical details and place names. Here toponymy has a sacred dimension; it represents a cryptic script, a language that structures space, time, and society.

Before society is created, founding myths construct sacred places and, through them, the enchanted space of the island. They allocate individuals through space, create the names of men (those of ancestors and of civilizing heroes), and at the same time connect these men with places. In other words, they generate a full-fledged sacred geography. Through myth, the land becomes a "homeland" and the scenery, a landscape rooted to the genealogical time of the origins.

Tanna's great myths enfold the entire island. A song is there also, a song that illustrates the mythical narrative in a poetic and allusive manner, sometimes in an ancient, archaic language that aligns symbols and metaphors, making it all the more difficult to understand the underlying text. The song generates a dance. Thus a fruitful relationship connects founding places and founding myths with the island's oral tradition and dance heritage. This alliance is still vigorous today.

Moving from group to group and from place to place, all mythical cycles are engendered through space. Each local group protects the part of the myth that occurs on its territory and refers to the neighboring group to know the next segment of the story. A mythical cycle is therefore a sort of discourse shared among groups that follow one another sequentially. As a rule, each group is allowed to deliver only that part of the story which focuses on its own area. The knowledge of myth-related toponymy is indeed perceived as locally "owned." More specifically, the fact that it has been committed to memory and transmitted from one generation to the next within a group is the best proof of both the authenticity of its origin and the legitimacy of the group's territorial rights.

As it moves through space, Tannese oral tradition generates clusters of place names. Each great mythical cycle may be considered a "road," with an origin and a sequence of meaningful places that represent as many transmission points. The departure point is primordial: it is a founding place, as expressed in the Bislama word *stamba* (from the English 'stump'). Thus, the man who is at the *stamba* lives at the founding place associated with the origins of his lineage and holds the lineage name, or customary title. As the "owner" of the entire myth, he is entitled to a right of precedence over other group members who refer to this myth.

In brief, the island of Tanna was fashioned in the course of a saga-like story emphasizing places and names of origin. I recorded the following segment of the story at Ipai and Loanatom on the northwest coast of the island; it explains the creation of the world.[2]

The Howling Horde of the Beginnings

The spirit Wuhngin (or Wuhngen) created land. It is neither a man nor a hero; Wuhngin is a genuine spirit and no one has ever seen it. Wuhngin was here at the beginning of the world. To create the islands, it created the land, and then stones to shape the land. Since then, Wuhngin's spirit has inhabited Mt Melen, whose summit in the south of the island is visible from all of Tanna. This mountain is regarded as a huge raised stone—the mother of all other stones and the first among the island's sacred sites. Its summit is a taboo place, out of bounds to most Tannese and certainly to strangers.

The land started its journey at the northeast tip of Tanna, moved westward and southward, and finally went back to its point of departure through the east. In the course of the land's travel, the island emerged, taking on the outline and dimensions that it has today. This land which gave birth to lands is called *numapten* 'the land's house', Tanna's name according to the west coast tradition. When the land arrived back at its point of departure, it prepared kava, drank it, and took a rest. Then the land dived into the sea and disappeared, re-emerging in the north, where it gave birth to the island of Erromango in the same fashion. It kept on traveling in that direction, creating new islands on the way. All such lands are seen as Tanna's daughters, since they appeared later, in the *numapten*'s wake: the island's traditional society thereby accounts for Erromango (called Ilmanga in northern Tanna), Aniwa, Futuna and, farther away, Emae, Makura, and Mataso (or Masaka), which represent the boundary of the known world. Conversely, Anatom Island, to the south, was born earlier than Tanna.

Because the land was bare, lifeless, and devoid of form, Wuhngin sent a hard substance: stones or *kapiel*. According to most oral traditions, such stones came from the sea. In others, they rose directly from the earth's core or occasionally, for instance in the eastern part of the island, from the volcano. But in all cases Wuhngin's breath made them appear. On the island's soft matrix, the stones created geographical shapes: mountains, capes and headlands, ridges and crests, rocks, and solitary stones. The *kapiel* liked to travel and make noise. When they arrived on the island, they generated a great commotion and went on a fantastic circuit, spreading out in separate groups making war with, and constantly opposing, one another. Because of this magical tumult and anarchical wandering, there was neither rest nor refuge in the land. The fighting and talking stones wore themselves out in unceasing competition. But in so doing, they made the world and scenery of the island.

The stones laid out roads *(suatu)*. Three major itineraries appeared in the magic circuit: in the western part of Tanna, they are called *nikoka-plalao* 'what encircles the canoe'.[3] The main road, named *kwoteren,* follows the shoreline around the entire island.[4] A second road parallels it halfway up the slope. Finally, a third road girdles the island through the mountain and crest line. The stones also established two offshore roads: one loop is at reef's edge, the other named *karipen* makes a wide circle around the island, on the open sea. (The *karipen* 'road of the great canoes' was deemed the safest for travel as it was away from the island and its potential traps.) These "stone roads" have names that are known throughout Tanna; they possess a "spirit" and a "breath." A string of hidden powers and meanings stretches along their entire course.

Stones moved along the roads for a very long time, not peacefully but in disorderly and quarrelsome ways. The stones on the mountain road were particularly aggressive; they were a howling horde, circling relentlessly through the island's enclosed space. Meanwhile, the stones that kept to the coastal road were trying to protect themselves. These shoreline stones became weary of their endless wandering. Eventually, the stone Wiwo stopped across from a channel in the reef named Lasum, in the Ipai area. Wiwo had a leg abscess that prevented it from walking: it withdrew from the round and hid itself at the water's edge. Others followed suit, such as the stone Waniko which had been moving around the island so much that it had a stiff neck. The shoreline stones settled down one by one, trying to hide. Ipai residents say that most were "children" or "women." Higher above, the howling horde of "men" were still fighting; they had set up "companies" *(nahwuto),* disparate troops that never stopped fighting and chasing one another. But weariness eventually caught up with them as well. They settled in clusters that were evenly spaced out along the roads. Peace reigned over the island for the first time.

Magical Stones and Places of the Origins

On settling down, the howling horde turned into a more peaceful community. Increasingly silent and immobile, the magical stones evolved into a web of redoubtable places whose supernatural powers are still active and rule the world. At nightfall, these stones come alive. Spirits

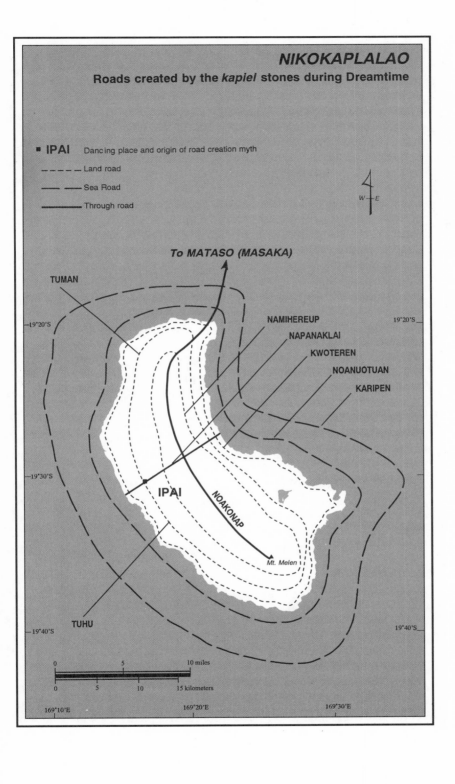

NIKOKAPLALAO
Roads created by the *kapiel* stones during Dreamtime

■ **IPAI**   Dancing place and origin of road creation myth

– – – – – Land road

— — — Sea Road

————— Through road

W—E

To MATASO (MASAKA)

TUMAN

NAMIHEREUP

NAPANAKLAI

KWOTEREN

NOANUOTUAN

KARIPEN

19°20'S   19°20'S

19°30'S

IPAI

NOAKONAP

Mt. Melen

19°40'S   19°40'S

TUHU

0   5   10 miles

0   5   10   15 kilometers

169°10'E   169°20'E   169°30'E

come out: they are the *yarimus* *(devel* in Bislama, or devils, as the missionaries used to call them). Eerie shadows in the night, these spirits take on a vaguely human shape and wander through the forest. The *yarimus* have their own roads, meeting places, sites, territories, and names. They feed on raw foods, taking tubers left for them in the gardens. At night, they can possess women in their huts or attack men belated on the trails. They have thorough knowledge of the life of the people whose territory they share and whose behavior they watch. The unknown individual, who at night slips into an area that is not his, is their favorite target of attack. They can kill or wound him seriously with their bite. The *yarimus* are considered to be outside the circle of humankind; most terminal illnesses and sudden deaths are imputed to them. According to Tanna's *kastom,* everything that exists on the surface of the island draws its power from the magical stones scattered thereon, which at night engender the frightening world of the *yarimus.* These spirits carry out the ancient life of the initial horde: pure magical powers, they wander about in the foliage of large trees or on hidden forest trails. Human beings worry about them and entrench themselves in bare clearings, behind fences. Sometimes Islanders leave half-sized swing doors in their gardens so as not to disconcert *yarimus* that need to move about. The world of wandering spirits, both near and dangerous, represents the stones in their liveliness and indicates that forces of a magical nature still dominate human society.

Tanna's *kastom* makes a distinction between "white stones" *(kapiel tuan),* all of which have a specific name and carry magical power, and "black stones" *(kapiel apen).* The latter are anonymous and represent inert forces that are neutral from the standpoint of magic. "White stones" alone are the repository of Wuhngin's sacred powers; they are inhabited by *yarimus.* As a general rule, each mountain, crest, or oddly shaped rock is a "white stone," and so are some specific submerged stones and crests of the fringing reef. In Tanna, everything that makes up a place and bears a name is a reminder of one of the phases of sacred time and represents a special mesh of the enchanted net.

Two major types of magical places are acknowledged: *kapiel assim,* simple rocks with a specific type of power, surrounded by variable proscriptions, and *ika ussim,* sacred areas endowed with multiple powers and surrounded by very strong prohibitions that the ordinary individual respects scrupulously. The *kapiel assim* make up a dense network of points scattered on both sides of the great roads of *kastom*—each point represents the settling down of one of the original wandering stones. Usually they are white coral stones with jagged edges; in some cases they are surrounded by a small sacred grove where the common people do not venture. These *kapiel* are mother stones, fragments of which may be broken off or gathered at their base. When enclosed in a basket or a *niko* (small wooden canoe), these fragments will carry the spirit of the mother rock. They will keep on radiating magical energy, even away from the spot where they originated.

The stone places weave a sort of net whose meshes, of variable width, cover the entire island. The great sacred areas or *ika ussim* represent powerful points on that net; multiple powers are believed to originate there. These sacred areas are kept as forests whose dimensions are a function of the strength of the associated proscriptions. Some are as big as two or three hectares, making up sacred woodlands which only the magician of the group *(yatamassim)* may enter. The extent of other sacred areas is even larger: mountains and entire hills represent gigantic *kapiel*. Mts Melen and Tukosmera are the best-known cases, but most mountains and reliefs on Tanna are deemed to be places which, to a variable extent, are under the influence of magical forces. An enchanted landscape emerges, made up of mountains and rocks that are attuned with the great forces of the cosmos.

Stones in Loanatom

The Loanatom coast aligns clusters of magical stones *(kapiel assim)* across from the reef channels—about fifty stones along a three-kilometer-long shoreline. For the most part, these "white stones" are located between the coastal road *(kwoteren)* and the reef-hugging loop *(noanuotuan)*. Each stone conveys a specific story, power, and meaning.

The loading stone, *lun,* is located at one spot of the *kwoteren* road to help passers-by who are hauling food. A little farther, the courage stone, *tuku,* grants those who are walking with their loads the endurance to go to the end of their journey. Farther on is a stone with the opposite meaning—the rest stone, *nura*. Weary of circling the island with the fighting stones, it left and hid below the road. It is associated with fatigue and rest, but it is also a dangerous stone because the spirits of the dead often choose it for their own respite. The *nura* stone is both a spot whose energy heals one's fatigue and a place to communicate with the dead.

Even more surprising is the traditional story about two rat stones: *kao tuan* (the white rat stone) and *kao apen* (the black rat stone), which the warriors left behind as a source of food for the troops that were following each other on the road. The *kao* stones explain the presence of rats in this part of the island. They also play a part in agrarian magic and hold a special power over the sun (to stop rain) and the catching of fish. Two other stones appear at low tide, in alignment with the rat stones. Called *ukas* and *kasawar,* they encompass a reef channel at Lowkatu Apen. Those two stones represent the rat's legs while the two *kao* stones

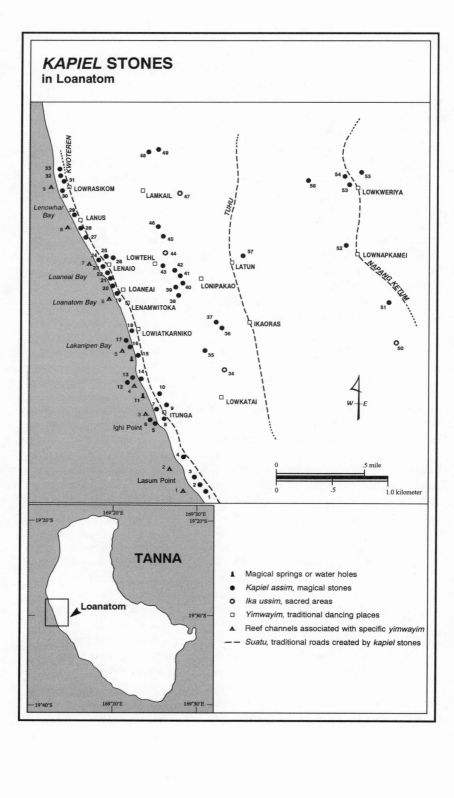

Stone Names

Coastline
1 Wiwo
2 Yeviakel
3 Lanekem
4 Keleplepen
5 Lowanangne
6 Lowaiyemnapus
7 Nepenrwatiken
8 Nim
9 Nipayarmanum
10 Tangalua
11 Lowaputil
12 Napatu
13 Lemanikapiel
   Yakis
14 Naipis
15 Yuwaniko
16 Ukas
17 Kasawar

18 Kihi
19 Kaleu Kanmita
20 Wuretam
21 Letektenun
22 Brahinel
23 Kasipapeun
24 Tekeu
25 Lun
26 Tuku
27 Lowanange
28 Nokuriawanimita
29 Lanus
30 Napangnisinalik
31 Lapangkumekume
32 Nokurmatuamin
33 Nokurabomin

Midslope
34 Lenura
35 Yemeltoseng

36 Kao Tuan
37 Kao Apen
38 Kihi
39 Napario
40 Wusmil Kao
41 Kutuhan
42 Yarimus
43 Wusmil Kwarwo
44 Nemenek
45 Lakur
46 Loweyarow
47 Lenakam
48 Kaniani
49 Lahikom

High Slope
50 Leniakis
51 Nura
52 —
53 Kemama

54 Napiworwor
55 Leuwalawuya
56 Wik
57 Buleng Buleng

Reef Channels
(1) Lenagne
(2) Lowanpatniko
(3) Niya'us
(4) Lowkanipen
(5) Lowkatu Apen
(6) —
(7) Lowanan
(8) —
(9) Lowagap

are its testicles. Tradition tells that the rat fornicates with the fish going through the channel. Fish scales wound the rat, with the exception of the blue coral fish whose skin is soft. Indeed, the rat is in love with that fish, and vice versa. The magic of rat stones operates at exactly that spot and allows for the catching of reef fish.

Near the midslope road, two other stones, *kutuhan* and *yarimus,* suggest further magical symbolism. The *kutuhan* stone is tied to the power of basket-making. Its shape vaguely evokes a seated woman weaving a basket; the intersecting streaks on the rock symbolize the basket's decoration. A lower cavity represents her sex. When the male stone, called *yarimus,* is introduced into the female stone, it can trigger sexual frenzy in distant enemy groups, which leads to discord and mutual extermination. Despite a seemingly joyful appearance, the *kutuhan* stone is particularly feared since it is one of the stones associated with the onset of war. Sex is dangerous.

Finally, some stones represent the source of cosmic powers. Here is their story:

When the *kapiel* stones were circling the island as warring gangs, there used to be constant fights, especially among the higher stones. One of the main reasons for these battles was the fact that no *kapiel* would accept that one of their number might become greater than the rest. The reed stone, *nuhying,* had gone to Erromango, where it had settled and acquired great power. Reeds had become the kings of Erromango and now covered the entire island. Tanna's jealous stones met at Imaya'une, in the heart of Middle Bush, and decided to punish *nuhying*. After drinking kava together at Loanpakel, six *kapiel* left for Erromango: *nekam* 'fire', *nematang* 'wind', *ming* 'earthquakes', *nihin* 'rain', *kalvalva* 'thunder', and *nemangat* 'sun'.

Ming and *nihin* triggered off a powerful earthquake, followed by torrential rains that flooded plains and valleys. *Kalvalva* lighted up and set the sky ablaze with its thunder, then *nemangat*, the sun, triggered off a great drought. *Nekam*, fire, attacked the vegetation and *nematang*, the wind, transformed it into a blaze. Charred to cinders, the reeds perished. The *nuhying* stone, now burned, was picked up by Tanna's *kapiel*, cooked in Luanumen (Lenakel), and shared with all the other stones on the island. A *kapiel* survived on Erromango. It climbed to the summit of Mt Warantap and from there harangued Tanna's *kapiel* stones: "Who ate *nuhying's* head?" No one answered. The Erromango *kapiel* then saw a stone called *lukassanga* and, speaking to it personally, repeated its question forcefully. *Lukassanga* was frightened: "This morning I saw *kapun* pass by with a leaf-wrapped parcel." "All right," said the Erromango *kapiel*. That very night, *kapun* was literally impaled by reeds rising out of all its body orifices and fastening themselves to the earth. Since then, reed-covered *kapun* has stayed where it had been sleeping. And reeds have invaded Tanna and deserted Erromango. (Loanatom oral tradition)[5]

Each of the six stones responsible for *nuhying's* death is at the head of an islandwide network of places. Each is able to generate and interrupt the cosmic or climatic power that corresponds to its name. The *kapun* stone is the stone of those who are afraid and search for a hiding-place (in other words, it has the power to conceal and discover fugitives). The *lukassanga* stone is the stone of betrayal, of those who cannot be silent. And the *nuhying* stone is the stone of reed reproduction; it is also associated with death-related magic. Fire-making is prohibited in all the areas that contain *nuhying* stones.

How Men Appeared

In Tanna's first tradition, free mobility is associated with warfare. When the stones were moving around the island in howling gangs, they had no name and were not endowed with specific powers. They were simply fighting tumultuously as they went. Besides their chance encounters, there was no connection among them. When they settled down, they received names and turned into places; the *kapiel* stones "sank" into the soil and became connected with underground powers. As places, they have been carrying the world's architecture and meaning ever since. The contrast between tumult and silence, rootedness and journeying, is at the heart of Tannese (and Melanesian) thought. Mobility is represented by the horde—a restless, bellicose, anarchical, statusless horde. Stability is "society"—the silence of those who know, secretiveness, territory, the birth of social functions and status, the advent of power. The wild horde progressively gave way to a rooted society.

For a long time, I believed that men were but the emergence of stones, in other words, that in Tannese thought men represented the diurnal side of the forest-based *yarimus* spirits' nocturnal world. The Tannese state that the magic stones are their *bubu* 'ancestors'. However, while the *kastom* people do identify with the stones of their territory, they do not necessarily claim a genealogical affiliation with stones; they only suggest that they are inhabited by the same "spirit" and share the same power. There is no real difference in nature between original stones and humans: the humans succeeded the stones, although not all stones engendered humans. The human phenomenon paralleled the slow emergence of biological life. Some stones gave birth to hawks, sharks, turtles, rats, birds, and so forth. Many of these animals eventually became people, while other stones gave birth directly to the first men. Therefore men are not the ultimate product of creation, but stand as just one natural element among others. They are neither less nor more sacred than animals and plants; indeed, they may transmute their appearance instantaneously.

The appearance of men was the result of a dispersion process from a few particularly meaningful stone places. The human phenomenon was very gradual, and Tanna's Dreamtime lasted over the span of creation while space acquired its final form and society its order. During that phase, the "first men" were stones as much as men. Rich in terms of nature, in other words, magic, these "first men" were poor in terms of culture, or *kastom*. They were not organized and therefore there were no links between them. Also they did not have real food and, most important, women did not exist among them. These stone men were living in a world of wandering and solitude, cold and asexual. They barely dissociated themselves from surrounding spirits. The "first men" appeared on a bare and treeless earth which was not ready for them. As they came out of the stones, they wandered in a cold mineral universe devoid of refuges except for the rocks they were sharing with the *yarimus*, those beings of nothingness. Deprived of places, the stone men had no identity; devoid of power, they had no secrets to conceal and spent much of their time talking.

According to the tradition from the western part of Tanna, the original form of vegetation on the black and sterile soil of the origins was a dark moss, a sort of small lichen that grows on rocks after the rain. This lichen emanating from stone was emulated by trees. The first tree grew close to shore, on Nemenek territory, near the current Loaneai dancing place. It was a banyan tree (*Ficus* sp) or *nepuk* in Tannese language. Since it was the only one, that tree was given a name: Nesis. The first men gathered round the tree, then banyan trees multiplied and the stone men followed them, peopling the shore first, the mountain next. Other plants emerged from the banyan tree: first the *nip,* a palm tree whose core is edible, then the entire cohort of coastal and mountain vegetation.

The real life of men could now begin. Trees were growing in dispersed order, so the men disbanded to take advantage of the trees' shade, fruit, and roots. Once they learned that specific plants correspond to specific *kapiel,* men could master the cycles that allow nature to reproduce. Yet men were not full-fledged beings—they lacked hot food *(hot kakai)* and especially the presence of women. These came into the world at the same time.

And Woman Came, at Last

In a small village at the edge of the vast White Grass plateau, a sort of savanna where, today, wild horses live in herds, an elderly man named Kooman[6] keeps the secret[7] myth that gives a clue to the emergence of woman and human food:

At first, only *kapiel* stones peopled the island of Tanna. In the reef off White Grass, there was a stone by the name of Noburbunemel. This stone was female. Farther north, straight up from Lownamilo, on the shore, was the male stone Kamtuwe. Kamtuwe loved Noburbunemel, and from their union a stone was born, called Kooman. Kooman grew up with his mother at Yetpalakamtiwe, close to shore, from where one can see Kamtuwe's rock.

At that time, stones did not even know how to make fire; they would dry and heat their food in the sun. They only ate roots of reeds, ferns, and wild fruit. One day, Kooman went hunting for green pigeons. He climbed to the top of the big tree Nesis[8] and built a hidingplace out of leaves and branches. A pigeon flew near. Kooman wielded his bow, but the pigeon went straight to him and landed on the tip of the arrow. Its appearance changed: it became a woman of flesh. Kooman shuddered and was so moved he nearly fell off the tree.

"Do not shoot," the woman said. "I come from another place, my name is Penoa.[9] Where do you live?"

"I live with my mother," Kooman answered.

"Who is your father?"

"My father is Kamtuwe. He does not live with us."

"How many houses do you have?"

"Two. One for my mother, one for me."

"Take me there."

Penoa and Kooman went on the trail along the coast. Once at home, Kooman hid Penoa, because he feared his mother's reaction. When Noburbunemel came back, she understood that something had happened, because her son was still shaking. She questioned Kooman, who told her about Penoa.

"Show her to me. She may just be a *yarimus* . . ."

Noburbunemel was mistrustful, but when she saw Penoa, her mistrust vanished and she was happy for her son. Penoa was indeed a woman because she had put ritual paintings on her face—something a *yarimus* never does. Noburbunemel prepared a common bed for Kooman and the unknown woman, then offered her dried fern roots, but Penoa did not want to eat. When the mother went to sleep, Penoa told Kooman:

"I do not like your food. Mine is better."

The next day, Kooman went into the forest to get the root of the *napatum* plant, which is better tasting, and offered it to Penoa, who again refused it.

"I have another name: Naunum,"[10] she said.

That same day, the mother again offered fern roots to Penoa, who did not eat them.

"I am going to go to the other side of the sea, very far away, where I used to live and where my food is. I shall bring it back to you. Do not worry, I shall return tomorrow."

Penoa went to the shore and entered the water; as she walked, the sea would open and then close behind her. She came back the next day. She was bringing taro roots, yams, bananas, coconuts, breadfruit, and fowl. She was carrying all these things on her back, tied together, and she leaned on a sugarcane stalk to walk. Her forehead was ornamented with leaves of island cabbage[11] which were tangling down her face; in her free hand, she was carrying embers—fire. On seeing this odd scene, Kooman and Noburbunemel became frightened and wanted to flee, but Penoa stopped them. She made a glowing fire, killed a chicken and cooked it, and finally broiled the yam. She then divided the meal in three portions. At first, neither Kooman nor his mother dared taste it, however when they eventually did, they were amazed.

"Kooman, my son," Noburbunemel exclaimed, "you are very lucky. You have just found a true woman and she has brought you the food of men."

Following Penoa's advice, the mother and her son prepared a large garden at Iken 'the place', on the coast. There, they buried all the stones brought by Penoa. These stones produced food and the garden went on growing, thanks to the magic that Penoa taught

Kooman. He called all the other stone men who lived on Tanna; at Iken, he prepared three large *niel*[12] and gave them away according to the roads his guests had followed. The foodstuffs went from hand to hand and spread throughout the island.

Kooman and Penoa were living together at Iken. A daughter was born, whom they named Nemei.[13] One day, Kooman's father Kamtuwe invited his son to an exchange of food, a *niel* that was to take place in the northern part of the island. Kooman and Penoa went there, leaving their child in Noburbunemel's care. They received a basket full of breadfruit and started on their way back. Kooman was walking ahead; Penoa behind him was carrying the breadfruit basket tied to her forehead.

At Iken, the child Nemei suddenly started to cry. Noburbunemel took her in her arms, but Nemei soaked her with urine. Furious, Kooman's mother put the child down and insulted her. At that very moment, Penoa felt pain rise through her breasts. She understood what was going on and started crying. Worried, Kooman stopped walking. Penoa suddenly untied the basket from her forehead and threw it down forcefully. The breadfruit scattered in all directions, with the largest fruit rolling all the way to White Sands.[14] [She said:]

"Your mother insults my daughter, I have been good with all of you but you are bad with me."[15]

Once in Iken, Penoa took her daughter back and walked to the seashore. She entered the water: the sea opened. Kooman's old mother followed her, crying; she wanted to stop Penoa but she drowned when the sea closed on her. Kooman had stayed on the shore, watching his wife and daughter disappear toward an unknown island and his own mother drown.[16] Penoa went to an island whose name only is known: Lapnuman. It is the country of the god Mwatiktiki, father of all foods.

Later, Kamtuwe had a second son, named Yepmol, with another female stone. Time was going by and Kooman was still sad. He wanted to look for his wife and daughter in the other world beyond the sea, but his brother Yepmol held him back:

"We all came out of the sea, stones as well as men. But for us that time has come to an end; we left the water, and now we belong to the land. Penoa and Nemei have left. Yet Nemei will come back because she was born on the island and she belongs to a race that is of this land."

As Yepmol had told, Nemei later returned to Tanna. Kooman "paid" for her by sending her mother one pig, one large yam, and a kava root. Kooman's lineage (Namiplopmatua) has lasted in both Lamasak and Lowkurus (southeast of Lamasak) until now. Between them, these two lineages share the White Grass region. They also share power over all the places associated with the mythical cycle of the arrival of food and the appearance of woman.

The Founding of *Kastom*

In this myth of great richness, the first man is "humanized" by the first woman. With woman also comes food. Man then evolves from a state of nature to a state of culture: by introducing him to the world of shared cooked foods, woman allows man to leap from one stage to the other. The myth also establishes the *niel,* a form of exchange that links men together. Accordingly, the one who receives food must give it to others, and doing so he behaves as man should—what Kooman did with the initial food, men must do repeatedly in the course of their lives. Man is distinct from stones in that he eats cooked food which he shares with his allies. *Yarimus* spirits eat raw food and do not share it: they are sub-human beings who keep their food for themselves. Rich in magic but poor in custom, spirits are not sociable.

To illustrate, Captain Cook and his companions never received a *niel*[17] during their stay on Tanna. The British navigators gave nothing of interest, therefore they received nothing of importance. They were regarded as familiar *yarimus,* not as real men.

According to Penoa's myth, food originates from Lapnuman, an island that moves like a canoe and occasionally appears in the distance; the Tannese may see it as a blurred shape on the horizon. Mwatiktiki is Lapnuman's king. This god with a Polynesian-sounding name sometimes floats on the surf by himself, with his feet resting on two coconuts, while he plays the flute.

When Yepmol spoke with his brother Kooman, he stated two great tenets of *kastom.* Men are *men ples* 'men of one place' and sons of the land, who must live where their place-bound fathers have lived. As to Nemei, Kooman's daughter, she had to come back one day, because the woman who has gone away must be given back: such is the rule of marriage exchanges. The road of blood-related alliances always goes back to its point of departure. And the man who gives his daughter in marriage must eventually see another woman return to wed his own son or a member of his own patriclan.

The eastern side of the island offers different and sometimes complementary versions of the myths. During the nebulous time of the origins, when men were stones and vice versa, a canoe landed at Sulphur Bay and Port Resolution. The hero Mwatiktiki himself was at the bow. A crew of male stones or *yani niko* (literally "the voices of the canoe") steered the boat from the stern; stones of female gender, or *naotupunus,* were in the

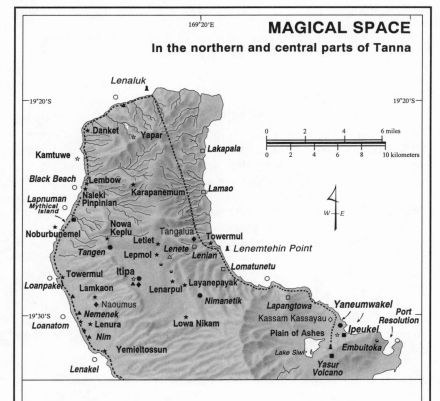

MAGICAL SPACE

In the northern and central parts of Tanna

169°20'E

19°20'S — 19°20'S

Lenaluk

★ **Danket**   **Yapar**   □ *Lakapala*

Kamtuwe ☆   □ *Lamao*

Black Beach   ★ **Lembow**
Lapnuman   **Naleki**   ★ **Karapanemum**   □ *Lamao*
Mythical   **Pinpinian**
Island

Nowa
Noburbunemel   **Keplu**   **Letiet**   **Tangalua**   ★ **Towermul**
Tangen   **Lepmol** ★   **Lenete** △   **Lenian**   ▲ **Lenemtehin Point**
Towermul   **Itipa**   *Lomatunetu*
Loanpakel   **Lamkaon**   **Lenarpul** ★ **Layanepayak**
◆ **Naoumus**   **Nimanetik**   □ **Lapangtowa**   **Yaneumwakel**
19°30'S —   **Nemenek**   **Kassam Kassayau** ◇   **Port**
Loanatom   ★ **Lenura**   **Lowa Nikam**   **Plain of Ashes**   **Resolution**
Nim   ☆ **Ipeukel**
Yemieltossun   *Lake Siwi*   ▲ **Embuitoka**
○ **Lenakel**   ■ **Yasur**
Volcano

0 2 4 6 miles
0 2 4 6 8 10 kilometers

W — E

Great sacred places of multiple magical powers associated with the first mythical cycles: appearance of *kapiel* stones and men; Semo-Semo's myth.

☆ Places of primeval multiple magical powers, associated in particular with the first appearance of human beings and *yarimus* spirits.

★ Places of multiple magical powers-- diversified and specialized, for example for healing purposes. Places where *yarimus* spirits first appeared.

Great sacred places of agrarian and weather-related magical powers associated with Mwatiktiki.

■ Places where (i) food magic first appeared and was redistributed, or where (ii) fire magic appeared.

□ Places associated with stones of *nusua* yam magic and stones of sun magic (east coast).

▲ Places where stones of *milu* yam and *ka'uye* yam magic first appeared (west coast).

△ Places where stones of taro magic magic first appeared (Middle Bush).

● Places where stones of pig and fowl magic and stones of hunting magic (rats, hawks, pigeons, and the like) first appeared.

○ Major places of fishing magic, linked in particular with the catching of turtles.

◉ Major places of beauty, poetry, or love magic: magical trees and springs.

Great sacred places associated with the appearance of evil magic.

◆ Places where evil agrarian magical powers, or *naomus*, first appeared.

◇ Places where poison magic, or *netuk*, first appeared.

The path of the dead.

---- Underground path followed by the souls of the dead.

▲ Entrances to the abode of the dead.

↩ Direction from which magical stones and food arrived.

center. The canoe held food stones: taro roots, yams, fruit trees, fish, shellfish, and so forth. In the evening following their arrival in Ipeukel Bay, Mwatiktiki, tired from the long journey, fell asleep on the beach while the stones of male gender were combing each other's hair. Taking advantage of that slumber and this inattentiveness, the stones of female gender stole the food stones and fled. When he realized what had happened, Mwatiktiki became very angry and hurled the following curse at the *naotupunus:* "You stole the food stones! From now on, you are to be the only ones to make use of them, as you will feed the others."

The *naotupunus* stones dispersed. On the east coast, Ipeukel is viewed as the redistribution center for Mwatiktiki's food. Ipeukel residents thoroughly remember the itineraries of dispersal and the names of the *naotupunus* clans that distributed foodstuffs through the island. As to Mwatiktiki, he stayed on Yenkahi (Ipeukel) territory at a place called Ensefa, a sacred area on the mountain north of Port Resolution.

On both sides of the island, east and west, the food stones scattered off from one ally to another and one place to another. Today, the areas that hold the stones of agrarian magic are deemed to be propitious places, places where the spirit of Mwatiktiki resides. But Mwatiktiki has a dark side called Naumus, its own malevolent spirit. When men do not respect the magical rules and ritual taboos articulated by Mwatiktiki, Naumus strikes them. He is the keeper of Mwatiktiki's law, his "policeman" as the Tannese say. Some clans of the original men *(men ples)* watch over Mwatiktiki's beneficial places; other clans watch over the places he has cursed. Clans control the magical power emanating from these places. For instance, they can stop famine or, just as easily, cause it. The role is powerful but also quite uncomfortable.[18]

9 Society of the Stones

> Everything that exists, in the strong sense of the word—
> be it a mountain, a water hole, an institution or a custom—
> is acknowledged as real, valuable, and meaningful, because
> it appeared at the origin of the world.
>
> MIRCEA ELIADE,
> *Religions australiennes*

In 1977 and 1978, when political issues and conflicts over land tenure (which I examine later) brought turmoil to the central part of Tanna, local customary groups endeavored to create a political system. To face the leaders of the Vanua'aku Christian nationalist party, Middle Bush "pagans" needed to designate those who had the right to speak in their name. To my surprise, the pagans' strategy was to look for the "aristocracy of the origins." As they searched for Tanna's "original clans," the pagans acknowledged the direct successors to the first men who had appeared on the island, in other words, the *rili men,* the real or true men who had obtained the original powers of *kastom* and spread them throughout Tanna. The pagans went back to the origins of their society and even to the creation of the world, the *stamba.* Doing so, they did not use a genealogical or time-based approach, but a space-based one.

The Canoe's World

After recollecting the primordial sacred places through which humans, then food, had emerged on the island, the pagans designated the genuine keepers of such places as the big men of *kastom.* Real power accrued to them. The *yani niko* 'voices of the canoe' were granted political authority. Because they represent the "first men" who have emerged from the stones, they are naturally in command of the political sphere as masters of Tanna's discourse. Not only are they associated with the first magical places created by Wuhngin, but they guard the great dancing grounds of old, which were also created at that time. One of these "voices" is Kooman, the hero of the White Grass myth (chapter 8). The "voices of the canoe" are also seen as the "surveyors" of territory and the authorities on land sharing, internal boundaries, and external borders.

Land is identified with political power: the men who control land—the "voices of the land"—hold power.

After the *yani niko* come the *naotupunus,* in other words, the local clans associated with the networks of places whose magic powers stem from stones of agrarian fertility. Mythology links such clans with the world of women; the *naotupunus* are said on Tanna to be "females." Life on Tanna rests on their magical activity. On the other hand, their connection with the sacred world of food excludes such clans from the political sphere. They have no "voice," only a type of power that is also a form of duty. Just as the *yani niko* clans represent the "voices of the canoe," the *naotupunus* clans are its "belly." Thus Tanna's first community seems to have evolved with a dual perspective: the forces of nature are split between masculine and feminine principles and, likewise, the original society itself is divided into male clans that rule the political sphere and female clans that rule the sphere of food-related magic. This partitioning of social status is the foundation of *kastom's* "canoe," the initial society on Tanna's soil, a society called *nepro.*[1]

Semo-Semo's Murder

In those times, the gods Wuhngin and Mwatiktiki reigned over Tanna, and the island space was sprinkled with sacred places and trees. In an unpartitioned political space, the only visible signs were the roads delineated by the howling stones and the natural edges of rivers. Only later did the original canoe disintegrate while space splintered into political "territories"; the story of that event is captured in another mythical cycle based on the murder of a malevolent hero. Again, the western side of the island is the birthplace of this oral tradition, which is held by the Ipai dancing grounds. The complete version of the myth appears here, as it was told to me by Nemisa and his son Yameu (from the Ipai dancing place) and by Niluan ("voice of the canoe" from the Lenamwitoka dancing place who, through his lineage, is also linked with Ipai).

Semo-Semo lived on Anatom. He was very tall and ate people. After he had eaten everybody on Anatom, he went to Tanna and the other southern islands whose population he exterminated. He would go back and forth between islands, eating their residents one by one, then return home to Anatom to rest. On Tanna, all had been devoured except for one woman and her child. Semo-Semo eventually got hold of these. He carried them to Yemieltossun, slightly to the north of Lenakel, a shoreline spot where he devoured the woman (see map 7). The child was a little girl who was toothless and nameless; Semo-Semo forgot her in the grass. Left alone, she dug out the root of the *namum mihien* tree, which she suckled like her mother's breast, then she fell asleep. Semo-Semo had gone to Anatom to look for other prey. The child was now the only living being on the island.

The little girl grew. Soon her teeth and hair appeared. She went to the *nia* 'kangaroo grass' that grew nearby and started to eat some of its root. Its slightly sweet taste is not unlike that of sugarcane. As the little girl continued to grow, she walked longer distances; soon, she heard the sound of the sea and went in that direction. At first, she was very frightened, but eventually she touched the water and then washed her face. She bathed in it and saw fish she was not able to catch; but she got hold of two crabs. She noticed two stones near the shore: she hit one that was ocher-colored and smoke came out. This was the *nekam* stone whose magical power is to give fire. The girl blew on the smoke, took some dry grass from the shoreline, turned it into a sheaf, and put it in the smoke. She blew again and the fire got to the grass; she then added some dry wood.

The girl started to live near the seashore, never going away from the fire and preventing it from dying out while hiding the smoke so that Semo-Semo would not see it from Anatom. She now took longer walks. She discovered the gardens of the men whom Semo-Semo had devoured; yams were still growing there. She followed the vines to a hole, unearthed the tubers, then gathered some cabbages that were growing nearby and prepared the first *lap-lap*.[2]

The girl was eating what grew in the abandoned gardens and also fish and crabs from the reef. She became a woman. One day, as she was swimming in the sea, she saw a floating *nolu* vine. She grasped it and played with it. The *nolu* vine penetrated her. Later the woman's belly started to grow: two children were moving within her. She used medicine to purify herself so that the children would develop harmoniously and her belly would not be too large.[3] Later, she gave birth to two boys. When they were bigger, she made bows and arrows for them to hunt birds and pigeons in the forest. She circumcised her two sons *(kawur)*; she built a wild cane fence *(nowankulu)* inside which she kept the children while their wounds were healing, bringing them food in the evening. When the wounds healed up, the boys came out and on that day, their mother made a big yam *lap-lap*.

The mother made a spear and taught the boys how to use it. She gradually taught them all the things a man must know—how to fish, hunt, build houses and cane fences, make canoes, work in a garden, plant yams, and so forth.[4] One evening, the two boys asked their mother:

"The island is big, but we are alone: are there other men and women elsewhere?" Their mother answered:

"I am the only human being here. A giant came to devour those who used to live on the island. The giant's name is Semo-Semo and he lives on Anatom. . . . If I call him, will you have the courage to kill him?"

The boys did not answer. They went back to playing, traveling around on their canoe, and using their bows. The mother had not given them names; they called themselves "Weli," the elder brother, and "Mimia," the younger brother. Still later, the mother asked the same question:

"Will you have the courage to fight and kill Semo-Semo?"

Weli, the elder son, did not answer. Mimia, the younger son, finally said:

"Mother, I shall kill Semo-Semo."

The mother prepared a big *lap-lap,* which she shared with her sons in the evening:

"Tomorrow, I am going to call Semo-Semo; if we die, we will have shared the meal of our death."

The mother prepared spears for the fight, which she planted in the earth at regular intervals from Yemieltossun to Lowanunakiapabao along the shoreline road, *kwoteren.* They climbed the hill above Yemieltossun and started a great fire at night. The mother got her two sons ready for war; she put coconut oil over their faces and hair, tied coconut husk bracelets to their arms, and attached sheaves of vines and white leaves to their ankles. Since then, the hill where she got her sons ready and where the fire was lighted has been called *Wuhngin Rodi Nekam Iken* 'the place where Wuhngin made the fire'. The three of them went to the spot where the first spears had been prepared and waited for Semo-Semo. The mother was wearing a new grass skirt[5] and in each hand she held sprays of reeds, which symbolize death. She was the first to hear the giant's breath as he moved in their direction.

"He is coming. Courage, my sons."

Weli, the elder son, started to shake, but Mimia comforted him:

"Brother, do not be afraid, today we shall kill Semo-Semo."

At Lowanunakiapabao the noise was spreading like a great wind originating from Anatom; the giant was getting closer to them. The sea was rising and becoming heavy.

"He is near. . . . He is coming our way," the mother said. To give courage to her sons, she started to sing. When Semo-Semo heard the song defying him, he shouted:

"Where are you, my nourishment? I am coming to eat you . . ."

The mother gave her sons their manhood names: Kasasow 'the one who shakes' for the elder, and Kaniapnin 'the one who kills danger' for the younger.

"Kasasow, Kaniapnin, *kiyaho* Semo-Semo . . ." the mother was singing, "Kasasow, Kaniapnin, you are going to kill Semo-Semo.

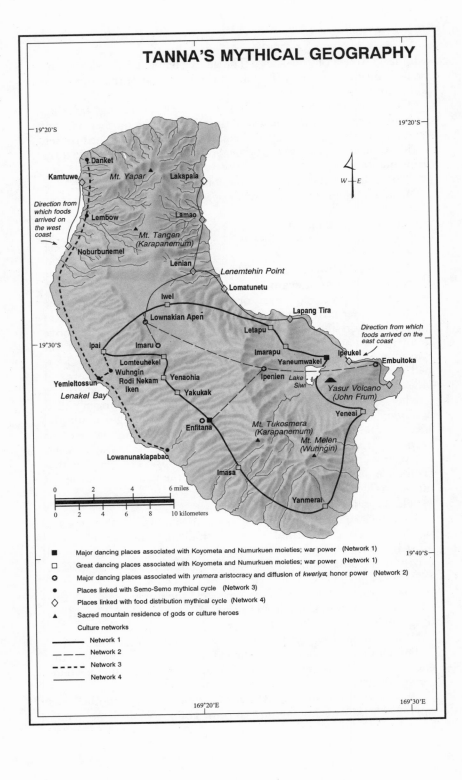

TANNA'S MYTHICAL GEOGRAPHY

19°20'S

19°20'S

Danket
Kamtuwe
Mt. Yapar
Lakapala

Direction from which foods arrived on the west coast

Lembow
Lamao

Mt. Tangen (Karapanemum)

Noburbunemel

Lenian

Lenemtehin Point

Lomatunetu

Iwel

Lapang Tira

Lownakian Apen

Direction from which foods arrived on the east coast

Letapu

Ipai
Imaru

Imarapu

Ipeukel
Embuitoka

Lomteuhekel
Wuhngin
Rodi Nekam
Iken

Yenaohia

Yaneumwakel

Ipenien
Lake Siwi

Yasur Volcano (John Frum)

Yemieltossun
Lenakel Bay

Yakukak

Yeneai

Enfitana

Mt. Tukosmera (Karapanemum)

Mt. Melen (Wuhngin)

Lowanunakiapabao

Imasa

Yanmeral

19°30'S

0   2   4   6 miles
0 2 4 6 8 10 kilometers

19°40'S

■ Major dancing places associated with Koyometa and Numurkuen moieties; war power (Network 1)
□ Great dancing places associated with Koyometa and Numurkuen moieties; war power (Network 1)
◉ Major dancing places associated with *yremera* aristocracy and diffusion of *kweriya*; honor power (Network 2)
● Places linked with Semo-Semo mythical cycle (Network 3)
◇ Places linked with food distribution mythical cycle (Network 4)
▲ Sacred mountain residence of gods or culture heroes

Culture networks
——— Network 1
— — — Network 2
- - - - Network 3
——— Network 4

169°20'E

169°30'E

. . . My children, you who shake and you who kill, you are going to kill Semo-Semo. . . ."

When Semo-Semo was very close, the two boys together threw their first spears at him, then fled along the *kwoteren* road. While chasing them, Semo-Semo was pulling each spear out of his body and eating it. He was shouting:

"You are running, but where to? . . . I am going to catch you and eat you."

The mother, who was running ahead of him, answered:

"What are you eating? You are not eating anything, and reed leaves are slashing your ass!"

She was insulting Semo-Semo, who was becoming angry and whom the spears kept on piercing; but he did not stop running and shouting. The chase went on all along the *kwoteren* road; the boys would run, stop, throw the spears they had prepared, then go on with their wild race. Ahead, the mother would encourage them. She was insulting the giant while waving her reeds: he was beside himself with rage. At the place named Lamwinu, above the Lenakel anchorage, a spear of *nape*, a hardwood, pierced Semo-Semo's belly. He fell to his knees, spat out his liver, but rose again and went back to the chase.[6]

"I am going to catch you and eat you," he shouted once more.

"Eat what?" answered the mother, who again insulted him.

Semo-Semo's rage was now at its peak, but he could not catch the fugitives and was almost out of breath. When Kasasow and Kaniapnin got to the top of the hill *Wuhngin Rodi Nekam Iken,* they reached the spot where they had set their last two spears. One was called *nepina,* the other *niseko.* Kasasow took the spear *nepina* and threw it at Semo-Semo; it struck his left ear and pierced his head. This time Semo-Semo fell to his knees, knocked out. Shaking his head, he tried to rise but failed. Kaniapnin then dispatched him with the spear *niseko,* which he threw into the giant's right ear. Struck down, Semo-Semo collapsed and fell dead on the hilltop.

The mother and her two sons drew near him with some apprehension, fearing that Semo-Semo might trick them or jump back to life. They called the red ant and told it to go over the body to make sure the giant was dead. The ant did so, biting the flesh and going over Semo-Semo's open eye, which did not blink. The black ant, whose bite is more cruel, also went over the corpse: it did not move.

The mother and her sons called all the island pigeons and birds, and these flew near the corpse. The two brothers asked the pigeons to go inside the body to ascertain the death once again, but they were fearful and refused. A small light-green bird was the only one to accept the task: it put its head through Semo-Semo's anus, looked thoroughly inside, and heralded his death. The larger red-colored brother of that bird finally decided to go inside Semo-Semo's body. He started at the anus, went through the entire body, and came out through the mouth.

"Are you sure he is dead?" the two brothers asked.

"Yes, he is dead indeed," the red bird answered.

But the pigeons were not convinced yet:

"You are lying," they said.

The bird went back inside Semo-Semo's body, this time through the mouth first and out through the anus:

"I tell you he is dead."

This time the pigeons believed the bird and all moved nearer. The red, green, and yellow-colored coconut lory, the green pigeon, and the scarlet robin went around the corpse.

"What are we going to do with it?" the two brothers asked.

They suddenly heard the chirping of all the pigeons that the ogre had eaten and that were still inside his body. They sharpened some bamboo and started to carve up the corpse by cutting off the head first, then the tongue, and finally the rest of the body whose pieces they put in a pile before them. Slightly to the side, they put down Semo-Semo's steaming intestines and everything these were holding came out, such as chickens, rats, pigeons, birds of all kinds. These creatures were speaking, singing, and becoming alive again. Kasasow started to allocate the pieces of Semo-Semo's body to the living beings around him.[7] To each he would give a name and designate a place that would be that being's territory, then he would throw a piece of the corpse there. But all these beings were too many. Kaniapnin intervened and advised his elder brother to do it differently:

"This is taking too much time, you will never reach the end."

Kasasow then named the territories two at a time, throwing them a piece of the giant's body to share. The chickens, rats, and birds went to the places that had been allocated to them.

When the division of the corpse was over, Kasasow and Kaniapnin threw the large intestine onto Ipai, at a place they called Semo-Semo. The sharp bamboo they had used to slice the body was thrown a little farther, at Lowkwerya.

The two brothers and their mother went to the northern part of the island. Since then, they have lived at Danket, in a barely accessible cave which the sea floods at high tide. The opening is guarded by a raised stone representing a warrior by the name of Yapum, who watches over Kasasow and Kaniapnin. Inside, two tall stones personify the heroes of the mythical cycle. Their mother is situated higher, in a sacred spot. Upon reaching the end of her path, she told her two sons:

"I am old and I have become ugly. Let me hide myself, I no longer want anybody to see me."

The mother's stone is near the cave ceiling, in a secret and damp spot from which the water falls drop by drop down to the faces of her two sons, just as her milk used to feed them. These drops are the mother's tears. At the foot of the two statues, one notices fish bones, remnants of the meals eaten by Kasasow and Kaniapnin. At night, they go out to fish; their fishing lines appear as streaks of color on the neighboring reef.

A magician by the name of Nowkahut reigns over Danket, which is a secret spot—but all Islanders know about it. The master of the place holds magical war powers. When officiating, he can awaken the powers that are concentrated over Kasasow's and Kaniapnin's stones.

The "Original Murder"

Undoubtedly one of Tanna's most beautiful and meaningful mythological narratives, the giant's story can be seen as a founding myth par excellence. Semo-Semo's murder introduces social organization and territorial division on the island. Earlier mythical cycles represent a series of fragmented geographical episodes that move from stone to stone and place to place and explain such and such local power; they do not attempt to incorporate any global perspective. By contrast, the vision underlying the Semo-Semo myth encompasses the entire island's political space while giving a cogent explanation of its partitioning.

Following Semo-Semo's killing, human beings emerged in their present, final form. Until then, they were undifferentiated magical beings such as stones, birds, and sea residents that could transmute their appearance and move freely through space. When territories were created, all beings were in the same motion bequeathed "flesh," a symbolic identity, and geographical roots. They could no longer change their appearance or propel themselves through space as they pleased. Identity and territory went hand in hand: to be human was to be from somewhere, to have a name, and to belong to a "canoe." The stone men became *men ples,* that is, men who identify with a place. The founding heroes then left the visible world and joined the eternal slumber of places and stones.

All through Semo-Semo's myth, poetry and emotion emerge as the storytellers convincingly relate the impact of each scene. On Tanna's west coast, the mother and her two sons are considered the mother and fathers of the Islanders as well as their ultimate source of support, should an external danger threaten them again. Another striking feature of this particular myth is woman's central role. Civilizing heroes in Melanesia and

Polynesia are generally men. In this case, a woman holds the major role. Such a "feminist" viewpoint is rare in Vanuatu, particularly in the strongly patrilinear societies of the archipelago's central and southern islands.

According to Ipai storytellers, the nameless mother of Kasasow and Kaniapnin is the symbol of womanhood and the essence of motherhood. Through woman, the community of men not only revives but finds its way to civilization anew. It is she who rediscovers fire-making, gardening, fishing, and hunting. After conceiving the challenge to Semo-Semo, she chooses both the tactics and the grounds. The mother starts the fire that is to attract Semo-Semo on a hill called *Wuhngin Rodi Nekam Iken* 'the place where Wuhngin lights the fire': at such time she is not only a woman, she is Wuhngin, Tanna's god. In other words, the mother's powers and deeds are identical with those of the primeval god. Her role is a decisive one throughout the fight. Here, woman appears as the warriors' partner and encouraging figure. In the confrontation that she dares initiate, she gives men the courage to challenge, and the intelligence to outwit, the enemy; her sons' victory is also hers. The warriors apply the strategy told them by woman and do not launch a frontal attack that would be lethal for them. Faced with brute force, they use tricks and extend the scene of the operations. The long-winded chase that follows allows them to multiply the number of blows. Thus, speared on all sides, driven into a frenzy by the mother's insults, and exhausted from the race, Semo-Semo eventually expires.

Kasasow is afraid, as his name indicates. Although he is the elder, his younger brother inspires him with courage and, indeed, directs him. This dialectical rapport between older and younger brothers is present in many Melanesian myths, notably the Tangaro myth in the northern part of the group in which the youngest brother keeps on making up for his oldest brother's stupid, malevolent, or despicable deeds. Here, the relationship is more subtle. Kasasow is the leader, while the one who pushes him to act and wields real power stays in his shadow. In many respects, the power system in Tanna follows that rule. The man who represents power acts on behalf of another who pushes him into the foreground—insofar as true "chiefs" do not show themselves.

The killing that helps human society to emerge is akin to the "foundation murder" analyzed by René Girard (1978). Tanna's social organization is granted a sacred basis by this initial act of violence. Semo-Semo is the victim—a malevolent figure undoubtedly, yet a victim—whose death allows for the building of society as Tanna's "canoes" spring from the corpse. Although the island is divided from a political standpoint, it is made an organic whole by the sacred deed of violence that links it with its creation.

The Birth of the Society of Canoes

Semo-Semo's myth and song conclude with the roll call of the groups born of the giant's shared body. The first names are recited individually, the following names two by two, and each is associated with a "tribal" group designated by a generic name and a place. Each place is both a dance site and the nexus of a territory. Each territory is a "canoe" or *niko*. The single outrigger canoe has turned into many canoes, and space is no longer the open structure of the origins but a world now partitioned into over one hundred independent territories.

As a rule, each tribal group avails itself of one piece of the giant's body or one of the animals or foods that were found in his bowels. Thus the Nalhyaone of the Lamlu dancing place received Semo-Semo's skull, the Lowkhamal Namasmitane from south of Kokawite-Iken got a man's ritual belt covered with the ogre's blood *(mitane)*, hence their name Namasmitane 'the blood on the belt', and so forth. Some groups received pieces that were less noble, for instance, a group was given the contents of Semo-Semo's intestines and is said (by other groups) to owe its inception to the giant's excrement. Others are better endowed: the north side as a whole is identified with Semo-Semo's heart, which the Nomtowasne group received. Associated with the back-bearing muscles, the Kasarumene at White Sands are a pivotal group bearing fundamental values. Giving honor where honor is due, Ipai, as the myth keeper, is identified with Semo-Semo's intestines, a human being's live power and magical root according to tradition. The Ipai group is the only one to bear the Semo-Semo name, which entitles it to tell the entire myth.

By calling the canoe names two by two, Kasasow and Kaniapnin have laid the foundations of an alliance that affects the entire island. Paired from their inception, neighboring groups acknowledge their kinship and proscribe any act of war between them. This type of alliance has no other basis but the myth. The sharing of Semo-Semo's corpse is like the ending to a play: the community of the origins is now divided and set within a specific territorial order while being simultaneously united by propinquity-based relations of alliance. Hence the society of canoes is neither conflict-prone nor divided into friends and foes. Further, this society does not carve up space: it organizes space by naming it. In that perspective, the Semo-Semo myth completes the shaping of the world initiated by Wuhngin.

An Egalitarian Society

The community born of Semo-Semo's killing belongs to the original mythical time of the *nepro* which all Islanders consider their "paradise

THE LAND CANOES

Traditional territories and groups in Tanna

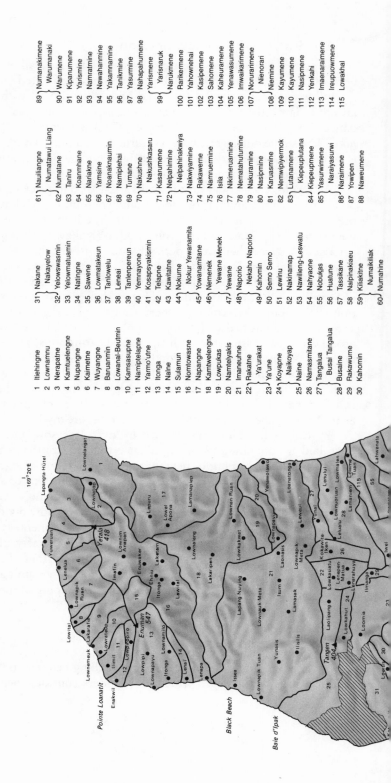

169°20'E

1 Itiehingne
2 Lownammu
3 Nerapatne
4 Kamtuelengne
5 Nupangne
6 Kaimetne
7 Wuyangne
8 Baruanmin
9 Lowanal-Beutmin
10 Kamsasupne
11 Namiptelapne
12 Yarmo'utne
13 Itonga
14 Naine
15 Sulamun
16 Nomtowasne
17 Napangne
18 Kamtwelengne
19 Lowpukas
20 Namtelyakis
21 Imaneuhne
22 Rakatne
  Ya'urakat
23 Ya'une
24 Koyapne
  Naikoyap
25 Naine
26 Namasmitane
27 Tangalua
  Busai Tangalua
28 Busaine
29 Rakawurne
30 Kahomin

31 Nakane
  Nakayelow
32 Yelowswasmin
33 Yelowmatuamin
34 Natingne
35 Sawene
36 Lowmatakeun
37 Tanlowelu
38 Leneai
39 Tanlenpereun
40 Yemnayone
41 Kosapsyakismin
42 Telapne
43 Kawitatne
44 Nokume
  Nokur Yewanamita
45 Yowanamitane
46 Nemenek
  Yewane Menek
47 Yewane
48 Naporio
  Nekaho Naporio
49 Kahomin
50 Semo Semo
51 Lewinu
52 Nakinamap
53 Nawileng-Leswatu
54 Nahyaone
55 Nobukas
56 Huatune
57 Tassikane
58 Nalpinakiaeu
59 Kiliakitne
  Numaikiliak
60 Numahine

61 Nauliangne
  Numatawui Liang
62 Numatane
63 Taniru
64 Koanmhane
65 Nariakne
66 Yamsine
67 Noanaknaumin
68 Namiplehai
69 Tumane
70 Nakushne
  Nakushkasaru
71 Kasarumene
72 Nelpahimine
  Nelpahinakwiya
73 Nakwiyamine
74 Rakawerne
75 Namruermine
76 Isila
77 Nikimeruamine
78 Nematahutumine
79 Nakuramine
80 Nasipmine
81 Karuasmine
82 Nemwipiyermok
83 Lutanamene
  Kiepeuplutana
84 Kiepeupmene
85 Yasurwimene
  Naraiyasurwi
86 Naraimene
87 Yowipen
88 Naweumene

89 Numanakimene
  Warumanaki
90 Warumene
91 Kipanumene
92 Yarismine
93 Namratmine
94 Newahanmine
95 Yakammamine
96 Tanikmine
97 Yasumine
98 Nahapahumene
  Yarismene
99 Yarisnaruk
  Narukmene
100 Rarikermene
101 Yahownehai
102 Kasipemene
103 Sahomene
104 Kaheuramene
105 Yenawasumene
106 Imwalkarimene
107 Noruraimene
  Nienorari
108 Niemine
109 Kayumene
110 Kayumene
111 Nasipmene
112 Yenkahi
113 Imaenaraimene
114 Ireupuowmene
115 Lowakhal

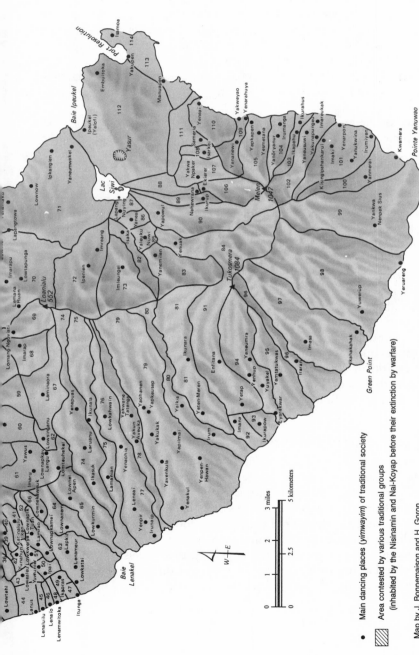

● Main dancing places (*yimwayim*) of traditional society

● Area contested by various traditional groups
(inhabited by the Nisinamin and Nai-Koyap before their extinction by warfare)

Map by J. Bonnemaison and H. Goron

© ORSTOM 1986

Map 9

lost." To the Tannese, the word *nepro* evokes the era of a simple society. Groups of "male" status keep watch over the territory, groups of "female" status feed it. There is no political structure beyond this organizing principle. Each "canoe" is the equal and the ally of its neighbor and this united community is without war. It is said that at the time of the *nepro,* "men have no war weapon, they are only playing like gangs that throw fern sprigs at each other." In short, this simple society is the ideal society of the mythical time of origin. Canoes are equal, *men ples* complement one another: exchange is the only formal linkage between them. Everything that is received must be returned along the same lines. At that time, neither kava nor pig is known and the only sacred food is the sea turtle *(yao).*

Two of the great rites of Tanna's contemporary *kastom* refer to the *nepro* society. The first rite, the *niel,* entails the sharing of food among allies. Excluding any form of profit-making, the *niel* does not designate a winner or a loser. Tanna's first society has no knowledge of debt, that powerful mechanism of social stratification which prevails in the graded societies of the northern part of the group. Here, what has been received is strictly given back, and what is owned is given away with the expectation of receiving it back from one's ally. The *niel* rites often deal with a specific food, for instance, a yam *niel* is exchanged for a taro *niel,* a banana *niel* for a sugarcane or fish *niel.* Today, gifts of pigs are added to the agrarian *niel*s. The aesthetic side prevails. When a group invites its ally to its own dancing grounds, it decorates them completely with the gifts it is about to give. Yams (or another item) make up huge piles at the center of the grounds while all surrounding banyan trees drip with long braids of entangled yams that tumble down from the highest foliage. This ritual concludes with dances that last all night long, as each of the two networks of alliance succeeds the other on the grounds until dawn. The great dances of Tanna originate in the *niel* custom and glorify the magical fertility of Tannese gardens.

The Sharing of the Turtle

The second and supreme rite of Tanna's original society involves the sharing of food from the sea turtle *(yao).* Some shoreline groups own magical stones that allow them to catch turtles in the bays where these occasionally lay their eggs. The groups operate for the benefit of the largest dancing places, which hold the right to cook the animal. Once captured, the turtle is the object of ritual exchange and sharing that enhances the bonding of local groups while reflecting their levels of precedence. The group that has caught a turtle forwards it through the set paths of alliance toward the dancing place that has ordered it. The animal is transferred from one group to the next and paid for at each stop with an equivalent gift (represented today by a hairless pig),[8] all the way to the group that owns the right to cook it. In some cases, for example, when the turtle is captured without having been paid for in advance by another group, the live animal is left free to choose its fate. By itself, it may move in the direction of the road where it is to be sacrificed.

After being cooked, the skull, which holds the turtle's magical power and intelligence, is given to the oldest man of the *yani niko* clan who eats it in secret, thereby absorbing the sacred animal's decision power and wisdom. The turtle's body is then divided into five parts. Each leg and shoulder is given to one allied group according to the direction of the four great roads that originate at the dancing grounds. As to the central part of the back, repository of the vital force, it is cooked in a hot stone oven and eaten by the cooking group. This sacred meal, called *numanim* 'the turtle's blood', only involves "brothers" who live on the same territory.

The sharing of the turtle is a symbolic form of alliance, and the roads followed by its various body parts represent the directions of such alliance. Through this ritual meal, the *nepro* community began to delineate a societal organization. Political hierarchy appeared to the benefit of both the great founding places where turtles were cooked and the *yani niko* that had the right to share them.

The turtle ritual is not based on any acknowledged myth. In eastern Tanna, oral tradition holds that Mwatiktiki's canoe brought turtles along with the first foodstuffs. On the western side of the island, the turtle is associated with Wuhngin; when eating it, one absorbs Wuhngin, one communicates with the original sacred force.

During the sharing, the "voice of the canoe" clans do affirm their precedence over the clans of agrarian magicians. The latter cook the turtle for the former, who then distribute it to political allies. Yet this organization is not one of true chieftains because power in the *nepro* society only refers to founding areas, in other words, to *stamba* places, of which there are many.

When one conjures up Tanna's original community, one confirms to some extent the first impression of Cook and his companions who described Tanna as a "leaderless society." The men from the canoe territories are free and practically equal. Insofar as each individual can refer to a place of origin, he has a name, a portion of power, and therefore a dignity that makes him the equal of his allies. Concurrently, relations of antecedence make reference to all the various places and stones where power originated, yet they do not involve political power as such. The individual who is at the "stump" of a specific power is only the founder of a relationship, which then evolves freely through space. Each part of the network is needed to maintain the relationship, and each is also independent.

By spreading their powers over a number of places, the men of the *nepro* society have willingly destroyed the possibility of central power, whatever form it may take. These men have woven space into an organic wholeness, where each part is both autonomous and interdependent with the others. The *niel* and turtle linkages entail neither allegiance nor domination in any form, provided all units uphold the three components of the system: rules of antecedence, egalitarian exchanges, and processes of alliance.

Ipai's Power

The Ipai dancing place, keeper of Semo-Semo's myth, was dug and leveled by hand. Ipai means "to plunge." The site plunges steeply down into the earth, which is the source of all powers and magic. Not only was Ipai's prominent position established in the myth, but the big men of this dancing place avail themselves of a final power.

According to the Ipai tradition, Semo-Semo could not be a mere *yarimus* 'spirit', contrary to what most Islanders believe today. For the people of Ipai, the magical ogre was, in fact, a turtle. The sacrifice of the turtle replicates Semo-Semo's foundation murder: those who eat the turtle eat simultaneously Semo-Semo and Wuhngin, the initial force of the world. Ipai shifted the act of violence on which Tanna's first community was based to the rite of turtle killing and sharing, which represented a way of eating the island's founding hero and partaking in his magical power. As the pig had not reached Tanna's shores at the time of the *nepro,* the turtle, considered eternal because of its longevity, was the only animal that could embody Wuhngin's sacred spirit.

When Kasasow and Kaniapnin were dividing up Semo-Semo's corpse, they made two piles, one for the body parts, the other for the steaming intestines. After their task was done and everybody had left, there remained only intestines. In the giant's body, the men from Ipai then discovered the symbols of a new power: the *kweriya,* or hawk, and the ritual belt, or *tut* (chapter 10).

The *kweriya* is the denizen of the sky and the sacred animal of Tanna's second society. The ritual belt symbolizes political power. When common men walk behind the one who is wearing the belt, they are literally pulled by the force emanating from it.

The people of Ipai who found the two symbols in Semo-Semo's intestines hold the last secret of the power of *kastom*. A new aristocracy—the *yremera*—rose from Semo-Semo's murder, and a new society—more sophisticated and perhaps more warlike—emerged.

Thanks to this discovery, Ipai and the west coast tradition play major roles within *kastom*. When the egalitarian society of the *nepro* ended, the *kweriya,* or hawk, society began. The two traditions united or, more precisely, one gave birth to the other. No longer did the island's western shore need to use the traditions of the eastern shore to complete its cultural genesis (see chapter 10). Thus, Ipai is the foundation of the island, being the root of its first society and the cradle of its second society.

10 Society of the Hawk

> [To the traditional man,] space . . . is like a clearing
> which communal myths have reclaimed and orga-
> nized in the midst of an immense, unknown, and
> hostile world.
>
> GEORGES GUSDORF,
> *Mythe et métaphysique*

On the island, nothing is ever removed from memory: as each cultural system is layered over the previous ones, spatial networks emerge and new places contribute to the density of the island's cultural and magical space. According to the myth of the creation of territories, the first society of *kastom* relied on a network of strong nodes and kept a balance between the cultural traditions of the island's western side and those of the eastern side. Equality-based exchanges prevailed among deeply rooted, allied territories, allowing for a relative social peacefulness.

The equilibrium of this "simple" society was shattered when several "heroes" appeared in the course of Tanna's mythical time. As they contributed new rites and new powers, these heroes gave another shape to the original social matrix. Kasasow and Kaniapnin, the heroes of the Semo-Semo myth, were Tanna's first forefathers. Later, the eastern and southern parts of the island were particularly rich in comparably strong individuals such as Karapanemum, Kalpapen, Kasiken, Tangalua, Kaluas, Masaka, and the like. These powerful and occasionally frightening cultural heroes are still living today in the familiar neighborhood of villages and dancing grounds. They have the gift of spatial ubiquity: they can extend their multiple powers, ad infinitum, into a variety of places. Tanna's most prestigious lineages keep watch over the places where linger the fragments of power contributed by heroes. In the process, the lineages have acquired the magic substance of such places.

Men of the Hawk

The hero-based tradition set up new networks of power and alliance; networks of enmity also appeared. When the society of equals, the *nepro,* broke down, the island started to change. The history of men

146

began, steeped in rivalry and constant competition, where honor was at stake.

At this stage, the founding myths of the island's east coast differ from those of the western side. As far as the people of the White Sands region are concerned, their history began at the foot of the Yasur volcano, where a new hero by the name of Kasiken appeared. A man from Ipeukel on Sulphur Bay, Kasiken was the son of Mwatiktiki, the hero of foods. He reinstated the custom of *niel* exchange, turning it into the more sophisticated *nekowiar* ritual which is also known throughout the island under the name of its main dance, *toka*. At the foot of the Yenkahi volcano, while listening to the sound of the wind in the sacred trees of the Yentare headland, Kasiken was moved to create the *toka* dance. He went to his canoe's dancing place at Embuitoka in Ipeukel, danced the *toka*, and gave three gigantic *niel* or heaps of presents to his hosts. There, for the first time, he showed the great crest crowned with hawk feathers, the symbol of his new power, or *kweriya* (in the Tannese language *kweriya* means "hawk").

The "voices" of the neighboring Kasarumene (Yaneumwakel) canoe were jealous. They killed the Ipeukel hero. Buried in various spots on the island, the corpse kept on speaking; eventually it was transported to Itipa, in the heart of Middle Bush, where it still is. But Kasiken's message did not vanish. His brother Kalpapen went on teaching it to the other canoes on Tanna. Those who had the right to carry the sacred crest made up an invisible aristocracy spreading from dancing place to dancing place by means of the great *toka* festivals. They became the *yremera* 'lords', a kind of honor-based nobility that took precedence over the "voices of the canoe."

The giant *kweriya* crest consists of a two- to three-meter high bamboo trunk covered with white hen feathers which are sprinkled with and crowned by black hawk feathers. The regal bird's domain is the sky, whose glory is symbolized by the crest. Thus the men—the *yremera*—who, starting from Kasiken, have received the right to hold the hawk symbol represent a new aristocracy whose kingdom is the sky. Their power is higher than that rooted in the land of the traditional "voices" of the *niko;* the ritual cycle of the *nekowiar* celebrates their glory.

The new ritual could only be created by a man from Ipeukel, belonging to Mwatiktiki's lineage. Kasiken used the ritual exchange, or *niel,* created by his father Mwatiktiki to set up a new ritual cycle that magnifies food exchanges to the ultimate degree. The showing of the *kweriya* is the climax of this ritual. Stating they are Kasiken's sons and Mwatiktiki's grandsons, the men of the Ipeukel canoe are the creators of the *nekowiar,* whose purpose is to honor the *kweriya.* Today, the whole island acknowledges such prerogative.

By means of the *nekowiar* ritual, the diffusion of the hawk symbols followed the paths of alliance. From these sprang new lineages of aristocracy within *kastom*. The initial *toka* dances were performed on several dancing grounds (such as Embuitoka, Ipenien, and Enfitana) that now hold the largest *kweriya* and represent the founding places of the new network. The diffusion process is still operating today (see map 8).

Toka Dances and Nekowiar Ritual

The *nekowiar* ritual follows straigthforward rules. One group invites another to dance the *toka* on its territory; it itself dances the *nao* in honor of its guests. Each of the two partner groups makes up a dance company with all of its allies.

Chants and dances must be entirely re-created for each *toka* since the visitors expect the unexpected. Magicians and poets from the White Sands area, for example, go to the Yentare headland where Kasiken had found his inspiration for the initial *toka* dance. There, at the foot of the magical tree *nesesa,* they slowly chew the branches and gaze at the sea. In the evening, when the kava starts to have an effect and the mind drifts, Kasiken prompts the words and the rhythms of a new chant. This practice exists everywhere in Tanna. Each great canoe has access to its own magical trees, where the inspiration strikes for the chants and dances of *kastom.*[1]

The festival lasts twenty-four hours. It begins in the evening with *napen-napen* dances performed by the women from the *nao* group, that is, the host group. Their faces painted and their hair decorated with hawk feathers, the dancers wear colored grass skirts covered with odoriferous leaves *(nesei);* they perform as a group. As they sing, they strike leaf-woven baskets holding the magical stones that make them fertile (women's "medicines"). Around them, other dancers form a circle. This nebula-like circle is called *kawua;* all those, men and women, who attend the festival participate in it freely. The night belongs to the *napen-napen* dancers and to the *kawua* circle which unceasingly swirls around them. Meanwhile, the dancers who are to perform the *toka* stay among themselves, hidden in the bush a little farther away.

The *napen-napen* and *kawua* dances begin slowly at nightfall then become increasingly frenetic as sunrise nears. Shortly before dawn, the swirling *kawua* groups hurl themselves toward the center of the dancing place, then move back. This rhythmic pattern stops abruptly when the darkness of the night starts to lift: all is quiet again and the dancers leave the scene.

In *kastom*'s days, this night festival had a sexual connotation to some extent. The guests of the *kawua* were dancing, men and women together

—a rare event as far as traditional dances are concerned. With the help of darkness and closeness, sexual advances were allowed, provided the lovemaking was discreet and short-lived. Daylight would put an end to all this and what took place during the night was cleaned up—or "paid for" as the Tannese say—by the blood of the pigs that were sacrificed the next day.[2]

The men dancers of the invited *toka* group arrive solemnly at dawn, preceded by the *kweriya,* the symbol of their honor. Several men from the clan of the *yremera* aristocracy carry the ceremonial crest. In their midst walks the *yremera* who holds the title but whom nothing sets apart from the others. All perform the *toka* dance which they have rehearsed out of the public eye for months while fasting and avoiding any contact with women.

As an evocation of the *niel* exchange custom, the *toka* dance is always based on agrarian themes praising the fertility of Tannese gardens and the cult of giant yams. Moving in a circle, men stamp the ground with their feet and clap their hands. The dancers who make a circle symbolize the yam mound, whereas those who move away from the circle represent the growth of vines. The *toka* dance is always performed with a branch whose end, painted white, represents a beak: as they move this hook, the men pretend to attract presents to themselves and simulate the joy they will feel when receiving the gifts that are to be offered to them later on. There is no musical instrument here, not even a drum; the chanting, the sound of footsteps, and the hand clapping give the beat. When the *toka* is over, the host group participates in turn by showing its own *kweriya,* then performing the *nao* dance. As the performers dance, they hit the ground with large tied sheaves of cane symbolizing the many piles of presents to be given away to the *toka* group. Later, in honor of its guests, the *nao* group performs other dances on various themes.

At the end of the afternoon, the host group "pays" those who have come to dance the *toka.* In the course of a giant gift-giving of pigs, each animal is carried forth in turn, some on a wooden stretcher held by several men. While chants and dances are being performed, dozens of large hogs are offered, including the *kapia* pigs with little or no hair, which are the most valued. Fifty to sixty pigs are killed, then aligned in parallel at the center of the dancing place. To this *niel* are added gifts of kava and ceremonial yams. The *toka* group parades among the offerings, and takes possession of them: each dancer chooses the animal that he will take back with him. Some time after the ceremony, the *toka* group will give away a number of animals equal to the number received. This sober ceremony, called *menuk,* is held out of the public eye. It completes the *nekowiar* cycle and settles all accounts.

Today, the *nekowiar* tends to be an exchange-based form of competition. The *toka* group frequently offsets the pigs it has received with a bonus in quantitative and qualitative terms, in other words, not only more pigs but pigs of higher value. As the new debtor, the *nao* group must compensate the surplus at the next ritual; it generally raises the stake as well. The competition lasts long after the completion of the *toka,* kindling an exchange loop that never comes to an end.

Three Images of Power

Tanna's dual society has a dialectical nature: each phase of its cultural development stands in contrast to the previous one. The first society, the *nepro,* implied the sharing of food and an exchange ideology based on equality; it involved neighboring or fairly close groups on a small geographical scale. The larger scale of the second society meant much bigger chains of alliance which, covering the entire space of the island, facilitated the diffusion of the *nekowiar* ritual and led to a new aristocratic society associated with the *kweriya* symbol.

A tug of war between antagonistic forces and ideologies is at the heart of Tanna's society, steering it into constant renewal. The juxtaposition of opposing forces and traditions is such that power is never held by a single individual, but by a network of individuals dispersed over the various places and clans of the territory. Men inherit an identity and a memory that position them within a larger world and on this or that side of the mythical tradition. As a result, society stands at the edge of chaos, each of its fragments being both autonomous and inseparable from the remainder of the network. The island stays united from a cultural standpoint through the dialectical process and the complementarity of each of its traditions, but it is divided politically by their perennial rivalry. Tanna probably wanted it that way; no central power could ever take hold on the island.

According to the island's oral traditions, Tannese society includes three explicitly defined social functions. These functions correspond to three groups of different status involved in separate types of activity; they can also be seen as three images of power. Keeping at the front of the canoe, the *yremera* is the canoe's "honor" and living emblem. As such, his power—symbolized by the hawk—is linked with great ceremonial exchanges, the sharing of food, and the control of the traditional roads of alliance that allow for these activities. The *yani niko* or "voice of the canoe" represents political will: keeping at the back of the canoe, he steers it in war times. He has authority over the territory, because he is heir to the "first man" who appeared on it. Indeed, the *yani niko* keeps land for the others and is in charge of land sharing. His role is to highlight the *yremera's* glory and to speak on his behalf. Finally, the *naotupunus* works with agrarian magic: he holds the sacred powers immersed in the canoe's places and is the sanctioned mediator of supernatural forces. As the canoe's belly, he keeps in the middle.

First comes the honor, second the political will, third the magic. In metaphorical terms, the *yremera* is the canoe's emblem, the *yani niko* its helmsman, and the *naotopunus* its belly. While the tradition of the "voices of the canoe" *(yani niko)* originated on the western side of the island, notably in the Ipai area which gave birth to the Semo-Semo myth, the hawk tradition, that of the *yremera,* gave rise to a second society on the eastern side, in the Ipeukel (Embuitoka) area.[3] The hawk tradition may be linked with the phenomenon of the Polynesian outliers and therefore with a cultural influence from Samoa or Tonga. This influence is particularly obvious in the White Sands area, notably with respect to the local language (D. Tryon, pers comm). With its equality-based ideology and its "voices of the canoe" as masters of the land, the myth of the *nepro* corresponds to a very ancient Melanesian tradition. More recent are the symbols of the *kweriya* (hawk) and the tapa belt *(tut)* which, along with their honor-based ideology, may have appeared in the twelfth and thirteenth centuries AD, or perhaps later, two or three hundred years ago. Mwatiktiki, Kasiken's father, is the first Polynesian hero. With him, the tradition of cultural heroes began to flourish on the island.

These two traditions also differ from the standpoint of the transfer of titles. Within the original lineage of each canoe, clan elders choose the *yani niko* on the basis of their human and intellectual qualities—their actual title is irrelevant. By contrast, an *yremera* receives his title as a child: he is neither "elected" nor chosen but receives his power through the height of his title. On the one hand, a society geared toward equality selects its "chiefs" among the most ancient lineage. On the other, a society leaning toward aristocracy and symbolized by the selective carrying of the hawk feather inherits its leaders. These two types of power blend and co-exist within each canoe in apparent harmony. Thus, Tannese society seems to be a syncretic combination of "Melanesian" and "Polynesian" elements. The man at the helm directs the canoe, yet the canoe reveals itself through its emblem and feeds itself thanks to its magicians. Far from creating different societies, the various cultural contributions that emerged on the island or reached its shores helped to enrich the amazing metaphor of the canoe. This metaphor in constant renewal allows for cultural unity on the island and ensures its continuity in the midst of change.

The Split Powers

There is no economic function involving producers as such, since all Islanders—except perhaps the highest *yremera* of the past—produce enough by themselves to live on, in practically identical amounts. The mode of domestic production that prevails on the island does not allow for specialization: the various households live the same lives and get identical "revenues" in terms of material goods. Traditional society is geared toward equality from an economic standpoint, but it also involves a definite hierarchy from a cultural and political standpoint. Apparently, political power has no real connection with the sphere of daily economic activities.

Yet power, the overriding concern of the Tannese, is there for the taking. Each mythical cycle tends to erect a new source of power which is immediately contested by the coalition of existing forces. For instance, if the people of a dancing place rise above others, their political ascent causes another dancing place to emerge elsewhere, bolstered by all concerned until a balance of power is reached. In this way Tanna's aristocratic society keeps falling back onto a de facto egalitarianism: because they are many, powers offset one another, and permanent competition eventually destroys big men.

Tannese ideology does not validate the concept of castes or social classes insofar as the economic substrate remains undifferentiated. Indeed, nearly all Islanders share in one type of power to a smaller or greater extent. The space of the whole island is sacred, and the *man ples* who is rooted in his land and lives there in all legitimacy is also sacred. Each great Tannese canoe has its "voices," emblems, "bellies"; each canoe is sovereign with respect to its rituals, its land, and its magic, and each is equal to the others. All men of the canoe take a more or less direct part in one of the three power functions.

To sum up, Tanna's society, originally a simple, interdependent entity, grew increasingly complex. In a first phase, canoes sprang from the shared body of the same victim: society was but the reunited sum of its territories and each canoe stood equal to the others. Subsequently, distinct power nodes came into being and stirred the dynamics of history. The split of the island into moieties gave rise to a society where, once again, political divisions were apparent.

The Two Moieties

Oral traditions of the east coast tell of the arrival of a canoe at Yaneumwakel, a canoe steered by Karapanemum. This new hero was bringing four "stones" that moved ashore in staggered order. The first and second stones, Buga and Netuk, represented the pig and evil magic respectively; the others were two men named Koyometa and Numurkuen. To welcome the latter, the men of Yaneumwakel divided themselves in two equal moieties—some chose the stone Numurkuen, others the stone Koyometa. This partitioning process propagated itself in all the great dancing places on the island; each place became split into two sides facing one another. From that day onward, Tanna abided by the "law of the two canoes." The myths also suggest that the appearance of the pig and the new techniques of evil magic occurred at the same time.

According to the ideology that prevails in eastern Tanna, the two moieties—Koyometa and Numurkuen—are phratries that correspond to two brothers born of the Tangalua lineage (the sea snake) whose founding places are at Yaneumwakel on the east coast, and whose consonance, related myths, and symbols are Polynesian. This is further indication that the moiety system is a late addition, which occurred soon after the *kweriya* and the *yremera* chieftainships were introduced. More specifically, everything in this second tradition comes from the eastern part of Tanna: the *kweriya* was born in Embuitoka (Ipeukel), the two moieties in Yaneumwakel. The two competing tribal groups (Kasarumene and Yenkahi) of the White Sands area—they are still quarreling today—share the major sites associated with this legacy. Embuitoka (Yenkahi) finds its roots in the magicians' tradition: from a political standpoint, the *yremera* represent the revenge of the *naotupunus*. On the other hand, Yaneumwakel (Kasarumene) may be seen as the place where the *yani niko* reacted; they created the two rival moieties to hold power once again through warfare and to offset the power of the *yremera*.

The current view is that Numurkuen is the elder and therefore the more powerful of the two brothers. He owns the stones of magic; he speaks little because he has secrets to keep, but his words carry much weight. Koyometa, the younger brother, is aggressive—like all those who come late in a world already held and managed by others. He is impulsive because he has no secrets and no power; he speaks loudly and often without rhyme or reason, without really thinking. His elder brother has one word, but he has several and he tends not to keep any of his promises. In brief, he is not as serious and hardworking, and he represents a rough force next to the elder's serene strength. He is often thought to instigate war. The Koyometa race is one of warriors, while the Numurkuen race is one of powerful magicians.

On the Europeans' arrival, island terminology was enriched by the metaphor of the *manshipi* 'merchant ship', which became associated with the Numurkuen. The peaceful merchant ship had several holds out of which came various goods as well as men with multiple positions and powers. As for the Koyometa, they were connected with the world of the *manwawa,* from the English *man-of-war;* its hold was devoid of goods and it knew only one function, warfare. This terminology, now abandoned, was used in the White Sands region.

Known in that area as the *Shipimanwawa,* the last great war pitted the merchant ship against the man-of-war. The merchant ship won.

Order through Warfare

A "good peace" is one that comes only through the completion of a "good" war—at least the Yaneumwakel tradition says so. In this respect the "law of the two canoes" ended the confusion of previous times. Accordingly, ritual warfare always involved the same opponents and came to an end on a stipulated signal. Standing together in peace as they did in war, members of the same moiety[4] belonged to the same road, that is, to a canoe that extended beyond the boundaries of Semo-Semo's territories. As a consequence, the horizon of both alliance and warfare processes became considerably wider.

The Yaneumwakel tradition affirms that it has set society in order. Channeling violence into a ritual procedure, the "voices of the canoe" have "civilized" society. In other words, Tanna's "second society" has attempted to control warfare by making it look like a prestige-based competition in the *nekowiar* style. War was, and is, no longer the chaotic confrontation of local groups, but that of two roads of alliance. These meet on the initiative of big men, at a designated time and place.

At first, the law of the two canoes was associated with exogamy of the moieties to some extent. For safety purposes, marriages were set up along one's own road of alliance, within one's moiety-related canoe. Exchanges of women from one moiety to the other validated the return of peace in the context of alliance rituals occurring after a war cycle. As a consequence, a third group carrying the "blood" of both moieties gradually appeared. That phratry is called Nuolaklak in Middle Bush and Kouatkasua in White Sands. The Nuolaklak's role is to serve as a liaison between the "two canoes." They carry the message of one to the other and facilitate the arrival of peace. In practice, they are often accused of playing the opposite role by stirring up hatred, spreading falsehoods, and spying.

Each land canoe integrates the principles of this dual society. One or the other phratry predominates within each such canoe; in principle, the minority moiety is welcome but stands aside in relation to the controlling moiety. The exceptions to this rule are twelve strong nodes on the political network where the two roads intersect. There, Numurkuen and Koyometa live together as equals (see map 8).

Theoretically, the two moieties co-exist but do not merge. The places of one and the other are separate, and each interacts more frequently with the corresponding groups in the neighboring territory than with the adverse groups within its own territory. During the tense or conflict-ridden times of the past, the two parts of the canoe used to clash. At other times, one side tended to believe that the other was the source of all problems.

Nineteenth-century wars between phratries led to the partitioning of the original territories and, in most cases, to the eviction of the minority. Yet the "law of the two canoes" had not called upon the phratries to separate. On the contrary, they were meant to live together on both sides of the same dancing places. The two networks had not been created to shed blood but to surpass themselves and do "great things" through permanent competition, including, but not limited to, ritualized warfare.

The Winners' Order

The current ideology of the two canoes disparages the Koyometa who are seen as troublemakers and warmongers. Furthermore, they are associated with the image of the man-of-war, which coastal residents used to fear, especially in the White Sands area where the ship *Curaçoa* had shelled shoreline groups (see chapter 4). But here as elsewhere the prevalent ideology is that of the victors. It is mostly the Numurkuen who refer to these past events and identify their adversaries as *manwawa*. As for the Koyometa, they hardly speak of that era, as if somehow their defeat had led to a moral setback and, by extension, to a feeling of inferiority in political terms.

In fact, the *Shipimanwawa* never came to an end—its aftermath is still perceptible today. Previous wars used to take place within the context of *kastom*. By contrast, in the course of the *Shipimanwawa*, *kastom*'s leaders witnessed the birth of chronic warfare, a process which they could not control. White beachcombers and peddlers aggravated this process by marketing weapons and ammunition; they also located fugitives and sold them to labor recruiters.

The only known version of this formidable war is that given by the Numurkuen. The following account originates from Lemana-Ruan, at the foot of the Loanialu mountain, on Tanna's east coast:

> The two sons of Tangalua (the sea snake) lived together at Yaneumwakel. In those days, the two moieties intermarried and lived on good terms.
>
> Yet the elder was tired of his younger brother's jealousy. He decided to demonstrate his superiority once and for all. In order to determine who would win a fight, he used premonitory magic: he took the shark stone—a dangerous stone that calls for war—and put it in a basket with the stones Numurkuen and Koyometa; then he wrapped the basket and its contents in leaves of the type used for *lap-lap* cooking. The magic pointed to the victory of the Numurkuen, so the elder brother challenged his sibling.
>
> To wage this "war by consent,"[5] a meeting was set up on the Siwi ash plain, at the foot of the volcano. Several hundreds of warriors

took part in the fight. In accordance with the divination magic, the Koyometa warriors were seriously defeated, and an order was given to pursue them. A number of Koyometa took refuge in the Ipai area; many spread out among predominantly Koyometa groups on the west coast or in Middle Bush. Other Koyometa belonged primarily to the groups living at the southern edge of White Sands: these fled to Green Point, in the south of Tanna. Stalked by their enemies, they were smoked in inside the Yankeva Nenai caves, where they perished. Eventually, the war was stopped by the Numurkuen *yani niko* of the territory where the final battles had been taking place; the last Koyometa fugitives owe him their lives.

Within the losers' territories, such as Ipai, both the power associated with the *kweriya* and the political leadership of the *yani niko* moved into Numurkuen hands. More seriously still, the fugitives' territories and places went to the Numurkuen moiety. The names, identity, and status of the losers who were dead or who had fled were granted to certain subgroups within the winning clans. These subgroups occupied the losers' land, creating a new and irreversible situation. As a result, the island in turmoil was divided to the very core of its territories. There was no longer any apparent way out except through the victors' order. A new society seemed the likely outcome, facilitated by the arrival of Presbyterian missionaries in the nineteenth century. Welcomed by the winners, who joined their cause, the missionaries unknowingly justified the victors' territorial takeover. The pagans' resistance became rooted primarily in the Koyometa bastions of Middle Bush and the west coast, in other words, among the losers of the war of the canoes, who did not accept the new territorial and political order (see Part Three).

Tanna's hawk society attempted to implement a strong type of power by inventing honor and also by dividing the island into two moieties, yet the attempt was unsuccessful. Ultimately, it appears that power in the unruly island can never be whole. When the *kastom* men investigated their history at the end of the 1970s, they focused on the first society, or *nepro,* which today is still regarded as a "paradise lost." They wished to revive the society of their stone ancestors. To these men, the social and ritual elements of the second society appeared debatable, even dangerous, with the conspicuous exception of the *nekowiar* cycle. In their eyes, the society of honor and moieties had been activated within the course of human history and not by Tanna's ancestors. For that reason it was no longer part of the saga of the origins.

11 At War

"Long stil faet, i no gat sori."
"When a war is stolen, it is without mercy."

A man from Tanna

In their myths, the Tannese make the distinction between the *nepro*'s age of peace and a subsequent age of war. It would be a misinterpretation to see Tannese society as a fixed "structure" reproducing itself identically through the generations; on the contrary, that society appears to have a political history. Not only are island groups aware of this continuous unfolding, but their search for a solution to the historical disunity issue is at the core of the contemporary political debate.

Why the Fighting?

In itself, the partitioning of men on different territories does not entail war since that partitioning follows natural boundaries. More specifically, the territories created by Wuhngin make up a "nature" which cannot be the cause or purpose of fighting.

In the image of their ancestors of the howling horde, however, groups turn into pugnacious, easily offended gangs locked into a continuing competition. In peaceful times, exchange rituals represent the arena where this rivalry is acted out. As seen in chapter 9, a *niel* is a gift that implies reciprocity either through an equivalent gift or through the provision of a similar service. Although it is based on equality and generosity and is meant to ensure peace, the *niel* exchange may lead to opposite results in practice. Gift giving for the purpose of domination is perceived as such by the one who cannot reciprocate to the same degree and who subsides into feelings of inferiority and wounded pride. Conversely, the one who gives too much becomes frustrated. If gift giving is not duplicated through reciprocity, it creates debt and therefore destroys the initial equality. Because of this potential risk, today's exchange rituals are still characterized by the detailed accounting and strict equivalence of gifts and return gifts. Breaching this rule in the smallest way may go against

157

the original purpose, thereby turning a pact of alliance into an offense while depriving one party of its goods and the other of its honor.

According to oral tradition, the first of Tanna's great wars to involve major groups took place at White Sands, in the area of the volcano. The Yaneumwakel canoe had invited the Ipenien canoe for the purpose of proceeding to a ritual exchange of green pigeons *(nowamenek)*. One of the two parties gave less in return than the other. This was perceived as an insult, and a meeting was called in the ash plain near Lake Siwi—to fight. The Ipenien war leader, Masaka, had won the *nowamenek;* a big man and a hero, he was famous for his hunting skills. He led the battle against Yaneumwakel troops, but he and his group, smaller in number, were defeated. The bodies of the Ipenien warriors and their allies were thrown into Lake Siwi. Masaka, unharmed, fled by the northern road. He crossed Middle Bush, left Tanna, and ended his long escape at Mataso, in the Shepherd Islands, where he released Mwatiktiki's pigeons, which had been unknown there.[1]

Another traditional narrative accounts for the beginning of warfare in Middle Bush. Two groups were confronting one another, pretending to be at war. When small stones carried by the tide reached the shore, some men used them as projectiles. One group leader was wearing a wild taro leaf on his arm as a sign of his status. After he was killed, his body was thrown into Lake Siwi but would not sink despite the heavy stone tied to the leg. Eventually, the victim was buried at Enfitana, in the southern part of the island. Thereupon the war immediately rekindled, pitting all canoes of Tanna against each other.

While the oldest myth in the oral tradition explains the origin of warfare, another explicitly mentions the partitioning of the island into two political moieties: the Koyometa and the Numurkuen. Thereafter, the nature of warfare evolved in the eastern part of the island (see chapter 10).

Fighting in the *nepro*'s early wars was fair in its own way: *"tufala i faet blong agree,"* which in Bislama means "both sides agreed to fight." Yet there could also be confrontations without any rules. That other type of warfare is called *stil faet* in Bislama—the "stolen war," the war that one is not allowed to wage. It is likely that Tanna's history unfolded in dramatic fashion at the Gordian knot of the transition from *faet blong agree* 'war by consent', or war of honor, to "stolen war," or war without laws.

For the Glory of Heroes

Tanna's society allows for constant rivalry between "equals." Within this context, fighting by common accord is not an aberration which destroys society. On the contrary, it is seen as a ritual. Neither is a war of honor the antithesis of exchange ceremonies; it actually extends that particular type of connection through other means.

In the past, big men used to compete with one another nearly constantly, with the lack of central political authority and the de facto equality and autonomy of each canoe within the social nexus facilitating their rivalry. Ultimately, big men's reputations rested on the recurrence of both war rituals and exchanges of ceremonial goods. Extreme quickness to take offense seems to have been the hallmark of their social lives. To restrict its effects, all meetings of distinct groups were carefully formalized through rituals. The smallest transgression of precedence rules was perceived as an insult that could only escalate into warfare.

Traditional wars were rarely associated with economic greed or purely material needs. In the context of Tannese *kastom,* goods that are produced beyond subsistence standards are assigned to be "given away" during cycles of domestic and political ritual exchanges. Therefore, why fight to grab from others that which will be offered in any case? The very concept of stealing has little meaning within traditional society. Goods are not hoarded; rather, they circulate constantly. One is rich from one's gift giving and from the quality of the resulting social relationships. Accumulating goods is useless in this respect. Likewise, the opposing party's territory can be conquered and plundered but it can never be usurped. In other words, one will feud with an opponent but one will not take his land. As a rule, land grabbing is a boundary the *kastom* men do not have the right to cross since land belongs to the canoes, within the limits defined by Wuhngin. No one may modify this territorial order which goes back to the Semo-Semo myth and sets the Islanders in their places.

To use a specifically Tannese metaphor, big men are "stones" first; but they are also "trees" that grow tall. While trees fight to dominate and conquer the realm of the sky and its glory, they do not thrive by intruding on the territory of others. Each tree must remain faithful to its roots; it can expand into greatness only on its own land. In the past, warriors who had invaded the territory of their opponents would withdraw. Warfare had designated a winner and the honor of one hero had been enhanced, which seemed enough.

Peace always meant a return to the pre-existing territorial status. Keeping the land of enemies was useless since, in traditional terms, land was not owned but used and circulated upon. Horticulture was an itinerary: gardens moved every year within the territory, going back to their point of departure after a long fallow period of twenty to thirty years according to customary norms. It was more important for an individual to hold the right to circulate within his territory and that of his allies than to keep the land to which he was entitled for his own use. Shifting horticulture implied a flexible use of space and excluded permanent tenure or individual ownership over the territory. By extension, conflicts about boundaries were avoided.

Today, given increasing population pressure on the island, changes in the land tenure system, and the birth of the right of ownership where there used to be only a right of circulation, land tenure conflicts have become crucial.[2]

Fighting in the Arena

The uncertain outcome of ritual wars was made sacred by the blood of those who were to die. The territory supplied the arena. To fight, there were places; to find allies, there were roads; and there were spatial rules and taboos to respect. Warfare took place in the open, under the eyes of all, through coded combat. Women, children, and the elderly were not affected by an activity that only involved men, more precisely "true men," these being the *yani niko* 'voices of the canoe' whose status qualified them for political power. In order to fight, a man had to be no longer beardless, an essential sign that differentiated children from adults. On acquiring a beard, a man obtained the right to have a wife . . . and the duty to fight for the honor of big men, or of himself.

Agrarian magicians were not present on the battlefield, an indication of their lesser political status (chapter 12). In symbolic terms, they were women, respected for the magical procedures whose power they mastered while being concurrently excluded from the arena of political authority and rivalry. For this reason, the Ipeukel territory, which contained the original places of agrarian magic, was deprived of the formidable honor of being involved in the traditional wars of the past. As a rule, the same prohibition concerned the men from the northern part of the island, regarded as the "daughters of Yapar." According to the myths of the origins, Yapar was the ancestor of all northern inhabitants and also the wife of the hero Kaluas, who was from the south. The mandatory neutrality of these "women-men" meant they could not participate in warfare activities. This was particularly the case of Imafin residents, also the masters of circumcision rituals and renowned agrarian magicians.

Today, the people of Imafin, in the northern part of Tanna, and those of Ipeukel, in the east, are eager partisans of the John Frum movement. This millenarian movement developed in places either associated with traditional agrarian and fertility magic or devoid of customary political power. Groups from these areas were the first to become Christian, thereby obtaining a form of political power which *kastom* had never granted them. When, disappointed by the mission, they moved away from Christianity, they did not go back to ancient *kastom* but created another *kastom,* that of "John Frum" (see Part Three). Not only did the new religion offer another explanation for the world, but it gave these groups a major political role.

Combat never involved both parties directly, only their allies. This major rule of warfare derived from the existence of blood ties between neighboring territories. A brother could not kill his brother-in-law, nor a nephew his maternal uncle. The space of *kastom* was a world where Islanders could name human beings as well as places. Warfare was prohibited in that domestic and familiar space where all were allies or even close kin, ensuring physical peace. Yet civil peace was not guaranteed— because spatial closeness often brought out the keenest confrontations. Paradoxically, war was possible where there was no conflict, but it was ruled out where antagonisms were present. The network-based culture that turned neighbors into kin meant that Islanders had to achieve their end, fighting, in a roundabout way. To battle with one's neighbor, the solution was to ask a third party who was sufficiently remote to be able to discharge the obligation. A distant foreigner would come to shed the blood that close kinship and propinquity prevented one from shedding. There is a certain duplicity attached to *kastom:* what one cannot do oneself, one can always have done by someone else—or one can do it in the name of a third party. Within such a system, the most rigid law itself generates the parry that allows it to be circumvented.

The War Path

Roads of alliance operated in the same network fashion as marriage rules and exchange rituals. If a canoe wished to settle a quarrel with its neighbors but could not fight with them, it would ask those "who were behind it" to fight on its behalf. The path of alliance was transformed into a path of war.

War coalitions rested on each partner's freedom of decision. The call to war traveled unconstrained: each ally contacted whoever he wanted to follow up on the invitation. Any partner could halt the message. The disagreement of an ally on the path of alliance forced one to turn to other roads and search for other alliances.

"To cut the banyan tree"—the explicit metaphor for a declaration of war—meant that the messenger gave his allies a branch cut from a banyan tree, which passed from one individual to the next. To accept the branch was to accept the underlying message, to pass it on to allies, and to enter the coalition oneself. When each belligerent had organized a war party, the challenge was launched. "By common agreement," an appointment was set up to meet in a neutral and open space. The ash plain next to Lake Siwi, outside the Ipeukel territory, was one such area, the White Grass savanna on the west coast was another; occasionally, other places were cleared by fire. Once the time and place were known, warriors would ready themselves for war as if they were going to a festive event. They shunned the world of women and followed food prohibitions to harden themselves to invincibility. On the eve of the fight, they bathed in sacred water holes or in the vicinity of warm springs. This ritual bath, called *amatua,* cleansed warriors from their previous contacts with the world of women. It also protected them from evil spells and magic tricks cast by their enemies. Magicians on both sides endeavored to bring about a victory for their camp, while visionaries dreamed, predicted victory, or advised on a strategy for the battle. After the *amatua,* men smeared their skin with odoriferous leaves and plant substances that made it oily; they painted yellow and red lines across their faces. *Yremera* high chiefs gave rooster or hawk feathers to those they believed would be their best representatives on the battlefield. In short, warriors left prepared as for a dance, beauty-related magic being as essential to warfare as invincibility-related magic. War represented one of the focal points of societal life: networks of alliance and leadership systems were strengthened by it. Painted and decorated with feathers, leaves, and flowers like today's dancers, the warriors were handsome—war is also a show.

Shields were unknown, but throwing stones, skillfully handled, were feared weapons. Several types were available, such as the slightly curved *kako* stones thrown by means of a liana sling which the user twirled at arm's length. Later came the *kasawaso* (or *kasoso*) stones, a specialty of Yenkahi residents (Ipeukel).[3] Each warrior kept several of these stones in the basket he took to war. Another weapon was the great war bow made of ironwood, which was about two meters long. Finally, for close combat, there were spears and a club (*nal-nal* in Bislama).

The fight in the field was preceded by speeches to intimidate the enemy and grant courage to the warriors. There were also special chants and dances. Fighting was rarely a pitched battle: rather, a series of fights took place between individual warriors on a front that undulated back and forth. There and then, those who had the reputation of being great fighters, in other words, the heroes in each camp, showed their bravery under the watchful eyes of all. The death of one of these "heroes" often put an end to the fighting. The party to which he belonged pulled back while the winners stayed on as masters of the battlefield.

The Path of Alliance

The true protagonists, those who had initiated warfare, watched the contest from afar; their involvement was limited to magic procedures for their allies' benefit. In due time, these big men would decide to put an end to a war in the field, provided the contestants had respected all rules. The *faet blong agree* was terminated either because a winner had emerged or because there had been enough casualties on both sides.

When they designate the end of warfare, the Tannese use another metaphor: "to lower the sail of the canoe," which means to put an end to the canoe's wandering, to calm it down, and to make it go back to the serene haven of peace.

As a matter of principle, a great war must end with the preparation of a *nekowiar* ritual, or *toka,* whereby the opponents meet again, this time with peacemaking in mind. A *nekowiar* means completion and reconciliation. Without it there can be no genuine political peace between old enemies. Conversely, if the conflict lasts in the hearts and minds of some, or if one component of the alliance system still disagrees, the *nekowiar* ritual cannot be organized.[4] In this case messages will not circulate, the whole mechanism of the pairing of dance companies will be hampered, and fighting will rekindle eventually. The basic purpose of the *nekowiar* is to reconnect the ends of the roads which the war has severed, thereby re-establishing territorial continuity. At this time the *yremera* 'lords' of honor, who were silent during the fighting, go back to their position at the front of the canoe while the *yani niko,* the voices of the canoe, organize the ritual and direct the "men-women"—the *naotupunus* or agrarian magicians—whose work will bring forth bountiful gardens. The Tannese say that the *nekowiar* ritual is in the image of the *katik,* a very strong liana used for building outrigger canoes. The *nekowiar* mends lost unity, links nations together, and "ties the canoes" *(alise niko).* This ritual makes the war path a path of alliance once again.

In parallel with the peace ritual, various events facilitate the settlement of the conflict once and for all. The protagonists exchange sisters and daughters for marriage purposes. They may also exchange rights of sovereignty over certain parcels of land *(silen)* located on their territory, thereby formalizing the new alliance and inscribing it in the land. Dead warriors are "paid for" in pigs, women, land rights: the loser forgets his defeat and the winner his victory. Songs in the guise of poems are created to remember the confrontation and celebrate the names of its glorious heroes. Such are the principles of traditional Melanesian warfare when it occurs under the aegis of the *yani niko,* who are the canoes' political "voices."

The Network War

Warfare by common accord allows for a self-contained release of violence. A confrontation takes place, but within limits, notably with respect to the number of casualties, the required presence of noncombatants in the background, and the territorial integrity of the groups concerned. Insofar as the parties involved choose to proceed through allies, society's concern is obviously to control violence. War also enhances the glory of big men, who can both launch it and stop it.

As mentioned earlier, Tannese society operates through a system of spatial networks within which autonomous but constantly interacting groups are allocated along roads; these bear names and are said to have preceded the appearance of mankind in the course of the creation of the world. Each mesh of this net must be able to communicate with its neighbors. A steady flow through the linkage-based chain allows for messages to circulate, move around the island, and even radiate toward neighboring islands. Should one link be skipped, the chain is broken. Exchange rituals and the exchanging of women for long-distance marriages are no longer possible. Missing out a link may be a risky proposition: if A refuses to communicate with B, all individuals behind A and all behind B will also be deprived of a connection. They will need to find other "doors" and other intermediaries; they will have to forge new roads. The outbreak of a war between geographical neighbors tears the fabric of social relations linking dancing places together. As a result, the island goes back to its initial partitioning, preventing the emergence of any large-scale design. An uncontrolled conflict precludes any long-distance relationship, impedes the working of exchange systems, leads to consanguinity in marriage, and isolates groups from each other.

This type of warfare must therefore be avoided: others must fight in lieu of the groups concerned. Both canoes turn toward those who are behind them, bypassing direct confrontation. Once the war is over, enemy groups that had become indirect adversaries are able to resume normal relations as neighbors or *niel*. Thanks to this system, an alliance network and its roads can stay open at all times and incorporate a great number of segments.

The split into two moieties or phratries, Koyometa and Numurkuen, was well accepted initially, and was perfectly adapted to the network-based "road" system. The ideology of the two big canoes penetrated to the core of each local canoe as it helped create two groups with a distinct political identity in each mesh of the net. Two continuous chains of alliance now circled the island. Whenever the Numurkuen of a specific canoe were in conflict with their Koyometa counterparts, they asked all island Numurkuen to settle the dispute in their place; the Koyometa did likewise. The code of alliance became simpler and even more efficient, and messages circulated freely among allies with the same political identity.

As a result, networks of alliance became considerably more open.

Messages circulated around the island faster and the big men who had initiated them could gather larger numbers of individuals. A missing or hostile link in the spatial nexus of relations was no longer an issue. Thanks to the allied phratries, the open circulation process represented a shift toward greater political unity on the island. No longer was society made up of one hundred autonomous, even anarchical canoes. Now two mimetic moieties encompassing all canoes were supervised in a few strong nodes by big men who constantly interacted with one another (see map 8). The whole system rested on their interaction. Those big men, both Koyometa and Numurkuen, controlled their own local groups; they initiated warfare and halted it at will. The quality of their agreement upheld the social order. In other words, *kastom* now reflected a type of power whose dual nature implied a dialogue between its leaders. But this involved a great risk: if the dialogue stopped, the "war among canoes" could take a turn for the worse.

The "Stolen War"

Born in precontact times, this fighting without rules is uncontrolled by society. Secrecy and cunning prevail. If one group wishes to settle its quarrel with another by means of a "stolen war," it will close off all openings through which the enemy would be likely to escape or receive help from its allies—it is said that the first group "shuts doors." All geographical neighbors are told to be silent. Closing their roads and refusing to transmit messages, these neighbors play deaf. The opposing group, isolated and wrapped in silence, can no longer send off or forward a message: with no available outlet, caught in the midst of a hostile mass, it is trapped. The first group acts unexpectedly by means of a deadly raid, a surprise killing at night or, preferably, at dawn. The group attacks hamlets on enemy territory. Its goal is not to pit itself against the adversary, but to annihilate it. For this purpose, the "obstruction of doors," that is, of roads, is essential. The victims lose any chance of being saved as their allies close off their territory and do not respond to the message asking for their help.

In practice, the rejection of fugitives seems to have been uncommon. Allies can be forced to remain silent and neutral—which in itself represents a betrayal of their status—but they cannot refuse to grant survivors access to their territory. In discreet terms, they are said to "leave their door ajar." Fugitives do not stay on that territory, as the enemy is too close and their presence is potentially dangerous for their allies, but they are allowed to cross it to escape from group to group until they find a safe haven.

It may take several generations for those who have fled to go back to their original territory. The fugitives become "drifting" men, without land, roots, or power, and entirely at the mercy of their hosts. The losers' land is now a dead territory. Often the winners raid it, then scatter "poisons" and "spells" over it before departing. In most cases, a "stolen war" leads not to the conquest of one's opponents' territory but to its destruction. On a lesser scale, some acts of "stolen warfare" consist of laying an ambush on a path, murdering the adversary or adversaries, and walking out.

"Stolen warfare" entails the execution of one individual or, occasionally, of an entire group. In the eyes of the men who carry it out, the execution is less a normal act of war than an act of "policing." The executioners do not make peace with those who are punished and on whom they impose their law; the latter's submission and, if needed, annihilation is what matters. There is obviously no ritual ending to acts which are themselves beyond rituals. Customary justice and the law of big men are generally dispensed through "stolen wars." Thus, a man (or a group) that has become an "outlaw" deserves death, either because he has circumvented the hierarchies and precedence rules of traditional society or insofar as he has disturbed the social order—the most serious and also the most frequent accusations being those of witchcraft, black magic, and women's abduction. Having placed himself beyond the rules of *kastom,* he does not deserve to be treated according to those very rules. He will be executed by stealth, in utter silence.

By definition, a "stolen war" establishes the authority of a winner, creates a loser, and expels a number of fugitives. Initially conceived as a war to dispense justice, a "stolen war" can also be entirely political. In the past, some individuals used it as a means to eliminate their rivals and impose their authority. In short, they brought disarray to the social order under the pretext of defending it.

Drift and Tragedy

At a certain juncture in Tanna's history, it seems that the warfare process went wrong. Wars that had begun in customary agreement ended as wars of extermination, and society lost its control over them. Island history became an incoherent sequence of acts of war—with winners and losers. Formal Melanesian warfare degenerated into wildcat warfare. What happened?

Most Tannese believe that the institutionalized partitioning of the island into two patrilinear canoes exacerbated the war process, thereby contradicting the division's initial purpose. Each local conflict became a global political matter involving the entire island and setting each moiety against the other. This explanation is too general, however. In the matrilinear islands in the northeast of the group, such as Ambae and Pentecost, there was also a system of moieties, which were structurally exogamous. Yet that system did not generate comparable effects. Besides, the accounts of the first generalized wars pitting Koyometa and Numurkuen on Tanna suggest that they occurred under fairly strict control.

A more detailed explanation is given by the oral tradition of the Yaneumwakel dancing place, according to which the island became overpopulated at one time. Land was in short supply, famine was a threat, and local conflicts were increasingly difficult to master. In order to ease the island's demographic strain and re-establish their authority, the phratries' big men launched a great war named *kapakol*. For peace to return, they deemed it necessary to decrease the number of Islanders and stir up a "war by consent." The great fight entailed heavy casualties, but this was one of its purposes; it led to the extinction of some groups. The aftermath of the war was such that a genuine reconciliation could not occur. The two canoes, Koyometa and Numurkuen, started drifting apart and interacted subsequently as if they were antagonistic "nations."

The argument linking population imbalance and intensified war is plausible, if difficult to investigate in historical terms. An overriding concern of traditional society was the issue of overpopulation in a closed space with no outlets.

At the core, the dual canoe system carried the seeds of its own polarization and demise. As one winning party emerged, the canoes' political equality was shattered. So was the agreement among the phratries' big men, all of whom were positioned on the network's strong nodes. As an institution, the moiety system defeated its own purpose. Used initially to better regulate warfare, it became an unmanageable mechanism that led society into permanent confrontation. Unregulated fighting was born when the two moieties locked themselves into mimetic rivalry. No longer could the various territories keep their relations in a state of equilibrium through the alternation of war and peace. Eventually, two kindred population groups sharing one territory turned into enemies.

The critical phase when society switched to unregulated warfare corresponded to the time when the patrilinear moieties ceased to intermarry. The ideology of the two canoes initially specified that the two moieties had to exchange brides upon each ritual or peacemaking occasion. Marriages between phratries came to an end probably because peace did not return, or returned in unfavorable circumstances. As a consequence, each moiety reorganized its own marriage networks. The roads of war alliance alone supplied the networks of marriage alliance, and bloodlines that had once mixed Koyometa and Numurkuen now each excluded the other. Warfare came full circle: the absence of peace made marriages between the two moieties impossible and the lack of marriages made a return to peace unlikely. The logic of an ever increasing rivalry led to a point of no return.

As marriage alliances between phratries vanished, so did peaceful coexistence. At best, the moieties parted geographically as they carved out their respective political space. At worst, the dominating half expelled the minority half or even exterminated it. Once again, each canoe's territory came to represent a politically homogeneous entity populated by a "single blood." Such was the case at White Sands where most defeated Koyometa minorities and groups were forced into exile; as they dispersed, they had to find hospitable lands on the island's western side. Gone was the harmonious spatial distribution of moieties in each mesh of the territorial network. Tanna went back to a state of internal disunity. Areas under the control of the Numurkuen came into being, and so did areas controlled by the Koyometa.[5]

The *Shipimanwawa*

In the nineteenth century, the last great war on Tanna—the *Shipimanwawa*[6]—began in formal arena-style fashion and ended in the chaos and anarchy of a "stolen war" with guns and powder. The many repercussions of the *Shipimanwawa* became the source of today's acute territory-related issues, including most geopolitical divergences on the island. The war played havoc with traditional territorial structures. Entire groups fled; they no longer live on their territory and do not venture back. Others were exterminated, and no one dares to deal with their dead land *(tet land* in Bislama). Also, the winners inhabit some of the conquered territories even though *kastom* excludes such right. A huge territorial problem now lies at the heart of Tannese society. *Kastom* was meant precisely to avoid this type of issue.

War tactics changed in the course of the *Shipimanwawa*. Firearms had just been introduced: their use intensified warfare. Far removed from the customary confrontations of the past, fratricidal fighting spread everywhere, accompanied by conquest and pursuit. Combatants had guns, and meetings in the open gave way to confrontations wherever the dense vegetation allowed for tricks and maneuvers. Close combat, in which great warriors used to distinguish themselves, was replaced by ambushes and fighting carried out over medium-range distances. A tactical approach and a feel for the terrain prevailed over strength and courage. Arena-style behavior was no longer an option.

Tanna's contemporary society cannot be understood without referring to the context of crisis and disarray that existed at the time of the missionaries' arrival. The *Shipimanwawa* was cut short and "Christian peace" took over island history. Yet, fundamentally, nothing had been settled.

Territorial conflicts and political rivalries were latent during the entire colonial phase but resurfaced on the eve of independence. They contributed additional arguments and resolute fighters to the modern political parties whose aim was to dominate the whole island; their quarreling began in the early 1970s. Once again, Tanna was a battlefield.

12 *The Return of Magic*

> Magical thought is not to be regarded as a beginning, a rudi-
> ment, a sketch, a part of a whole which has not yet material-
> ized. It forms a well-articulated system, and in this respect
> independent of that other system which constitutes science.
> . . . It is therefore better, instead of contrasting magic and sci-
> ence, to compare them as two parallel modes of acquiring
> knowledge. Their theoretical and practical results differ in
> value. . . . Both science and magic, however, require the same
> sort of mental operations and they differ not so much in kind
> as in the different types of phenomena to which they are
> applied.
>
> CLAUDE LÉVI-STRAUSS,
> *The Savage Mind*

In the nineteenth century, Presbyterian missionaries endeavored to
thwart all forms of magic, which they saw as satanic practices; however,
they unwittingly contributed to their rebirth. When most Tannese made
the decision, from 1940 onward, to follow the new path described by the
John Frum prophecy, the Islanders were declaring that they were taking
back most of the sacred powers seized by the Presbyterian theocracy. The
grand return to *kastom* was, first and foremost, a renewal of magic. The
men of Tanna thereby regained the convictions they had earlier lost.

The Magical Function

Each clan, each man with a *kastom* name holds a fragment of power.
In total, these powers define both the society of the island and its space.
Traditional powers are connected with stones and plants; more precisely,
stones become magical in conjunction with certain plants. Once the
leaves are rubbed against the stone and various other ritual gestures are
observed, a magical effect occurs as expected. As a rule, the individual
using a stone must belong to the clan connected with that stone; he communicates with the spirit of the stone by spitting. Spitting acts as a signal
through which the magician enters the world of spirits and is acknowledged by them (Lindstrom 1980).

Numerous forms of magic are practiced in Tanna. In this respect, the entire island is like a "pantheon," a sacred space peopled with local "spirits." Each of these spirits has its own territory, places, roads, and specific power—just as men do. That parallel universe mirrors gestures and aspects of daily human life. There, each illness has its specific place and "remedies." So do various human qualities, such as intelligence, good speaking abilities, honesty, enterprise, and keeping one's promise. Thanks to the adequate remedy these traits can be strengthened among one's friends or weakened among one's foes.

Magic rests on the dual principle of hot against cold. For instance, an unfortunate event, an illness, or a mediocre crop are attributable to a conflict between one and the other. The magical function operates by restoring balance and harmony. According to the Tannese, men represent the concept of "hot" and women that of "cold."[1] Wuhngin made the first stones, or *yani niko,* emerge from the sea—these were men. In turn, Mwatiktiki made the food stones, or *naotupunus,* appear—these were women or, more accurately, a fellowship of men whose totem and female symbol are "cold." Work in the gardens involves both men and women: the *naotupunus,* as "men-women," fulfill this creative symbiosis within themselves.

Since the *naotupunus* belong to the peaceful, fertile world of women, the moral code of war traditionally spared their lives. The Tannese say that the entire island "ate from their hands." Those hands could not be severed.[2] Agrarian magicians would return to the foreground when ceremonial cycles ushered in an era of peace. At such time, true women were exchanged as brides and bountiful ritual goods were presented. Therefore peace among true men was possible thanks to the female universe.

Today, Islanders from the central part of Tanna also say that agrarian magicians are *yolat koken* 'men of inferior status'. Acting on the orders of big men who reward them, these political servants are seen as men of duty, not men of power. An area of the dancing grounds devoted to Mwatiktiki is reserved for agrarian magicians when they drink kava. They are respected insofar as they carry on a dialogue with invisible forces.

The Islanders' conviction that they master fundamental magical powers buttresses their self-confidence. A Middle Bush magician, a master of banana magic, told me one day with a big smile: "You, the white people, you believe you are the best, but you are small next to the black people. . . ." When I asked him why, he answered: "We have the stones." What does the power of an airplane represent next to the power that makes a tree spring up and develop? What importance do mechanical forces have next to those of life? Tanna's magicians know the secrets of the magical nature that surrounds them and are no longer in awe of the skills of Westerners.

Agrarian Magicians

Agrarian magicians make yams grow, and grow well. Today they use their magic only when great rituals are undertaken. The process is always the same—each magician uses his own garden to perform agricultural tasks which the entire community around him repeats in turn. While yams are growing, he lives by himself, away from women in particular as their contact might imperil his bond with the magical force of the stones. He only eats foods he has prepared for himself and he does not drink water. More specifically, he eats "hard" foods of broiled tubers and he can only drink kava, which he prepares and drinks alone in the evening near his stones. This life eventually leads the magician into a state of consciousness propitious to visions and dialogue with supernatural forces, which has the effect of making him appear puzzling to outsiders.

The magician's first ritual act consists of washing the magical stones encased in their little wood outrigger canoe. He does so with water from the sea or from a sacred spring. He then rubs the stones with the leaves and bark of their plant associates, the knowledge of which he is the only possessor. For example, yam-related magic procedures are associated with the leaves of *narwiru* (*Cordyline* sp), which are Mwatiktiki's personal symbols. The magician spits on the mixture and voices incantations to Mwatiktiki. When everything is ready, the small canoe holding the stones is wrapped in the leaves and buried in the magician's garden.[3]

In all other respects the magician is a model gardener. He is the first to clear and prepare the soil, plant, and finally harvest the crop. From the magical garden *(nemayassim)* cultivated by the magician and his kin emanates a supernatural force that is transferred to other gardens within the community.

Today, the magical work itself ends with a feast celebrating the full growth of the first plants. In the case of yams, the festival is called *kamaru nu* 'to tie the yams'. When the vines are blooming, the magician removes the first-grown yams from his own garden and distributes them among the members of his group. In exchange, group members "pay" for his work with a banana *lap-lap,* a pig, a hen, or a kava root. The magician is now a man like the others: at last he can sleep with his wife, drink water, eat *lap-lap* and "soft" foods. As a rule, his magical duties last six months, from the clearing in August to the festival in March or early April—it is a hard life.

In the magical garden, now deserted, what has not been eaten on the day of the festival is left for Mwatiktiki and assorted wandering spirits. In the other gardens, taboos are no longer operational—in particular the taboos preventing children, menstruating women, and men after recent sexual intercourse from circulating through the gardens in their fertile phase. Gardens are now open to all and festivals and ritual exchanges can be initiated.

The magician's duty was gratifying in good years, thankless in bad years, and dangerous in the case of natural disaster. Today the magical function has been streamlined. Instead of several men as in the past, a single individual fulfills the task and abides by the related taboos. He is often assisted by his real or adopted son who is to replace him after learning about the process. While the magician always carries out his duties when a great ritual is being prepared, the timing is more flexible in normal years: generally the magician is only away for a few days to "wash" his stones and plant yams in the sacred garden.

The yam magician is also a sun magician. Shortly after clearing the land and as many times as necessary until the outcome materializes as expected, the *naotupunus* spits and rubs the sun stone with selected leaves, then hangs it in a basket above a fire which he starts and keeps going with a special type of wood. When rain is wished for, the magician who owns the rain stone washes it near a spring, rubs the stone with specific leaves, and deposits it in running water. If one wishes for the rain to stop, the stone is removed and dried; it is now the turn of the sun magic to operate. Similarly based on the use of magical leaves are procedures whose purpose is to have the winds come or go. In the past, before outrigger canoes were to leave for other islands, it was believed that winds could thus be moderated or made to blow in the right direction.

The various types of plants used in traditional horticulture hold their own magic. Besides yams, such plants include taro, bananas, kava, island cabbage, sugarcane, and the like. There are also magical processes for pig husbandry purposes—to cure a pig's illness, to have the animal grow well, and to have it return safely when it is lost. Other magical procedures involve hunting, fishing, fighting the rats that devastate gardens, in addition to war, love, and so forth. The list is nearly endless; each group has its own techniques, stones, and traditions. Further, magical practices are like goods that may be borrowed or exchanged between villages. Not only does the magician work for his group, he is able to serve an entire network of alliance in this respect.

Tanna's Enchanted Gardens

Enhanced by magical practices, traditional gardening evolved into a ritual. In this light the beauty and fertility of gardens on the island are a tribute to the glory of Mwatiktiki, the god of foods. The Tannese employ unchanging techniques and follow an identical calendar year after year; on a small scale, the magician's garden represents the perfect version of that traditional model.

Generally, traditional gardeners comply with cultural criteria to a large extent. The Tannese look for beauty and quality: they try to obtain impressive roots which they can give away. This attitude leads the *kastom* men to spend more time growing roots for gift-giving or exchange purposes than harvesting yams for consumption. In a traditional garden, yams that are to be used for ritual exchanges are called the yams of the *yremera*. The other yams are *yolat koken* or subject yams. Whereas the *yremera* or "aristocratic" yams are grown for their individual size, the *yolat koken* yams are grown for eating and their yield is therefore considerably higher.

Each clone of a ceremonial yam is carefully accounted for while it grows in its own ecological niche, a hole within a mound. At the top of the clone classification are the great ceremonial yams which stand out in terms of various criteria, such as the size of the mound, the mound's position at the center of the garden, the depth of the hole, and the care given to vine tutors. A traditional garden is thus organized around the great mounds used exclusively for "aristocratic" yam production.

The purpose of Tannese horticulture is to set up gardens whose organization parallels that of human life. Like human beings, yams are associated with certain myths of appearance, territories, founding places, magical stones, and a given hierarchy. Cultivating "aristocratic" yams is the equivalent of creating a work of art. A Tannese garden is not homogeneous, rather it is a mosaic of mounds made up of as many ecological niches. The traditional mound *(toh)* varies according to the type of soil, the value of the yam plant it shelters, and the skill or imagination of the mound builder. When setting up a garden or building a mound, the horticulturist is free to carry out his aesthetic vision. Some gardeners set up gigantic mounds that may reach four meters in diameter at the base and over two meters in height.

The building of a *toh* begins with the digging of a hole whose depth may reach one meter. The hole is then filled with a mixture of humus, friable earth, and ashes of plants and vines burned during clearing. Ashes act as a natural compost. The magician adds the leaves which he has used to clean his stones during the phase of magical preparation. The next step is to build a one- to two-meter-high mound in the axis of the hole, using surface soil obtained from scraping the earth in the surrounding area or, if needed, digging shallower holes. The earth is carefully kneaded by hand to make it as crumbly as possible. On a smaller scale, a great mound duplicates the overall organization of the garden. Thus the great yam plant rises in the central axis while on the sides grow the *katuk toh*, which are border yams of a round or short type, and sometimes shoots of larger yam plants grown only for consumption.

In February, plentiful vines begin to cover the mounds. At that time, kava plants are set between these mounds; they will be kept in the fallow

A TRADITIONAL YAM GARDEN
(Loanatom area)

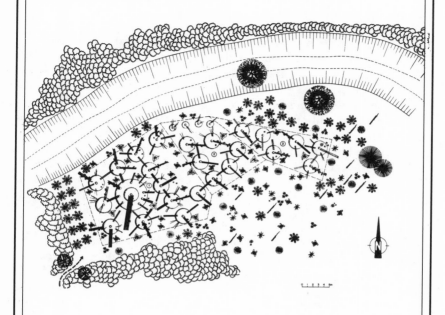

①	Nemisa's garden -- 345 square meters	▬	cane stakes
②	Yameu's garden -- 144 square meters	⌇	yam vine
③	Yawakalamus's garden -- 115 square meters	🌿	kava plant (*piper methysticum*)
creek		✳	banana tree
vegetation			Minor crops
banyan tree			taro
coconut tree		✳	corn
	Major crops		sugarcane
	giant mound (*maktamel*)		cassava
	traditional mound (*toh*)	•	island cabbage (*hibiscus manihot*)
∘	small mound (*toh to'inio*)	·	leeks
		—	yam plant (*kopen*)

Joël Bonnemaison and Hubert Goron 1978

garden for another two or three years after the yam harvest. To hold up
the vines, the gardeners set tutors made of cane. These stakes are slightly
slanted and extend over one side of the mound. A line of tutors on a great
mound can be eight meters long; it is four meters long on the average.
The quality of the yams is determined by the length and sturdiness of the
vines, and also by the sizes of the hole and the mound. The largest frame-
works of tutors are built at the center of the garden while the others are
organized star-wise around them. This architecture is all the more complex as some tutors stand on mounds that are facing one another.

On the bare soil of December, a brown-colored mosaic of mounds
holds a superstructure of dry off-white canes that look like scrawny
arms. This odd architecture, this abstract geometry is short-lived. The
fast-growing vegetation soon covers cane tutors and mother mounds.
Twisting themselves together in long sweeps, vines and young shoots
take over the garden. At this time, called *narua,* the garden has the same
colors as the surrounding forest. The bush is then so dense and thick that
even wild pigs get lost in it, as the Tannese say.

Traditional gardens, which are maintained in the areas where *kastom* prevails on the island, are more or less numerous depending on the
circumstances. There may be fewer gardens for several years; but when a
major local ceremony is being planned, more come into cultivation.
Rather than the beautiful *kastom* gardens, however, most Tannese now
cultivate "modern gardens" where all the plants are mixed. Cassava predominates, and neither holes nor mounds are used for yam plants, which
are simply buried in the ground (yam *kopen*). Modern gardens involve
less work; plants are cultivated for consumption purposes, not for gift-
giving. Yet, of all islands in the group, traditional horticulture and *kastom* gardens are best represented on Tanna. This is not a matter of
chance: by renewing *kastom,* the John Frum movement has boosted the
role of magic and, along with it, the world of enchanted gardens.

Springs, Plants, Stones, and Places

Magic deals with places, vegetation, and water. Nearly all Islanders
know about certain plants, which they use to treat common illnesses. By
tradition, more elaborate medicines belong to specific families, with any
patrilineage on the island holding a number of these. Finally, for major
illnesses, there are secret medicines known only by a few medicine men
or *kleva* 'clever men'.

These learned men of *kastom* are both genuine botanists—they have
a thorough knowledge of plant therapies—and visionaries. When a disease occurs and common cures are ineffective, one goes to a *kleva*. The
medicine man examines the case, then goes into a period of fasting and
confinement. Like the agrarian magician during the phase of plant

growth, he hardly eats, stays away from his wife, and drinks only kava in an isolated part of the bush. At night, dreams bring him an understanding of the specific problem. He identifies the illness and addresses the patient to the stone and the magician that can cure him or her; in some cases, the medicine man provides his own specific plant therapy. Plant medicine is nearly always made from several kinds of leaves and bark that have been left to steep in water. The pharmacist Pierre Cabalion has described the process:

> Pathological symptoms are ascertained with another logic than that of Western semiology and it is often difficult to interpret their labeling. Which term should one adopt to translate the names of acknowledged illnesses . . . such as kava illness or shark, raw yam, banana, and taro illnesses? The common belief is to attribute the causes of an illness to various spirits called devils or ghosts. By fighting these natural entities [the medicine man] can make the patient recover. On the basis of such convention, formulas which have no *a priori* physiological effect are called medicine since their purpose is not to heal directly but to expel spirits from the victim's body. (1984*b*)

Other types of magic are associated with trees, springs, and water holes. Running water in particular is linked with very ancient traditions. Water washes bodies just as it washes stones; more specifically, water in association with trees is considered the "source" of music. When those who have the responsibility to create new songs go near certain springs and trees, the noise of running water and the rustling of leaves in the wind generate a sound environment which the songmakers reproduce. It is said that one just needs to be there, to stop thinking, and to wait; music will not fail to arrive. Songmakers, who create poems that are sung, hold their office formally. Poets are seen as magicians, and the making of songs is a social function like any other, inherited patrilineally and associated with a particular title.

Running water carries further powers. For instance, a sacred spring can "wash off" spells, heal some illnesses tainted with impurity, and boost one's vigor. Weaned infants are bathed in it so as to grow well and be protected against evil magic. Women purify themselves after menstruation, and yam seedlings are dipped before being planted. At the time of the ceremonial harvest, ritual prohibitions protect spring water so that it does not come in contact with something "impure." Springs are also associated with love magic. In Middle Bush, for example, an individual who is made to drink the water from a particular spring will fall in love. The woman whom a man has chosen is no longer able to sleep and will go by herself to the one who wants her. Many other water-related powers are known to the Tannese.

In addition, there are, or were, stones for warfare and war-related skills, stones for courage and strength, stones for intelligence, for union and disunion, stones that "carry" the languages spoken by men, stones that designate a territory, and finally stones for the forms of magic tied to divination and evil spells; certain springs and trees are also linked with beauty and love magic. These stones, places, and springs refer to a personalized type of power, a power always embodied in one man and one local lineage.

Tabu Men

In nearly all cases, the territory of great canoes, or pairs of canoes, encompasses a sacred area *(ika ussim)* whose powers are multiple. Sacred areas may be used to put a spell on a distant enemy—or even an entire group in the case of war. To each sacred area is assigned a priest, *tabu man* in Bislama or *yatamassim* in Middle Bush language. The *tabu man* is in permanent contact with the magical world of *yarimus* spirits and is vested with the spirit of the "stone." Other men keep him at a respectful distance; for example, he drinks kava by himself in a reserved area of the dancing place.

The *tabu man* acts only on the order of the "voices of the canoe," who reward him. Because his power is double-edged, he is able to erase the harm that he might provoke. Being halfway between the world of human beings and that of *yarimus* spirits, a *tabu man* is perceived as dangerous. People say that he "puts on other eyes at night." A *tabu man* can see *yarimus* and participate in their lives, notably in their activities of warfare and lovemaking. During the day, he recovers his human eyes and comes back to live the life of mortals. For this reason, he is assigned the duty of feeding *yarimus* so they do not plunder gardens. To fulfill his mission, the *tabu man* uses his own garden and sets aside a space consisting of a yam mound around which grow samples of all the plants that are being cultivated. This symbolic patch is never harvested. In some cases, the yam mound carries a small cane scaffolding that represents the house of the *yarimus*.

The great sacred areas are frequently connected in pairs near traditional routes. They are also found in other territories, under different names. Sacred areas thus make up supraterritorial networks which cross Tanna along an east-west line, with a "heart" generally located on the island's central road and "hands" that spring out on both sides of the island.

To the south of Middle Bush, for example, the Layanepayak sacred area extends over nearly three hectares of woodland (see map 7). It is guarded by the direct descendant of the *yarimus* who, before settling down to "sleep" here, used to eat human beings. The present-day *tabu man* enters the Layanepayak sacred area in his *nambas* 'penis sheath' after he has undergone various sexual and dietary taboo-related purification processes. Among other things, he must remove smells that are too human since they may antagonize the *yarimus* spirit. The sacred area is all the more dangerous as one gets closer to the center of it. As he walks, the *tabu man* shakes with fear; the least mishap under the rules of the place causes deaths and illnesses.

Another network of magical places, and one of the most feared, is located in Middle Bush. Here, the stone containing the *yarimus* is entirely submerged in the water of a stream. To cut wood anywhere nearby is prohibited, and any injury or fall means death. The *tabu man* breaks a branch of specific wood over the rock while pronouncing the name of the man aimed at; the latter literally comes under a spell and dies without delay. This type of speech-based magic dates back to the original society of the *kapiel* and to the *nepro*. According to traditional ideology, this magic used to be the "prison of the chiefs." It represented the means of enforcing obedience and of punishing those who disregarded the code of social relations.

By comparison with the *ika ussim,* the numerous *kapiel* places are generally peopled with more easy-going *yarimus* spirits; in such places the villagers' simple magic is enough. Some varieties of magic are forgotten and no longer in use. With the passage of time, what was a supernatural environment has become somewhat ordinary, as if its human residents, rooted in magic yet tired of the extent of their powers, had ceased to believe in them.

Black Magic

More consequential is the *netuk,* which is the practice of black magic. The *netuk* corresponds to Tanna's second society, that of political moieties; Karapanemum is the master of it. Informants versed in traditional ways are usually less communicative about the *netuk,* because all Tannese still fear it. In 1978, there were rumors that black magic had returned to the northern part of the island: magicians were striking entire villages and scores of suspicious deaths had occurred. In the area where I was staying at the time, I did not meet one man who doubted the reality of such practices.

Black magic differs from place magic. For it to operate, one needs to obtain some material item belonging to the victim, such as hair, cigarette butts, food scraps, strips of clothing, and the like. The items are wrapped in special leaves and laid in a package which the magician places in contact with the *netuk* stone. Several magical processes and incantations are then used. Struck by fever and headache in the morning, the designated victim lies down and dies by the end of the day. Any such death is the sign of black magic. The men who practice it are sorcerers. In contrast, stone magicians of the *nepro* society are linked with specific places and are under the authority of the voices of the canoes. Sorcerers are more frightening because they make use of a secret and dangerous technique that is beyond the community's reach. Further, this "wild magic" travels from person to person through purchase or exchange and cannot be controlled. When a suspicious death occurs, accusations are easily brought forth as a result, and those who may own *netuk* stones are eagerly hunted down.

Netuk witchcraft has been "enriched" by new procedures originating in particular from the islands of the northern part of the archipelago. The new magic is said to operate by means of ashes resulting from the burning of special packages called *nelapen,* a procedure borrowed from witchcraft as practiced on the island of Ambrym and known in Bislama as *su*. The ashes are mixed with the kava or food of the individual whose death is wished for. This form of witchcraft is practiced among family members; in some cases it may actually be used for beneficial healing. Since *netuk* magic is associated with the world of the spirits of the dead, incantations are addressed to these night wanderers. Young men usually own *nelapen* packages, acquiring them on trips to other islands in the group.

The New Shamans

The magic of space and that of dreams have been revived in contemporary times in step with the growth of the John Frum movement, all of whose leaders were and are clairvoyant.

Clairvoyance within traditional society was a privilege granted to some lineages. The *yanmik* was a sort of *shaman* whose spirit went to meet the *yarimus* and obtain from them the sought-after secrets; there were stones for this purpose. Today the function has changed and, to my knowledge, there is hardly any man or woman who is able to play this role in contemporary society. On the other hand, the so-called *yemelait* 'visionaries' have become more numerous. In fact, any individual, man or woman, who has dreams may pride himself on his power of vision and prophecy. The *yemelait* shows no outer sign of "possession." His spirit leaves his body during the night to carry on a dialogue with the dead; during that time he discovers the mysteries of illnesses, the meaning of current events, and the lessons thereof. Traditional *yanmik* spoke with the spirits of the "stones" whereas the *yemelait* are in contact with the dead, either recent or known.

In the last few years, magic has slipped toward communication with the hereafter. The mineral world of *kapiel* and spirits is still present, but today's Islanders are moving away from it and toward the new magical practices. Magic is increasingly leaving the stone-related and spatial context within which traditional society had enclosed it to appear as a "free" and uncontrolled phenomenon. Without status, roads, customary name, and specific "stone," even as he or she lives in a place contested by others, a man or a woman may attempt to practice this new type of magic and eventually carve out a position of some success. In this context, dreams and psychic techniques are within reach of anyone.

The John Frum movement has accelerated the trend. Its leaders generally have neither "stone" nor specific customary status, and they are often "transplanted." Their power rests on their visionary abilities. A new type of social mobility is thereby acknowledged whose effects are to parallel the appearance of another Melanesian society.

Dialogue with the Dead

The Tannese know that the "country of the dead" is located deep within the earth. Death is not where being is broken off, but a change of place and a plunge into a new space whose entrances are nature's terrestrial and submarine pits. In direct contact with the country of the dead are the stones that go down into the earth via an invisible bedrock, the roots of great trees that penetrate the soil, and the sources that spring from underground.

Yet no one knows that world. It is subterranean, but where is its location? And who knows its name and the type of life that one lives there? People simply say that a deceased individual has "gone down," in other words, that he or she has left for an unknown destination. The mysterious path of the dead is at the core of contemporary clairvoyance and divination, while the world of dreams allows one to travel toward the world of those who have departed. Today the universe of John Frum supporters is nearly entirely built on a dialogue with the dead, a dialogue which is not part of original *kastom* but is based on a belief of recent origin.

In the past, the dead from coastal villages were wrapped in mats, fastened to a stone, and thrown into specific passages through the reef, where sharks would devour them.[4] In Middle Bush, they were set up in a sitting position, covered with mats in underground caves. Today the dead are buried in a specific area near the dancing grounds. If the right rules of mourning and funeral ritual are not observed, if burial in the ground or at sea does not occur in the right place and in the right circumstances, if the pigs needed for the funeral meals are not sacrificed, then the spirit of the deceased cannot follow the road leading to the entrance to his new abode. He is doomed to becoming a wandering soul. He loses his places and roads while he mingles with the *yarimus* spirits and partakes of the lives of those chilly beings of nothingness.

That fate is shared by those who are killed at war and whose bodies fall into the hands of enemies: they will never join the warm fellowship of men who preceded them in death. As an extension of this idea, the Tannese state that they were not eating an enemy they had killed but a *yari-*

mus. They only anticipated events, because the individual who was not buried in the ground (or at sea) within his clan's area lost the opportunity to enter the country of the dead. He was no longer a man and he would never be an ancestor, therefore he was a *yarimus*. The same risk affects those who die far from Tanna and whose bodies are not returned to the island. Buried in an alien land, they will not find the road to the abode of the dead.

Generally the deceased are still interested in the affairs of the world. At night, their spirits are on the prowl near the places of men, often finding a receptacle in the "totem" plants that grow on their burial place. They are the ones with whom psychics endeavor to communicate.

The Tannese believe that the dead are still closely related to them personally. Whereas ancient generations mostly attempted to protect themselves from the dead through rituals, the trend is now in the opposite direction. Part of today's traditional society is trying to carry on a dialogue with the dead in order to draw on new sources of knowledge and power. However pervasive the world of "stones" and *yarimus*—it still commands respect, particularly in terms of magic related to food and agrarian fertility—increasingly a whole new universe of magical practices is being superimposed on it.

The Song of Kava

Playing a larger role in this magical context is kava drinking, which unveils the world of dreams. Today its practice is considerably more widespread than before. Kava drinking takes place almost daily. It is a social gesture as much as a mystical one; the beverage makes the legs heavy but liberates the mind. Before they begin drinking, the pagans shout toward the bush *(tamafa)* to warn their ancestors and herald the purpose of their prayers. The trance, or sacred drunkenness, that seizes them is seen as the sign of a dialogue with the supernatural world. At nightfall when the participants show the onset of drunkenness, all is suddenly quiet on the dancing grounds. In small groups, the men move to their respective spots, sit down, start small fires, pull out clay pipes and, in silence, "listen to the song of kava" which comes to them, and in which, in their own words, they are immersed like "rain." Children, who are not entitled to drink kava, but prepare it for their elders, go from group to group bowing and, in a low voice, ask the drinkers if they wish for a second cup.

The practice of kava drinking among *kastom* supporters is strongly linked to the contemporary renewal of magic and clairvoyance. The song of kava is not really the song of the living, but that of ancestors. It stands at the core of mysticism on the island.

Men from the Kastom area of the Nivhaal-speaking region of southwest Tanna, gathered for a meeting. In 1986, followers of the movement numbered over sixteen hundred spread over more than thirty hamlets. Daily wearing of the penis wrapper *(nagwil)* was common throughout the area. (Text and photo by Kirk Huffman, 1990)

Jonson Kowia of Yakel, southwest Tanna, a visionary and leader of one of the major Kastom factions. Strict adherence to *kastom* and avoidance of modern politics characterize this community, which filters out tourists and alien influences. (Text and photo by Kirk Huffman, 1990)

Before playing the panpipe *(talei nao)*, a youngster from Tanna's Nivhaal-speaking region counts song verses. His panpipe is exactly the same as those collected by Captain Cook in the Port Resolution area in 1774. (Text and photo by Kirk Huffman, 1990)

Traditional sand play. (Photo by Kirk Huffman, 1990)

Tom Yopat, an *yremera* from the Imanaka John Frum group, tying a yam vine to a cane stake in Imanaka, on the northwest coast of Tanna.

Traditional yam mound with slanted stakes rising from both sides of the mound. Tanna's traditional gardens are designed like works of art.

In the course of a *nekowiar* in Enfitana (1977), members of
the invited *toka* group watch their hosts dance the *nao* in
their honor. The *toka* is a stick whose beak-like end, painted
white, symbolizes a hook; with it, dancers pretend to pull
toward them the presents set on the ground by the host
group, their ally.

Children of the *toka* group watching *nao* dancers. These hit
the ground rhythmically with tied sheaves of cane symbolizing the piles of presents to be given away.

Nao dancers gathering around their dance leaders. They
make a circle to represent a yam mound; cane stalks used as
stakes for the yam vines rise from the mound.

After receiving their share of traditional food *(lap-lap)*, *toka* dancers accept prized gifts from their hosts: big shiny pigs, aligned at the center of the dancing place, which they select after careful consideration and take back with them. They are expected to reciprocate later with a gift of equal or higher value.

A yam *niel*. The giant tubers, flanked with sheaves of cane, are ready to be offered to allies. A *kastom* big man and master of gift-giving rituals stands in the foreground. (Photo by Editions Delroise)

During a *niel*, or festival of food exchange, the dancing place is entirely decorated with giant yams while smaller yams hang down from tree branches. The aesthetic dimension of rituals of alliance is highly regarded in Tanna—how one gives is more important than the gift itself. (Photo by Editions Delroise)

As in all great rituals of alliance, the *niel* is always followed by a slaughtering of pigs, exhibited with kava roots. The number and value of the pigs give a measure of the importance of the ritual from a political standpoint. Each animal is "signed," often with a knot or an external mark that identifies the giver; later, in the course of another ritual, a pig of equal value must be returned to him. (Photo by Editions Delroise)

Food magician *(naotupunus)* Kiel and *yremera* Noklam
Niko, two *kastom* supporters from the Lamlu dancing
place in Middle Bush, one of the strongholds of Tanna's
revolt and core of the Kapiel movement in the 1970s.

Although copra is the only marketable good in Vanuatu today, it
is relatively rare in Tanna. In Loanatom, a shoreline village with
little land, the coconut grove extends over just a few hectares.
Niluan (foreground) was a John Frum leader and customary chief
who held the power of the *yani niko* 'voices of the canoe'.

PART THREE

FIGHTING ON THE ISLAND

We are talking on and on, but in truth we are crying over our lives.

John Frum supporter, 3 January 1980

13 The Pagans' Resistance

> The men from Tanna have an air of self-assurance that
> strikes the observer. They have a fixed look of wickedness.
> . . . Their language is high-sounding and harsh. They are
> quarrelsome and always carry knotty clubs similar to Asian
> bludgeons. Being mistrustful, they never part from their
> weapons.
>
> > EMILE MICHEL, *"La tentative de colonisation
> > belge aux Nouvelles-Hébrides . . ."*

When the Tannese refer to their past, they reconstruct a train of events,
which they order from a specific inception point. In their eyes, the world
gets its meaning from the sphere of the origins and the metaphor for history is not so much a forward movement as a stream flowing back to its
source; the ultimate meaning of the human adventure is not buttressed by
a vision of the future but by one of the origins. Besides, the Islanders' perception of the past is not time bound. Time is not understood as a chronology or a linear progression but as a motion through space that comes
and goes, hovers over one place, then another, just like a winding road
that always returns to its starting point. After arising from a place of origin, time unfolds in association with various other places, which fix this
ongoing motion in the Islanders' memory. When mapped together, these
places do not appear strung along a main axis; rather, they are dispersed
in starlike fashion around the founding site. There is no point of arrival,
nor even a "course of human history." As for the road traveled, it has no
major bearing in itself. The point of origin is the only reference that
really matters: a focus of meaning, it gives cohesiveness to the whole.

To the Tannese, the arrival of the whites represented just one moment in a series of even more essential moments. It was as if the impact of
the historical events surrounding European contact had broken on the
island shores in multiple separate waves. Relying on their extensive memory, the Tannese integrated these splinters without having to change their
own image of the world.

English Settlers on Tanna

The arrival of the whites represented more than sheer contact, however—it was akin to a shock wave that hit certain areas with maximum

strength, spreading in an uneven pattern through the island. Some regions and some groups sustained the blow directly, such as the shoreline areas of White Sands in the east and those of Lenakel and Loanatom in the west. Other regions such as Middle Bush and the south were spared to a certain extent.

Following James Cook's stay in Port Resolution, which went well but ended on a sour note, there had been no real contact with outsiders except for an occasional whaling ship. When the crowd of sandalwood traders reached Tanna, safe mooring grounds became favored locations. There, a large number of inhabitants were interested in trading and soon acquired a taste for tobacco, iron tools, and firearms in particular.

Tanna's major ports of call were Port Resolution, Waisisi on the east coast, and Black Beach Bay on the west coast. Farther south was Sangalli, now called Lenakel Bay. The first recruiters were operating without rules. In Tanna they found gullible workers and "volunteers" for the Australian cane fields far away. Yet the island had a bad reputation at the time, and all Europeans roaming through the Pacific thought the Tannese were cruel and dangerous warriors. For example, royal commissioners from the Belgian government visited the New Hebrides archipelago in 1861 in their search for a possible site of colonization in the Pacific. After meeting Reverend John Paton in Port Resolution, they described him as a man subjected to continuous hostility: "He is a genuine martyr to duty, so wicked, so very wicked are the natives toward him. He is to be pitied for he gets nothing, neither help nor acknowledgment. Once he had to defend himself bodily. . . . As he talked about his family problems—he has had his share of these—and what he had gone through in Tanna in the previous three years, the poor missionary could not help crying. He is tolerated in the island but has no authority here whatsoever" (Michel 1948, 153).[1]

By the end of the 1860s white settlers were moving to the northwest coast of the island, attracted by the area's empty land. The first settler was the recruiter Ross Lewin, about whom little is known. A former sailor of the Royal Navy, Lewin participated in the various facets of "human traffic" in the South Seas; he may have played a part in the deportation of Polynesian labor to Peru. Through the sandalwood trade, he also acquired an experience of the Melanesian insular world. Lewin built a reputation by walking on Malakula's inland trails from the south to the north along with a band of gun-carrying Tannese (Docker 1970, 42–43).

Lewin settled in Tanna in 1867. According to deeds at the Land Tenure Office, his first purchase was 197 hectares at Lenakel Bay. Other white settlers bought land on the northwest side of the island, in particular at White Grass near Ipak Bay (185 hectares), and around Black Beach

Bay (671 hectares). Such was the case, in 1868, of Donald MacLeod, who was to make a fortune later as a Caledonian Company agent. The settlers planted some cotton on the western side of the north-central part of Tanna, where the open savannas were fertile: one could sow White Grass lands and harvest the following year. Besides, on that side, the few inhabitants seemed to welcome the settlers; the bulk of the population lived inland. The Islanders were not opposed to white settlement. For instance, Thurston, passing through in 1871, was offered, without him asking for it, a plot that was "well located, accessible, and undulating, could be used for farming and stock breeding, and extended over several miles." He turned it down because, he said, "I do not like Tanna, the coast is inaccessible and the inhuman natives make up a category of unclean, despicable, and repulsive individuals" (Thurston 1957, 77).

For several years, the northwest coast of Tanna sustained a small population of settlers. Lewin shipped out a first cargo of cotton bales in 1870. His coral stone house overlooking Lenakel Bay was guarded by dogs; his dutiful employees were recruited on other islands so they would not think of leaving. Lewin gave numerous presents to a number of Melanesian "chiefs" who benefited from his presence on the island and supported him, to the extent of supplying him with women and a labor force. The Tannese, however, ceased to appreciate Lewin and his cohort of "white kings" fairly rapidly. The newcomers soon came across formidable adversaries—especially when some of the settlers began to expand their land holdings.

The people of White Grass say that one day a white man called Tom, a cotton planter on Ipak Bay,[2] met a high-ranking chief, an *yremera* of the Rakatne group, on his way back from his garden; he had worked in the rain and was covered with earth and mud. Tom derided him quite bluntly: "You are dirtier than a pig, at least a pig cleans itself when it rains, but you wallow in mud." Humiliated, the *yremera* did not answer, but later he summoned Taha, a man from the Rakawurne group, to do justice on his behalf. Taha lay in ambush in a corn field near Tom's hut. Attracting the planter outside with some noise, he killed him with a single gunshot. The body of the unfortunate settler was cut up on a dancing place in Middle Bush and shared later with allied groups in the course of a ritual anthropophagous ceremony.

On the west side, according to oral tradition, several white men perished likewise, one after the other—including Ross Lewin, the most famous and the most dangerous of all. The day of his death was set when, in 1874, he shot an Islander he had accused of stealing bananas. In retaliation, a Tannese warrior killed Lewin while he was resting under the veranda of his house one afternoon. The British Admiralty investigated his death and concluded that he was fully responsible. No reprisals were carried out.

Only a handful of besieged whites were left in 1875. By the following year, all were gone. Silence returned to the west coast of Tanna now rid of its "kings."[3] Twenty years later, recruiters still hardly ventured into the Loanatom and White Grass areas, which they considered unsafe (Hagen 1893). Today, little remains from that era of risk-taking and confrontation. The horses of White Grass have multiplied into wild herds since they were introduced by the English; there are also some abandoned cotton plants, and a few memories that the Tannese did not care to turn into myths, so insignificant was this episode in their eyes.

Two "Very Christian Kings"

Since the sandalwood-trading era, most Europeans had settled near the seashore, rapidly acquiring the reflexes of Islanders for whom the first crest line of hills represented the border of a "taboo" world, a dangerous world. In most islands of the group, a split had always existed between people on the coast and inland people: it became even wider on that account. The Presbyterian missionaries and their Samoan teachers respected that frontier. On the beaches they often crossed paths with European traders and adventurers. Hatred reigned in that small world; each clique passed on the worst gossip about the others, running the risk of thwarting the undertakings of all.

As described in chapter 4, Christianization was slow in the making and the first generation of missionaries did not convert anyone. In 1875, a recruiter noted in his ship's log: "The mission had been established for many years, but there were no converts in my time. HMS *Curaçoa* made it lively for the natives in 1867" (Wawn 1973, 26). The first conversions to Christianity took place in Kwamera on the southeast coast where, in 1881, Reverend William Watt baptized six Islanders and three children (Guiart 1956b, 123). The first Presbyterian missionaries had reached Tanna more than thirty years earlier.

Ravaged by internecine wars, the west coast embraced the religion of the whites even later, with the exception of a large new Christian village on the Lenakel coastal plain; it was given the "exotic" name of Sydney, translated later as Isini. The process of Christianization developed rapidly after the first conversions, however. In the early years of the twentieth century, Waisisi and White Sands on the east coast and "Lenakel-Sydney" on the west side became the strongholds of the missionary system. Big villages developed in those areas, continuously increasing in size through the influx of converts originating from elsewhere. But Middle Bush remained resolutely pagan. The inhabitants of that area do not recall ever seeing white missionaries, as these did not venture into what to them appeared as the last bastion of paganism. If a *manbus*[4] wished to be converted, he was disavowed by his community and therefore had to leave his land and settle in a shoreline Christian village.

For the "pagans," as they started to be called—all groups in Middle Bush, residents of the southern hills, and a few small indomitable groups on the shores of Loanatom—Christianity did not come in the exotic guise of white missionaries but in the more familiar and probably more dangerous form of their own newly converted Melanesian brothers. These eager Christians called themselves the *skul* 'those of the school' in Bislama; in their eyes, the proselytical battle they carried on against pagans illustrated the struggle of light against darkness. Christians rejected pagans on the side of the damned as *yapinap* 'men of the night' allied to the demonic magic of the *yarimus* 'spirits', to which Christians gave the name *devel* 'devil' in Bislama.

The era when Christians from coastal areas dominated inland pagans is known as Tanna Law; it extended the era of the *Shipimanwawa*. As decreed by the new converts, mission law was to prevail on the island and *kastom* had to be eradicated. Two Melanesian figureheads, Lohmai in Lenakel and Kaokare in White Sands, were both appointed as "chiefs" by the missionaries. Far from simply being assistants to the ministry, these "Christian chiefs" asserted themselves as political leaders. In a society like the Tannese, with its egalitarian bent and multiple power levels, the selection of two major "chiefs" went against the entire traditional political system. It opened a door to abuse and, without fail, generated a reaction of rejection. This wrong move on the missionaries' part explains why, early on, resistance to Christianity came to be political rather than religious in nature.

To implement their policy, the new "Christian kings" first created what they called a "police," which was a local militia made up of zealous, physically strong Christians. Local courts were set up to carry out the Tanna Law order now in effect. Initially, the new men in power aimed at putting an end to traditional warfare and at opposing evil magic. This phase was widely accepted because it fulfilled the innermost wishes of an entire people decimated by warfare and haunted by the fear of war-related poison magic. No one had yet been able to pull the island away from the cycle of "stolen wars"; these had become increasingly deadly owing to the use of guns. There was also the intractable issue of the refugees and defectors whom war had uprooted in great numbers and who lived outside their territories of origin. A complete peace appeared the only viable policy, which happened to be the missionaries' solution. This approach may explain why close to two thirds of the island population was converted rapidly after 1890. To become Christian meant to choose

the side of peace. Further, Tannese society, rife with discords and desta-
bilized by strife, thought that Christianity would bring unity to the
island. The first European missionaries, such as Watt and Neilson, limited their political power to reaching this aim.

Such wise tactics were not adopted by the second generation of missionaries who settled on Tanna in the early part of the twentieth century.
Upon their arrival, they found the place conquered—at least for the most
part. Peace prevailed. Thanks to its network of teachers, elders, and
"Christian chiefs," the church had control over the entire space of the
island. The newcomers, MacMillan and Nicholson in particular, were
politics-minded above all and endeavored to create a Christian order,
which ushered in the second phase of the Tanna Law era—the best
known and the most lamented.

Not only did Tanna Law assail the pagans' "dissolute customs," but it
also struck at the foundations of traditional society. Polygamy was
banned. So were the festivals of ritual exchange[5] because they included
night dances, which the ministers assumed were obscene and sexually
permissive. The magnificent *toka* ritual, especially, was castigated on
account of the *napen-napen* night dances involving men and women
together. The anathema spread to all chants and dances within Tanna's
kastom. Transporting kava on trails became so difficult that the plant
became the very symbol of the pagans' resistance. As for the *yowanem*,
awkwardly translated as "sacred prostitutes," whose role was to sexually
initiate young men of high birth from allied groups (and who would later
get married and start families), their function was prohibited and
severely condemned by local courts headed by the missionaries or their
assistants.

The "new order" revised territory-related rules. Ancient taboos on
travel were lifted: men and women now had the right to move freely and
to go and live wherever they wished . . . in particular in the Christian
coastal villages. The missionaries also acknowledged the ownership
rights of de facto land occupants, which froze a situation in turmoil: war
victors kept the lands they had conquered while the losers had to stay in
the areas where they had taken refuge. Wars and rituals being banned,
any return to the original territories—as previously was the case after
each war—became impossible. Territorial chaos was perpetuated and
made worse, for the benefit of the winners of the *Shipimanwawa,* that is,
the Numurkuen phratry (chapter 10).

In the White Sands coastal region, some groups held no real rights
over the lands they lived on; they took advantage of the situation by
becoming converts. The Christian chief of that area, Kaokare, acted
as a lord, distributing land to his Christian subjects and taking it away
from those who remained pagan. Whether they intended to or not,

European missionaries systematically favored the status of coastal Christians against that of their pagan adversaries, who were pushed back inland and lost their customary rights.

Although serious, land issues were not the determining factor in the onset of the pagans' resistance, however. Land issues did have a sharp impact, but only after the end of World War II when population growth resumed. What seemed unbearable from the beginning was Christian domination in its cultural and political aspects, in particular the fact that pagans, with their "degraded" customs, were being persecuted. The cornerstones of the resistance appeared in areas like Middle Bush among Koyometa groups in particular. "Cultural" warfare erupted between coastal people and inland residents.

The Heyday of Tanna Law

Tanna Law reached its height in 1905—when Christian courts were created—and ended only in 1925, when the European district agents of the Condominium administration introduced secular power to the island. During that twenty-year phase, fines, forced labor for road maintenance, whippings, and other forms of humiliation were used against the pagans. For example, it is said that an *yremera* who was a big man of the Rakatne group in Middle Bush was seized, his penis sheath *(nambas)* removed and replaced by *nangalat* leaves, which cause severe itching, and the man shown thus to the women of his group.

This era is fairly well known thanks to the eyewitness testimony of the Englishman Wilkes. He was the first district agent to be sent to the island by the joint administration. As soon as he arrived in 1912, Wilkes —who was a jurist by training—raised his voice against the principle of the potentially arbitrary and utterly illegal local courts. In a letter to the British Resident dated 31 December 1913, Wilkes noted some of the "laws" enacted by these courts:

1. No one shall feed his pigs on the day of the Sabbath.
2. No one shall henceforth wear his hair straight.[6]
3. Anyone touching a French lifeboat with his hand shall be jailed for three months.
4. Anyone going aboard a French recruiting ship shall be jailed for six months.
   Ad infinitum ad nauseam. (FRA, translated from the French)

In another letter dated 10 March 1914, Wilkes wrote that on Anatom and Futuna, which were entirely Christianized, the leaders of the Christian party had ordered that "any native who did not attend the Presbyterian service be bound hand and foot and whipped in public" (FRA, translated from the French). The harsh Tanna Law especially affected the Islanders who went with recruiters to work on plantations elsewhere in the archipelago, and incidents occurred regularly between ship captains and the island's Christian party. In November 1910, for example, two French recruiting vessels, the *St. Michel* and the *Tam-Tam,* were not able to reach Tanna's shores. A *Tam-Tam* lifeboat was intercepted and the seamen imprisoned by the missionary himself, Dr Nicholson, at the head of troops armed with automatic Winchester rifles. According to the recruiters, the "minister's militia" also shot at the *St. Michel* to make it sail away. This affair caused a great stir in Vila where the newly established Condominium was already confronting contrary forces. In its November 1910 issue, the settlers' paper *Le Néo-Hébridais* violently attacked the Presbyterian mission. As an official survey carried out by the Condominium government pointed out: "The missionary-doctor has set up a complete administrative system in [Tanna]. There is a small army; he, Nicholson, sovereignly dispenses justice, handing down fines as well as forced labor or jail sentences. More specifically, the condemned men are sent to a tribe other than their own. There, they have to find their own food and maintain and build roads joining missions or linking these and native villages" (*LNH,* no. 14, Dec 1910).

The *Tam-Tam* affair led to the tumultuous visit of the *Kersaint,* the first French warship to call at Tanna, in November 1912. As the French vessel got nearer, the Christians, forewarned by the missionaries of the "devil's" coming, vanished in the bush. The pagans saw allies in the French Navy and greeted the sailors with chants and dances. On the beach, Commandant Roques, the French captain, and Dr Nicholson, on horseback, confronted one another. Nicholson refused to let the French sailors go through his property to meet the pagans, even though this was the only possible route. Acting as mediator was the Condominium district agent, Wilkes. Meanwhile, "[t]he missionary threatened to shoot in the head the first French sailor who moved past his fence." A distinctive phenomenon associated with Tanna was already present, namely, that whites staying on the island for too long became somewhat deranged. To avoid an international incident, the French captain—whose restraint Wilkes praised—gave in and went back to the ship. "However, [Roques] was able to free the Mission's prisoners and leave them a letter of support from French Resident Commissioner Repiquet allowing dances and recruiting for Noumea, among other things. . . . It does not seem that [he] could speak to the pagans owing to Dr Nicholson's opposition" (Guiart 1956*b,* 141).

The visit of the *Kersaint* took on a symbolic meaning. Wilkes's reports to his administration and the fact that Nicholson had gone a little too far in that particular case brought about the first challenge to Tanna

Law by Vila's joint authorities. In 1913, Christian "courts" were definitively terminated and replaced by a Native Court presided over by the district agent with the help of local assessors, either pagan or Christian.[7] Only the district agent could inflict jail sentences and fines, the mission being unequivocally relieved of such "duty." In a December 1913 letter to the British Resident Commissioner, Wilkes wrote that the pagans' reputation for savagery and cannibalism was merely the pretext for political ascendancy over the island: "When I arrived in Tanna, the Christianization of the island through methods that are akin to political pressure had been moving fast ahead. Nonetheless one cannot say the pagans are savages. . . . On the contrary, many are gentlemen by nature, most have spent five, ten or fifteen years in Queensland, all are quiet, courteous, and well-behaved. A large majority speak English intelligibly" (FRA, translated from the French).

Missionaries could not forgive a statement of this nature. During the four years Wilkes stayed in Tanna, the Christian party unceasingly asked for him to be recalled. But Wilkes kept on fighting. In 1914, he obtained from the two powers in Vila a joint letter granting the pagans the freedom to drink kava and to dance. The 1914 Presbyterian synod reacted fiercely to the decision, accusing the district agent of favoring immorality on the island of Tanna. Wilkes was also accused of not acting firmly enough in banning sacred sexual initiators *(yowanem)* and of opening a "brothel" which generated venereal diseases (Guiart 1956b, 144).

For Wilkes, the final blow came from the British Resident, who yielded to pressure from the Presbyterian mission. Wilkes relinquished his position in 1915. Isolated and "dropped" by his Resident, he decided to volunteer for the European front as an officer. He never went back to the group. Beside his letters, which reveal a man of great culture and sensitivity, Wilkes left no other written testimony about his action on Tanna. In him, the pagan community lost its best supporter.

Once Wilkes was gone, British High Commissioner King replaced him with an entirely different man. James Nicol was the engineer aboard the British Residency ship *Euphrosyne*. He ruled over Tanna for nearly thirty years, until his death by accident in 1944. Like the missionaries, Nicol was a Scot; he acted as the political ally of the mission. However, the support Nicol gave to the Presbyterian missionaries did not mean he was their unconditional ally. A Catholic priest who visited the island in 1923, looking for a plot of land, was warmly welcomed and even supported by the British district agent (Monnier n.d.a, 9). Nicol did not openly repudiate Wilkes's decisions, in particular regarding the local courts and the Christian police force. Yet the court over which he presided pronounced numerous judgments of a nature to please the new order's most zealous followers.

In 1920, a protest from pagan leaders reached Vila through the European traders established on the island. Kaokare, the Christian chief of White Sands, had a woman seized by force to marry her to a Christian; this woman was one of the two wives of a pagan named Johny Kapalu. Because Kapalu protested, Nicol condemned him to one year's imprisonment with no possibility of remission. French Resident Commissioner Repiquet questioned this judgment in a letter to his British colleague:

> The Condominium district agent in Tanna is not responsible for reforming local customs but, on the contrary, should prevent them from being violated. Mr Nicol misused his power when he tried to eradicate the custom according to which Tannese men may have more than one wife. Therefore, the sentencing for this fact of the man named Johny Kapalu . . . appears to me to be entirely illegal. In addition, the granting to the man named Nanapo of one of Johny Kapalu's wives seems an arbitrary act for which no justification was given. Finally, it is unacceptable that Tanna's courts may inflict one-year jail sentences without the Resident Commissioners being apprised of such convictions and the purposes thereof. (Letter, 4 Nov 1920, FRA)

In the same letter, the French Resident Commissioner complained that he never received any report about the island from the Condominium district agent. He was thus held "at bay," with Tanna a de facto British stronghold. The letter did not appear to have much of an effect. Nicol went on supporting Tanna Law. While large Christian villages were set up, polygamy was outlawed and traditional magicians harassed. Indeed one of Nicol's first decisions was to rule that all "magical stones" in Tanna be cast into the sea. In short, cultural repression reappeared under the aegis of a dual power, both political and religious. The pagans also lost their last allies in the guise of local traders whom the Christian party endeavored to eliminate, replacing them with lay mission assistants (Guiart 1956b, 129). In addition to their trading duties, the lay assistants had to serve the mission: such was the case of Carruthers at White Sands. Eventually, the political-religious power took over the economic sphere; it controlled the copra trade network, copra being the only economic resource on the island.

The mission tried to strengthen its hold by purchasing land. Its goal was to put all coastal areas under the umbrella of a Presbyterian Land Trust Board. At the time, rumor had it that the joint powers were to share the archipelago between them, with the northern islands going to Great Britain and the southern islands to France. To remove Tanna from French reach (or such was the Presbyterian argument), the Presbyterians bought land directly from the Islanders,[8] in particular in the areas adjacent to what was already in the hands of the mission, namely, White

Sands, Port Resolution, and Lenakel—the island's main safe anchorages. For instance, Dr Nicholson bought nearly five hundred hectares along the Lenakel coast. The Presbyterian purchases took place in 1904, followed by a request for registration by the Joint Court and, in 1914, preliminary surveying. Pagan groups reacted vigorously to such events. From a legal standpoint, the transfer only meant that the mission was holding land on behalf of the Melanesian beneficiaries. Yet, in practice, customary space was replaced by a "missionary space" in the most populated coastal areas, and pagan groups were now under siege in Tanna's mountains and plateaus. Further, the Islanders felt they had lost their last chance for autonomy. In its shoreline strongholds, the new power tightened its control, requiring residents to abide by the letter of the new moral code and attend religious services under penalty of banishment. Tanna Law was scoring total victory. Its proponents held full-fledged power over the island.

In Middle Bush, previously little affected by Christianity, small bands of converts began proselytizing among groups mostly composed of Islanders transplanted after internecine wars. Small churches were built. When the church bell rang for the evening prayer, silence was shattered for those who were drinking kava nearby. The bell became the very symbol of divisiveness: in the evening Christians and pagans would go their separate ways, the former to church, the latter to the dancing place *(yimwayim)* to drink kava.

Pagan Renaissance

Christian police, followed by gospel preachers, had invaded the territories of Middle Bush pagans. Feeling trapped within their island, the pagans tried to find a means to communicate with the outside world. They called on the local traders who were still in Tanna; most did not like the mission. They also contacted those pagans among them who, despite the prevailing ban, had been recruited to work on plantations off the island.

The pagans' major concern was whether the law being forced upon the Tannese represented a universal law. Adopting a pragmatic attitude in this respect, they did not so much wonder whether the missionaries' message was right or wrong; they only wanted to know whether the Presbyterian law did rule the rest of the world. Should the answer to this question be positive, any resistance on their part would be fruitless. But if such were not the case, the pagans had allies outside their island who were within their reach—the issue was to find the "road" toward these potential allies.

In the second decade of the twentieth century, a messenger was sent

out from Middle Bush, whose mission was to explore the world at large.
The messenger's story, now a myth, is told below as it was conveyed to
me on the Koyometa dancing place of Le'uluk by its keeper.[9] Like the
other great myths of *kastom*, this story is associated with a complex of
dances and chants and delineates the roots of the problem.

The Presbyterian mission began in Anatom, then it went to Tanna
where it landed in Kwamera. From there it moved first to Aniwa
Island and then back to Port Resolution, expanding toward Waisisi.[10] In Lenakel, the white ministers selected Lohmai; in White
Sands, they chose Kaokare. These two chiefs devised Tanna Law
and created a police force to uphold it. *Kastom* had to hide. The
white ministers did not implement Tanna Law; the two chiefs did,
distorting their words.[11]

The Ipeukel Meeting   At a gathering in Sulphur Bay,[12] without the
missionaries, the men from Middle Bush asked the chiefs:
"Where does this new law that wants to bury *kastom* come from?
Who ordered it? Which road did it follow to get here?"
The two Tanna Law chiefs answered that the order did not originate in Tanna but from a powerful country on the other side of the
sea: America. Once the meeting was over, everybody went home.
Sios Natingen, a man from Le'uluk, went along with Yapon, who
was from Lamlu.
The two men returned to Lownhim.[13] What they had learned at
the meeting made them sad. When they were asked about it, Yapon
answered:
"We only got hen feathers from it."
The men of Lownhim drank kava together. Then, one by one, the
men left; Sios Natingen and his brother Ya'uto stayed on the dancing
place a little longer.
"Brother," Sios said, "I understood what Yapon meant. He is furious, because he thinks the new law exists only in Tanna. But we
must be certain of this. Go to the other islands of the world and
come back to tell us whether what is true here, as we are told, is also
true there. Does Tanna Law exist in the countries of the whites? Do
the whites believe what the missionaries are telling us?"

The Pagan Messenger   Sios and Ya'uto walked down to the coast,
toward the Lenemtehin headland.[14] When they saw a ship, Sios
Natingen lit a fire on the beach. They were seen from the ship and a
boat was sent. The captain hired Ya'uto as seaman. The ship
belonged to Dick Pentecost; men from Lifou[15] made up the crew. As
the ship was sailing toward Noumea, the pagans' emissary and a
Lifou sailor named Willy Pea became friends. Ya'uto told him the
purpose of his trip. The voyage continued to several islands of the
world: Lifou, Noumea, Sydney, and several other countries.

After three years, Ya'uto returned to Tanna with Willy Pea. They held a great secret meeting in Lenemtehin and told what they had seen: the Presbyterian ministers were lying, the new law did not come from America, and the whites themselves did not know about that law. It existed only in Tanna, it was but a Tanna Law. When they heard the news, the pagans were extraordinarily joyful—they danced all night long. Dances were also performed in Iwel and then on the other Middle Bush dancing places.

"Those of the Law are lying. *Kastom* will be reborn," sang the *kastom* men.

The Christian Response   Spreading like fire in the whole of Tanna, the news reached the Christian camp, which reacted immediately. A man brought to Sios Natingen a message from a Lenakel Christian, a message that derided the pagan camp:

"I tied all your customs to the top of a banyan tree in Isapiel: kava, the *kawur*, the *nekowiar*, the *kweriya*. . . . If you want them back, come and get them here, where I live . . ."

"I do not carry the *kweriya*, I do not have the right to, since I am not an *yremera*, but when I go to Isapiel, all the things you tied to your tree will fall by themselves to my feet. I will just stoop and gather them . . .," Natingen answered.

Sios Natingen decided to send a band of warriors to retrieve the sacred symbols of *kastom*, which had been placed on top of the Isapiel banyan tree in derision. The young warriors were close to leaving when they were told that the Presbyterian militia from Lenakel had left for Middle Bush that very day. This looked like the right opportunity, so the pagans decided to go and meet them. Later the two groups met as expected.

After observing one another in silence, they lined up to shake hands. It was a trick. When the pagans' leader, Yamus, lowered his head, the pagans jumped and seized one of the Christians. The others fled, abandoning the prisoner who was restrained and taken to Middle Bush. Later, one of the prisoner's brothers reappeared, holding a gun called Misis.[16] He aimed at the *kastom* men, who freed their prisoner.

Meanwhile, Kaokare, the Christian leader from White Sands, had sent his policemen to Yaohanen, in the southern part of the island. There, a *kastom* man called Yassum defied the Presbyterian militia, killing one of its members. The others captured Yassum and took him to White Sands hanging from a pole by his hands and feet, just like a pig.

"They are going to kill him," Ya'uto warned, "then they will come and get us. They know that we are the ones who decided that *kastom* should resist."

All fled except Nimayen, a Koyometa[17] of the Numaine canoe, who refused to leave the village. During the night, the Tanna Law policemen surrounded the hut where Nimayen was sleeping with his two wives. He tried to use his gun, but his cartridges did not work and he was captured. The men of Tanna Law broke the wooden *niko* containers used for kava drinking, seized the magic stones, and set fire to the houses. Nimayen was bound hand and foot and taken to White Sands. There, he was tied to a tree and given hen excrement to eat. Before fleeing, Ya'uto had warned him:

"They will take you, they will tie you up, and they will keep you prisoner. You will have to wait. . . . But one day two ships will arrive to set you free."

The Two Ships   Nimayen was fenced in. He was counting the days on his fingers; every morning he would climb to the top of a tree and look at the sea. When asked about it, he would answer:

"I am looking at my home . . ."

His wardens thought he was sad on account of the two women he had left behind. Yet the day came when Nimayen saw two great ships that were circling around Waisisi Bay and getting closer.[18]

Sailors and soldiers went ashore, and the Tanna Law police force fled into the bush. Seeing Nimayen on his tree, the sailors greeted him. As for Kaokare, he had gone into the bush and found a hiding-place, a hole within the roots of a banyan tree. The news about the outsiders' arrival went quickly around the island. Knowing that an ally had come, the *kastom* men greeted the sailors and performed dances in their honor. The first ship was French: its name was *Makriko*. The name of the English ship is not remembered, however its captain was called Mr King.[19]

Wishing to speak to the sailors, the *kastom* men went to Yaneumwakel to find a man by the name of George Nakoa who could speak a little English. The man was so old and sick that he had to be carried on a wooden stretcher covered with leaves. The sailors' leader already knew what had happened in Tanna:

"We have not come against the mission and the English ministers," he said to the men of Middle Bush. "We have come because the Christian leaders and policemen have erred against you."

The sailors arrested several Tanna Law policemen and took them to the ship. They asked the *kastom* men what they wanted them to do about the prisoners.

"Just tie them up to poles by their hands and feet, as they did with us, and slowly go around the island to show everybody that their time is over, then release them."

So the sailors did. The *kastom* men danced once again to thank them for their visit. Pigs and hens were killed, kava was offered.

"We have to go," said the sailors, "but soon a man will come, sent by us. He will stay in Tanna. This man will come to help you. What happened in the past will not happen again."

"You must tell those of the mission that their time is over," Ya'uto answered on behalf of his camp. "If they wish to forsake *kastom* and go with the *skul,* they can do so on their own, but they should not come and impose their law on us. *Kastom* belongs to us."

Later the two Condominium district agents arrived as promised: the Englishman was walking in front, the Frenchman behind.[20] Ya'uto asked that a real French leader, a capman, be sent to live with the Englishman in Isangel, far from the White Sands stronghold of the Presbyterians.[21]

The Pagans' Store   That day *kastom* finally scored a victory. Later a great gathering was organized in Lenemtehin for the purpose of granting *kastom*'s leadership to Ya'uto, but he turned it down: his status as an agrarian magician *(naotupunus)* was not high enough for him to aim for such a position.

Ya'uto's friend Willy Pea opened a store in Lenemtehin. He was selling stick tobacco, cigarettes, rice, salt, and pipes, which the *kastom* men were exchanging for coconuts. *Kastom*'s enemies learned about it and were jealous; they surveyed the area and discovered the store. One night, a man from the island of Mare[22] arrived, went into the hut where Willy Pea was sleeping, and severed his head with a knife.

Ya'uto organized a great festival and called all the big men, one by one, to Lenemtehin. To each he gave a gift, sharing the entire "cargo" that remained in the store. When giving out each item, Ya'uto said:

"Do not forget that what I give you has a name. It is called Willy Pea."

In a mythical form, this story illustrates the views of Tanna's Melanesians on a series of major events. For the people of Middle Bush, it is a tale of victory: *kastom* recovers, and it does so by dispatching a messenger. The answer comes via a Melanesian brother from Lifou, then through the Condominium, which imposes a lay type of power over the island. As a result, the myth behind the overpowering Tanna Law is shattered and the law definitively thwarted.

Also dealing with the messenger's story is a song that celebrates a major event and therefore takes the form of traditional Tannese poetry:[23]

> We wrote everywhere, all the way to Vila
> The missionary Gidi read the letter[24]
> He crossed the piece of paper out[25]
>
> Nulak decided to write
> About what men were carrying in their hearts

This was written in our language
We put together the names of the two canoes
That of the Englishman and that of the Frenchman[26]

The message went off, it enunciated
It repeated once again
The others answered thank you
They always said yes, they never said no
They understood everything[27]

In Lenemtehin Sios lit the fire[28]
Ya'uto helped him
The others were afraid
They lit the fire so that everything would be known
So that this story may go on and never die.

In this type of poem, the chronology and description of events are not essential. What is emphasized here is the symbolic meaning of such events, along with place names and names of participants. Everything else is a metaphor—in this case, the letter calling on the delegates, the crossing out as a symbol of Tanna Law, and the fire alluding to the messenger's departure. Through the power of suggestion, such texts of oral literature have much to say about the pagans' resistance. Once convinced that their fight was legitimate, *kastom* supporters believed the Condominium administration was their best ally against Tanna Law. The pagans celebrated the various stages in the progression of lay power over religious power as victories for their own camp. Thus, the calling of the French warship—the *Kersaint*—was the first breach of Tanna Law, even though the facts related in the myth seem amplified and sometimes more symbolic than real; Wilkes's brief but momentous stay was the second; the third was the arrival of the French district agent, whose power was supposed to balance that of British District Agent Nicol; and the fourth was the move of the joint administration to Lenakel on the west coast, a more neutral place than White Sands, where the Presbyterian mission had its headquarters.

Undoubtedly, the most important and mysterious personality in the Middle Bush myth is Willy Pea, the black brother from the outside world who advised *kastom* followers to resist. Willy Pea went to the secret place of Lenemtehin to bring the *cargo* to Tanna's pagans; until then the *cargo* had only reached Christians on the coast, with the whites as intermediaries. This was the fifth and final breach of the power held by the Presbyterian mission and the Christians. Political power had already been divested of its mythical quality, and the mission's economic power came next. Following Willy Pea's ritual-like murder, the island's *kastom* men stood united in their stand against Tanna Law.

Willy Pea is regarded as a cultural hero. Indeed this black man who came from elsewhere saved *kastom*. The final episode when all his possessions were named and redistributed is suggestive of Semo-Semo's myth: it was not his body which was divided up, but his goods, in other words, the symbols of the new society. Although the *kastom* men were guilty to some extent of letting him be killed, they became united again through the objects they received from him. Overcoming their divisiveness, *kastom*'s advocates made up a single body.

Did Willy Pea exist? There is no written evidence to confirm the existence of a copra maker from the Loyalty Islands who was murdered on the east coast of Tanna and who secretly inspired the pagan camp to resist. Yet Middle Bush inhabitants vouch for his existence and state that his story was kept secret in fear of the mission.

Middle Bush's *kastom* men found their cultural hero in Willy Pea. Whether he was real or not, this black messenger imparted a new life to their society and heralded fairer times to come. The "other side" killed him, but his sacrifice solidified *kastom*'s alliance network. With the exception of their epilogues, the respective messages of Willy Pea and, later, John Frum have the same meaning.

The "False Christians"

In marked contrast with the events in Middle Bush, the irruption of the white universe hit a coastal society in decline, whose culture was less than resilient. Nearly all men from coastal areas had already worked in Queensland or elsewhere; many groups had fled or were in exile. This uprooted world had also fallen prey to epidemics. Apparently, its only means of survival was the European mission.

By the early part of the twentieth century, coastal Christians were not all of one mind, however. Groups still secretly attached to traditional values played out subtle tactics to keep some of their independence vis-à-vis Christian strongholds. Settling for peace, they took on a Christian veneer; such was the case for the Loanatom and Ipai groups. If John Frum had not appeared at Green Point in the south, the prophet could have done so on the equally underpopulated northern coastal area near Loanatom and the empty White Grass region.

When the Presbyterian mission began marking out land, a Kanaka who had worked in the Queensland cotton fields told the Islanders about the meaning of land surveying. As a result, Loanatom residents decided on a common front regarding the Presbyterians' territorial expansion: the creek between Loanatom and Lowkatai became a "border" that the surveyors did not have the right to cross.

But the people of Loanatom and Ipai had harbored another concern for more than a generation. In the nineteenth century, a twenty-hectare piece of land on Loanatom Bay had been sold in exchange for firearms to English traders. The sale was all the easier as none of the Islanders agreed about the land, which had been conquered in the course of the *Shipimanwawa*. The sellers themselves had no specific rights over it. Although the land had not been used by the buyers, people knew it had white owners. The Islanders were worried: they thought that Tanna Law proponents might take it over since, in their eyes, the British buyers could only be the mission's allies. Preparing for such a possibility, Loanatom residents endeavored to attract French or other traders whom they knew were not connected with the mission. In their eyes, the traders would be of help to market copra and could protect them against another Tanna Law-inspired territorial expansion. But the copra makers that did come only set up temporary collection points. Still empty, the land in Loanatom was like a threat and even more, an obsession.

In the early 1920s, Vila's Catholic bishop, Monseigneur Douceré, received a delegation of Tannese men who wished to offer him that piece of land for free and also asked him to send a "French missionary."[29] The visit was mentioned in a report to the French Residency linking that specific request and the issue of an official French presence on Tanna:

> A group of natives went to see Msgr Douceré, vicar apostolic, and asked for a Catholic missionary in Tanna. Mr Repiquet, the French High Commissioner, intended to send a French district agent to the island. Such idea was not to the taste of Mr King, the previous British Resident Commissioner in Vila, who upon learning about it exclaimed: "But France needs to save money, why do you want to create a new position?" However, no one in Noumea wants to sign up because the new civil servant would be paid in francs in an island where the pound [sterling] is in use. Besides, Msgr Douceré has no missionary available right now and it is a pity for we must strike while the iron is hot. (Captain Husson's report, FRA)

For the "false Christians" of Ipai, the Catholic option was one of last resort. It would prevent the "empty" land in Loanatom from being taken over by the Presbyterians—a good illustration of the fact that, during the early part of the twentieth century, groups situated on the coast or in neighboring areas had no alternative, conversion to Christianity being mandatory to a large extent. Ipai residents were looking for a church that would be less threatening from a political standpoint. In this respect, or perhaps because of its reputation as the church of the devil, the Catholic Church appealed to them the most. On his first visit to Tanna in 1932, Father Bochu of the Vila-based Marist mission bought some land in Lenakel, in the heart of the Presbyterian stronghold. Of themselves the people of Ipai advised Father Bochu to settle in their area instead, on the famous Loanatom plot. The Catholic mission purchased it from the Land Tenure Office and the "false Christians," relieved, found a way out of their dilemma by becoming Catholics—in name only.

A Christian "Dialogue"

The rival mission did not appreciate the move. In April 1933 the French district agent in Tanna, a physician called Legrosdidier, received a letter from his colleague MacLeod, the Presbyterian missionary–physician based in Lenakel. Without comment, the Frenchman forwarded it to the bishop's office in Vila.

Tanna, 3 April 1933

Dear Dr Legrosdidier,

In the course of a purely professional visit this morning, I regretfully had to speak to you about an issue of which I had just been informed.

My elders and deacons, as well as several persons from the village of Loaneai,[30] have told me of their concern regarding your preparations for installing a Catholic priest in one of your stations.[31]

Undoubtedly you will not share my opinion, but I am convinced that this act will have harmful consequences. I have seen the Roman Catholic system at work in Scotland and I do not wish to see it here again. It will then be my duty as a Christian to warn the natives against that religion.

Given the essential differences between our respective viewpoints and aims, I trust that you will understand that our friendly relations will henceforth be unsuitable as long as your intentions are the same, at least this particular intention. However, I am at your disposal regarding medical matters. (CMA)[32]

Puzzled about the tone of the letter he had received, the French physician and district agent wrote an answer the same day. He was sent a second note, which reinforced the message.

Tanna, 4 April 1933

Dear Dr Legrosdidier,

Your answer makes me realize that some aspects of my letter are not particularly clear to you. Let me add the following details:

First of all I am surprised that you do not quite understand the reasons why we must stop seeing one another. You openly state your confidence in the natives and you are actively helping a representative of your religion settle here. That religion is entirely opposed to ours. As long as you only fulfilled your functions of physician and French district agent, there was no obstacle to our friendly relations, but now that you give your help to a project which undermines our work among Tanna's inhabitants, it is obvious that such relations cannot continue: the natives would not understand it otherwise.

I realize what the religion in which you have been raised represents for you, but it is also obvious that, as per your own words, you do not seem to be very knowledgeable about the tremendous differences between our two faiths: these differences are exactly the same as those in existence at the time of the Reformation in the sixteenth century.

Regarding Catholic priests, I have known some personally in Edinburgh and I cannot truly say that I have fond memories of them, or that I consider them as interesting individuals.

You probably did not read the biographies of popes and the public surveys concerning the lives of priests in New Zealand and other Pacific islands. . . . From the most ancient times [*sic*], history has been sullied by acts performed by Catholics against men and women of my religion. I do not share your wife's opinion that "Is not Christ the same Christ everywhere!" Do look at your teachings and ours, your ritual and ours, your Bible and ours, your deified Virgin Mary, your worship of saints, your confession booths, the absolution from the priest's hand, your theory of the purgatory, your Mass, your devotion to the pope and the formality surrounding the one who should first be the servant of our humble savior. All these things, and many others, are shocking to us, as they are to any sincere Protestant; they are absolutely contrary to the words of Christ in the Gospel.

You must not be surprised therefore if I see it as my duty to show the errors of such doctrine to my flock. Things being as they are, it would not be fair for me to act this way while still going to your home and staying on good terms with you.

Dear Mr Legrosdidier, I have no issue with you personally. As long as your religion was a private matter, we had friendly relations, but as soon as you try to introduce it to people who in thirty-five years have been transformed from the status of cannibals and atheists to that of peace-loving Christians, we can no longer see one another. (CMA)

The historical reference was precise: the sixteenth century and the era of the wars of religion in Europe. Dr MacLeod had reason to be mistrustful, for when Father Bochu and his successor, a Spanish father named Martin, settled in Loanatom, they saw over a hundred "converts" within a few days, all asking for baptism, confession, and the "medal." One of the Ipai pagan leaders, Sell Noklam, was the first to ask for baptism, albeit under three conditions: the Catholic mission was to use only two hectares out of the plot's twenty; it should open a store where he and his group could find a plentiful supply of tobacco; and it should open a school where children would learn to weigh copra *(we em i save long kilo)*, because he had had enough of being cheated by traders. Given these three requests, Noklam and his group were ready to accept the *skul* of the Catholics. However, against the local priest's wishes, Monseigneur Doucéré refused to open a store in Tanna.

The Presbyterian façade of Ipai and Loanatom villagers gave way to a Catholic faith that was no less of a veneer—but it was a faith they had chosen, if only for tactical reasons. By necessity and philosophy, the Marist fathers kept the low profile that had been the policy of their order since its arrival in the group.[33] Their ministry was only moderately successful; as soon as John Frum appeared, that segment of the west coast adopted, with one exception,[34] the millenarian prophecy which is still, for the most part, its own today.

The Messengers of John Frum

Slightly to the north of Loanatom reside Islanders who are now John Frum supporters. They relate an odd tale in which Loanpakel Bay near Imanaka, on the island's west side, plays a role identical to that of the Lenemtehin headland on the east side. Monuments are located in both Lenemtehin and Imanaka. More contemporary in appearance, the Imanaka cement memorial imitates the monuments in many Christian villages on Tanna which are dedicated to the memory of the first missionary and the first converts. The Imanaka monument honors the last pagans. Here is its story:

> Karapanemum, Tanna's black god, used to reign over the island. The Presbyterian mission arrived, bringing Tanna Law along, and *kastom* had to hide. Pursued and stalked like wild cats in the bush, the big men hid *kastom* under the leaves of the forest. No longer was there any *yremera, yani niko, naotupunus,* or *yowanem;* Karapanemum had become voiceless.
>
> One day, the big men of *kastom* held a secret meeting in Lenemtehin. They decided to defend *kastom* and their pledge went all around Tanna.[35] Yopat, big man of the Nakane canoe, belonged to the *skul* but still kept *kastom* in his heart.[36] He went to see a white man in Lenakel by the name of Jack Sapet, to whom he used to sell his copra.[37] Yopat asked for Sapet's advice: Did he know a country somewhere that could help *kastom?* Did he know a road to get there?
>
> "It is easy," said Yopat. "If you want all of us to go to jail, you just need to repeat what I told you. But if you want to help, do it and do it quickly. Send our message to the country that can help us."
>
> Jack Sapet agreed; he for one did not like the mission. He asked to meet other big men, all of whom confirmed Yopat's message. He promised to personally carry the names of these men and the letter

they dictated to him, then he left. It is believed he went to South America. . . . Time went by until one day a ship anchored in Loanpakel Bay.[38] A tall, brown-skinned man who looked like a half-caste went ashore. He was holding a big book. The man's name was Mr Lani and he had come from South America.

"Don't be afraid," the stranger told Yopat. "I am a friend. I come in the name of Jack Sapet. In this book all your names are already written down."

The foreigner walked to the hills all around. He had instruments; he looked through large field glasses and put stones on the hilltops. When his work was over, he went to Yopat.

"Who is Tanna's first man?" Mr Lani asked.[39]

"His name is Karapanemum,[40] but he is not the first man, he is a spirit, a devil," Yopat answered.

"If Karapanemum is indeed the first man, then he is neither a spirit nor a devil, he is God, your God, and only he can help you. Tell me his story."

A man from the northern part of the island called Nimakepa'us told Karapanemum's story: "Karapanemum used to have a fence[41] in northern Tanna.[42] *Skul* men invaded his house, burned the forest around it, and turned it into gardens. Since then Karapanemum has been hiding on top of Mt Tukosmera."

"Someone who lives in America knows Karapanemum," added Mr Lani. "I am going to tell him what is happening here and he will return to save *kastom*. I am only his friend. I have put something on the mountain that will prevent your lands from ever being stolen by the whites. The one who lives in America will come later. If he cannot come himself, he will send a boat that will take you to America. Do not be afraid of this boat when it gets here, because it will be silent, it will be like a moving island."

Mr Lani was not seen again, but the man whose coming he had announced arrived later in Tanna. His name was John Frum. First he hid at Green Point, where everybody went to meet him in secret. Yopat shook his hand: John was white, he was wearing a hat, pants, a jacket with shiny buttons, and he carried a walking cane. John said:

"I have come back to save *kastom*. Each of you should go to his land, to his dancing place, and drink kava in the evening. Let go of warfare and poison magic *(netuk)*, these are bad customs, but keep the others, they are good. If the *skul*, if the French or the English pursue you, do not ever be afraid, I shall return to tell you what to do."

John Frum left, and the big men of Tanna's *kastom* gathered once again in Lenemtehin. They asked the French to come to Tanna to protect them from the English who were walking behind the missionaries. And John Frum returned a second time.[43] Today, Tanna Law is dead and the days of the mission are over; those of *kastom* have yet to begin. John will return for the third time.

This story was first told in public in 1978, when all John Frum supporters from the north-central part of the island met around the Imanaka monument. The narrative is somewhat similar to the Middle Bush story. Like the pagans, the "false Christians" on the west coast were seeking a way out of the island; the trader Jack Sapet became their messenger to the world. Ya'uto, a Tannese, returned with a black brother from Lifou, whereas Sapet, a foreigner, was followed by another foreigner. Mr Lani and Willy Pea had the same role, but the former was evolving in a more millenarian context. Originally from Latin America, Lani prepared the path of John Frum, who is perceived here as a white man. Lani saved the lands of the Tannese; later, John Frum was to save *kastom*.

Was Lani, Imanaka's cultural hero, a true figure? In all accounts where mythology is the driving force, the narrators are more interested in uncovering the meaning of an event than in describing it. In this case, the narrative's primarily symbolic components cloak possibly true events with wonder and magic. The Imanaka story suggests that Lani was a surveyor. Between 1910 and 1915, topographical triangulation was carried out in Tanna and geodesic markers were placed on the major high points. One marker was set on Mt Tangen near Imanaka in White Grass. The surveying predated the registration of a number of plots on Tanna's west coast in the name of the Presbyterian Land Trust Board. Did the Condominium surveyor who did the work play the role of a forerunner within the millenarian John Frum movement? Did he speak with coastal inhabitants, who worried about the threat of Tanna Law on their territories? Was he told Karapanemum's story and did he encourage local residents to resist because he himself harbored some hostility toward the Presbyterian mission? Everything is possible, yet nothing is certain.

There is another issue. Most topographical surveys of the time concerning Tanna are signed by a James Fletcher, in particular the reports concerning White Grass and the island's west coast. Was he also the author of the famous letters originally published in 1923 under the title *Isles of Illusion?* Robert James Addison Gerard Fletcher was indeed a surveyor in the Condominium around that time. His letters reveal his strong personality, anticonformism, and lack of sympathy for the Presbyterian mission. Besides, Fletcher had come from South America and spoke Spanish fluently. Are "Mr Lani" and Fletcher one and the same? There is no direct evidence to confirm it, because Fletcher did not mention having traveled to Tanna. According to former British Administrator William

Stober,[44] the author of *Isles of Illusion* never worked in Tanna (pers comm). Perhaps a namesake endorsed the topographical reports about the island.

Compacts of Alliance as a View of the World

All Tannese oral traditions, be they ancient or recent, follow the same tiered pattern. They refer to founding places which themselves refer to guardian groups; placed in a sequence, these narratives anchor a cultural system from which originates a political system. Such is the case for the various oral traditions dealing with the Islanders' resistance to Tanna Law. Thus, the protests of both Middle Bush pagans and coastal millenarians were linked to a process of reconstruction of the past which extended into a political compact of alliance. This gives a clue about the way Melanesian society interprets the events affecting it and simultaneously uses such assessment to rebuild itself in the moment.

Among coastal millenarians the John Frum movement simmered for a very long time. The final phase—the Green Point events (see chapter 14)—represented the emergence into the open of an expected, already announced phenomenon. The early millenarian stand delineated in the White Grass myth developed within uprooted, decimated groups that had lost part of their cultural memory. As they resorted to John Frum, those groups re-created *kastom* and thereby re-established an identity for themselves. The resistance movement coalesced when pagans on the coast opposed the Presbyterian mission's territorial expansion. For the pagans, the first step was to save their territories. They recovered their culture only later, as expressed in the Imanaka myth which focuses its symbolic approach on the role played by the surveyor "Mr Lani." Perhaps for the same reason, Imanaka was also the only village where I was allowed, along with the surveyor Hubert Goron, to conduct a complete land survey. We were turned down everywhere else. Imanaka accepted us, because here surveyors are not feared. Besides, Goron had a full red beard and he spoke very little, a trait that appealed to the local John Frum supporters: they found him mysterious-looking, and perhaps in the likeness of the earlier surveyor.[45]

The Middle Bush myth developed in a different context. In the inland area that is Middle Bush, the mission was never a real threat to the pagans' territories[46] and, further, the impact of the white clash was subdued. Here, *kastom* was never lost and even less forgotten. To resist, local pagans did not need to rely on a comforting millenarian message. The Middle Bush myth is more tradition-bound than the White Grass myth, which creates a new tradition. Inland pagans were pragmatic and deemed it essential to strike an alliance with the Condominium administration that could protect them from missionaries. Accordingly, they saw the arrival of district agents as a decisive victory for the camp of *kastom*.

Although these two traditions differed with respect to their approach to the past, they had a common purpose, which was to stand in the way of Christian power and re-establish *kastom*. Both were born when the Tannese tried to secretly reorganize their society as they set up the origin myths that would facilitate its renewal. Eventually, the Melanesian cultural fabric started to mend. Population decline stopped around 1910, and emerging compacts of alliance gave meaning to the Europeans' arrival on the island scene, laying the foundation of a new cultural resistance.

14 John Frum People

High waves are breaking
They rejoice the heart of Tanna's peoples
Every Saturday there is a great action
Mwatiktiki and Karapanemum
Call for America. They say
Ah Weh . . . We are here, in the middle of the sea

JOHN FRUM song, Imanaka

The advance of this movement remains our major concern and worry: it calls for great and thorough vigilance.

Letter from French District Agent Jocteur,
25 September 1947

For the John Frum people,[1] the story began, or rather began anew, at Green Point, in the southern part of the island.

John Frum's First Appearance

In Tanna, all stories start with rumors and end as myths. At the end of 1940, James Nicol, who was Tanna's British district agent and sole representative of the Condominium government, heard about unusual events that had been taking place at Green Point over the preceding two years. A stranger would appear in the evening on the Lematekerek dancing place, on the slopes of Mt Tukosmera, at the time when men, their minds clouded by kava, hardly make the distinction between reality and illusion. Silently, he would walk across the dancing grounds. His skin was relatively fair, like that of a half-caste. He wore a jacket with shiny buttons and a European hat, and he leaned on a glowing stick.

A hut was built for him; the stranger would usually go there in the evening to "heal" the sick by means of a syringe; he would give shots without ever showing himself. A crippled woman was healed and the people started to believe that Karapanemum, Tanna's black god and Mt Tukosmera's resident, had returned to the society of men. The news was carefully hidden from the whites, who did not suspect anything. This was made easier by the fact that Green Point was isolated and that islandwide communications were generally difficult, only allowing for person-to-person contact, which could be carried out in a discriminate way.[2]

The stranger never spoke. Shortly after the miraculous healing, and once all had come from around the island to see him, he suddenly stopped appearing. Green Point was quiet again, but the wild rumor spread everywhere else in Tanna: Karapanemum had returned among men, he whom all missionaries had labeled as their personal enemy and the incarnation of the devil. And all the newly converted Christians, probably harboring both fear and a secret hope, now looked toward Green Point. The first silent appearance of "Karapanemum" took place in late 1938 or in 1939; the exact date is unknown. Some time later, after the rumor had circulated around most of the island, the stranger appeared once again. He gave out his name, John Frum, and invited Tanna's big men to come and hear him.

Still wearing the same jacket with shiny buttons, John Frum only spoke at night, at a distance from his listeners, in a magical halo that blurred his facial features. Whether the figure was real or not was no longer an issue. What fascinated the men of Tanna was the discourse they were hearing. In their own language, John Frum was announcing great events and the concurrent departure of the whites. Then, he said, a new world would emerge; Tanna would be reunited with Erromango and Anatom, the island terrain would become flat, the elderly would be young again, and garden work would cease. The Tannese had to ready themselves for this advent, or parousia.[3] For it to occur, four conditions had to be fulfilled. The Islanders had to chase the whites out of Tanna, send people from other islands back home, cast European currency into the sea, and reinstate traditional customs, in particular night dancing and kava drinking (O'Reilly 1949, 195).

As for the name John Frum itself, John referred to John the Baptist, the forerunner who had heralded the news of the coming of Christ to Jews, and Frum stemmed from the English word *broom,* the image of a broom being used in the Tannese language to designate the act of cleansing. In other words, John Frum was going to purify the island and prepare it for a parousia, a millennium that would establish a new society. "John's" actual discourse was probably less organized and more obscure, mixing up prophecies and visions with practical and moral advice. But the central argument was there: the return to *kastom* meant the rejection of white society in all its aspects. Once this rejection had been accomplished, a new era would begin.

The message went around the island. At a big secret gathering at Green Point, John spoke again. Among the big men attending the meeting were Lohmai's successor, Nako, who was the Lenakel Christian chief set up by the Presbyterian mission, and Kaokare, the old Christian chief of White Sands. They all drank kava together, thereby solemnly breaking the law of the Presbyterian mission.

These events were kept secret and, for a while, outside authorities noticed nothing but an apparent agitation in the minds of the Islanders. This respite allowed for the belief in John Frum to deepen and for the doctrine to be delineated more precisely. No longer did John need to appear, everywhere in the island men would hear his words in their dreams and propagate his discourse through various themes. A new religion was being collectively organized, a religion that the people of Tanna wished to give themselves. Meanwhile, the island pagans did not get involved in a story which was not theirs; they only encouraged the Christians to drink kava again.

In November 1940, Nicol made a move. In a letter to the British Resident, he stated his intention to enquire about some strange events at Green Point. Nicol noted the name John Frum for the first time without paying much attention to it. The district agent did complain that all "chiefs" or assessors sent there to gather information for him seemed troubled or, at the very least, disconcerted upon their return.

On 16 April 1941, the movement suddenly burst out into the open. First, there was a rush on trade stores in the course of which Islanders used up their entire cash savings. Shortly thereafter, the personnel of the dozen white employers based in Tanna stopped working. In one day, over one thousand pounds sterling were spent in the stores. The most serious event occurred on 11 May, "the fateful Sunday" in the words of a Presbyterian minister (Calvert 1978, 213), when only eight Melanesians attended Presbyterian services in the breadth of the island. It was as if the Christian people of Tanna, a vast majority until then, had vanished entirely. To the ministers' despair, the men who had abandoned the churches were now walking the paths of John Frum.

Crushing the Dreams

The missionaries and the British district agent had perceived the wild April spending spree as an intolerable gesture. But the defection from churches was seen as a call to insurrection. Definitely alarmed, the Condominium initiated a policy of repression that would last sixteen years.

The white power's counterattack began on 21 June 1941, when Nicol asked for additional police in order to strike fast and hard. A few days later, he went with twenty armed policemen to Lematekerek. His enquiry on the scene of the appearances led him to put eleven persons under arrest. One of them, by the name of Manehevi, was suspected of setting up the show. The village and "John Frum's hut" were burned; the prisoners who were deemed guilty of giving the word were moved to Isangel. The name John Frum was banned and no one could utter it under penalty of imprisonment. Eventually, Manehevi confessed that he had played the role of John Frum. Nicol had him tied to a tree for twenty-four hours across from Lenakel Bay so that everyone could see he was not a supernatural being. In fact, Manehevi may have been the wrong person. All Islanders affirm that Nicol had arrested a "false John Frum," and that the genuine Frum was still in hiding in Lematekerek. Nicol was said to be the victim of a staged event, with Manehevi as scapegoat.

Researching the topic in the early 1950s, anthropologist Jean Guiart was the first to reach that conclusion (1956*b*, 164). But the real identity of the man who played John Frum is secondary. At the time, all Islanders, or nearly all, were expecting someone who would rescue them from the ascendancy of the Christian ministers.

Tanna's leaders gave £100 to the British district agent—in a spirit of submission, according to Nicol, so ashamed did they feel of their gullible acceptance of the apparitions. The leaders acknowledged their delusion; that sum of money was to compensate the British administration for expenses related to police intervention and prisoners' upkeep. But today's John Frum groups remember another version of the incident. According to them, Nicol levied a tax of £100, threatening the leaders with deportation and imprisonment if they did not gather the money. The people of Tanna paid the tax because they hoped they would no longer be pursued, but the repression intensified. Forty years later (1980s), the Islanders still recalled Nicol's broken promise and the unsettled debt. After the payment, Nicol showed no more concern for the matter, convinced he had stifled what might have otherwise turned into political rebellion. The prisoners were transferred to Vila.

The Sons of John Frum

There was a new twist to the John Frum affair a month later. At Green Point, the police had overcome an isolated, sparse population. More seriously and spectacularly, the action moved to Ipeukel, in the eastern part of the island, one of the largest Christian villages and, until then, a stronghold of the mission. The Ipeukel tradition used the John Frum myth but "redesigned" it. John had appeared on the slopes of Tukosmera—hence its filiation with Karapanemum—but he had lived hidden in Ipeukel earlier; three children, his sons, proved his presence. Thus Ipeukel was the place of origin chosen by John Frum, Green Point being just the location where he had first appeared in the public eye. Pursued by Nicol's police, John had left Tanna, but his three sons—Isakwan (Isaac the first one), Jacob, and Lastuan (the last one)—were living in Ipeukel and represented his word.

The Ipeukel movement was actually instigated by Nambas, the village's Presbyterian teacher[4] and one of the mission's most trusted pillars.

Imbued with biblical culture, Nambas knew about the white world, enough in any case not to like it. According to all witnesses, he had charisma. Nambas gave the John Frum movement a doctrine and also a more subversive and anti-European ideology than that of the Green Point–based John Frum.

Once informed about the Ipeukel movement, Nicol reacted with similar ruthlessness. This time, all those he suspected of propagating prophecies were arrested. The most influential leaders in the village—nine men including Nambas—were deported and jailed in Vila. A young man named Tom Mweles took up their message, but was seized shortly after and transferred to Vila with two of his companions.

Yet the movement was moving forward and getting stronger: restrained in one place, it would reappear somewhere else. Nicol had an array of repressive tools but had not anticipated the mechanism of propagation through dreams. To detain a prophet did not stop the prophecy: another Islander, farther on, would also "dream" and move into the field left vacant by repression. It seems that the first arrests, in particular that of Manehevi, the presumed "real John Frum" from Green Point, only facilitated the transition to the prophets' "imaginary John Frum." Since John could not have a physical presence, he manifested himself in the dreams of those who started to be called John's "ropes." These ropes connected him with the rest of humankind. They began to multiply in Ipeukel, Lenakel, and the other Christian centers. Prophecies carried a similar message about rejecting European money, rejecting the mission, and restoring *kastom,* in particular the ancient pagan practice of kava drinking. In this context, jailing "the leaders" was useless for everywhere new prophets were stepping forth. Tanna, the mystical island of visionaries, was being swept along by this irresistible tide as it joyfully rediscovered its pagan gods and its *kastom.* In his letters, Father Martin wrote that the tide was also pulling in the Catholics: "Pagan dances are very popular right now all over Tanna" (August 1941). "[People] care little about religion, their priest, their church, and the like, about as little as wanting to know if there are people on the moon. [They say]: 'We want to become pagan again and let go of the things of the whites'. Chiefs gave the order to perform pagan dances and all are quite willing to obey. Our people are just like the others!" (October 1941, in Monnier n.d.*a,* 29).

These were difficult times for Nicol. In 1941, a year of turmoil, he was fighting on two fronts: first, in White Sands, which for the most part had adopted Ipeukel's beliefs and where the villagers fervently protected John's sons, three small children who could hardly be arrested; second, in Lenakel where Nako, the Christian chief for the west coast and Lohmai's successor, had also turned to prophesying. Today, Ipeukel villagers say that Nicol threatened Nako with these words: *"Sapos yu i holem law orda blong John, mi putum iron long fire, i hot nao; OK, mi putum iron long ass blong yu, yu staon [sidaon] long em.* (If you continue to obey John's orders, I'll put an iron in the fire until it's red-hot; then I'll bring it to your ass and make you sit on it)." Nicol suspected that Nako had given the order to abandon the churches, an order that had been widely followed on the west coast. Nako was eventually deported to Vila and died in exile.

The British district agent was the only one to play an active role on behalf of the Condominium; at the time the French were still represented by a physician who was not involved in "politics." Nicol really felt he was dealing with anti-British sentiments that were all the more dangerous as the events in Tanna were taking place during World War II. The war context may explain Nicol's brutal reaction.

American Brothers

The movement was thrust in new, surprising directions by a number of factors, such as the leaders' exile to Vila, the local climate of repression, and the dramatic events simultaneously taking place at the other end of the world. Already rooted in Tannese mythology, the belief in John Frum was now becoming a true eschatology. The winds of war were getting closer to the Pacific Islands, portending the "final event" to the Tannese. At this time, the Vila exiles revealed that John Frum, who had been of indeterminate nationality until then, was in fact an American. Renewed spending in White Sands stores and the squandering of English money added to Nicol's concerns. What could the district agent do against a revolution of minds that was not attacking him directly but was developing as if he did not exist? Unless he imposed a totalitarian regime—in the modern sense of the word—and tried to subdue minds, which he was unable to do, Nicol was reduced to watching things slip from his grasp.

Prior to these events, in 1939, Nicol had carried out a census indicating 3381 Presbyterians, 656 Adventists, 72 Catholics, for a total of 4109 declared Christians (71.3 percent of the island's population); the 1659 pagans (28.7 percent) were mostly located in the southwest and on the Middle Bush plateau (Guiart 1956b, 151). By June 1941, less than a hundred Christians remained, the other Islanders being either undecided or enthusiastic advocates of John Frum. In Guiart's insightful words: "For the Presbyterian mission in particular, failure was all the more complete as the great majority of its teachers and elders vanished in the turmoil. The missionaries told a bitter tale: all the men they used to trust, to the very last one, fooled them about the real meaning of what was going on and tried to mislead them before openly choosing the other camp" (Guiart 1956b, 162–163).

Tanna's Christian kingdom collapsed in one blow, without the use of violence or any subversive plan. The new John Frum myth and the power of dreams were enough to shatter it. Nearly all Presbyterian model villages—carefully laid out around a central lawn where church, school, and bell were in proximity—became empty. More than any discourse or deliberate stand, the spatial redistribution of population that followed meant the end of the missionary era. So far as they were able, the Tannese went back to their original territories and waited for John's return.

By itself, Tanna had obtained its freedom. The colonial organization had lost its missionary foundation, and the authorities responded with a repression policy that only succeeded in making the movement more legitimate. The exiled leaders turned into martyrs. And since John Frum was communicating with them, they also became prophets. No one could stop John Frum; he was reborn with each arrest.

As of mid-1941, in a context that included the expectation of a parousia, the ineffective repression, and the dismay of both administration and religious authorities, John Frum supporters were elaborating, day after day, their American metaphor. In the midst of the war in the Pacific, the news that the US army had reached the group crystallized the millenarian aspects of the movement. The appearance of the United States of America amounted to an explicit illustration of the John Frum prophecy: John was American, his army was coming in, and the parousia announced by the prophet had just begun. In the whole island, there was renewed exultation and enthusiasm. Overwhelmed, Nicol wrote to his administration: "Vila is full of Americans. Many others will come to Tanna. The US dollar is the newly-announced currency, Americans are blacks, they are soon going to govern the islands, free all prisoners, and pay them wages. This is what is said in the island" (O'Reilly 1949, 199).

A large labor force was needed to build the military bases in Vila and Santo from which the US Marines were to attack the enemy in the Solomon Islands. Nearly all adult male Islanders volunteered to help John Frum's fellow Americans. Nicol noted in his report dated 13 August 1942: "Practically all Tannese men are ready to go. They are totally convinced that John Frum is going to come from America, so they are only too happy to help him. To argue with them serves no purpose. . . . Their stay in Vila will at least have the advantage of being a change of scene for them" (O'Reilly 1949, 200).

In a lesser known episode, island magicians went to the sacred Danket cave in the northern part of Tanna (see map 7). Within the cave, in the guise of two stones, are the heroes who rid the island of Semo-

Semo. There, the magicians performed specific rites that were meant to contribute to the success of US soldiers, in other words, John Frum's brothers. The victory of the Americans over the Japanese was also that of the Tannese.

John's Return to the Northern Part of Tanna

In October 1943, John Frum was back in Tanna. The northern part of the island—the land of "men-women" and agrarian magicians—was set ablaze; no longer subdued, it specified its own version of the myth. John Frum appeared in the dream state to Nelawiyang, a man from Itonga in the Green Hill area, who claimed he had a personal alliance with President Roosevelt and gathered nearly all northern groups behind him. He organized them into a "police" that undertook to build an airstrip on a hilltop in order to accommodate American airplanes. A few skeptical or rebellious individuals were beaten up and fled. The Green Hill corps would clean the airstrip in the daytime and, at night, dance and drink kava in John's honor.

Nicol dispatched a patrol that rapidly turned back when confronted with Nelawiyang's partisans. For the first time, the Melanesians did not let themselves be stopped without resisting and challenging the district agent's authority. Nicol urgently requested additional police from Vila. On 16 October, Nelawiyang went to Isangel on his own to discuss matters with Nicol, who used that opportunity to take him prisoner. The next day, supported by their fellows from the west coast, John Frum supporters from the north arrived in Isangel to ask for Nelawiyang's release. On 18 October, Nicol's men and the John Frum "police," armed with a few guns and clubs, faced one another. A fight was avoided thanks to the joint efforts of Nelawiyang, who restrained his troops, and Nicol, who cleverly re-established order without the use of weapons. But the district agent sent this telegraph message to Vila the following day: "I am losing my grip on the situation. Practically the whole of Tanna is siding with Loiag's (Nelawiyang's) supporters. Send one hundred men as soon as possible" (O'Reilly 1949, 201). In one of his previous letters, Nicol had estimated that Nelawiyang's "police" were 250 strong, a considerable number given the island's population of approximately six thousand at the time.

The additional police force arrived on 20 October. Two US officers came along, including a major in full dress whose task was to reveal to the Tannese that the Americans were friends of the English and that the whole John Frum story was but a fantasy. The scenario which consisted of having "genuine Americans" go to Tanna to demythify the prophet was to be repeated several times thereafter, always unsuccessfully. In the meantime, the British militia went to Green Hill and fired with machine guns over the heads of John Frum supporters. Forty-six of them were arrested and transferred by ship to Vila for sentencing, while an apparent stillness returned to the northern part of the island. The aftermath of John Frum's last apparition had been thwarted in the same brutal way as the earlier unrest.

Nelawiyang was given a two-year jail sentence; ten of his companions were condemned to one year in jail, and all others to three months. By comparison with the heavy sentences against the leaders of the Ipeukel movement—who were only accused of a misdemeanor—the verdict affecting Nelawiyang was relatively moderate. Yet the British administration, and notably Nicol, no longer seemed to believe that the movement would soon come to an end. As Nicol wrote in one of his last reports, shortly before his accidental death,[5] "Undoubtedly the John Frum movement is not the affair of one man or one small clan. It is supported and inspired by an island-wide belief" (O'Reilly 1949, 203).

The Song of the John Frum from the North

The northern John Frum people remember all these events. In particular, they vividly recall the denunciations, humiliations, and bad treatment inflicted on them at the time of their arrest. A song refers to their misfortune. Here is my translation, in free verse, of the version from Itonga in the north:

> At nightfall I went back home
> But my bed was burning hot[6]
> I do not know who made this report that denounces us
> Yet in the leaf basket which was given to me[7]
> I saw a piece of paper at the bottom on which two names
>   had been written, Jo and Jack
> Then I realized they had denounced us
> For them I sing this song.

> The order to attack us went around Tanna
> The Isula canoe must be attacked[8]
> Thunder strikes in Lamanspin Assim[9]
> Gun noise and barrel smoke are around us
> The corporal is holding his gun toward us
> He is pointing his bayonet at us
> This is the way they are treating us
> And for them I sing this song.

> We are chased on the long, winding trails
> At dusk we are locked up
> At morning dew the door is opened

> We are doused with cold water
> At nightfall we are locked up again
> And in the morning the prison is emptied
> All nations of Tanna are here[10]
> For them I sing this song.

This poem shows how northern Islanders perceived the Green Hill events. The John Frum were denounced by two Islanders and, confronted by modern weapons, could do nothing. Violence took over. The "long trails" on which the partisans were pursued is a metaphor for deportation from the island, the sentence they feared most. The door that opened in the morning and closed at nightfall was that of the crowded jail. Also, the prisoners were drenched in water so they would shiver in the coolness of the night and wake at dawn, still shivering. Yet humiliation and violence were ineffective: the men within the prison represented all the island "canoes" re-establishing their shattered unity. The song is dedicated to the memory of these men.

Administrative documents do not report the brutal acts of the police as they arrested the so-called rebels, who had no weapons. In all its refinement, the dousing that took place in the overpopulated cells twice a day was meant to crush the wills and tame the minds. The people of Green Hill remember this ruthlessness, which is mentioned in the song. When Tanna's revolt was crushed in 1980, a similar ruthlessness prevailed in the same Lenakel jail.

The contrast between the "historical" version that appears in written sources and the more concrete version of Tannese myths and songs is obvious at each stage of the repression era (1940–1956). While the historians refer to judgments and prison sentences, sometimes heavy, sometimes light, the Tannese conjure up humiliations, brutal deeds, and police violence. Rather than the prison sentences inflicted by European judges, John Frum partisans remembered the police action at the time of their arrest. One would hardly understand the movement's evolution and strength if one were to forget that, in the eyes of the John Frum, repression was never moderate but was always perceived as an injustice—worse, as an injury. Often, repression was preceded by denunciation by those Islanders who had remained faithful to the mission. Adding insult to injury, repression was carried out by policemen who were fellow Islanders. The anti-authoritarian stand that characterizes John Frum groups is rooted in their perception of these past events.

Nelawiyang (or Neloiag) never returned to Tanna. Labeled in Vila as mentally unbalanced, according to British reports, he escaped from jail and lived by himself for three years in the inland part of Efate, on a diet of wild taro and fruit. After giving himself up to the authorities, he was sent to the Noumea psychiatric facility.

Nelawiyang is vividly remembered in the northern part of Tanna; Islanders consider the Imafin dancing place to be the guardian of his message. Nelawiyang, it is said, has not returned to Tanna but neither is he buried in Vila. Having become one of John Frum's "ropes," Nelawiyang keeps traveling.

With Nicol's death in 1944, the founding phase of the John Frum movement came to a close. "Events" still happened, although they lost some of their intensity and dramatic flavor. Perceived as John Frum's great adversary, Nicol belonged to the saga of the movement: for John to be great, he had needed a great foe. Although Nicol's successors had less influence, they carried on his repressive policy with equal conviction and even more harshness, ignoring Nicol's remarks in his last reports about the ineffectiveness of his policy of violence.

The Prophet Hunt

Nicol was replaced by two district agents. For the first time, a full-fledged French district agent was to play a real political role in Tanna. *Condominium oblige,* the new British and French representatives governed the island jointly. Soon they were living a few steps from each other, above Lenakel Bay, on the Isangel hill that was now Tanna's administrative center. The two district agents immediately felt that the situation was alarming. In a letter dated 16 January 1945 to his Resident Commissioner, the British agent, Gordon White, gave his views on the matter:

> I have the honour to report that the John Frum cult is far from dead on Tanna. . . . I can see it is a growing menace at the present time and it is growing fast. With a complete change of government authority here since the death of Mr Nicol, there will very soon be a showdown and the New Authority will be tried out. I can only hope it will be able to control the situation as well as Mr Nicol did on the last occasion when we all came very near to losing our lives over it. One has to live in Tanna to realize the seriousness of the John Frum movement and I believe it is a serious thing. (BRA)

For his part, French District Agent Jocteur stated the same concerns. In his eyes, the only possible policy was force or, as he euphemistically called it, "the hunt."

> The John Frum movement is still active and if nothing is done to stop it, [the situation] could become very serious. . . . In the name of Tanna's white population, I ask for your support and emphasize our request regarding the four dangerous gang leaders[11] who are now free in Vila— they should be expelled from that town and sent very far away, where

they can no longer communicate with their people. . . . I ask you to uphold both the punishment and the expulsion. This is the only way for the natives here to actually realize that the government is the strongest. . . . I shall go on with the hunt, I have obtained new information. (Letter to French Resident Commissioner, 8 Feb 1945, FDA)

These letters reflected the fear of an uprising, a fear shared by the whites who lived on the island—mostly traders and a few civil servants. One by one, the John Frum leaders eventually returned to Tanna at the end of their sentences. None of them made any difficulty about signing a statement of loyalty toward the Condominium, yet all immediately resumed "subversive" prophesying. Accordingly, the district agents expelled the "dangerous gang leaders" once again. As Vila was deemed to be too close to Tanna, they were exiled to Malo and Lamap on the island of Malakula. But they continued sending messages through Melanesian seamen who worked on the boats plying the waters of the group.

The curious affair of the "label raiders" broke out in April 1947. The store owned by the trader Bannister, in White Sands, was stormed by several John Frum disciples who climbed over the counter and pulled off the colored labels from the canned goods for sale. They did so especially with respect to the red, blue, and yellow tags. Bannister intervened and questioned the raiders who told him that John only tolerated the colors black and white. Although nothing was stolen, the district agents, faced with an opportunity to prove themselves, decided the case was serious. The villages of Letapu and Loearfi, from which the "label raiders" originated, were encircled by the police and burned down. Fourteen individuals were arrested. The remaining population was condemned not only to build new huts along the road but also to be kept under supervision by "loyal" Christian assessors.

Yet the raid on Bannister's store represented only a ritual gesture (Guiart 1956b, 189–193). The clans from the Mt Tukosmera area were related to Karapanemum and could not use ornamental colors; they were only allowed black and white. Some White Sands visionaries extended this adornment taboo to the whole of their region on account of the original link between Karapanemum and John Frum. The colored labels on goods in European stores became the only casualties of the new prophecy. As always, Europeans in Tanna were sensitive to whatever affected their own values about money, goods, and trade stores, and overreacted.

Gordon White stated at the time that he and his colleague had the situation well in hand, but that new incidents were to be expected: "The John Frum movement is not extinct in any way, all we can do is wait for its next manifestation and deal with it even more harshly then" (Letter to British Resident Commissioner, 24 May 1947, BRA). As for Jocteur, he wrote in his report dated 11 April 1947: "We must inflict heavy sentences followed by banishment, because people fear them, especially when they face the possibility of not seeing kin or country ever again. . . . Therefore we must be strict, without pity or mercy. . . . Tannese natives respect and fear the use of force, they consider lenience as a sign of weakness and try to take advantage of it. . . . The Tannese would be up to killing all Europeans on the island if John Frum requested it of them" (FRA).

A new incident gave the district agents an opportunity to demonstrate their philosophy about law and order. In September 1947, a Christian assessor denounced Ipeukel villagers for receiving coconuts from their leaders in exile in Lamap. Not only did the nuts symbolize the banished leaders' spiritual presence, but the fact of having planted them at the center of the village represented an act of rebellion. The armed militia encircled Ipeukel at dawn. The population was gathered to unearth the subversive coconuts, which were confiscated, and the village came under threat of being burned down and displaced. Ipeukel's exiled leaders were sent to the island of Malo, farther north, where they were confined on a settler's plantation. The French district agent wanted to expel these leaders from the group.

Condominium Em I Finis

Tanna's white population had been growing steadily and by 1952 amounted to about thirty individuals, both French and British in approximately equal numbers—a change from Nicol's time when all Europeans (about ten of them) were British. The larger number of whites, either civil servants, traders, or clergymen, became associated with the harsher repression policy of the post–World War II era. Just as much as Melanesians, whites played their part in feeding the rumor mill and many among them kept pressuring the district agents to adopt a tougher stand.

In 1952, the John Frum were heard from again, on the island's west coast this time, with what could be called "the *nesei* holders' affair." The *nesei* is an odoriferous plant which Tannese dancers wear during rituals. To be understood, this affair must be placed in the extravagant context of the times. Demarbre and Bristow had replaced the previous district agents. The Frenchman and the Britisher did not get along and the Islanders relished any opportunity to exacerbate their ongoing dispute. In 1952, the rumor was that John Frum had announced his forthcoming return aboard American ships. Again, he advised his followers to spend all their money in trade stores or to get rid of it for good; he also told them to drink kava, even during the day, and to wear *nesei* leaves on their arms as a sign of anticipation. Further, a "Jack Navy" had been appearing in the visionaries' dreams. Jack Navy was the name given to the fair-headed, bearded English sailor whose image was on the packs of

Players cigarettes sold in Tanna. In people's minds, Jack Navy had one of John Frum's faces. Night dances resumed and the Islanders kept watch over the coast while a millenarian ambience developed once again in the Lenakel region.

These events were taking place as the rift between the two district agents was widening. The Frenchman was involved in infrastructure projects such as maintaining existing roads and beginning the construction of the road across the island from Lenakel to White Sands, which was then called *la route de France* 'the road of France'. With little funding and labor available to him, Demarbre set up a system of mandatory work: each assessor had to supply a given number of free laborers per district. As a result, the Frenchman became particularly unpopular. His British colleague Bristow was able to stop the practice and emerged a champion of liberalism. The visionaries from the John Frum—also known as Jack Navy—movement gave an astute interpretation of the discord. They heralded the forthcoming death of Demarbre, then hinted that Bristow was "John Frum's hidden son" or, according to some versions, the son of Noa (Noah), a biblical figure of much importance within the John Frum belief system. The assessors eagerly related these interpretations to the two district agents.

Soon the antagonistic position of the two men became a matter of public record. Demarbre favored harsh repression whereas Bristow, true to his new mythical persona, believed it was not justified. Christian assessors were eager adjuncts of the administration; most were also mouthpieces for the Presbyterian community, which was then consolidating and getting stronger. These assessors started to spread the rumor of an uprising by John Frum groups. The Middle Bush assessor said *wan samting long bifo* 'something like before' was actually in preparation, the sign for it being the wearing of *nesei* leaves. Demarbre wrote to his Resident Commissioner: "Wearing the *nesei* is now widespread on the west coast, this is signed John Frum. . . . People refuse to produce copra. Yet Mr Bristow thinks the situation is normal, nothing seems to worry him" (Letter, 25 June 1952, FDA).

Demarbre decided to act on his own and launched a new repressive cycle. Twenty-two persons were arrested and tried. Several among them were sentenced to three years' imprisonment for "dreaming" and "spreading rumors." The British district agent eventually joined in—although the tone of his letters indicates that he did so reluctantly and that he even tried to minimize the extent of the repression. Yet, in Demarbre's eyes, Tanna had been on the brink of a generalized insurrection. Apparently, the movement was stifled; John Frum partisans became silent. According to one Christian assessor, the movement of *nesei* wearers, called "Union," heralded the end of the Condominium—*Condominium em i finis*—as well as the flight of the whites, Demarbre's death, and the disclosure of Bristow's true identity as Noa's son. This affair was the last one to bring about a repressive action on the part of the administration, at least on such a large scale.

At this juncture in Tanna's history, the number of John Frum partisans who had been arrested between 1941 and 1952 reached 126—nearly one jailed or deported individual per fifty inhabitants.

The John Frum Movement Acknowledged

The joint administration began to wonder about the effectiveness of its repression policy, all the more as it could hardly extend banishment sentences once they had expired. According to the new French Resident Commissioner in Vila, Pierre Anthonioz, a liberal policy was now called for. In the words of the anthropologist Jean Guiart, the "repressions that followed one another after 1940 had been implemented haphazardly and without overall vision" (1956b, 220). Not only had the repression policy failed to solve the issues, it had actually multiplied and exacerbated them. British Administrator G. Barrow emphasized another aspect of the John Frum movement: "The core message of this movement is: Tanna belongs to the Tannese and must be freed from all foreign control" (1951). The Presbyterian mission had already changed its approach to acknowledge the validity of *kastom*'s values, accepting in particular the right of Christians to drink kava.

A postwar colonial power lacking confidence, a Christian ministry suddenly condoning customary values, the action of a few men willing to help turn the page: all these factors contributed to the return of the individuals still in exile and the official ending of the repression era. The autonomy of the "seditious" cult was fully acknowledged when the last prisoner, Nakomaha, went back to Ipeukel in 1957. After sixteen years of repression, John Frum was no longer a forbidden name. Yet Tanna was to live through an ultimate crisis.

On 15 February 1957, forty-five days after Nakomaha's return, red flags[12] were raised on the Ipeukel dancing grounds. The entire John Frum island community was present: about two thousand people were waiting for John's return. Shortly after, the two resident commissioners went to Sulphur Bay where the red flags were handed to them without difficulty.

A few months later, in May 1957, an American warship, USS *Yankee,* called at Tanna. At the Resident Commissioners' request, the commander in full uniform spoke to John Frum partisans in Ipeukel, letting them know officially that no one in America knew a John Frum. Ipeukel residents concluded that these Americans were false Americans, or else unimportant men who did not have access to great secrets. The administrative power intended the gesture to be a subtle one but it actually had opposite effects. On 17 July of the same year, a "Tanna Army" headed by "General" Nakomaha suddenly came out of the bush where, in total seclusion, it had been in training for three months. Their faces painted with ritual colors, wearing a white T-shirt on which the letters T-A USA (Tanna Army USA) had been painted in red, and holding "guns" made of bamboo with sharp red-painted tips, several hundred young men marched in step, then walked on toward Isangel. Emotion ran high among Tanna's Christians and also among the whites, who believed they were back in the island's days of turmoil. But Tanna's army only wanted to meet John Frum. Once in Lenakel, it disbanded without incident or violence.

In line with their new policy, the two district agents successfully negotiated the return of the bamboo guns, the only weapons ever owned by John Frum partisans up to that time. About the military display by the Tanna Army, French District Agent Duc-Defayard was to write in his report: "Despite the attempt to conceal it, the sedition was obvious, yet belligerence was absent" (report on John Frum movement, 1959, FDA). The administration's new goal was to let the situation "rot."

Building a John Frum Order

Nearly ten years after the "fateful Sunday," a new census delineated Tanna's religious situation as of 1950. Out of 6650 individuals stating their religious preference, there were 973 Presbyterians, 675 Catholics, 331 Seventh Day Adventists, 2571 customary pagans, and 2109 so-called neo-pagans, in other words, John Frum people (Barrow 1951). Although they made up substantial groups in Lenakel and White Sands, the Presbyterians (14.6 percent) were still largely below their prewar numbers. The self-declared John Frum supporters represented 31.7 percent of the total. Traditional pagans, who had stayed on the sideline during the decade and had enjoyed the sight of Tanna Law enemies fighting among themselves, represented 38.6 percent. The 675 Catholics (slightly over 10 percent of the total) were John Frum partisans in disguise; their Catholic label had helped them escape the district agents' repression policy. When the era of violence came to an end in 1957, most of them let go of their religious façade and stopped going to church, especially in Ipai, Loanatom, and White Sands (Lownow). One may therefore estimate that John Frum disciples represented more than 40 percent of the island population in 1950. Neither the repression nor the false news about John's return could counteract the thrust of the movement: in 1957, nineteen years after the first apparitions at Green Point, the John Frum "road" was still thriving. Former British District Agent Alexander Rentoul, who had replaced Nicol while he was on leave, deemed it a sort of spontaneous "political" rebellion primarily directed against an alienating missionary power.

> I believe that this movement . . . was first prompted by the dissatisfaction with the Mission, and that it had no connection with Communism or other outside influence. The Tannese, in my opinion, are not the sort of weak minded natives, likely to be influenced by such teachings, and are quite capable of starting a movement of their own. . . . [T]he object of [the John Broom ("John Frum") movement] was to sweep (or "broom") the white people off the island of Tanna: Tanna for the Tannese was their slogan. (Rentoul 1949)

The administration did acknowledge the movement, while expecting it to "self-destruct," in the words of French District Agent Duc-Defayard. His British colleague suggested a new policy: "What the Tannese need is the implementation of a social, political, and economic order in which they can participate and from which they can expect to benefit" (Barrow 1951). In the concluding part of an article published earlier, Father O'Reilly had expressed the same opinion: "The best response is education, along with political and economic development" (1949, 208). The "seditious" John Frum movement, hitherto a clandestine presence, had to confront not only the administration's sudden open-mindedness, but also the risk of legitimacy.

The long exile of Ipeukel leaders, the symbolic role played by Ipeukel itself, its position in the new cosmology, all these factors pointed to the village on Sulphur Bay, which became vested with the title of capital of the John Frum movement. The major rituals of alliance, such as the *nekowiar,* had originated in Ipeukel, a place of great meaning to island magicians. Devoid of political power within *kastom,* Ipeukel did not belong to any of the two warlike phratries, Koyometa or Numurkuen, and, as the heart of peace, was not allowed to participate in the wars they waged: through the *nekowiar,* its traditional role consisted in reuniting what wars had set apart. After becoming a Christian stronghold at the beginning of the century, Ipeukel had forgone all *kastom* practices. Kava drinking had resumed, but very few magical practices had survived, and generally the villagers did not know much about *kastom,* with which they wanted to re-acquaint themselves. The former Presbyterian teacher Nambas, a thinker and strategist for the movement who lived in Ipeukel, copied the two models he knew, the Presbyterian Church and the US army, organizing the movement along the lines of the church model, while the religious ritual emulated the US military parade. In this unusual assemblage, the flag was an object of worship, and the Tanna Army's parade the high point of a religious ritual.

Nambas named some "missionaries" to spread the new faith and especially several *boss blong John* who became the movement's political representatives in each canoe. The organization of the new John Frum community patterned itself after the traditional "path of alliance." The John Frum road begins on the east coast, at the founding place of Ipeukel, crosses the southern part of Middle Bush, and branches off to several places on the west coast, notably Imanaka and Loanatom. Each node of the itinerary is a "door" (*get* in Bislama) where a *boss* holds the authority. There are twenty-six of these *boss*es. Accordingly the John Frum network is a cluster of interdependent nodes linked together by the path of alliance.

Thanks to this organization, all John Frum groups are connected with each other even though their respective villages are spread throughout Tanna. The Tannese say that, like the sun, the roads on their island begin in the east, end in the west, and then plunge into the sea. In this respect, the John Frum road is no exception to the design of customary alliance networks: it originates in Ipeukel, ends toward White Grass, and disappears into the ocean. But it goes farther than all others, for it reaches the dream country—America.

The John Frum Ritual

At first the religious ritual consisted of morning and evening collective prayers; flowers were offered at the red crosses newly erected at the center of the villages. However, daily prayers soon became a thing of the past and, likewise, visionaries replaced the early John Frum "missionaries." Other symbolic elements endured, in particular the red cross emblem and the flag ritual. The red cross is deliberately based on the Christian symbol in order to convey the message that John Frum disciples are not true pagans but are on the side of the *skul* or, better, that they have a *skul,* a church of their own. The red color represents blood; it was selected by reason of its universality. A complementary explanation was given to me in Lownow (White Sands): Nambas chose the cross for political reasons, thinking that this Christian symbol would protect John Frum supporters from renewed repression on the part of their Christian "brothers."

The US flag refers to the mythical and fraternal America that is John's country, and in this respect a great day for the entire John Frum community is the anniversary of the day the flag was raised for the first time, marking the end of the repression era (15 February 1957). On that day, an impressive ceremony takes place in Ipeukel, a ceremony which in terms of magnitude and symbolism matches *kastom*'s *nekowiar.* Groups follow a similar procedure as they make up companies of dancers and singers and arrive by their own traditional roads. At dawn comes the parade. Several hundred young men with bamboo guns dyed red, the letters USA painted on their chests, march on while a "major" gives the beat. This drill at the foot of the flagpole represents an essential moment for the John Frum; it is their *toka,* their bamboo guns are the sticks with beak-like ends of the famous dance, while the US flag raised on the day of the festival represents their supreme emblem, in other words, their *kweriya* (see chapter 10). In the afternoon, there is a continuous show of customary and "modern" dances, as well as numerous mimed skits. Then, as in the great customary rituals, Ipeukel villagers give away cooked food *(hot kakai)* to all their allies who have come to dance and parade in honor of the American flag.

The Fridays of the John Frum People

Having lost the taste and remembrance of the traditional *nekowiar,* the John Frum of Ipeukel have created a new *nekowiar* to honor the American flag. This event is a sort of apotheosis that only takes place once a year. More common are the weekly celebrations in Ipeukel. Friday is a holiday for John Frum disciples who, by contrast, work with ostentation on Saturday, the day of the Adventists, or on Sunday, the Presbyterians' and the Catholics' day of rest. On Friday evenings, the entire community is invited to Ipeukel to sing and dance in John's honor, and accordingly each of the twenty-six "doors" on John's path tries to send a company of singers. The John Frum converge from the whole island, walking for a full day in some cases. They meet their leaders, "the ropes of John," where they always sit—under the Ipeukel banyan tree.

The ritual is an immutable one. Under a kiosk built of plant material, the "companies" follow one another in succession throughout the night, interpreting the songs they have created. Boys and men, seated in the middle, sing and accompany themselves with a guitar or banjo. One of them may use a small drum for further rhythmic effect. Seated around in a circle are the young women and girls of the singing group, often with babies in their arms. With their high-pitched voices, they constitute a second choir. Singing along and dancing in the open along the sides of the music kiosk, in an increasingly more relaxed ambience, is the public—which sometimes numbers several hundred people. The men move back and forth on their feet, singing the choruses together, clapping their hands, and punctuating their movements with numerous whistle blows that pierce the night. A compact group of women dances on each side of the kiosk. Like undulating bronze columns, animated with shouting and laughing, they move rhythmically with the singers—advancing into the light of the kerosene lamps that shine on the building, then back to nocturnal darkness. Their faces are painted and they wear a *gras sket,* a multicolored pandanus fiber skirt that goes down to their ankles and elongates their figure. At the foot of the Yasur volcano, which rumbles periodically, this nocturnal show is not lacking in beauty.

Like the *napen-napen* night dances that open the *nekowiar* cycle, the pulse of the dancing and singing crescendoes until morning: the last chants are sung in a spirited way and repeated by all just as the first light of dawn appears. Exhausted, singers and dancers give out a final burst of energy before suddenly stopping at daybreak. Looking for sleep, some participants disperse under the tree canopy. The most courageous immediately start on their way back, to the other end of the island in some cases.

The creation of John Frum songs is an ongoing process, and the community has its own poets, many of whom are also knowledgeable about the magic related to enchanted places, springs, and trees. The magnitude and duration of their poetic success vary; some songs are "classics" that all disciples know and sing together. With the same suggestive and poetic tone as traditional chants, the songs represent the movement's oral tradition and celebrate its saga. They can commemorate a noteworthy event —a political issue that has affected the John Frum people, or a leader's journey—or conjure up a basic element of the John Frum cosmology such as John's return, America, Karapanemum, Mwatiktiki, *kastom,* and the like. Some chants are choruses made to be endlessly repeated, others are verses that are sung. An example of the latter is the northern song mentioned earlier, with its traditional structure and modern theme—Nicol's repression.

To reach young people, the movement leaders have not hesitated to adopt a contemporary item such as the "string band," a modern type of band with guitars that is widespread in Vanuatu today. The Friday festivals are a cultural success, facilitating as they do the creation of an entire John Frum folklore and body of poetry. They focus on dance but are also a social event; some disciples have only this opportunity to meet and interact. News or rumors circulate, various tactics are organized, and if need be a command is initiated. Seated on the roots of the central banyan tree, the leaders of the movement, the elders in particular, talk, while young people sing and dance unconstrained through the night and are free to intermingle. Sexual or romantic affairs often begin during these weekly gatherings, a feature common to most night festivals within *kastom.*

In the years that followed 1957, close to one thousand people used to sing and dance in the name of John Frum every Friday night. The size of the group decreased thereafter, stabilizing at the end of the 1970s at between two and three hundred people on average, in addition to the

Ipeukel population. For John Frum groups located far from Sulphur Bay, in particular those of the White Grass and Lenakel region, the walk takes a full day. Taxi service is available yet expensive, even when an entire group shares the cost. In most cases, the travelers who begin their journey to Ipeukel on Friday morning only return home on Saturday evening. When repeated every week, the trek to the central part of the east coast represents a great loss of time and energy. In his White Grass village, Kooman once told me: "All my life, I have walked on John's trails, my hair has turned white on the Ipeukel road."

For this reason, John Frum partisans from the west coast eventually decided to set up a center of their own. In the late 1970s, one to two hundred people would meet in Imanaka to dance on Saturday evenings. Imanaka has its own foundation myth, as mentioned earlier, and has tried to play a role similar to Ipeukel. In February 1979, after Ipeukel unfurled its flag, Imanaka also flew the US flag and organized a drill that was nearly identical to the Ipeukel ceremony. [13]

The John Frum movement has built a cohesive and structured community which, as of 1980, included three thousand to thirty-five hundred persons. The disciples belong to various groups that are rarely neighbors; instead, they are staggered along the traditional path of alliance crossing the entire island, from Ipeukel to White Grass. This figure correlates with the number of people who attended the annual flag-raising ceremony at the mid-February festival in the years 1978, 1979, and 1980.

Against all odds, the movement has essentially succeeded in keeping its unity, for two reasons: first, the charisma of its leaders whom the repression policy of the Condominium turned into living symbols and, second, the resourcefulness of a man like Nambas, the ex-Presbyterian teacher, whom all official reports described in his day as a very dangerous individual. What was once a conglomeration of scattered, helpless groups evolving into a cultural void and oriented neither to Christianity nor to *kastom*, Nambas shaped into a genuine community. In the process, this community created its own *kastom*, using syncretic rituals that were half-modern and half-traditional. Many Islanders had had a vision; as the vision became a reality, it heralded a surprising and unexpected future.

Not only did the issues raised by Tanna Law and the *Shipimanwawa* need to be settled but also the clans of agrarian magicians *(naotupunus)* were eager to obtain the political powers to which they had been denied access by reason of their symbolic female status. The creation of John Frum represented a means to that end. In this respect the John Frum movement has strongly emphasized the revival of magic, which, as noted earlier, was the traditional domain of *naotupunus* clans.

15 *The Bible Revisited*

> Mythology consists of preserving the concept of eternity in
> the category of time and space.
>
> KIERKEGAARD

Much has been alleged about the John Frum's thought processes. Some
of their adversaries in Tanna have described the John Frum as not only
illiterate and credulous, but also fundamentally illogical. Shrouded in
mystery and traumatized by sixteen years of repression, they did keep
silent, which served their opponents well. The John Frum feared violence
and ridicule. They never revealed or explained anything to the whites or
the Christians on the island, exposing themselves all the more to rumors
and cursory judgments.

John Frum supporters agreed to speak openly about their beliefs in
1978, when they were finally granted the right to fly their flag. This new
right signaled that times of injustice were over and that their real identity
was officially acknowledged. Instead of a fragmented, disjointed discourse, the John Frum were able to reveal a full-fledged original belief
system. The "cargo cult" aspect of the system is superficial, as I indicate
later.

The John Frum Origin Myth

The John Frum do not reject today's world as such. Neither does
their millenarian-style approach imply that they are severing their ties
with their pagan past. Their purpose is to restore *kastom* as the best path
leading to the new and perfect world promised by John Frum. The message is syncretic; it is both "modern" and "traditional." Although the
John Frum approach can have an unsettling effect on Western minds,
used to thinking in more exclusive terms, it is consistent within its own
frame of reference.

The system of thought held by John Frum believers rests on a number of vivid metaphors which, in their own way, nourish this thought,

241

replenish it, and continuously lead it toward new developments. Like all great Melanesian myths in Tanna, the John Frum founding myth today is splintered into numerous local versions and episodes. Here is the version given to me by one leader whom Nicol sent to jail in 1947 for a "dreaming" misdemeanor. During a *nekowiar* event in Ipeuruk near Lake Siwi, a Middle Bush pagan introduced me to him with the following comment: "This one will tell you about John Frum, because he used to know him." The man agreed to relate the myth if I would visit him at his home in Lownow a little later, adding: "We were silent before, but now John's flag is flying in Ipeukel and we have decided to reveal that which was hidden." Groups making up the "Ipeukel path" use this particular version of the myth as their compact of alliance.[1]

Wuhngin created Tanna, the stones, and the plants. From the plants emerged the first men, who were Karapanemum, Kalpapen, and Noa;[2] they were black. Noa had three sons: the eldest, Ham, was black, the second, James, white, and the third, Set, a half-caste. Noa's three sons had many children. At that time Tanna contained the animals of creation mentioned in the Bible: elephants, lions, zebras, cows, and so forth. Karapanemum and Kalpapen lived together on top of Mt Tukosmera while Noa lived on the Yenkahi mountain above Ipeukel (Sulphur Bay), near the Embuitoka dancing place.[3]

   The island became densely populated. Karapanemum and Kalpapen called Noa one evening and all drank kava in Eneihai at the summit of Mt Tukosmera. They advised him to build a big boat and to leave the island with its overly large population and its animals. Noa began to build his boat in one of the Yenkahi mountain creeks. Many laughed at him then, especially those from Middle Bush. When the boat was ready, Noa called it the *Ark* and informed Kalpapen and Karapanemum.

   A flood hit Tanna, the animals and people who had boarded the boat were saved, those who had not done so perished. Kalpapen boarded the boat which then set sail on the sea, steered by Noa. Staying by himself on the submerged island, Karapanemum took refuge in an underground cave, keeping Tanna's stones and plants with him. First, the boat went in the direction of Port Resolution. However, the bay was closed off because magicians had raised a mountain so as to protect the roads of sacred turtles from the flood. Ham's sons were steering the boat; but when they saw in the distance that the flood had receded, most black men dived and went back to Tanna. Set's sons replaced them at the helm. The first island where they landed was Samoa, and Kalpapen told Noa to leave a man there. A half-caste stepped ashore. This happened in all the

islands of the world, those of Polynesia and those of Africa. To each
Noa gave a name, leaving a half-caste and some animals on it.

The sons of James were now at the helm. After landing in many
places, they arrived in France; Kalpapen ordered the large animals
such as elephants and lions to be moved ashore along with them, but
there was none left. Kalpapen retorted: "Well, we shall call this place
'it is finished'." The capital of France has been called Paris ever
since.[4] Eventually the boat reached its ultimate destination, Big
Land, the last country in the world. Noa had the remaining animals
step ashore: horses, cows, and bulls. All were good animals. The
last men still on board, a few white sons of James and the last black
sons of Ham, landed together.[5] Noa also disembarked and threw
down the hammer with which he had built the boat: he called this
big country *Hammer Iken* 'the Country of the Hammer' or 'the
Country of Americans'.[6]

Kalpapen gave Noa, who was staying in that country, a book and
a pen, entrusting him with the mission of gaining wisdom *(casem
wise)*, in other words, knowledge. Then Kalpapen moved on.

Still later, the whites returned to Tanna. Although they held the
fruits of knowledge that Noa had given them, they kept these for
themselves. Missionaries also came and built churches and schools;
they pretended to teach the truth to the men of Tanna, but everything they were saying, the men of Tanna already knew. The Tannese went to church anyway because big men had told them: "Let us
take what the whites are giving us. Our time has not come."

Finally John Frum, Noa's son, arrived. He is American, but he
carries Karapanemum's blood. He said this to the people of Tanna:

"Whites have the power of Knowledge. Blacks have the power of
Life. Knowledge without Life is nothing. Whites possess the book
and the pen, you possess the stones and the plants. The pen and the
book help make airplanes and submarines. But the stones and the
plants help foods to multiply, pigs to grow well and return when
they get lost, they help the sun to rise, they help rain-carrying clouds
to reach the island and fill the springs and the creeks, they help the
thunder to rumble, the tide to go up and down, the turtles to get to
the island. . . . Whites have the book of Knowledge, they believe
they are knowledgeable, yet they know nothing. Your power comes
from the stones, from your medicine and plants, from your water,
from kava. For everything that lives, there are stones and plants.
These powers are yours. The stones and the plants are the stick on
which humankind leans to walk; if you do not use it, life will disappear from Tanna and also from the rest of the world. Blacks will die,
so will whites."

Noa spoke thus through his son John. John Frum did not speak against whites, he said that blacks and whites are brothers, since all originate from Wuhngin. Some of the Islanders thought they had to leave the schools and church of the whites and toss their money into the sea, but they misunderstood the message. John Frum only said that the teachings of *kastom* should be followed again. Missionaries are against John, but John has never been against them. Missionaries have always hated stones and plants, they have already thrown many into the sea, and they are searching for still-hidden stones and plants to do likewise.

The Tannese now hold three types of magical power: the stones and plants of food magic, those of weather-related magic and natural phenomena, and those of illness and healing. Such stones and plants are important, but there are others, which hold the final powers. These ultimate stones and plants will come out of Mt Tukosmera only when Karapanemum, who keeps them, leaves the mountain that has been his hiding place from the origin. John Frum can make Karapanemum leave the hidden world, because he is the only one who owns the key to this last road.

Everything will then return to its original state. Men will lose their old skin and will again live forever. America, the last and largest country in the world, will be connected with Tanna. The road joining them will be open and the sons of Ham, James, and Set will finally meet. Neither the Condominium administration, nor the missionaries, nor those who, today, belong to political parties have understood this vision; they are not aware of the reasons why the Tannese are waiting for John Frum to return, and consequently they have obstructed—and still obstruct—John's road.

Tannese Paradise Lost

The myth has several variations. In Imanaka, for instance, it is said that Noa was not black but white. Also, some details differ with respect to the circumstances surrounding the *Ark*'s departure and voyage to America. In some versions, the whites are blacks who lost their original color: they were churned by waves over white coral stones when they swam after the flood. The myth corroborates the fundamental position of Ipeukel and its Embuitoka dancing place within the John Frum cosmogony. Nambas's stroke of genius was to turn a universal biblical hero, Noah, into a local hero, thereby making Embuitoka the founding place of the world.

Likewise, Nambas reversed the identity of the major characters and geographical places mentioned in the Bible. The Garden of Eden that existed before original sin was not a mythological place which missionaries were unable to locate on a map. Full of intellectual arrogance, missionaries ignored what the Tannese had known for a long time. "Paradise lost" was nothing but the society of *kastom,* the *nepro,* or society of origin; its kingdom was Tanna, the mystical cornerstone of the world, whence the ark, the fabled canoe of John Frum partisans, set sail.

In the same vein, the warring phratries of the Koyometa and the Numurkuen transcribed the story of Cain and Abel. Abel's murder was akin to Kasiken's and in more general terms represented the ending of the peaceful *nepro* society. Since then, men have gone mad and their story has been one of intense misfortune.

Accordingly, it is easier to understand what is meant by the following words, which John Frum partisans often repeat: "Everything the missionaries spoke about, we already knew." In their eyes, the Bible is a story that occurred in Tanna. As for European missionaries, their lack of awareness made them take part in a large-scale quid pro quo: they thought they were unveiling the mystery of the world to Islanders who were in fact directly associated with the origin of that world.

The John Frum and the pagans share the same longing for their sacred roots, which they situate in the space and time of the original society, the *nepro.* Yet, like the Christians, the John Frum expect a messiah who will put an end to the human age through a second, and final, advent. In other words, John Frum mythology makes Christianity "pagan" by merging it with island lore, and it also has a Christian message, thereby giving *kastom* a meaning that is both messianic and universal.[7] Ipeukel proponents of the John Frum belief system have elaborated a syncretic approach that blends the two aspects harmoniously; they have attempted to include both terms simultaneously and reconcile what they believe are the best and most compatible features.

Other Versions of the Myth

By contrast, John Frum groups from the southern and northern parts of Tanna have generated more radical versions. The south, for example, condemns Ipeukel for "stealing" John Frum and keeps faithful to the tradition of the first appearance at Green Point. In this case, John, as Karapanemum's son, heralds a strict return to *kastom* and the ideal *nepro* society. Inputs from Christianity are kept to a minimum: the millenarian spirit is here, but the associated set of beliefs has been left out. The groups near Mt Tukosmera consider Karapanemum their mythical ancestor, and their rivalry with Ipeukel is compounded by the issue of the movement's leadership.

One of the most astonishing derivatives has been elaborated by some very small, relatively isolated groups living on the slopes of Mt Tukosmera. According to their version, John—Karapanemum in fact—left the island on an American ship at the end of the war in the Pacific, shortly after Nicol initiated his repression policy. The Queen of England was looking for a husband at the time. She invited the world's big men to come and visit her with a view to choosing the most eligible. Karapane-mum, also known as John Frum, introduced himself, emerged victorious from all trials, and conquered the hand and heart of the Queen. Philip, Duke of Edinburgh, is actually a man from Tanna pretending to be a white man; he is waiting to go back to his island to re-establish his true identity. His real family lives on the slopes of Mt Tukosmera.

In Tanna nothing is ever truly out of the ordinary. Besides, our British friends seem to be able to trigger such transfers of identity onto themselves. In 1952, for example, District Agent Bristow was regarded as Noa's son. The French do not seem to get implicated in similar situations —could the needed distance be lacking? In any case, the British Residency informed Prince Philip about his mythical identity. He generously sent a signed photograph and several old-fashioned clay pipes. In September 1978, British Resident Commissioner John Champion went to Yaohanen to give away these presents to the prince's "family members," who gracefully accepted them. The Islanders took the opportunity to remind the Resident Commissioner that Britain still owed them one pig, which a former British district agent had promised them fifteen years earlier. With scrupulous attention, John Champion discharged the obligation incurred by his country. Around the time of independence, these southern John Frum partisans did not join their Ipeukel allies in supporting francophone moderate parties: their family links prevented them from adopting the latter's anglophobia.

In the northern part of the island, *kastom* John people have erected black crosses in the middle of their villages, heralding a new version of the myth. The color black symbolizes their links with traditional *kastom*. Whereas Ipeukel villagers support a *kastom* that is also a *skul,* in other words, a church whose symbol is a red cross, northerners from Imafin, Ehniu, and Lenatuan[8] maintain that John Frum is a road leading only to ancient *kastom.* Black is the skin color of the Tannese, and the black cross is made of ironwood; the hard, rot-proof ironwood tree is deeply rooted in island soil—and island past. In symbolic terms, the black cross refers to the *niko apen,* the dark canoe of ancient times. It stands in stark contrast with the new syncretic religion developed in Ipeukel.

This revival of the black canoe is surprising, for Tanna's northern groups were among the first to be converted to Christianity. By the end of the nineteenth century, Imafin (a dancing place used by the magicians from the northern part of Tanna and by the masters of circumcision rituals for the entire island) already existed as a Christian village, the result, like Ipeukel, of the clustering of pagan groups previously scattered in surrounding traditional sites. Imafin was a Christian stronghold where *kastom* and "pagan" beliefs were eradicated more deeply than in the south. Here, John Frum was neither Noa's nor Karapanemum's son: he reincarnated into Nelawiyang, that unfathomable prophet who, in 1943, gathered around him the entire population of northern Tanna and was later labeled insane by Condominium authorities. His disciples claim that he is to return to the island at the time of the final parousia.

Of all John Frum movements, the northern version is probably the most unusual. No longer is there in this case a "real" *kastom*—in the way groups in Middle Bush and the southern part of the island have implemented it—nor a "real" Christianity—in the way it is experienced in established churches. With its black crosses, the northern version tends to look like an esoteric messianic sect. The Ipeukel-based John Frum regard that offshoot with some suspicion.

The Broken Gun

A myth recorded in the northern part of Tanna (in Ehniu) illustrates the debate between paganism and Christianity, a debate which is at the heart of the John Frum creation:

Four generations ago lived an *yremera* from the Ehniu dancing place called Yapum Kassol. At that time the coast was dangerous, because from their boats the whites would capture people and take them away. These white men were called *yarimus enao neta'i,* which means "spirits from the bottom of the seas." Yapum Kassol was fishing on Loanpakel Bay when he was abducted. Under the threat of guns, some white men took him to Queensland to work on a cotton plantation. When Yapum Kassol returned, wars were still destroying Tanna and poisonings were decimating its people.

Yapum Kassol believed that missionaries should be helped because they alone could make peaceful times return. First, he converted his group and they all went to Imafin to establish the first Christian village. Then he left on a mission boat called *Satalina* to convert the rest of the island. He went to White Sands where, in Yakai, he raised the first house that sheltered a white missionary. People remember this quite well, because it was the first time they had seen a house with a roof of corrugated iron. Once the missionary had settled down, Yapum Kassol went back to Imafin where he rested for a month. Then he left for Lenakel. He chose Isini—which was unpopulated at the time—as the site for the first Christian village on the west coast. He prepared a large garden, then built a church. Pagans came and were converted [to Christianity]. Peace returned to the island.

Yapum Kassol went back home. He took a gun, broke it in two pieces, and in front of his group planted the iron barrel at the center of the Laouiapup dancing place:[9] "My road is finished, peace and unity have returned," he said. "Tanna is going to become a Christian island. This is thanks to me. So the law for us black men will now be that of the broken gun."

People went to church but, on Yapum's advice, a few men in each northern canoe kept the memory of old *kastom* in their hearts.[10] They continued to drink kava and to dance on their ancestors' dancing places at night. As Yapum Kassol got older, he became closer to these men. Because he had known the world of whites very well and had lived among them, he did not really trust them. Just before his death, he advised a complete return to *kastom*. In his eyes, the only message to retain from white men was to stop waging war.

When Yapum Kassol died, well before John Frum appeared at Green Point, the whole village of Imafin abandoned the church. The people of White Sands and Lenakel, who had not understood the situation, became furious and, with the help of the English "capman," sent Tanna Law against Imafin villagers, but to no avail.

The Tannese from the northern part of the island had accepted the church's message of unity and peace, then they had returned to *kastom*. Not only is the broken gun the sign of their evolution, but it is also the sign of John Frum: the black barrel of the gun has the same meaning as the "cross" that came later from Ipeukel.

In this myth, northern Islanders assert themselves as the earliest Christians and the last of the pagans. The first Islanders to convert to Christianity, they were even used as agents for the conversion of others. Subsequently, they were also the first to abandon the Presbyterian church. As a result, northern Islanders were affected by the backlash of Tanna Law, an order they had helped set in motion. On their own, they completed the full cycle of mental and cultural conversion which the other island communities followed later on. The myth of the broken gun also underscores Yapum Kassol's complex personality. In his old age, "the missionaries' good friend" openly revealed that he was moving to the pagans' side. Kassol had obviously been fighting the battle between Christianity and *kastom* within himself.

The Golden Age

In its sheer diversity, the forging of the John Frum myth, or rather the forging of the myth's multiple versions, rests on a common background of ancient beliefs extending far into Tanna's culture and collective unconscious. This has undoubtedly given the myth its strength and enduring power.

The "Christians" who wanted to go back to ancient ways often had but a partial knowledge of old customs. Indeed, after two generations steeped in Christianity, many among them had forgotten tradition. The world of *kastom* was, and is, split into several localized fragments, each fragment claiming itself as the point of origin of a more or less essential part of *kastom*'s powers. Therefore any attempt to reinstate a unified, authentic *kastom* soon appeared a near-impossible challenge. *Kastom* also became a myth, which, giving meaning to the world by virtue of the image and the feeling it evoked, was a vision more than an explanation or a theory of the world.

All Islanders of the John Frum persuasion believe that when history ends, the simultaneous revival of Tanna's earliest past will help re-establish the unity of the island. This return of the long-lost golden age will only take place through a miracle that will allow for current contradictions to be transcended. "America" is the miracle, as John Frum reinstates fellowship between the separated brothers from America and Tanna. To the reunited island society will correspond a reunited world society, because the end of history can only refer to its beginning. The final knot of history will have its denouement where it started, in Tanna's sacred places.

Beyond Alienation

The anti-European stand of the John Frum movement in its early days should not be construed as one of its major characteristics. This stand did not so much precede the administration's repression as it was an effect of it. According to the argument of the anthropologist Worsley (1968), the John Frum movement should have gone from "cult of passive resignation" to "secular liberation movement," yet this did not happen. After the movement was acknowledged by the authorities, it set itself up as a religious society, the main purpose of which was to keep the word of John Frum. No political gesture was intended when John's "soldiers" surged from the bush with their bamboo guns in the course of the famous 1957 Tanna Army episode. As already mentioned, the "soldiers" paid no attention to the whites; their only wish was to meet John.

When political independence became a matter of discussion in the early 1970s, the movement adopted the following position: neither for nor against independence, but for John Frum. Subsequently, the members of the movement did oppose the nationalists, but only because they saw them as a threat to their own independence. In the debate between "moderates" and "nationalists," the John Frum were less committed than their pagan allies. The John Frum criticized their allies for being too politicized; southern and northern John Frum groups even left the political sphere altogether. Yet the Ipeukel movement, under the influence of Mweles, remained faithful to its alliance with the moderate parties. The Ipeukel-based John Frum shared an anglophobia inherited from Nicol's repression and did not trust those whom they saw as the heirs to Tanna Law.

In addition, the John Frum movement was barely influenced by the various Condominium policies that came to be implemented in Tanna. These policies aimed at injecting more democracy into public life and, more successfully, improving the island economy. Producers' cooperatives were set up and new crops introduced, such as vegetables for the retail market, coffee, and pineapple. As early as 1957, the movement turned down the administration's offer to open schools on its territories. The John Frum did not expressly want greater "political democracy," "economic development," or better "education"; although they were not opposed to these Western creations, their specific aim was to remain secluded and replenish themselves from their own vision. The more generous policy of the administration was almost as ineffective as the previous approach, when the John Frum were treated as rebels.

Too often the John Frum belief system is simply seen as a cultural response to a process of political alienation: in other words, a "cargo cult" whose followers escape from political and economic domination or even oppression by a flight of their imagination. The underlying assumption is that millenarian groups in Oceania are fascinated by European civilization—at least in its material aspects—and that they embrace an ideology based on envy, frustration, and powerlessness that makes them drift into irrationality. Millenarian groups are also assumed to have no autonomy in terms of decision making and analytical thinking, and no inner substance. They are defined not in terms of who they are, but of what they are expecting, which will never come. The John Frum are therefore seen as "losers" who set themselves up to lose again. Their attitude of refusal is symbolized by the famous response *mi no wantem* 'I do not want' in Bislama: an attitude which, in the eyes of the adversaries of the movement, characterizes the John Frum coalition, dismissed as a gathering of "strong heads." This disparaging judgment turns John Frum disciples into "reactionaries" who are guilty of rejecting the modern world; it also opens the door to any and all repressions.

Such an approach also fails to recognize the movement's creative uniqueness. The essential part of the John Frum vision is not the expectation of cargo, but the freedom of choice of a society that produces its own system of images and myths to fit its process of change or, more exactly, its encounter with the external world. Rather than a cargo cult, the John Frum's millenarianism is an expression of Christianity within the time and space parameters of the island.

Nostalgia for the Great Space

Underlying the John Frum's utopia is the memory of a golden age. Their wish to return to the Great Time of the beginnings is enhanced by their vision of an enclosed, isolated world that is also a fragment of a Greater Space. A Great Time predates man's presence; likewise, a Great Space predates human settlement. The Islanders' identity is passed on from generation to generation through the places that delineate their social status and land rights. These places only exist by virtue of their own linkages, now severed, to a Greater Space.

Although the island of Tanna is a sacred creation and in that sense one of the absolute places associated with the foundation of the world, it is not the ultimate measure of that world. Today, the John Frum still wish the Great Space could be whole again. They see themselves as isolated particles in a splintered universe; they believe that the men of the *nepro* society were able to use roads that offered an infinite number of links with the rest of the world. In their eyes, the unity of the world entailed the oneness of their own island. At the time of the origins, the hundred or so canoes on Tanna made up a single canoe, and space, undivided from a "political" standpoint, was only punctuated by important places and connected by roads. These roads were unconstrained by the island's physical boundaries.

According to the traditional Tannese vision, the Great Time of the origins was experienced in a Great Space characterized by a thick web of great roads. Where these intersected, great places emerged. In essence, the Tannese "rebels," the John Frum, wanted to rediscover that Great Space, which had been the source of their forebears' magnificence and happiness at the time of the *nepro*. Along those lines, the John Frum approach bears little relation to a cargo cult established on the basis of materialistic or political principles. In the same vein, the John Frum people did not try to cut themselves off from the world at large but to set a genuine encounter with it while searching for their own roads. They aimed at rediscovering their former powers and, more profoundly, their true identity. Finally, contrary to an often-stated opinion, the John Frum, although distrustful of the island's white residents, the representatives of the administration in particular, were far from being xenophobic.

Tanna's subsequent misfortunes stemmed from its isolation: the network-based society of Tanna suffered from not being able to belong to a more encompassing and global network. Further, Tannese society revolted against "white power" because the colonial system was dominating and acted as a shield between the island society and the rest of the world. In this respect, it is interesting to compare modern and traditional visions of utopia. The modern vision often searches for the road that will make it possible to travel toward an ideal island. Inversely, Tanna's utopian vision is to find the road that will make it possible to journey out of the confining island.

A Fascination with the Old Testament

The story of Tanna and perhaps of Melanesia as a whole is, first and foremost, that of an immense disappointment with the West. When the first Europeans arrived, with their strange and colorful garments, pale faces, ever-present guns, and large boats looking like floating houses, they were seen as reincarnated forebears or else as new cultural heroes who were bringing another type of wealth. There was no colonial or religious alienation at the time, and even less a historical "defeat"; but what prevailed instantly was an attitude that reflected the early beginnings of a "millenarian" approach, in other words, the intense feeling that something was coming from beyond the earth and was meant to shatter the limits of the Islanders' world. In the eyes of the Tannese, time—their time—was reaching its point of completion, the world of gods was merging back with the world of men, and island space was moving into a larger world. A second coming was at hand.

Disenchantment soon set in, however. The white sailors were coming and going on their boats filled with goods. They knew about the road linking the island's enclosed world to the boundless and essential space beyond, but were not divulging its secret location. In order to find out, many Islanders agreed to go aboard European ships and set sail toward distant horizons. As a result, whites ceased to appear as new gods. Whites were now perceived as the inhabitants of other fragments of the Great Space, who happened to be better off in some respects (materially and technologically) and worse off in others, such as morals.

A John Frum leitmotif is that although whites are powerful, they are not good. Whites like money too much, they do not take care of their elders, and in their own country the powerful crush the poor. Yet no morality is possible among individuals without their being to some extent equal, and first of all in economic terms. In that sense, whites are seen as unethical.

Missionaries arrived next, and they asked nothing better than to disclose their secret. Tannese myths were suddenly compared with Christian myths. Never may a people have listened with so much zeal to the endless discourse of the tenacious bearded missionaries who had come from their native Europe to deliver the Gospel to "savages." Tannese millenarianism was already latent among Melanesians at the time of their very first contact with outsiders and in this context missionaries conveyed a biblical message rich in images, symbols, and tales which the Islanders rephrased to provide answers to their own questions.

For doctrine-related and didactic reasons, Presbyterian missionaries focused on the Old Testament as they wished to prepare minds for the understanding of the New Testament's more radical mysteries. In line with their own cultural viewpoint, Tanna's Melanesians paid special attention to the myths of the origins. The Islanders accepted the early phase of the biblical message and transferred it to their own mythical and geographical world. Hardly satisfactory in their eyes, however, were the denouement of this message, as reported in the New Testament, and the central role granted to European churches. The "evangelized" sifted their evangelizers' teachings and secretly worked out a local version of Christianity that matched their own view of the world and the pivotal role they thought they would play in it.

When John Frum appeared at Green Point, shattering the Presbyterian religious consensus, the Islanders' interpretation of Christianity surfaced, and a syncretic construction helped revive the traditional millenarian dream. The Bible became part of the greater book of Tanna's *kastom,* Christian myths developed into local myths, and Noah entered Tanna's traditional pantheon. The biblical flood became closely linked to myths from the island's eastern shores, according to which the sea had gushed out of the volcano and advanced upon the land. The Melanesians felt they knew more than the missionaries in many respects. In particular, their own myths remedied the lack of geographical accuracy in biblical writings.

John Frum allowed for continuity between *kastom* and Christianity. In the Islanders' eyes, John was not the one who would conclude the history of men: instead, he was taking history back to its source. As the last of the island's heroes, John Frum was returning to his black brothers separated from him by the flood. The Tannese were rediscovering their universal identity while keeping from the Bible what appeared essential to them, such as the affirmation of a forthcoming millennium centered on Tanna and the consciousness of a real world that was wider and more fraternal.

At this juncture, Jesus of Israel was replaced by John of Tanna and his name forgotten. In Christian thought, the New Testament completes the Old Testament but, in the singular John Frum-inspired transposition, the Old Testament completes *kastom* and the New Testament is left out. Thus, Tannese metaphysics leans more toward a Judeo-pagan religion of the beginnings than toward the Christianity of the Gospels. All things considered, Presbyterian missionaries were not logical vis-à-vis their own faith when they denounced the John Frum as relapsed and basically dangerous. Rather than going back to their original paganism, the John Frum were returning to the source of Christianity by putting it in the light of their own tradition; they were also building their own church.

"Fools of *Kastom*" and "Fools of God"

Against the backdrop of the Tanna Law era, some unusual white actors, the ministers of the reformed Presbyterian Church, played their parts. Using an approach based on "Calvinist fundamentalism," they placed the conflict in the Manichaean context of the fight of light against darkness, or good against evil, thereby increasing its dramatic intensity and causing the Islanders to harden their position. Because they wanted to institute not only a faith but also an evangelical society, European ministers confined the society of the island within the naked walls of an austere temple. Tanna was turned into a stage for a tragedy that still endures. To the extremist "folly" of the Christian project corresponded the extravagant "folly" of the Melanesian response; John Frum is the fruit of that story.

The missionaries introduced a form of centralized politico-religious power but were overtaken by their own creation. The new society assailed the old, which led to a fratricidal war among Melanesians. Heirs to this new "war of the canoes," the John Frum were also seen as Christian perjurers. Yet the John Frum were not so much against the ministers or the whites as against some of their fellow Islanders, whom they blamed for wanting to impose, and benefit from, a foreign order over the entire island.

The surprising outcome is that the Christians re-created *kastom* and that the pagans won—perhaps the single such case known in Oceania. Suddenly island churches were empty. The Presbyterian mission was not able to recapture lost ground until several years later, and only in part.

Today, each camp still attaches a different meaning to the island's history. A traditional rite of alliance would normally have helped to settle the issues at hand yet was ruled out at the time. As Christianity divided the island, it also posed the formidable problem of how Tannese society was to function, since traditional roads were cut off and rituals prohibited, except for those of the Presbyterian Church. Social and cultural confusion prevailed: the island was in a state of implosion. John Frum provided the means to transcend Tanna's splintered society; the primary purpose of the John Frum approach was just as much to reunite society as it was to develop a religious belief system. However, far from reuniting Tannese society, as it believed it could in its early phase, the John

Frum movement caused further division and became a new faction in the island's religious kaleidoscope.

America

To explain the permanency of the John Frum movement, one can refer to, first, a multi-layered local culture that has allowed for a millenarian vision focused on the golden age of the past and, second, a local history replete with acts of political and cultural divisiveness. Yet these factors do not tell us why the millenarian approach of the traditional golden age turned into an "American millenarianism." Many reasons may be invoked, but none can thoroughly explain the extraordinary extent to which the Tannese identified, and still identify, with their chosen allies who live beyond the seas, in America. The freewheeling imagination of visionaries cannot be reduced to a set formula, and even the most penetrating analysis would fall short of explaining it fully.

The logic of Tannese thinkers differs from that of Westerners but is just as profound. Nourished by myth, their thought processes are not irrational; the Tannese find links between signs and images, and their purpose is less to reach a deductive explanation of the world than it is to give a sharply focused and comprehensible picture of it. A picture that can impart renewed meaning to the destiny of men, make space enchanted once again, and be a source of inner emotions.

From the "dialectical clash" between Christianity and paganism has emerged not a lifeless synthesis but a new myth that finds its expression by means of images and through which John Frum partisans project their vision of the millennium onto America. Accordingly, the inner and outer journeying beyond the island will help the Tannese solve the contradictions that keep them imprisoned. As the Islanders depart on this fantastic journey, they will also return to the source, since the American metaphor is nothing but the "road."

A great ritual exchange is planned for the "day of encounter." Yet one would mistake means for ends if one were to say that the movement's only purpose is the expectation of American riches, as would be the case for an ordinary cargo cult. What takes precedence is the strongest road of alliance ever imagined. In the eyes of the John Frum, the reciprocal exchange of goods is a manifestation of the quality of this alliance, not the end goal itself. For that matter, the John Frum believe they are equal to their partners. When they receive the source of American magic—which originates in the book and the hammer—they will give away their own stones, in other words, the source of nature's magic. Technology against Nature: the trade-off is not as unequal as it appears.

The Star Metaphor

The concept of the soon-to-come merging of the worlds was expressed by a metaphorical drawing set on the ground in Lenatuan, in the northern part of Middle Bush. At the origin of this newly created village stood a visionary inspired by the Imafin-based movement of "black crosses." In February 1979, a French television crew went to Tanna to shoot a documentary film about "John Frum." Dr Bernard Fonlupt of the White Sands French hospital and I were their guides and interpreters. The John Frum of Middle Bush invited us and disclosed their "founding image" in front of the cameras.[11]

Inside a bamboo fence, on bare soil, two stars are outlined with stones laid end to end. The first star represents Tanna and the present universe. At the center is a stone symbolizing the array of current powers; roads start from this central node and end in each point of the star. All these roads are the pathways of the modern age, and those who now walk them belong to churches and political parties. Since the roads lead to an abyss, the men who follow them are bound to plunge into a void. A single road comes out of the world of the first star. It breaks through the world's boundary, moves beyond it, and joins what is separate. John's people have been following this hidden road in a long march of their own. The road leads to the second star's secret world.

Only visionaries have had glimpses of that other star. They tell little about it, only that roads are many and unobstructed, that ancestors live there, and that death and old age are unknown. At this time, the roads of the world are disjoined but they are meant to connect once again.

The impact of the star image is reinforced by the fact that the star is also the symbol for America, as the Islanders realized by looking at the planes and armored Jeeps on US military bases during World War II. When John Frum disciples raised the star-spangled banner on Ipeukel's central pole on 15 February 1978, they made it clear that it was not a foreign symbol but a symbol common to the American and Tannese nations.

America is Tanna and Tanna is America: the technological power of the newest and most powerful nation on earth is linked to the most ancient and traditional nation. Together, modernity and tradition buttress Tanna's millenarian dream. In the minds of the John Frum, this somewhat paradoxical approach is always associated with a passionate, often moving, affirmation of the beauty of Tanna's *kastom*. John Frum partisans have translated their many dreams and contradictions into an unusual strategy; in their view, modern time will come to completion in the fabled harmony of Tanna's genesis. The island's history tore society apart, but the island's space is that of Arcadia.

16 Kastom *and Nation*

As indeed we have seen nearer home, wherever history has left an electorate divided not by theories or political figures . . . the popular appeal of which may shift from time to time, but by more or less immutable differences of culture, language, education or religion, minority groups may abandon hope that the complexion of an elected majority can ever be changed or that their rights can be safeguarded. In these circumstances a conventional system of undiluted majority rule does not work. . . . This applies particularly to the islands of Santo and Tanna, where the factions are most evenly divided and where for years tension has been correspondingly high.

JOHN CHAMPION,
24 June 1980

The Impossible Unity

In the mid-1960s, Iolu Abbil, a young Tannese, was sent to London to study business management and accounting. On his return, Abbil joined the management team of the British Cooperatives Department and was called upon by the two resident commissioners to sit on the newly created Advisory Council of the New Hebrides. The council was to pave the way for a democratically elected Assembly and facilitate the political evolution of the group. Iolu Abbil belonged to the council as a representative of the southern islands. Wishing to know the opinion of the people he was representing, Abbil decided in 1968 to set up an advisory body in Tanna through which traditional power holders and church representatives would meet regularly in customary fashion.

Iolu Abbil's more ambitious long-term goal was to set up a kind of "customary parliament" that would deal with general and local issues. The original name for that organization, *yani niko* 'the voices of the canoe', illustrated the link with *kastom*. Not only would the *yani niko* emphasize projects benefiting the island as a whole, but it would focus on community development, rather than entrepreneur-led capitalistic development.

Despite this generous attempt, the *yani niko* could not overcome the island's inherent contradictions. John Frum groups mistrusted churches as much as they mistrusted the two administrations; they refused to send any representative to the new organization. Pagans followed suit upon learning that the meeting place for the *yani niko* council was on the grounds of the Lenakel Presbyterian mission. Although, in its founder's mind, the council was not meant to have specific links with the political sphere, it came to represent a crucible for the antagonisms of the past.

Iolu Abbil later became one of the National party[1] leaders, and the council he had set up to unify the island appeared to his opponents as a mere tool of his party. Eventually, the *yani niko* council was given the new name *Nikoletan* 'Canoe of the land'. The adversaries of the Presbyterian mission believed the Nikoletan represented a renewed attempt to set up a structure of central authority. In their eyes, the Nikoletan would reunite the island under the aegis of the educated elite originating from Christian anglophone groups.

In July 1975, given the Nikoletan's focus on development and local jurisprudence, its members asked that it become a local council officially recognized by Condominium authorities. British District Agent David Browning actively supported this request, to the extent of recommending that the Nikoletan be turned into a council elected by the entire island population. However, the French district agent opposed the suggestion, noting that the project was supported by only part of the Christian population. Infuriated, the British district agent sent a letter to his French counterpart: "It seems to me that in the last few months you have constantly discouraged local political initiatives and only tried to support movements which clearly tend to be influenced by colonialist and reactionary elements" (letter, 2 Aug 1975, FDA). French Resident Commissioner R. Gauger gave the following response: "In an island like Tanna, which is greatly divided, the obvious political tendency [of the Nikoletan] may bring the population to hasty conclusions. This project is too crucial for it to be finally compromised by too much haste in the matter" (letter to British Resident Commissioner, 12 Aug 1975, FRA).

Because the two authorities disagreed about local representation for the Tannese, any form of political evolution was severely constrained in this respect. As a result, the political scene became static and the two camps continued their one-upmanship, if only on their own turf. With the Nikoletan affair, the French district agent and his British counterpart came to disagree more strongly than ever before, although their mutual antagonism had found a more dramatic expression earlier, in the course of the Fornelli affair.

The Man Who Would Be King

The adventures of Antoine Fornelli, short-lived as they were, caused a psychological jolt that had immediate repercussions on Tanna's political scene. Off the island, even Noumea newspapers and the Australian press reported the story. Noumea journalists used to refer to the self-proclaimed "king of Tanna," while the Australian press recounted each new development of the Fornelli affair in a tone that was both indignant and mocking. The two residencies, French and British, attempted to play down the affair by making it look like a banal event verging on comedy—*commedia dell'arte*. Yet in the course of this affair the island's old demons were awakened, and tragedy was barely avoided.

Antoine Fornelli was originally from the island of Corsica. A decorated veteran of the French Army, he was earning a living as a gunsmith in Lyon when he bought a plantation in the northern part of Efate. He had seen it advertised for sale in *Le Chasseur Français*.[2] Shortly thereafter, he moved to the New Hebrides, where he started collecting firearms of all types and was indifferent about caring for his property. There, he extended a generous welcome to all visitors. Although he was not involved in politics as such, Fornelli seemingly caught the fever that seized local Europeans in the early 1970s, with the approach of independence. Fornelli was particularly worried about the influence of the Presbyterian Church and the anti-French stance of the new independence movement. The first Tannese he met were workers on his plantation who originated from the northern part of the island. An islander himself, Fornelli showed specific and probably genuine interest in the history and customs of Tanna. But he went further: fascinated by the millenarian attitude of his work crew, he began to imagine that a new destiny was waiting for him on that island.

In the early part of 1973, Antoine Fornelli left for Tanna. Did other people, in particular local UPNH[3] politicians, appeal to him or was he influenced by the French district agent in Tanna, who had confided to him: "Help me, I know that I am going to bed at night, but I am not sure whether I shall be awake the next morning?"[4] Fornelli did not tell anyone about his motives, yet they were undoubtedly political. His purpose was to foil the action of the National party on Tanna by means of a "*kastom* party" that would abide by the law and militate for a politically moderate agenda akin to that of the UPNH.

At the time Fornelli was about fifty years old. He had a well-adjusted and solid personality, and many found him congenial. Tanna inspired him. Fornelli traveled at first with a French friend and with his Melanesian wife, who originated from the northern part of the island. "Tony," as the Melanesians called him, and his companions journeyed directly to Imafin, in the land of the "black crosses," where Sasen, the local leader, received them. Between Tony and the Melanesians from the northern John Frum faction, the rapport was immediate. Fornelli spoke little, all the more as he could hardly use Bislama at the time, but he was a good actor and mastered the art of meaningful gestures, symbols, and finery, often inspired from the military. Every day Fornelli would go diving beyond the reef, and he always gave away a large catch of fish. The new-comer seemed to know neither fear nor fatigue and openly scoffed at the ministers and the local political leaders, who belonged to the opposing party. Sasen and the northern John Frum believed Fornelli was the champion who would facilitate their return to the political arena and thwart the Christian militants of the National party, whose increasing activity within the John Frum fief worried them.

In May 1973, a considerable number of Islanders, between six and eight hundred, gathered at Lovieru, near Lenatuan, to hear Fornelli. By no means all of them were yet convinced and many attended the meeting out of curiosity. Iolu Abbil and some National party representatives came to contradict. In a speech that was translated by one of his friends, Fornelli developed two themes: "Progress is going to come to the island (in the guise of roads, hospitals, harbors, tourists, and so forth); the big men of *kastom* are the only ones who can dictate laws to Tanna's inhabitants" (Tony Fornelli, pers comm). To implement such a policy, Fornelli announced the creation of a movement called UTA *(Union des Travailleurs Autochtones* or Union of Indigenous Workers) and distributed membership cards. The acronym was obviously chosen because of its analogy with that of the French airline company UTA. Tom Mweles, the leader of the Ipeukel-based John Frum, attended the meeting; demonstrating his visible support for Fornelli, he claimed to inspire the newcomer behind the scenes. When Fornelli's opponents asked him who would pay for all the "goodies" that UTA had promised, Mweles responded with a few brief, hardly audible sentences. All the John Frum in the audience nodded knowingly.

After the Lovieru gathering, Fornelli stated he could account for 1300 memberships on the island of Tanna. Actually, this was the number of cards that he had given away. His followers were mostly limited to the John Frum networks from the northern and north central part of the island, in other words, to a few hundred partisans. As for the pagans in Middle Bush, they stuck to a wait-and-see attitude. On the side of the National party's political leaders and the Presbyterian Church, however, there was talk of a "very serious threat." Once again the island yielded to the delights of rumor, and the slightest word or gesture on the part of the protagonists was amplified. According to some reports (all of them false), Fornelli was providing the John Frum with weapons. Also, it was said that nationalist militants were risking their lives and that ministers from the northern part of the island were threatened daily.

Fornelli went back to Vila shortly after the meeting. While he was away, the political scene did not calm down; instead, new developments occurred, including further political polarization. At a synod in Tanna in

January 1974, the Presbyterian Church declared that it favored a speedy evolution toward political independence.[5] Meanwhile, the movement launched by Fornelli was getting organized in full secrecy. The name for it was no longer UTA but *Forcona* 'Four Corner', and Tannese emissaries were shuttling back and forth between Fornelli and his partisans to ensure contact. Fornelli returned to the island in January 1974. He spent two days in Sulphur Bay with the Ipeukel-based John Frum, who sided with his cause. No longer the movement's guiding force after this visit, Fornelli was swept along by his supporters. The John Frum were now seeking to set up not a political organization connected with the Vila-based moderate parties, but a movement that would pave the way toward their own independence.

After watching with satisfaction the Forcona rise against the anglophone nationalists, the French district agent started to worry about the drift of the new movement. Fornelli himself was floating on a cloud and, far from taking fright, endorsed his partisans' cause. In Fornelli's mind, the political stakes of the New Hebrides had vanished, to be replaced by the cause of the Tannese nation, the cause of *kastom*. From that time onward, all outside observers reported that he had become insane. The Presbyterian minister in charge of the White Sands mission, Reverend Ken Calvert from New Zealand, was to write that "one simple soul called Antoine Fornelli . . . on his periodic visits to Tanna where he was lauded by the new leaderships believed that he was actually helping to liberate the people from the fearful repression of the Government and the Mission" (1978, 215). Such was indeed Fornelli's belief, but it did not necessarily imply that he had gone crazy. However, Fornelli's European friends who had been with him on previous trips deserted him at this time. As far as they were concerned, the adventure was going too far and they feared for their safety.

A critical phase was ushered in by another meeting which took place in the northern part of the island on 24 March 1974. In front of eight hundred people, Tony, dressed in white and sporting a red paratrooper's beret with a shiny metal star, raised the colors of the "Tannese nation"—blue background, yellow circle, green star—stating that "this flag is the flag of unity, peace, and *kastom*." Political leaders were named to represent the four corners of the island: north, south, west, and east. Each received a metal pin with a star in the middle. The Forcona movement was born. Mweles, who was the guide of the Ipeukel-based John Frum and the new leader for the east corner, was named *kastom*'s chief while Sasen, the north corner leader, became the flag custodian. Sasen also received a Mauser dating back to World War I; the German rifle symbolized the armed forces guarding the flag. An even greater event was sched-

uled for 22 June in Imafin. Tony would then be publicly enthroned as
"chief" and spokesman—"voice of the canoe"—for the Tannese customary nation, and independence would be "officially" proclaimed.

Groups that had a stake in the movement held unusual ceremonies.
A star was drawn on the soil of dancing places and everyone asked to
step to the center. The ones who stayed outside the star were excluding
themselves from the new nation. Among the John Frum, all "took the
plunge." Plywood signs showing two red lines over a blue background
marked out the paths and villages involved in the movement. No longer
did Islanders venture far from their villages. The spirit of war was back
in Tanna, which worried many. The Australian trader Bob Paul[6] decided
to organize a counter-meeting with the representatives of Tanna's Christian groups, following which the two district agents were petitioned;
if these could not enforce law and order, the Christians indicated they
would organize a militia to settle the affair and remove the flag of
sedition.

The Imafin Flag

Yet Fornelli was not treading over illegal terrain. He was more a
symbol than a leader of the movement, and he was secretly keeping the
gendarmerie (the French police force), based in Vila, informed. As
Fornelli saw it, his role was not to stir up a rebellion against Condominium authorities but to organize *kastom* supporters along political lines.
In his speeches, Fornelli emphasized the friendly role of France, Britain,
and Australia and even envisioned their support for the "Tannese
nation." However, the term *Tannese nation* did cause a stir.

French District Agent André Pouillet wanted to travel to the northern
part of the island but guards stood in his way at the entrance to the "new
nation's" territory. Following this incident, Condominium authorities
feared they would lose their sovereignty over the island. In May 1974,
the two authorities signed a joint decree prohibiting the wearing of uniforms, the raising of flags, and any illegal gathering. On 18 June, a squad
of the Anglo-French police journeyed to Imafin, the stronghold of Sasen
and his group. Neither Pouillet, the French district agent, nor Fornelli
was on the island; David Browning, the British district agent, led the
operation single-handedly. While the police dispersed the Forcona
guards, Browning seized the flag and the old gun—"1884 model, made in
1916." Some blows were struck with the butts of rifles, in exchange for a
few punches.

The next day Fornelli landed in Tanna, along with a free-lance
photographer, François Giner, and was told about the Imafin incident.
Fornelli reacted on 23 June. In an astounding letter addressed to both the

Queen of England and the President of the French Republic, he announced his sovereignty over Tanna and gave eight days to Condominium authorities to leave the island. All over the New Hebrides, people made jokes about this letter, even though it was never made public. The most significant excerpts follow:

To Her Majesty the Queen of England, to the President of the French Republic.

Some time ago, this people took a liking to me, especially the majority that was still attached to its culture and age-old customs. With its help, given the indifference of local authorities and with a view to offsetting the actions of the National party and the Presbyterians, actions that I considered destructive, I set up a small Nation with the chiefs from Tanna's various regions and groups. Originally the natives named the movement Forcona, to allude to the four cardinal points that divide up Tanna as a whole. In view of the extent of the movement, it was converted into a Nation.

The Assembly was submitted to a gathering of eminent Tannese and approved democratically and unanimously; the colors representing this Nation were raised and approved by all. . . .

On 18 June 1974, a handful of fanatics in French and English uniform burst into the village of Imafin, in northern Tanna, without any sort of warrant; after ill-treating Mr Sasen, the village chief, they entered his hut through violent means and seized two emblems owned by Tanna's customary Nation, namely:

a flag with the colors of the young Nation,

an old unusable gun meant to present arms to said flag and be the symbol of the force on which any nation has to lean.

This aggressive act carried out in military attire is called a strike by commando and unquestionably represents an act of belligerence.

Whether or not the young Nation of Tanna is recognized by France and England does not change the facts. . . .

After consulting with all of Tanna's eminent citizens and being given a mandate by them, I demand:

(1) The return of the two emblems to the very spot where they were stolen, inside chief Sasen's hut in Imafin.

(2) That the two district agents who are responsible for this degrading act be immediately and without delay removed from office and expelled from Tanna. In any case no longer will their safety on the island be ensured.

(3) That the new district agents appointed by the authorities undertake to maintain friendly and constructive relations with the local leaders of the young Nation.

For all of Tanna to receive satisfaction [on these matters] an eight-day notice is hereby given. The allotted time will end on Monday 1 July 1974 at 6 PM. Thereafter, if no answer has been received, armed hostilities will begin in the entire territory of Tanna against the Condominium's presence on the island. . . .

Such action will end only through the plain and clear termination of Condominium status over Tanna or through the destruction of the young Nation.

Whatever the outcome of this conflict, and so that a young Nation may affirm its right to live in conformity with its laws—which emanate from age-old customs—and its wish to take from the civilization that others want to impose over it only what it deems favorable, if this entails for the great Nations to inflict a blood bath over this Nation, so be it. In any case, there will be no reflection of glory on their flags.

> The territorial leader of the young Nation of Tanna,
> Signed: Fornelli

> (FRA, translated from the French)

The version addressed to Giscard d'Estaing, president of the French Republic, included a few words which Fornelli wrote down on a separate page: "I am responsible for my acts only before the French people to which I belong, and my sole consideration in this matter is to uphold the presence of my country in this remote corner of the Pacific, at least from a cultural standpoint."

The ultimatum was carried to the two district agents by the photographer, who then left the island. In any case, Tony was bluffing. He had no armed forces and no wish to reach that stage. However, his partisans armed themselves with bows, arrows, and spears—all of these paltry weapons, even by comparison with the limited forces of the Condominium police force. Fornelli's real purpose was to bring about the involvement of a commission of inquiry. He also wanted to plead the cause of his movement and attract international attention to the island of Tanna. Fornelli sent the few men who owned antique shotguns back to their homes in the northern part of the island.

In Vila, the affair was labeled "dramatic" and the letter by Fornelli, now considered a "lost soldier," was taken seriously. On 29 June, the two district agents, Pouillet and Browning, landed in the northern part of the island, leading a joint force of forty Melanesian policemen followed by two French *gendarmes*. After a night hike, the column captured the village of Imafin in the rear. Sasen and the "rebel's" bodyguards were ambushed at dawn and arrested. Fornelli diverted his pursuers for a while before letting himself be caught. He was not armed, no shot was fired, and the use of arrows and spears remained entirely symbolic. Forcona leaders were jailed in Isangel where they were tried by the French district agent as part of his local duties. The four Melanesian leaders of the movement who had been in charge of island "corners" were given jail sentences, all of which were later reduced to one month. Fornelli received a heavier prison sentence—eighteen months—and was sent to Vila. There, he was tried a second time. The final sentence was one year in jail with no possibility of remission, along with a five-year prohibition from entering the New Hebrides. Tony was kept in Noumea's Camp Est prison where his only political visitors were several leaders of the National party who wished to confer with him. They told the Forcona leader that they did not see him as an enemy but as a victim of the colonial system.

On Tanna, the John Frum were again living in fear. They believed that the repression they had previously experienced for sixteen years would soon resume and sweep down on them. Rumors circulated, spread especially by the Christians, according to which the John Frum people would be deported to New Caledonia or Australia. On the west coast of the island, some John Frum families were evicted from disputed lands. Meanwhile, several groups—National party followers, the faithful of the Presbyterian Church, and other anglophones—saw the defeat of the John Frum and the downfall of Fornelli as their victory.

Toward Polarization

In factual terms, the Fornelli affair was only a minor event. There was a tragic atmosphere but no actual tragedy, thanks to the restraint of several participants, Fornelli in particular. Yet the Islanders were in a state of shock. While the John Frum were traumatized by their defeat, their adversaries were now convinced of their own future supremacy. Each camp had known fear in turn during the affair, and that fear engendered a feeling of resentment. Many events that were to affect the island later were born of the split that had resurfaced. In this context, the raising of the Forcona colors came to represent a symbolic gesture of sovereignty which had numerous imitators, including Fornelli's opponents.

The affair also bolstered antagonistic positions to such an extent that the political quarrel occurring in Vila on a national scale was transposed locally in terms of civil war. National party militants were cheered by the defeat of the Forcona movement. But the John Frum were at a loss now that Tony, their hero, had disappeared from the island. The Fornelli saga had meant much to them: their long march had ended, they had begun to speak out, they had taken revenge from past humiliations—and their adversaries had trembled. After the affair, the John Frum searched for a shield that would protect them from the 1940s-style repression they now expected. The French district agent on the island immediately offered his protection. In exchange, John Frum groups from the west coast and from the north and middle north areas, which had steadfastly refused schools, accepted the French instructional system they were offered.[7] With some bitterness, Tanna's Presbyterian minister witnessed the sudden change:

> With the demise of the "Four Corner Movement," it was not long before the French Administration turned to direct intervention in order to regain the confidence of the John Frum people. . . . The new French propaganda had a compelling logic about it. If summarised, their education policy might read: "If the National Party wins, and they get independence, then you will be in trouble because the National Party is just the educated younger generation of your old enemies, the Christians. But, if you support us, then we will protect you. We will not let independence come until you are ready. But first you must send your children to school. We will make special schools for you with European teachers to help you catch up quickly. These schools will be free, whereas you have to pay to go to the British schools which are inferior. Only natives teach in them and tertiary education finishes at Pacific island universities which are below world standard. Our schools on Tanna will teach you the same as any school in France, and you can finish up in the University of Paris which is one of the best in the world." (Calvert 1978, 215–216)

Another consequence of the Forcona movement was that relations between the two district agents deteriorated, sharpening the conflict between their respective political views about Tanna. Although the Englishman and the Frenchman did collaborate when Fornelli's adventure turned illegal, they did so with an attitude of contention rather than cooperation. In the British view, the French were playing a dangerous game with a moribund *kastom* and, through deliberate sabotage of New Hebridean independence, were also jeopardizing the unity of the young state, which the British identified with the Vanua'aku Pati (VP). Browning even added that the John Frum movement would have died long ago had not the French district agent been personally supporting it and deluding it with promises. In reply, Pouillet accused his counterpart, along with Browning's entire administration, of unilaterally supporting a single political party that dominated the country and compromised its unity; further, Browning was as far as he was from complying with the rule of noninvolvement required of all civil servants. Generally, one district agent obstructed any political move initiated by the other. The same antagonism existed, in a sharper mode, at the level of the two police forces and their local leadership. Yet in his own way Pouillet had panache; he and Browning did maintain courteous, even friendly, relations for the duration of their tenure. In this respect the district agents were not imitated by their respective subordinates and fellow citizens on the island—teachers, traders, technicians, and the like, many of whom had not been on speaking terms for a long time. As a consequence, the most politically committed Islanders "found their bearings": the British against the French, the Christians against the pagans, and the John Frum against all, at least at that time. The battle lines were clearly drawn, it seemed.

The sparring between the two district agents did not go unnoticed by their superiors. Although the two residencies had to support their respective positions and clientele, they could not allow the quarrel to worsen. Keith Woodward, the far-seeing civil servant in charge of political affairs for the British Residency, noted in this respect: "It would really be a pity if the relations between the two district agents reached the point of mutual suspicion on the matter of their sectarian links with the various political groups operating in Tanna" (letter to the French Residency, 11 April 1975, FRA). In fact, both sides had gone well beyond the stage of mutual suspicion. Yet it was not so much the European district agents who controlled Melanesian groups on the island—as they accused one another of doing—as these groups themselves, which manipulated the district agents into adopting specific behaviors.

The same thing can be said about the role played by Antoine Fornelli. Fornelli was neither crazy, nor Machiavellian, nor bought off, but undoubtedly he was a megalomaniac to some extent. The man was genuine even in his political itinerary, as he drifted from the UTA movement to the Forcona nation. He followed his partisans more than they followed him. Eventually, he joined their cause completely. In his supporters' eyes, Fornelli symbolized the hero, the ally who brings together dispersed local forces and allows them to stiffen their resolve again. The former Forcona leader Willy Kuai, who had been in charge of Middle Bush, told me once: "We are believed to be Tony's partisans, it is not true, he is our partisan: by coming to Tanna, he has not come to promote himself, but to promote *kastom*." Fornelli acknowledged this and was particularly bitter toward French policymakers. While detained in Isangel he drew his own conclusions about the affair. A formal letter which he wrote to the French Resident Commissioner to explain the reasons for his action ended: "A Nation of 12,000 souls within which there is no Englishman, or Frenchman on a permanent basis, has not been able to rise politically by its own means and in peace. This Nation will always find in its path the weapons and despotism of powerful nations still encumbered with outdated colonialism. Born on 24 March 1974, the Nation of Tanna was overthrown on 29 June 1974" (FRA).

Accompanied by Tahitian friends, Fornelli returned to Tanna aboard a sailing boat in 1977, adding another chapter to the tale of his adventures. Delivering a speech in Imanaka, he stated that he wanted to bury three things under the tree of *kastom:* "the Bible, the French flag, and the English flag." After this speech he was immediately expelled from the island (W. Urben, pers comm). The story was not over: Fornelli reappeared in 1979. In 1980, he journeyed to the island of Espiritu Santo, then under a blockade, and offered his services to Jimmy Stevens. Fornelli attempted to set up a "defensive guard" in the Vanafo camp, but gave up when he realized that weapons were lacking and that no real defense was possible.

Fornelli's memory is alive in the northern and central parts of Tanna. It has been invoked by both camps in each phase of their ongoing political fight: by VP militants, who feared Fornelli would return with weapons, and by John's partisans and *kastom* supporters, who were waiting for him. Whether he was conscious of it or not, Tony joined the legends and archetypes of an island that prizes symbolic heroes and uncommon personalities.

Kastom and Politics

Tension decreased slightly after Fornelli's arrest. Each political cell set up its own network of alliance: the Presbyterians were on one side, the John Frum and customary pagans on the other, to be joined later by a few Catholic groups based in Loanatom and Imaki. New leaders emerged, whose discourse grew increasingly radical. Nationalist militants accused their adversaries of playing into the hands of "puppet" parties that were bought by foreign interests and followed the Europeans' lead. The other side questioned the authority of a political party which, controlled by Protestant missions and organized according to a model that was breaching *kastom,* wished to create a strong and centralized state that it would hold alone. Yet although voices were raised, public order was never threatened.

The French district agent and UCNH francophone leaders searched within the ranks of customary groups for potential Melanesian political leaders. It was a waste of time, however. In Tanna, the moderate movement had—and has—always been richer in charismatic leaders, visionaries, and prophets, for want of an educated elite experienced in the modern style of political debate. This tragic lack of leaders who could communicate in the name of *kastom* was the great weakness of the movement. By contrast, the National party had less militants at the outset but was able to turn out leaders at a fast pace. The National party attracted Kawenu College graduates and also some of the higher echelon Melanesian employees of the British administration and anglophone Protestant churches. Using a revolutionary, modern language that appealed to these young adults, it referred to a "Melanesian nation" and validated its cause by relating it to the struggle for emancipation of Third World peoples. *Kastom* supporters, on the other hand, felt deeply within their rights and had their own commitments; they spoke about power within the boundaries of their island but were less prepared to deal with the national and international dimensions of the political debate. While the young Tannese who belonged to moderate groups remained faithful to the *kastom*-based discourse, those with a certain level of schooling often preferred the nationalist rhetoric. Between the metaphors dealing with *Nation* and those dealing with *kastom,* the choices were not always obvious. As said in Bislama by many of the Tannese who decided to stay in the background, "*Ol i fasfas, i gat tumas tink tink*" 'Everything is mixed up, it is very confusing'.

The first elections ever held in the group took place on 10 November 1975; the members of the Representative Assembly of the New Hebrides were to be elected.[8] In his monthly report written shortly before the ballot, A. Pouillet, the French district agent, harbored few illusions. The general opinion was that the National party would win:

> At least one third of the voters will not cast their ballot: out of timidity or total lack of interest, or else because the distances to cover are too great. Out of the remaining two thirds, a majority will vote for the men of the National party who are well-known and active and who started campaigning and infiltrating the Christian communities a long time ago. The remaining voters will hesitate, casting their votes for the UCNH whose platform is rather vague and which offers no valid candidate here. (July 1975 report, FDA).

In most islands of the group, a majority of votes were indeed cast in favor of the National party. It won 59.5 percent of the national vote and obtained seventeen representatives as against ten for the moderate parties. However, Tanna was one of the few places, along with Vila and Ambae (Aoba), where the National party was defeated: out of 3941 votes cast, 2071 (52.6 percent) and 1833 (46.5 percent) were in favor of the UCNH and the National party, respectively, the balance going to an independent candidate. The Tannese elected two candidates under the moderate (UCNH) label, representing, respectively, the John Frum and the Kapiel, the latter being the new Middle Bush customary pagan party. Voters elected only one National party representative, Iolu Abbil.

Moderate partisans considered this score a victory, although it primarily indicated that the island was split into two nearly equal blocs. Yet even without real political leaders, *kastom* and John Frum supporters had succeeded in commanding attention vis-à-vis the well-organized National party. Tanna's Christians, who had links with the National party, were all the more surprised at not winning as they held a rather low opinion of their adversaries (Wilkinson 1979). As a result, they ascribed their defeat to the French district agent's political maneuvering. If we look at voting patterns throughout the group, however, Tanna's specific pattern is less surprising. As an overlay of maps would show, the influence of the National party closely correlated with that of the Presbyterian and Anglican churches; Tanna was the only island in the group where the anglophones had no majority role.

The political activities of the anglophone Protestant clergy clearly benefited the National party. In his book *Beyond Pandemonium* (1980), Father Walter Lini, an Anglican minister who was then general secretary of the National party, acknowledged what he called "the church connection." The areas of moderate voting were those dominated by minority churches, such as the francophone Catholic Church and the Church of Christ in western Ambae. There were only two exceptions: Santo and Tanna, which took a stand against established churches and did so because they espoused the idea of *kastom* itself being a "church" in opposition to all the others.

Until then, *kastom* had been a vaguely delineated cultural term without political message, which each camp could manipulate as it pleased. Now *kastom* suddenly connoted a "political force." Vila's moderate leaders understood this transformation and adopted the argument. In Santo, Jimmy Stevens, leader of the Nagriamel, a messianic movement based in the northern islands[9] and similar in terms of structure to Tanna's John Frum movement, was increasingly talking about *naked pipol* 'naked people' whom he contrasted with *man skul,* the churchgoers who are clothed. Also, some moderate leaders suddenly became self-appointed guardians of *kastom.*

In the eyes of Tanna's *kastom* partisans, their victory at the polls meant that the other side had to stop talking, join their camp, or abide by their law. Such is the rule of consensus in traditional society: everybody must be in agreement before a decision is made, and the minority can only be excluded or silent. At a meeting, no *kastom* partisan ever suggests taking a vote; simply, matters are discussed until unanimous consent is reached. "*Wan tink tink nomo*" 'one thought, no more'. In other words, no group can afford to be divided. To the followers of tradition, the voting system introduced by European nations represented a "game for whites," entirely foreign to the art of local politics, and even dangerous. The Islanders "played the game" but did so in their own way, bypassing "democratic compromise," which to them was a meaningless concept. Besides, the Islanders perceived the voting process as a contest, and therefore did not condone its repetitive nature because it implied permanent political instability. After the election, the Tannese concluded that first, since *kastom*-affiliated groups had won locally but lost at the national level, they were now masters of the island, and second, what was happening elsewhere in the group was no longer of any concern to them. Such thinking would later prove to be a miscalculation.

Meanwhile, another political crisis was brewing in the capital. The

Assembly's elected majority of National party representatives felt that it could not speak out on account of two factors, namely, obstruction by the two resident commissioners, and the presence of non-Melanesian members who represented the sphere of "economic interests." As a result, the entire National party majority resigned. The island of Espiritu Santo also had its share of turmoil. The Melanesians, half-castes, and individuals of French stock who together made up a large francophone group in Luganville aligned themselves with the Nagriamel movement. To that movement belonged non-Christianized Melanesians from the bush. All actively and resolutely opposed the National party. This rapprochement gave the party the opportunity to criticize both the collusion of the Nagriamel movement with certain foreign interests and the major role played by Santo's European residents.

The turmoil in Tanna had other roots. In 1976, an apparently minor incident revealed the symbolic dimension underlying local antagonisms. A Melanesian teacher within the British school system, who was in charge of the National party in White Sands and was also one of the direct descendants of Christian chief Kaokare, drew a poster of a man with a pig's head. Because it was supposed to represent *kastom* and, more specifically, Riniao, one of the two Yaneumwakel *yani niko,* the poster was immediately seen as an "insult to the chiefs." Protest meetings were organized in several places. To the Melanesian turn of mind, an insult is often more hurtful than acts themselves. Confronted once again with the Christians' contempt, *kastom* supporters decided to send a letter to John Champion, the British resident commissioner. The letter's contents reveal the authors' heightened sensitivity:

> Once again, the people of your administration want to kill our *kastom.* One of your teachers has put up a poster mocking *kastom* on a wall in one of your schools and your district agent, Mr Norris, has done nothing. You think, Mr Champion, that we are fools. But you are wrong. We know much. . . . We know that the policy of your country consists of setting up Presbyterian and Anglican missionaries to do the work of the Colonial Office. Those missionaries are the biggest colonialists in the [New] Hebrides. . . . You want them to govern the New Hebrides, but do you, Mr Champion, remember Tanna Law, our forebears in chains shown naked to women, [do you remember] Tom Mweles and so many others who went to jail because they were defending our *kastom,* [do you remember] what your ministers, Watt, MacMillan, and Nicholson, did, [do you remember] their Presbyterian police forces armed with Winchesters and Sniders, their courts that sentenced our forebears to fines, jail, or forced labor because they were working for the French, [do you remember] Mr Nicholson who forbade our ancestors who had worked for the French to come back to Tanna, [do you remember] Indians in the USA, Aborigines in Australia, Maori in New Zealand, and the like?
>
> We remind you that we are the ones who bear the name of Tanna.

You have offended us. We give you ten days to answer us. If in ten days
you have done nothing, we shall take a great decision.[10]

The letter reflected the themes that united *kastom* supporters. *Kastom* partisans did not so much attack the National party as they did the Tanna Law episode and the Presbyterian Church, which in their eyes was the party's bedrock; they were to use the same approach in later circumstances. The British Residency chose not to answer their letter. Keeping their word, *kastom* supporters carried out acts of retaliation against National party sympathizers employed by French public and private organizations such as schools, hospitals, the Ballande store, and so forth. The wave of reprisals then proceeded to hit the Futunans who worked in Tanna, most of whom were close to the National party. This "witch hunt" was relatively effective: about fifty Futunans returned to their island shortly afterward, and most Presbyterian employees threatened by *kastom* partisans left their jobs. As a counterstrike, the Presbyterians, who made up the majority of Lenakel residents, prevented the women from Middle Bush moderate groups from selling their vegetables on the land next to Bob Paul's store in Lenakel, where an informal market used to take place on Monday mornings. From the division of minds and hearts emerged a form of territorial partition that would last until independence.

The Battle of the Flags

The political situation had worsened in the group as a whole. After National party representatives had left the Assembly in conspicuous fashion, the two supervisory powers decided to hold new elections in November 1977 and grant internal self-government to the archipelago. The National party, which had become the Vanua'aku Pati in January 1977, deemed such reform insufficient and was unwilling to compromise. In February, the northern part of Pentecost Island proclaimed its independence while refusing access to its territory by Condominium representatives. When the sixth VP congress chose English as the only language of instruction in primary schools, the francophones' widespread response was to side with moderate parties. Condominium authorities were having increasingly less credibility, and the country was falling into anarchy.

The seventh VP congress, meeting in Lenakel (Tanna), declared that the party would boycott the forthcoming elections because the two powers had turned down the conditions set by the nationalists in exchange for their participation. Among other conditions, the Vanua'aku Pati wanted the voting age lowered to eighteen; non-Melanesians would be barred from voting, and the elected majority would set up its own government without necessarily sharing power with its adversaries. Election day, 29 November 1977, was highly tense. On that day, the Vanua'aku Pati had decided to set up a "People's Provisional Government" and raise its flag in the territories under its control. In Tanna, all envisioned the forthcoming election as the next great battle, and the raising of the flag was a crucial and symbolic gesture in this respect. Local VP militants had chosen to fly their colors in Lenakel, in a Presbyterian area near the Nikoletan house and the British hospital. The moderates decided to stand in the way of this scheme. Gathered on the John Frum dancing grounds in Ipeukel, their leaders spoke: "In the past we were prevented from showing the red flag that John Frum had given us. Later, our fellow northerners who wanted to raise the Forcona flag were put in jail. And, each time, the Christians and all those who are with the Vanua'aku Pati today would laugh. Tomorrow, it will be their turn to cry."

From all corners of the island, more than one thousand *kastom* supporters walked overnight to reach a number of meeting places on the eve of 29 November, at kava-drinking time. After forming into "companies," the partisans set off again. As they were advancing from place to place toward Lenakel, the companies grew in size. The atmosphere had turned tense in the previous twenty-four hours. Among other fantastic rumors, it was said that a "New Zealand submarine"[11] had brought uniforms and firearms to the VP supporters in Lenakel. According to another rumor, *kastom* partisans were walking to their deaths. In the afternoon of 28 November, Hubert Goron and I were sheltering under a tree with a *kastom* supporter and waiting for the sun to go down before walking on. Without thinking about it, I told him: "It is hot today." He answered pensively: "Yes, but tomorrow we will be cold. . . ." On the Vanua'aku side, rumors were also being spread, according to which Noumea- and Vila-based white settlers had armed the John Frum and the Kapiel.

On 29 November, at dawn, the three or four hundred VP militants who had spent the night in Lenakel found themselves surrounded by more than one thousand *kastom* supporters, all of them wearing a red headband as a rallying signal. Confrontation was narrowly avoided, partly thanks to Iolu Abbil on the VP side, and Alexis Yolou, his cousin and leader of the moderate side, who not only were able to prevent violence but succeeded in setting up a dialogue. The two antagonistic forces met around the flagless pole in a fairly dignified manner: the speakers expressed themselves with talent and were listened to in silence by each camp. There was neither turmoil nor slaughter. On both sides, the decision was made not to raise a flag on the island as long as an agreement had not been reached. Some of those attending the meeting began to think that all was not lost and that a peaceful settlement was still possible. They were wrong.

The turn of events had been less favorable in Vila. Two processions of equal numbers, about four hundred persons each, had gathered in the capital. One side intended to raise the VP flag, the other wanted to lower it. The French police refused to intervene, but the British charged at the procession of francophone moderates, launching teargas bombs at very close range. Two people were seriously wounded, including a John Frum from Tanna. Elsewhere in the group, the historic day of 29 November showed mixed results. Although the flag of the People's Provisional Government prevailed in most territories of the archipelago, in several hot spots moderate Melanesians had ardently contested it. In other words, significant minority enclaves subsisted. Tanna itself was the only island in the group where such a "minority" could claim to be the majority.

The island now lacked the moderating influence of Iolu Abbil, who had gone back to Vila. Further, the power of the Vanua'aku Pati was in the hands of political stewards less favorably inclined toward conciliation. The Vanua'aku Pati set up the areas under its control in Lenakel, White Sands, and Waisisi as independent territories managed by newly designated "political commissars" and where the authority of the Condominium was not acknowledged.

In January 1978, another serious incident occurred while George Kalsakau was paying an official visit to Tanna. Kalsakau was prime minister of the Vila government formed by the moderate parties—the only parties involved in the 29 November election. Opponents from the Vanua'aku Pati invaded the landing strip and threw tree trunks on it to prevent the airplane from landing. Loanatom villagers cleared the strip after a short tussle. Alexis Yolou, just back from Vila, was the first to lead the charge of the moderates. He would soon assert himself as a major political leader.

Violence was spreading, starting with Middle Bush, where four men were seriously wounded in a series of fights. The French district agent left; André Pouillet had come to know the island well in the course of his nine-year tenure and, to some extent, could manage Tanna's turbulence. Pouillet's departure weakened the fragile authority of the administrative power. His replacement, Roger Payen, a former sergeant in the *gendarmerie*, faced even more difficult times in that he had practically no means of action.

On 12 February 1978, shortly before the annual John Frum festival, two to three hundred militants of the Vanua'aku Pati gathered again in Lenakel and raised the party flag. The next day, a tide of *kastom* partisans and John Frum people, singing war chants and armed this time with clubs and bludgeons, surged through the grounds of the Presbyterian mission. There were nearly seven hundred of them, headed by Alexis Yolou. Flag and pole, after being pulled out and hurled into a car, were triumphantly taken to Sulphur Bay. The reed houses of the Nikoletan, the VP headquarters in Tanna, burned down while a few party militants watched, powerless and with tears of rage. On both sides, the feeling of anger was overwhelming. *Kastom* supporters believed they had been provoked; nationalist militants were humiliated and thought their flag was nothing but a trophy in the hands of their adversaries.

Three days later, on 15 February 1978, all moderate sympathizers—about three thousand people—gathered in Ipeukel to attend the traditional festival of the John Frum. Because Mweles had announced that "something very important" would happen that day, the whole island was expecting a new flag. But which one? Among those who traveled to Tanna to attend the ceremony were Prime Minister Kalsakau and French Resident Commissioner Bernard Pottier. A television team was dispatched from Noumea, and many whites and officials were present. In short, it was the first quasi-official acknowledgment of the John Frum movement by external authorities. The British authorities alone refused to have anything to do with the event, although young District Agent Wilson did appear briefly at the end of the afternoon to assess the situation.

The festival began with a military drill. The John Frum, as always, marched in flawless order. On command, young men handled their symbolic red-painted bamboo guns; the word USA was inscribed in red on their bare chests. Then two men wearing US army uniforms dating from the time of the war in the Pacific solemnly raised the star-spangled banner of the United States of America on a tall bamboo pole.

Whether they were surprised or not, the officials in attendance remained impassive. Mweles and the other dignitaries of the John Frum movement shed tears of emotion as they saluted the US flag—their flag, "John's" flag. Mweles explained those tears by disclosing that he had finally realized his life's dream: he had raised the American flag, as John Frum had directed him to thirty-seven years earlier.

17 The Revolt

The Organization of *Kastom*

Three structures of political authority overlapped one another in Tanna in 1978. The legal structure, with two European district agents, one French *gendarme,* a system of assessors, and a dozen Melanesian police divided into British and French forces, represented the government of internal autonomy. The Vanua'aku Pati (VP) structure rested on a territorial partitioning overseen by "political commissars" and coexisted geographically with the network-based structure of *kastom.* Vanua'aku Pati and *kastom* systems spanned some of the same areas and, according to Melanesian logic, should have separated. Had such been the case, the territories under VP influence would have established an "independent popular republic" and the territories controlled by moderate parties would have set up an "independent *kastom* nation." *Kastom* supporters wished to partition the island and maintain a buffer zone, with an invisible "frontier" or demarcation line that could occasionally facilitate contact.

Had they parted from their adversaries, the leaders of the *kastom* party would have emulated their Anatom neighbors. On that island, the UCNH Catholics had settled on the east coast while the VP Presbyterians held on to their west coast bastion. However, what was possible on Anatom, with its small number of inhabitants, was much less so on Tanna because of two factors, rapid population growth and a tragic land shortage in some areas. No form of population movement that could help separate the adversaries was feasible, and within each political territory there subsisted enclaves that belonged to the other camp. Each majority group brought pressure to bear on its active minorities in order to "neutralize" them, either by obtaining their political silence or by striving to expel them. By 1977, all land tenure issues on Tanna had turned into

276

political issues. The two camps were no longer on speaking terms and foes stayed on their respective sides, ruling out any possibility of encounter. The cursed times of the *Shipimanwawa,* the "war of the canoes" between Numurkuen and Koyometa, were back, or so it seemed.

In Itunga, on the west coast of Tanna, I witnessed a kava ritual involving two opponent groups that were close neighbors. Some John Frum had given a traditional name to one of their children and, according to *kastom,* had to invite their neighboring allies or *napang niel.* The latter belonged to the Vanua'aku Pati, the adversary camp. The VP supporters came. Setting down their kava in the middle of the dancing grounds, they took the kava of the others in exchange. Then each group went to a separate side to chew the roots and drink the beverage. Once this was done, the visitors stood up and vanished. No one had said a word.

Tanna's "hot spots" were Lenakel, Middle Bush, and White Sands, areas with high population density and nearly intractable land tenure issues, most of which stemmed from the *Shipimanwawa* (see Bonnemaison 1987). Outbursts of violence would occur regularly, abating as quickly as they had started. Despite this climate of uncertainty, which allowed anxiety to flourish, *kastom* movements searched for the founding men best suited to hold power. Through this process, a structure was re-created in the shape of a net with a flexible mesh. This network encompassed the space of alliance; within it, the individuals who were promoted were linked by the roads of *kastom.* The dual nature of traditional power was observed in each node and, accordingly, the one who spoke and acted (the "voice" or *yani*) did it in the name of another who kept silent and seemingly did not act (the "big man" or *yremera*).

The Big Men of *Kastom*

Two moderate representatives had been elected in the 1975 elections: Charley Nako for the Kapiel movement and Aissa Nokohut for the John Frum movement. Nako and Nokohut were perceived as the Islanders who could best communicate the traditional word of big men in the modern political arena, and they had been chosen for that purpose. They were only spokesmen; they did not hold actual power. Nor did Nako and Nokohut have a special traditional status within *kastom* and the John Frum movement, respectively. An instructor for the agricultural extension services, Charley Nako had attended the French public school in Middle Bush. Among the John Frum, no one was really suitable for the role of representative, because they spurned school education, be it French or English. Nokohut was selected because he could write a little and knew about *bisnis.* The two representatives brought the word of *kas-*

tom to Vila, but they did so "under supervision" and after they had made a point of obtaining the opinion of Tanna's big men. Two major figures were behind Nokohut and Nako: Tom Mweles for the John Frum, and Noklam Assol for the pagans who had set up the Kapiel movement in Middle Bush.

The name of Tom Mweles has already been mentioned (chapter 16). Mweles is an authority figure for the John Frum, an inspired visionary within their ranks. His prestige is based on the sixteen years he spent in jail or in exile off the island, plus the fact that he is the sole survivor of the movement's "historical leaders." For that reason, Mweles speaks in the name of John Frum and introduces himself as being John's "voice." When he sent his men to tear down the Vanua'aku Pati flag on 12 February 1978 (chapter 16), Mweles justified his order with a few words: "John does not want this flag. Remove it."

The other authority figure, Noklam Assol, is a big man within Tanna's traditional society. As "voice of the canoe" *(yani niko)* for Lamlu, Assol belongs by blood and name to the island's most ancient patrilineage, from which stem the Koyometa people of Middle Bush. Noklam also owes his preeminent position to the fact that the Lamlu group used to represent the core of *kastom*'s resistance to Tanna Law: *kastom* was "in hiding" in Lamlu during those difficult times. Just as Mweles derives his power from John Frum, Noklam acts in the name of a deeper pagan "origin," which is the tradition that Yarris Ya'uto, from the Le'uluk dancing grounds, inherited from Willy Pea. Noklam's power derives from the myth about *kastom*'s resistance to Tanna Law. Ya'uto is the emblem of *kastom,* and Noklam speaks in his name; that is, Ya'uto is *kastom*'s *yremera* and Noklam serves as his "voice."

Mweles and Noklam Assol moved quite naturally into their positions as "political" leaders of the *kastom* movement. They could delegate their "voice"-related power to others in specific circumstances or places. Accordingly, Mweles named a spokesman, Isakwan,[1] who represented him at all great meetings. In addition, the big men who were dispersed along the John Frum's path of alliance represented Mweles's power in their respective territories. They delegated that power to others since the process of dividing up and delegating power could be infinitely repeated.

Similarly, Noklam Assol delegated his power to other men who extended his road to the boundaries of the island and even beyond. Such men were, of course, Charley Nako, the Kapiel representative in the Assembly, and Tom Kasso, a "*kastom* delegate."[2] Next to Noklam Assol stood his own brother, Posen. An outstanding public speaker, with a quick intelligence and a keen sense of logic, Posen played a major role within the *kastom* movement, for which he conceived both the operations and the theoretical foundations. He told me once: "It is a pity I did not go to school, I would have been a good minister."

By 1978, Alexis Yolou had begun to rise from the ranks of the moderate party, soon to be named Tan Union federation, that is, "land union," land symbolizing *kastom* (see chapter 6). Mweles was the first to acknowledge Yolou upon his return to Tanna, naming him to take on the position of Nokohut, who was perceived to be too old and insufficiently active as the John Frum representative. Alexis Yolou was a Catholic and former pupil of the Marist fathers at the Montmartre School in Vila. He was also a talented boxer, and his prestige was great among Tanna's youth. After joining the ranks of the UCNH in Vila at an early age, he deliberately chose to return to his native land to take part in the local political struggle. He was not yet thirty. Born in Loanatom, Alexis was the son of the dedicated catechist of the Catholic mission, Pierre Yamak. His lineage carried the traditional power of the *yremera,* the aristocracy of the island, and was associated with the Ipai dancing place. Through his mother, he was also Willy Korisa's first cousin. Korisa was pastor, political commissar of the Vanua'aku Pati in Lowkatai (near Loanatom), and future government minister—an example of family conflict brought about by the *Shipimanwawa.* The branch to which Alexis belonged lived in Loanatom; some still-pagan fragments had stayed in Ipai, while the rest of the lineage was in Lowkatai, one of the strongholds of the Presbyterian mission and the Vanua'aku Pati. Alexis lived on the small Loanatom territory of the old John Frum leader Niluan,[3] whose political "voice" he represented. As local leader, or *boss,* of the Loanatom-based John Frum company, Alexis Yolou became the political spokesman for the entire John Frum population on Tanna and was elected representative to the Vila Assembly under that label. Both Niluan and Alexis Yolou belonged to Koyometa clans transplanted in the course of the internecine wars of the nineteenth century and almost landless as a result. From the outset, these clans had opposed the Christian party backed by the Presbyterian mission.

Alexis Yolou was quite conscious of the contradictory, intricate nature of his political destiny. He had chosen to fight on the side of *kastom,* a world that he only knew in part. Educated in Christian schools, living in an urban setting for many years, he had married a young woman from Anatom and was an "urban citizen" who, perhaps, could have identified with the nationalist cause of the Vanua'aku Pati. Alexis did not, inasmuch as he shared the destiny of the John Frum Koyometa in Loanatom and felt solidarity toward the camp of *kastom,* even though his own vision was different. A nationalist, proud to be a *Man Tanna,* he belonged to that "lost generation" of francophone Islanders whom VP militants, as they opted for the English language, had rejected to the fringe of society from the very beginning. Was it this welter of contradictions that made him so popular—and feared by his adversaries? Whatever the case, many young people from *kastom*-based groups recognized themselves in him. Alexis Yolou spoke about the force of *kastom,* the better to link it with the modern world. None of these contradictions appeared to be an impediment in the eyes of the big men of *kastom* and those John Frum who had chosen him as their leader. The most clear-headed among them believed that Alexis Yolou was a fine leader who could pull *kastom* out of its entanglement with the past, a morass to which others wanted to confine it.

The Law of *Kastom*

During the two years (1977–1979) when *kastom* partisans believed they were politically autonomous, a series of conflicts, separate yet interdependent, kept reviving the antagonism between the two communities on the island. The first of these confrontations, and one of the most violent, occurred in Middle Bush. In the circumstances, the Kapiel pagan groups organized a "police force" and imposed their rule. Once again, the root of the conflict was a land tenure–related issue of territorial sovereignty going back to the time of the *Shipimanwawa.*

In Middle Bush, as in the rest of the island, the victory of the Numurkuen phratry had led to the exile of the Koyometa losers (chapter 10). Few in number and unconcerned, the winners did not take possession of their enemies' land but settled refugees from other territories on it. This buffering process introduced small "canoes" and allogeneous groups which, like as many defensive niches, protect the winners' territories from a possible return of the old Koyometa losers.

At the end of the *Shipimanwawa* in the nineteenth century, the Koyometa started to go back to their Lamlu territory, but cautiously and slowly, over several generations. As they returned, they collided with one allogeneous community, a Numurkuen group that had been left there by the victors to hold the traditional dancing grounds of Lamnatu. The first incidents broke out in the intense political climate prevailing on the eve of independence. Soon the boundary between the two groups turned into a site of confrontation. The Vanua'aku Pati coalition supported the local Numurkuen group while moderate parties championed the Koyometa claim. In Lamlu—that stronghold of pagan resistance to Tanna Law—the Koyometa, who numbered five to six hundred, wanted to reconstruct the traditional space they had held before the *Shipimanwawa* and, by extension, to restore their sovereignty over their places and their roads. Facing them was the Numurkuen group, slightly over one hundred people, who benefited—at least in an early phase—from the support of the Iwel Numurkuen who, four or five generations earlier, had installed them on that territory. The conflict was therefore triangular. At the outset Lamlu had to fight both Lamnatu and Iwel, rekindling the old conflict between Koyometa and Numurkuen. Lamlu's two adversaries differed markedly, however. Lamnatu residents were former fugitives and outsiders. Iwel residents were "real men" in terms of place and status; they were also members of the Nalhyaone canoe, in other words, traditional *napang niel* 'customary allies' of Lamlu's people through their "road" linkages, and unquestionably *men ples* (see map 9).

The confrontation centered on the territory of a small group called the Yahurne, a territory south of Lamnatu that the wars and epidemics of the nineteenth century had left deserted. Niere, "voice of the canoe" for Lamnatu, opposed Noklam Assol, "voice of the canoe" for Lamlu, who laid claim to that dead land. The *men ples* 'men of the place' were granted their wish by a ruling, first within *kastom,* then officially through a court presided over by the British district agent: since the Yahurne clan had once been a political satellite of Lamlu, the residents of the Lamlu dancing place should bring it back to life by taking over what used to be Yahurne land. On Niere's side, the case rested mostly on former marriage alliances with the extinct group, and his kinship-based arguments were not deemed valid enough to establish his sovereignty over the disputed territory. Political violence began after the verdict, in June 1977. Niere and his group—too many in number on this small territory—felt that they were the victims of an injustice. They refused to vacate the section of Yahurne land on which they lived, which included a cattle paddock. The men from Lamlu smashed the paddock fences. In the brutal fight that ensued, four of Niere's partisans were wounded, including one with a broken skull. The contested land stayed in the hands of the Lamlu attackers.

French District Agent Pouillet made an enquiry locally but could get only the accounts of Lamlu participants; British District Agent Browning was able to speak only with the people of Lamnatu. Although the two police forces were meant to act jointly, a precedent was set. Thereafter, French police received complaints only from groups allied with the francophone moderate parties, while British police recorded those of groups allied with the anglophone nationalist Vanua'aku Pati. As a result, the administration became practically powerless, which gave free rein to the adversaries. Had the administration wished to do more, it would not have had the means. The dozen police employed by the two powers on the island were themselves split along the same lines, precluding any involvement on their part should a major confrontation occur.

What was initially a land tenure question became a major issue dealing less with land use or land ownership than with identity and territorial sovereignty. In Tanna's contemporary society, conflicts about straightforward land tenure issues—that is, land use—ultimately find a solution. But conflicts are less easily settled as far as the identity and status of individuals themselves are concerned.

At this juncture, *kastom* partisans designated "*kastom* delegates," such as Tom Kasso, to promulgate rules and organized a police force to enforce them. At regular intervals, each group within the *kastom* alliance had to supply one or two young men who went to Lamlu or Ipeukel to serve on "*kastom*'s police force." These guards wore a red head-band and adopted the habit of carrying a *nal-nal,* a traditional war club. Among the John Frum, "John's guards" watched over the flag and protected Mweles, in addition to their usual obligations. The men with their *nal-nal*s did not enter VP-held territories but gave help whenever a conflict broke out at the edge of their own territories.

In April 1978, in Imanaka, Vanua'aku Pati militants interfered with night dances held in honor of John Frum. There was a fight and some people were wounded. Lowkatai's local "political commissar" and villagers prevented the French police from entering their village, a VP stronghold. In a reverse case, the British police wanted to make an inquiry about presumed arson on the VP premises on the day the Vanua'aku Pati flag had been seized in Lenakel, but were refused admittance to Middle Bush villages. Disillusioned, French Resident Commissioner Bernard Pottier wrote to his British counterpart: "As . . . we are well aware, the individuals at fault are present in both camps and we often do not have the means to act as firmly as is needed" (letter, 26 June 1978, FRA). Nonetheless, new French District Agent Payen decided to prohibit the carrying of war clubs—an order which was respected to a varying degree and which the John Frum criticized, seeing in it an attempt to curb their sovereignty and deprive them of a means of defense.

In August and September 1978, the island, already in a state of confusion, saw the tension escalate. Men from the northern part of Tanna were said to be using poison witchcraft, thus reviving the ancient *netuk* custom, which had officially disappeared over a century earlier. It was said that such men were descended from lineages of magicians who poisoned by using their stones as they wished, killing one person or another, generally for unknown reasons. Each new or recent death seems to have been liberally attributed to the magicians; a very ancient fear had resurfaced in the consciousness of the Tannese. The new "*kastom* authorities" decided to put an end to the phenomenon. At dawn, *kastom* police besieged a village in the northern part of the island. Suspects were tied up and taken to Middle Bush. Later dispersed to different villages, the prisoners were condemned to stay there for the rest of their lives under the watchful eye of *kastom*.[4]

The Commission of Enquiry

A Marist priest of British nationality, Father Sacco, was in charge of the parish of Loanatom, which included very active John Frum and Catholic militants. He and Bob Paul wrote to the two resident commissioners, relating that twenty-nine people had been seriously wounded and that Tanna's prevalent climate was one of violence. In their eyes, the local political scene was on the verge of anarchy:

> Tribal or sectarian disagreements have always existed in Tanna, but the current disintegration began with the advent of politics. Dissensions have become more pronounced. People have never understood what politics is all about; in their eyes it consists of joining one party and seeing all others as enemies. Many follow their party as if it were a cult, and with the same fanaticism as for a cult. The main event behind this explosive situation was undoubtedly the arson which the supporters of Moderate parties perpetrated on the Vanua'aku Pati offices in Tanna, yet one must also acknowledge that the raising of the VP flag was an unquestionable act of provocation in such circumstances. The attackers were armed with clubs [and] bush-knives. . . .
>
> Since mid-1978, there have been several cases of persons who have been seized, tied up like animals, punched, whipped, as well as intimidated and humiliated, so that in the course of a long imprisonment "confessions" can be wrested from them about witchcraft murders and the like. Those who feel they are the strongest threaten their adversaries in order to frighten them. They even have their own police force and cells. It is absurd to speak of custom in this case, this is nothing more than cannibalism. (Letter, Feb 1979, FRA)[5]

Ending their letter with a formal accusation against Gendarme Willy Urben, Bob Paul's personal enemy, who was blamed for protecting "war club carriers" and "hiring their services," the authors asked that public order be restored, that authors of violent acts be arrested, "whatever their political affiliation," and that the *gendarme* leave. Eventually, the two resident commissioners sent a commission of enquiry to Tanna, chaired by Justice Cooke, originally from Ireland. The commission made a number of recommendations that could only be construed as wishful thinking. However, the French Residency did transfer the *gendarme,* who was deemed to be overly involved with *kastom* partisans. Raised by an uncle who was a settler on Espiritu Santo, Willy Urben could speak Bislama remarkably well and had a keen sense of local politics. He was highly regarded by *kastom* supporters and hated by Vanua'aku Pati militants. Unquestionably, moderate groups were more vulnerable after his departure. The new *gendarme,* Lopez, was guarded at first, but soon adopted the same attitude as his predecessor, becoming in turn the target of VP demonstrations.

The commission of enquiry gone, the island's hot spots blazed up again. There was endless fighting in White Sands when the large

Yaneumwakel group, made up of John Frum supporters but a traditional enemy of the Ipeukel group, went over to the VP side. There were scuffles in Ikeuti, south of Enfitana, where the tug-of-war between different groups blocked the construction of a new road around the island. Also, a number of new flags were raised by moderate groups. The Forcona, whose supporters had remained faithful to Fornelli and had stayed in the background vis-à-vis other moderate groups, raised the flag of their movement in the north and in Middle Bush on 22 June 1979, the day of the "Tannese Nation."

In the course of a visit to the island in June 1979, Deputy Chief Minister Walter Lini tried to alleviate the conflict by emphasizing the need for a genuine council of apolitical leaders. But each camp had its own customary chiefs who did not wish to remain neutral when the stakes were so high. Amidst turmoil, rumors, and threats, roads were now blocked off, Islanders balked at crossing someone else's territory, women did not dare to walk to remote gardens, and those who had family ties but belonged to separate camps were not on speaking terms. In this climate, new elections were announced. They were to give the group a new Assembly, the last before independence.

The November 1979 Elections

The constitutional crisis in Vila had been alleviated through the creation of a "Government of National Unity" made up of five VP ministers and five moderate ministers. Gérard Leymang, a Catholic priest and the leader of the UCNH, was chief minister of the new government, with Walter Lini, the VP leader and an Anglican priest, as his deputy. Originally from Malakula, Leymang was a graduate of the University of Lyon (France); Lini was from Pentecost Island and had been educated in New Zealand. A return to unity through compromise was conceivable, as implied in the moderate leader's open-minded gesture vis-à-vis his adversary and the ecclesiastical status of both leaders. In November 1979, the Government of National Unity organized general elections to help designate the Assembly that would lead the country into independence.

Once again, tension was high in Tanna on election day. Standing as candidate for the John Frum was Alexis Yolou, who had just returned from a training course for civil servants in France and had not been on the island when political violence had occurred. *Kastom* partisans did not understand the significance of this vote and neglected to campaign, thinking they would easily win a second time because they had already won once. A census was carried out to set up viable electoral rolls but some *kastom*-affiliated groups refused to be enumerated, in particular in the south and among the northern John Frum who had joined the Forcona movement.

The nationwide elections, which took place on 14 November 1979, represented a "massive landslide" in favor of the Vanua'aku Pati, to use the words of *Nabanga,* the weekly newsletter published by the French Residency. The nationalist party improved its score in the group as a whole, with twenty-six elected representatives versus thirteen for the francophone moderates.[6]

More significantly, all islands expressed majority support for the Vanua'aku Pati, including Espiritu Santo and Tanna where it was previously a minority party. In Tanna, the Vanua'aku Pati came in ahead by a few votes: 2784 (50.6 percent) were cast in its favor, versus 2718 (49.4 percent) for the moderates grouped under the Tan Union banner.[7] This outcome allowed VP representatives to get three out of Tanna's five seats despite a transfer of only about 3 percent of the votes between 1975 and 1979.[8] Among *kastom* partisans, only the politics-minded militants had voted for the moderate candidates. Further, many incidents had taken place while *kastom* was sovereign on the island, and many excesses had been committed in the course of the so-called "witchcraft affair."

In Vila, the government was now entirely made up of VP anglophones. During the previous legislature, the moderates had set up the Government of National Unity by offering half of the ministerial posts to their adversaries. They expected a follow-up gesture that would grant them at least three positions. Nothing was forthcoming; the minority was excluded from the debates and turned into an opposition that had few hopes or prospects.

Before the Storm

Shortly after the elections, the new government organized an arts festival to be held in Vila. Every island was invited to illustrate *kastom* by sending groups of dancers and craft workers. The purpose of this cultural fair was to seal national unity under the sign of tradition and customs and allow each cultural area in the group to be represented. In Tanna, the Tan Union camp refused to participate, stating that *kastom* could not lend itself to a show organized for political reasons and least of all be part of a "festival" organized by its adversaries. On 27 November, roads were blocked off to prevent dancers from heading to Lenakel on their way to Vila. The same day, Burton Field, the airstrip at Lenakel, was also blocked off temporarily. Nevertheless, a number of dancers from Tanna's west coast were able to travel to Vila by boat. With the help of some Tannese who lived in the capital, they represented their island at the arts festival and performed customary dances.

The *kastom* people regarded this gesture as a ritual theft and, more seriously, as a deliberate insult. "We do not take up the customs of Christians by pretending to go to church," they wrote. "So why are they mim-

icking our chants and dances when their forebears used to condemn them
and they themselves have always spurned them?" (letter to the two resident commissioners, 28 Nov 1979, FRA). *Kastom,* which already ruled
its own territory, thus stated its sovereignty over Tanna's cultural heritage. On that there could be no compromise.

Tanna was overwhelmed by an array of conflicts. The construction
of the road to the south was hampered by the ongoing confrontation
between the two camps around Ikeuti, each camp laying claim to the
lands adjacent to the new road. Also, the Agriculture Department used to
give jobs primarily to francophone workers; as a form of payback, the
new anglophone agricultural officer dismissed Middle Bush workers who
belonged to the moderate camp. But the real bombshell occurred in
December 1979 when, to their stupefaction, the Tannese saw a Melanesian district commissioner from Ambrym, Jo Dalessa, move to the island
to replace the French and British district agents. On 6 December 1979,
the three movements, John Frum, Kapiel, and Kastom,[9] prepared a letter
which was signed by sixty big men and addressed to George Kalkoa,
minister of Home Affairs in the new government. The authors made no
secret of their views:

> We do not want the French district agent[10] to leave Tanna without our
> permission. He has always helped Tanna's *kastom* and knows about it to
> some extent. If the district agent leaves, there will be great battles. . . .
> The John Frum, Kapiel, and Kastom will obtain their own Independence
> and will join New Caledonia. We have been talking about freedom,
> peace, and unity. And what do we see? What you call reaching unity,
> peace, and freedom consists of dismissing a district agent when we want
> him to stay. We demand an answer by 15 December 1979. We, the
> Kapiel, John Frum, and Kastom state to you, George Kalkoa, Minister,
> that you give orders on Vate [Efate] but not on Tanna. Only Tanna's *kas-*
> *tom* gives orders on Tanna; only *kastom* has the right to decide whether
> the French district agent should leave or not. We shall accept another
> district agent in Tanna only when the region[11] is organized, after fair and
> clear-cut elections and according to the ways of *kastom.*
>
> You want to dismiss the French district agent because *kastom* has
> made mistakes, but what was done when the others caused trouble at the
> time the Kalsakau government was in power, and what was done when
> Tanna's Vanua'aku [Pati] blocked off the airstrip? (FDA)

Concurrently, political contact was made with Jimmy Stevens, the
leader of the Santo-based Nagriamel movement, with a view toward elaborating a joint platform in the name of *kastom.* The Vemarana nation
was meant to bring together the moderate movements based in the northern islands and centered in Santo. This project did not appeal to the moderates based in the southern islands, who thought it strayed too far from
the spirit of *kastom:* they decided to keep their freedom of action.

In fact, Jimmy Stevens's US advisors inspired and perhaps wrote the Vemarana constitution. These advisors belonged to the Phoenix group headed by the tycoon Michael Oliver. The Phoenix Foundation may be described as a US libertarian movement to the right of the Republican party. The foundation was then seeking an isolated land to build the utopian city of its dreams; liberalism had to be total, state control nonexistent. Originally from Lithuania, a survivor of Nazi camps, and a naturalized US citizen, Oliver wanted to create a state of free enterprise where American capitalists could seek refuge from the United States and what he saw as its rampant "fascist socialism" (MacClancy 1983). Oliver was searching for a Pacific island where the only responsibility of the local government would be to ensure the safety of goods and individuals, leaving residents free to organize themselves as they wished—in other words, an island where the Phoenix millionaires could prosper unfettered. The two men were suited to each other: by offering Michael Oliver a space in which to create his personal utopia, Jimmy Stevens found the powerful outside help he was looking for.

Adding another twist to the story, Fornelli journeyed back to Tanna from Noumea on a small sailboat. In Sulphur Bay, Fornelli had long talks with Mweles; the next day, he drove across the island openly, accompanied by a troop of about seventy "*kastom* guards." The US flag was waving from the front of his car. In Lenakel, Fornelli met with French District Agent Payen, still at his post, who gave the following account to the Resident Commissioner: "Fornelli appears self-assured. [He is] dressed in a light-colored bush jacket and wears a bush hat with the Forcona star. He is composed and makes an impression on his audience. The Forcona drink in Fornelli's every word, the John Frum and the Kapiel seem more circumspect. . . . His arrival is timely from a psychological standpoint. The John Frum and the Kapiel have lost the elections and are bewildered; he may take on the role of liberator" (report, 20 Nov 1979, FDA). The district agent did not know whether he was facing a friend or a foe and was uncertain how to behave. It was said that Fornelli had links with PALIKA, a New Caledonia Kanak independence movement. Payen noted that a crowd of onlookers had surrounded his office to catch a glimpse of Fornelli. In a letter addressed to the resident commissioners, the two *kastom* movements (John Frum and Kapiel) asked that Fornelli be allowed to stay on Tanna:

> Everything that Fornelli says, everything he has done, is for [the benefit of] *kastom*. . . . The English missionaries and Bob Paul have committed serious injustices against *kastom*. Mr Bob Paul has repeatedly used his gun against us and you have not expelled him, so why do you want to expel Fornelli who has never done anything, neither against *kastom* nor against the law? . . . If Fornelli must leave Tanna, the English missionaries and Bob Paul must go first. Then Fornelli will leave, but if they do

not go, Fornelli will stay. . . . If you force Fornelli, and him alone, to leave Tanna, there will be a great battle between the *kastom* people on one side and the missionaries and Mr Bob Paul on the other. Pay much attention to what we are saying, because these words really come from our hearts.

A good answer is a good solution. A bad answer is a bad solution. Do understand us. Thank you. (Letter, 24 Nov 1979, FDA)

The letter was a fruitless effort. Fornelli did not push his luck and, of his own accord, left the island aboard his sailboat. Yet his visit did strengthen the moderates in their secessionist longings.

The Independence of *Kastom*

On the first day of January 1980, in Lamlu, which was the stronghold of the Kapiel alliance, *kastom* supporters raised a new flag: a five-pointed yellow star on a green background with three yellow bars on the left. This act marked the official birth of the TAFEA nation, as indicated on a statement typed in Middle Bush and sent to the joint authorities:

Middle Bush, Tanna, 1 January 1980

Kastom-based Government of the TAFEA Nation

TAFEA means: T, Tanna
                      A, Anatom
                      F, Futuna
                      E, Erromango
                      A, Aniwa

These five islands are parting from the New Hebridean Government led by the Vanua'aku Pati and organizing themselves as a *kastom* nation, with the help of the governments of the following countries:

France, Noumea, Paris, Corsica, America.[12]

The TAFEA Nation wishes to receive aid for its budget in the areas of French education, *kastom* delegate, French hospitals, public works, agriculture, *kastom* police force, and so forth.

Sincerely
                                                                    (FDA)

The letter was not totally unexpected. In fact, the leaders of the *kastom* movements had explained the meaning of their gesture in an earlier letter addressed to the French and British resident commissioners:

TAFEA Office, 12 December 1979

To Your Honours the two Resident Commissioners of France and Great Britain in the New Hebrides:

The present letter is written in the name of the *kastom* leaders and inhabitants of the island of Tanna to tell you, the representatives of France and Great Britain, and also the other important persons in the World, that from now on *kastom* rejects the Condominium system and refuses to acknowledge the current Government of the New Hebrides. *Kastom* is independent wherever it exists, and it believes that it is free to ask any country for help with respect to its economy, schools, and hospitals. . . .

Kastom alone used to rule the earth and our island of Tanna. Later on, Presbyterian missionaries and then the agents of the Condominium government came [here]. All lied to us, because they said they would work with *kastom* and they [actually] worked against it.

Kastom stayed behind these men for a long time, seventy years.[13] But, today, *kastom* realizes that there is a big hole in the island, so it has decided to return to its original way of life. (FDA)

The authors used the term *hole* as an explicit reference to the departure of the French district agent, whom they considered an ally. When he left, the knot tied by Wilkes in 1910 came undone. Not only was the island symbolically confronted with itself, confronted with a big "hole," but *kastom* went back to its point of departure.

This unilateral proclamation of independence indicated a return to the traditional vision of political space. In other words, the *kastom* canoe was not an enclosed space but represented a road of alliance radiating toward four "islands" and potential allies (see letter of 1 Jan): Corsica, which probably never heard anything about it; Paris, which played deaf; Noumea, where some New Caledonians banked on a possible secession from the group; and finally the United States, whose ambassador posted in Fiji actually supported the Vila government.

At the beginning of 1980, five banners were floating over the island: the French and British flags over the Isangel administrative offices, the star-spangled banner in Ipeukel, the Forcona standard in Lenatuan, and the TAFEA flag in Middle Bush. The sixth flag was not visible, that of the Vanua'aku Pati, which held legal power. Emotions ran high, with tension and reciprocal aggravation in both camps. All Islanders were openly getting ready for a confrontation that would settle the issue once and for all. *Bai, yumi swim long blad* 'Soon we shall be swimming in blood' was the phrase heard on many dancing places in both camps at kava-drinking time.

The Meeting with the French *Chancelier*

The announcement of the French district agent's departure had generated much agitation, and the *chancelier* (assistant resident commissioner) of the French Residency in Vila, Peres, traveled to Tanna to hear the complaints of *kastom* supporters and try to make them listen to reason. The meeting took place in Middle Bush on 3 January 1980 and was attended by the main leaders of the moderate alliance. All spoke in turn, frequently asking direct questions of the representative of the French government. Their speeches and comments were recorded on tape; significant extracts follow. One may note the misgivings of moderate leaders about the ambiguous nature of French policy on issues of concern to them:[14]

TOM S. (Ipeukel): These days, the Presbyterian Church tells us about *kastom*. It did not use to talk about it before, it tried to kill it. Tanna's *kastom* would have died if John Frum had not come to the island. The Presbyterian mission and the British government wanted to wring his neck, but John Frum only came to help Tanna's big men. He never did anything against the Presbyterian mission and the British government: they are the ones that acted against him. The big men of *kastom* went to jail. They were punched and spent a long time there before they could go home. *Kastom* even gave £100 to the British district agent Nicol so the big men could get out.[15] Nicol put the money in his pocket and sent Mweles, Nikiau, and Nambas back to the Port Sandwich jail in Malakula, so that they would stay there all their lives and we would never see them again. Fortunately war came, and we saw them go back to Vila, all three of them. There, America gave them a flag, its own flag, and that flag we raised in Ipeukel. Now, there are no handcuffs for the *kastom* people, that time is over. We have raised the flag and won our freedom. Had we not flown that flag, the *kastoms* of the world would have died and we would be in jail.

ISAKWAN (Sulphur Bay): *Kastom* always stayed in its own country and never attacked anybody. When the capmen [the agents of the Condominium administration] arrived, *kastom* was no longer in its own country. The capman was walking in front, but behind him the Presbyterian mission was giving orders. Those two have kept on causing problems for us. The last problem was about the customary dances that were presented at the arts festival in Vila. Now, it is over, we are pulling out. . . . We no longer want to see agents of a government here. The word of John Frum told us that for forty years we would keep the prophecy;[16] we waited for forty years; the time of the prophecy is beginning now. We are willing for France to stay here to help *kastom,* but not the others. When we tell France to leave, then at that time and not before, she will leave. We'll escort her and shake hands with her.

AISSEA NOKAHUT (Ipeukel, Sulphur Bay): The position that the Presbyterian Church holds today used to be that of our big men. First the Presbyterian Church replaced them, then it threw them out. Later it pressured [Islanders] into following a law called Tanna Law, and our big men themselves wanted to kill *kastom*. John Frum arrived among us around

1938. He told us to go back where we used to be, and we did. The British government became very angry. It put our leaders in jail. . . . We gave £100 so it would release them, [but] it pushed them still a little further and they went to jail on another island, away from their fathers, mothers, and children. This is what made our hearts ache so much; since then we have not wanted to have anything to do with the Presbyterian side. We know that there is a government of the New Hebrides, but we [also] know that it sits on the lap of the Presbyterian Church. We are pulling out, but we are saying, our friend is France. She can stay in Tanna if she wants to.

TUK NAO (South Tanna): We are talking on and on, but in truth we are crying over our lives. . . . We are pulling out of the government, but we are looking toward France. If she wants to help us, she should do it, otherwise we shall stay by ourselves, we shall stay like this . . .[17]

NAKO (Middle Bush): *Kastom* never did any harm to English missionaries. They kept on doing us harm. So we are pulling out. It is over. If someone wants to hurt *kastom,* then *kastom* will hurt him. There is a day called the Last Judgment, and that day will pass judgment on us all . . .

ALEXIS YOLOU (Loanatom): A long time ago, when the Presbyterian Church came here, everybody followed it, everybody went to church. But for a man of Tanna to believe anything, he has to see it with his own eyes. If you tell us that you like us, we really want to know if you like us and we want you to show it to us. So we went to church, and then we pulled out; only a few kept on going. When VP politics came to Tanna, everybody went into it, then many pulled out. Today, you see, we are leaving Vanuatu politics, because we are afraid of it. I for one went into politics in 1971; I got involved because I did not want things like Tanna Law to happen again. We, who know nothing, do know that both the English and the French want to guide this country in their own best interests. The British government installed the Vanua'aku Pati and did so with a specific goal in mind. The English always do the same thing, they show you their queen who, in the front, is a woman, but, in the back, is a man; they give you independence in the front, yet they are still holding you from the back . . .

I want something that belongs to Tanna's *kastom. Seli Hoo,*[18] that's not a word from our language. There is another question which I am asking all Vanua'aku leaders. I attended a French school. But they proposed that only the English language be allowed in the New Hebrides; so why did we go to French school? Today, what they want is to wring our necks. Why not respect both languages? . . . We are told about democracy, but what does this word mean? The government tells us about unity, but what does it mean by that, when only one side is represented in the government?

THOMAS N. (White Sands): I want to ask you a question, Frenchman. You are coming from far away, you have gone a long way to come to us, and you have governed us for a long time. But can you still tell the difference between right and wrong? For us, what is right is to fight for the *kastom* of our ancestors. What is right is to give one's own child what was promised and not give it to the child of another. . . .[19]

ISAKWAN (Sulphur Bay): I also want to ask you a question. A lion is eating all the children of a country, he has nearly finished eating them. Who is going to kill the lion? Who is going to marry the queen's daughter?[20]

ALEXIS YOLOU (Loanatom): We saw it happen: the English used the Vanua'aku [Pati] and now they are winning. Everything that is in the hearts of the English is in the process of being completed, and that is to expel the French from the New Hebrides. Today it is the district agent's turn, Mr Payen, tomorrow it will be the *gendarme*'s. We all heard that Walter Lini has already asked Paris to make Mr Robert[21] leave, because he was helping the moderates too much. But if it is true that Mr Robert helped the moderates, who helped the Vanua'aku Pati? Didn't the English help it too? So why doesn't Walter Lini ask that Mr Stuart[22] be sent back to London?

NASE (Isangel): As a *kastom* supporter I have suffered too much in my heart with all these stories. The Presbyterian missions have been here for just too long. They have disrupted the life of the Tannese, they have waged war against *kastom*. . . . My father Narua gave away his land in Isangel so the district agents could establish themselves. When the Condominium boat anchored in Lenakel, the missionaries did not want the equipment to be unloaded, saying that the beach was theirs. The boat unloaded [the equipment] at the Lenami anchorage [in Loanpakel Bay] and my father called upon the *kastom* people to come unload the equipment and bring it to Isangel to build the district agents' houses. All this was done by *kastom* and not by the Presbyterians. If they wish, politicians may ask for the district agents to leave, but *kastom* for its part has the right to keep them, because it made them come here. . . . Now I can see that many houses have been built on my land in Isangel. If the district agents leave, the houses must revert to us. If the VP gets into Isangel, I'll drive it away. If the VP takes possession of the houses, I'll set fire to them.

Point of No Return

On 13 January 1980, French District Agent Payen left the island forever, leaving his key in the door. Whether this act was ill-considered or deliberate, no one knew. When the new Melanesian district commissioner—Payen's former deputy—wanted to come in, the door was locked and the key in the hands of *kastom* partisans who did not want to give it back. With its symbolic connotation, the "house-key affair" appealed to the Tannese.[23]

More serious events were in the making. On 28 January, one of the assistants to the Melanesian district commissioner was abducted by a group of moderates. Vanua'aku Pati militants retaliated by threatening Gendarme Lopez, the sole representative of the French government on the island. Moderates congregated and headed toward Lenakel to defend "their" *gendarme,* forcing the nationalist militants to move back. A report on the events heralded "deadly confrontations between these narrow-minded and primitive people" (FDA). It was an accurate prediction if not a perceptive judgment. The two camps maneuvered with subtlety, keeping the pressure on but bypassing frontal attack. If the moderates attacked a position, as they did in Lenakel, the Vanua'aku Pati left and then returned, speaking with great fanfare, when the place was empty, and vice versa.

The John Frum were getting ready for their yearly mid-February festival. They feared violence. Vanua'aku Pati militants were equally concerned and planned to block off all roads. A new letter was sent to the two ministers involved, Paul Dijoud, the minister for French overseas departments and territories, and Peter Dicker, his counterpart at the British Commonwealth Office. This time, the letter was signed by "ninety-three customary chiefs" on Tanna who had links with the Vanua'aku Pati, and by representatives of the Christian anglophone churches—Presbyterian, Seventh Day Adventist, and Assembly of God. Catholic Church representatives refused to sign the appeal, which in their eyes was entirely political. Rejecting any suggestion of secession, the signatories mentioned the loyalty of Tanna's population to the VP government and denounced the separatists while asking for a return to order on the island. The moderates were described as "a terrorist politico-religious organization, led by reactionary, so-called moderate, parties and manipulated by outside elements." The pro-Vanua'aku Pati signatories concluded: "If nothing is done, we will have to resort to defending ourselves on our own" (letter, 3 Jan 1980, FRA).

On the eve of the Ipeukel festival, in the course of an eventful visit to the island, Inspecteur Général Robert, the French Resident Commissioner, gave the key[24] of the French district agency's building to legal government representatives, thereby handing them the symbol of sovereignty over the Isangel hill, and over Tanna by extension. In the afternoon, Robert met in Lamlu with TAFEA leaders and asked them to stay within the law. Meanwhile, the Air Melanesia plane was landing at Burton Field with Jean-Marie Leye, the Anatom-born president of the Federal Party of Moderates, on board.[25] At once, Leye ran into a committee of Vanua'aku Pati militants. *Kastom* supporters were all in Middle Bush that afternoon to speak with the French Resident Commissioner, and Leye was completely alone. He was struck, humiliated, and thrust back into the aircraft, a gesture that angered the moderates considerably; they felt it was a serious provocation. "You started a fire up, it will have to be put out," shouted Alexis Yolou to his adversaries after rushing up to Isangel. During the night, each camp set up observation posts and got ready to settle the quarrel.

Despite this incident, the ambience of the Ipeukel festival was fairly restrained. A crowd of two to three thousand people watched the uncommonly solemn John Frum pageant, with its rich symbolism. The word in the island was that John Frum guards would march with uniforms and real guns, but they wielded only their red-painted bamboo guns. Three flags were unfurled. The US flag was in the middle, while the TAFEA banner on the left and the French flag on the right represented the "gates" allowing access to America. The contribution from the White Grass area was both novel and spectacular: a cavalry of about thirty young men, holding clubs and escorting the US flag. To feed all those who were attending the festival of the "John Frum Nation," Ipeukel villagers slaughtered and shared forty-one head of cattle that day!

For the moderates, the John Frum festival completed the earlier festival of the TAFEA. *Kastom* partisans had dared to fly their flags in Middle Bush and Sulphur Bay and therefore had achieved their goal. As far as they were concerned, political competition had come to an end. *Kastom* partisans were already "independent," with a full-fledged organization and a well-defined territory. Politics in Tanna was over. In the eyes of their adversaries, however, *kastom* supporters were now nothing more than "rebels."

An ominous truce stretched on until June. The two sides were getting ready for a decisive confrontation. The final escalation began on 18 May. In an incident near Loanatom, an important VP leader suffered the backlash of J.-M. Leye's ill-fated "welcome"; a fight broke out and the John Frum took some prisoners. Visibly, the point of no return had been reached in both camps. The next day, a group of VP militants seized Gendarme Lopez, tied him up, and tried to expel him from the island by thrusting him into an airplane. The mobile squad of the French police was dispatched by air from Vila and liberated the *gendarme,* preventing a large-scale confrontation with *kastom* partisans, then in the process of gathering before heading toward Lenakel. As the *gendarme* had become the favorite target of nationalist militants—who made up the majority of Lenakel residents—the French Resident deemed it wise to repatriate him. As a consequence, the island was left to itself. No longer was there an outside authority—even symbolic—that could come between the factions.

Tanna's Revolt

The last French *gendarme* left Tanna on 25 May. On 26 May, the moderates initiated a show of force. During the night, the cars used by cooperatives and French schools disappeared, "requisitioned" by the moderates. The next morning, they took over the airstrip, thereby preventing the plane from Vila from landing. At noon, a crowd of about seven hundred people invaded the Isangel administrative offices and laid siege to the police station, which was sheltering the district commissioner and his assistant (both Melanesians) representing the Vila government. A tear gas bomb launched to disperse the crowd triggered off a charge: the attackers forced their way into the office buildings and ransacked the quarters of the former British district agency. After the government police gave in, the district commissioner, Jo Dalessa, and his assistant were captured and taken to Middle Bush. The rebels swept back to their inland bastion for the night, making the serious tactical error of abandoning Isangel and the airstrip.

The next day at dawn, a British police mobile unit—twenty-four well-armed men and three European officers—landed in Tanna, whose airstrip had been reoccupied during the night by vp militants. Arguing that it was an internal affair, the French Resident refused to get involved. His real purpose was to let the moderate groups have a clear field, in the hope that they would gather strength and gain political concessions. As a result the British Resident acted on his own to restore the sovereignty of the new government formed by the Vanua'aku Pati. In an atmosphere of excitement, Lenakel residents swelled the ranks of the vp militants, who, of their own accord, joined the police mobile unit. Escorted by several Land-Rovers carrying vp supporters, the British force headed for Middle Bush to attack the "TAFEA Nation's" headquarters and liberate the district commissioner and assistant district commissioner. The battle began on the road. The "rebels" threw cartridges of dynamite and shot flights of arrows at the police; the latter fired with machine guns over their opponents' heads and used tear gas. After a short engagement, the *kastom* partisans dispersed. Several were taken prisoner. From Lamlu, besieged, all *kastom* partisans fled, with the exception of Noklam Assol, Posen, Kasso, and a number of other big men who stayed on, either on account of their age or out of dignity. The British police let vp militants act on their own. The TAFEA flag was seized, the government representatives freed. The prisoners, tied up, punched, and thrust into trucks, later found themselves in the Isangel jail.

After Lamlu's fall, Ipeukel became the last bastion of the moderates and the political center of the rebellion. It would have been impossible for government members to go there for talks: moderate partisans were flocking to Ipeukel from every corner of the island, joined by Alexis Yolou and his group, who used a boat, while the John Frum living in Vila hastened to return from the capital. Encircled on all sides, the village of Ipeukel was the symbol of resistance in the island; the vp forces triumphed everywhere else. With the help of the British special police force,

VP partisans invaded every village of *kastom* partisans in turn and arrested *kastom*'s main leaders, such as Tuk Nao in the south. An uncontrolled manhunt spread through the island, made easier by the return to Vila, on 30 May, of the British police officer, his subordinate officers, and half the mobile unit. Unrest was expected in the capital. During the night of 27 May, Santo's moderates had taken over Luganville; the government feared a similar attempt in Vila and drummed up its troops. Apparently the moderate parties had coordinated the events in Espiritu Santo and Tanna to force the central government to negotiate, with secession as their alternative.

That week brought great trepidation and turmoil to Tanna. Half the population lived in fear, and the bush and caves were full of people in hiding who had left their villages. From Isangel, rumors brought the tale of brutality and daily humiliation inflicted on the prisoners (as later confirmed by the prisoners themselves). In Ipeukel, the decision was made to free them.

The Tragedy

The action was planned for the night of 10 June. In the evening the men drank a single cup of kava and said the war *tamafa*.[26] All confessed to the spirit of John Frum, smeared their skin with coconut milk (a form of purity-related magic before warfare), and put flowers in their hair (representing mediation with their ancestors). The British anthropologist MacClancy (1983), who was in Ipeukel at the time, described their departure. Led by Alexis Yolou, Charley Nako, and Isakwan, about three hundred partisans left Ipeukel carrying traditional weapons and a few old rifles.

Watching the encircled village, the lookout men immediately saw their opponents' movements. Messengers ran out to Isangel where a "welcoming party" was organized. As they walked through the night for several hours, the "rebels," who were observed at all times, were unaware that the surprise effect on which they counted to deliver their fellow partisans would backfire. Near Lenakel, a group of about fifty *kastom* supporters led by Mariano, Alexis's brother, headed toward the airfield. They routed the guards of the VP forces and attempted to blow up the airstrip, to little avail. Meanwhile, Alexis and the main body of *kastom* supporters were reaching the Isangel hill across from the community center. A little farther on the British jail held the twenty-seven prisoners whom Yolou wanted to set free. His adversaries were waiting for him there.

Looking at the trap, Alexis Yolou immediately realized that he was not in a position of strength. The time was 3 AM. Before the John Frum and Kapiel lay a hollow lined with two hibiscus hedges. Across from the *kastom* people and on both sides, already encircling them, were the Melanesian members of the armed mobile squad, supported by an indeterminate number of Vanua'aku Pati militants, some armed with guns, and by workers from the Condominium public works teams. Suddenly, the lights on two Land-Rovers were turned on and their beams leveled at the "visitors." Had there been a formal attack, they would have known how to act, but in the circumstances they remained a compact group, indecisive and rooted to the spot as they faced their enemies' deployment. Then Yolou broke away from the group and walked ahead by himself.

Korisa, the minister who greeted Alexis, was also his first cousin; he led him to the community center to negotiate. According to all witnesses, their dialogue was almost friendly. Asked about freeing the prisoners, the minister told Alexis that they had to wait for morning to contact the government by radio, as he himself did not have authority to act on the issue. The John Frum representative requested that two representatives of the joint powers be sent to Tanna to take part in negotiations, and inquire into the matter of the maltreatment and humiliations inflicted on the prisoners; his request was granted. Outside, the *kastom* people, still clustered together, were sitting on the ground. Some were smoking, others were sleeping. The night was far advanced—it was close to 4 AM—and, owing to fatigue, excitement had dropped among Yolou's men. Yolou walked back to them and announced his decision: they would withdraw to Loanatom and wait until the next day to resume negotiations. A number of moderate leaders refused to leave, repeating their demands for the immediate release of the prisoners. A second discussion began between Korisa and Yolou, at the end of which the John Frum leader went back to his troops and gave the order to depart for Loanatom.

At that moment, events took a tragic turn. The moderates were starting to stand up in disorderly fashion; Yolou was walking toward them when shooting started. The police threw tear gas canisters straight ahead, while some militants opened fire at point-blank range. In the melee, the prisoners broke the prison door open and set themselves free. The moderates were assembled as a group and had no real means of defense. They sustained a direct attack that hit them from both the front and the rear. Thirteen were shot—one of them mortally—all of them *kastom* partisans.

The one who died, the only one during this tragic night, was Alexis Yolou, whose body was found around 6 AM a few meters from the site of the confrontation. The corpse showed several wounds from gunshots and a "blunt instrument," as the official report stated later. According to a letter dated 12 June by Dr Guidon of the White Sands French hospital, who was the first to examine the body, "After the injuries were examined, there was no doubt that Alexis Yolou had been struck on the spot and when he was down" (pers comm).

There are two conflicting versions of this tragedy. According to the official version, the moderates suddenly appeared to move toward the community center instead of shifting away from it, which triggered the shooting. In addition, the prisoners broke out, causing confusion. For their part, *kastom* partisans said they were standing up to leave, with no intention of fighting, when they were shot at point-blank range. They affirmed that they heard the order: "*Kilim olgeta, naouia, naouia* 'Hit them now, now'."[27] Some *kastom* partisans stated they also heard a comment after the order: "Fire up, they have no head,[28] they are idiots." Whether this was actually said or not, it tells much about the state of affairs between the two camps. On hearing the gunshots, the prisoners burst their door to free themselves. Earlier they had been told that, should their friends try to liberate them by force, they would all be killed by their guards. Alexis was in a critical position: he was separated from his men and very close to his adversaries, who were able to seize him. He did not die from his wounds, but from bleeding and lack of care as he was left to die on the ground. In the turmoil, several men heard him cry: "I have lost my children."[29]

The government version was that of the "slip-up": at night, the confusion created by uncontrolled movements had led to the tragic incident. According to the moderates, however, a trap had been set to kill the three leaders who were directing *kastom* troops. Isakwan and Charley Nako were able to escape, but there was no missing the mark for Alexis Yolou, Tanna's representative and spearhead of the John Frum movement. When he carried out the official inquiry, English Judge Graeme McKay was noncommittal. "Several versions of the events have been given, and it is obvious that the situation was very chaotic," he wrote in his report to the press. The McKay report made it clear that the British police used only tear gas. About the precise question of Alexis's death, McKay concluded:

> The information at our disposal leads us to believe that three or four different individuals are guilty of murdering or attempting to murder Alexis Yolou. Other charges may also be brought: bodily harm resulting in death, through random firing when people were nearby. All these points demand solid proof: this is the reason why, in the absence of new major evidence or a revelation by those who were involved in these events, I am not able to take into custody or charge anyone in the case of Alexis Yolou's death. (McKay 1981, translated from the French)

The airfield had easily been reopened and, in the morning of 11 June, the mobile squads of the two residencies landed on Tanna, a little too late. Struck down by tragedy, the whole island seemed in a state of bewilderment. In official circles and elsewhere, the Isangel murder "did not wash" and each side argued that the other was responsible. "The blood of Alexis Yolou will fall on his murderers," stated Resident Commissioner Robert on the Vila radio. "All of us are accountable for Alexis Yolou's death," said Resident Commissioner Stuart later in front of the Representative Assembly. Following the inquiry, Judge McKay resigned and left the group. The case was closed.

Alexis's murder resulted in the breakup of the *kastom* movement. Alexis had led Tanna's revolt; Tanna's revolt died with him. The John Frum and the pagans went back to the marginal status that they had known so well during the Condominium era, and the government was able to install its sovereignty over Tanna without meeting any resistance. Vanua'aku Pati leaders attempted to restore order and civil peace on the island. They also indicated that the rebels should account for their acts and that this matter would be dealt with as soon as the Santo affair was settled, the Santo affair being a secession attempt that diverted public attention for a time.

One month after independence, a US Navy ship anchored off the island of Tanna. On board were several national government members who wanted to show the John Frum that their defeat was complete: the Americans, who were the John Frum's alleged allies, were now the friends of their Vanua'aku Pati enemies—or such was the message. Yet in Ipeukel, the star-spangled banner was still flying and the John Frum were not swayed in their convictions. They had heard this tune many times before! The local VP political leaders did not get discouraged and organized "customary" ceremonies of reconciliation in September; again, some members of the government were in attendance. The main ceremony took place in the southwest part of the island. Another ceremony involved the residents of Loanatom, which was Alexis Yolou's village, together with those of Lowkatai, Minister Korisa's village. Also, the Vanuatu national flag was raised in Middle Bush at the very spot where the TAFEA banner had flown. Eventually, the John Frum of Ipeukel returned the VP flag they had snatched in February 1978; the police let the US flag fly over their village. The former moderate groups accepted the various political measures of "civil peace" initiated by the winners, but they did so in fear. These groups agreed that the courts should inquire into the matter of the post-1977 events. Yet they found it intolerable that the law was interested only in them, although their adversaries had been equally concerned in the breach of public order on the island.

The victors' justice came in January 1981. Judge Cooke settled the cases about the secession attempt by Santo groups, in the northern part of the archipelago, then he and his court headed south, accompanied by the mobile police units. One day in January, the police, bearing arms, encircled Ipeukel. The US flag was taken down, and the Vanuatu flag finally raised over the rebellious village that had become the symbol of Tanna's revolt. The people were ordered to raise the national flag every day and to lower it at night. As in the good old days, neighboring Christian villages were to keep watch. Next came the trial of the "rebels": 256 were condemned either to sentences ranging from one month to one year in jail or to fines. Without lawyers or any real trial, it was a travesty of justice. Judge Cooke carried on placidly, issuing his judgments in front of the accused, who for the most part filed past him in silence, one by one, village after village.

The two-day trial was attended by the Marist priest Arthur Tierney. Originally from Ireland, he had been based in Fiji and had just replaced Father Sacco in Loanatom. Father Tierney wrote,

> I want to say very clearly that British Justice died here on Tanna on Monday and Tuesday, January 19th and 20th. . . . All the accused were considered guilty before their trial. . . . During the interrogations of last month by the Mobile Police, each individual was coerced into signing a confession. . . . Not one of the accused was asked if he had anything to say in mitigation. The court was in a hurry to get back to Vila. I could go on with other details of this tragedy which ignored the custom way of life of the people and has broken the peace of this beautiful island. (Letter in *Tam-Tam* no. 27, 7 Feb 1981)

Tierney's letter gave examples of the brutality and humiliation to which the prisoners were subjected. He was expelled from Vanuatu.

The government wished to settle the issue rapidly and had the wisdom not to touch Mweles, prophet and living symbol of the John Frum. Sentences were relatively light for the most part. Yet only the camp of *kastom* supporters had to respond to the accusation of violence. Besides, as in the affair of the John Frum from northern Tanna forty years earlier, the "rebels" did not remember the court sentences, lenient as they appeared, but the winners' insults and gestures of gratuitous brutality. In other words, they remembered the humiliation.

Since then, the camp of the former "rebels" has kept behind a wall of silence. John Frum festivals are now celebrated in restricted circles. The camp of *kastom* bears the scar of Alexis Yolou's death, and the remembrance of the dramatic events of the early morning of 11 June 1980 will not fade for a long time to come. However, the memory of the tragic night has entered the collective unconscious and is already part of the oral tradition. Near the Loanatom church, on the grave of the young representative, his father and brothers inscribed these words: *"Alexis Yolou,*

30 ans, assassiné le 11 juin 1980 'Alexis Yolou, 30, murdered on 11 June 1980'."

To this day, a single high-level Vanua'aku Pati leader has visited the grave: Iolu Abbil, a native of the neighboring Christian village of Loaneai and the first leader of the Nikoletan, a short-lived attempt at unification. He was mourning his Tannese brother.

18 The Meaning of Tanna's Kastom

> Reason does not create its own themes but acquires
> them from myth.
>
> R. MEHL

As they delved into the memory of their past to search for a solution to the problems of the age, *kastom* supporters on Tanna had to deal with the contradictions and limitations entailed by this type of attitude but, on the other hand, were able to give their choice a truly epic dimension.

A "Hot Society"?

According to the Middle Bush tradition, the saga of the "stones" organized the world. Concurrently, a society was built, or rather several societies were organized, along identical lines within each "canoe" (or *niko*) on the island. It was the golden age of *kastom,* the *nepro* of the origins. Land was partitioned as canoes that followed natural features such as thalwegs,[1] crests, and watersheds, but there were no internal boundaries as such. A flexible webbing of space allowed one to find one's right place in society and stable roots within the land.

During that age of foundation, men were magic stones (see chapter 8). While they wandered about, they named places, territories, and themselves. When space had been completed and structured by places and roads, so had society. Nothing may be changed in that timeless universe which, situated at the beginning of time, results from the work of "stones" *(kapiel)*. Insofar as all its elements are place-related, society can live in peace.

As soon as the golden age of the origins disintegrated, men moved into a cycle of mobility and rivalry. Exchange turned into competition, which led to warfare; the unity of the island was shattered; time became steeped in reality. The cold timeless society of the origins became a hot historical society whose time was—and is—broken up by events.

History involves Islanders in a perpetual and dangerous movement, whereas the ideal society of *kastom,* which existed before people appeared in their human form, is outside chronological time. *Kastom* finds its meaning in the wish of its people to return to the time and space shaped by the magic of the origins. That mythical time stirred *"la grandeur indéfinissable des commencements,"*[2] in the words of Lévi-Strauss (1966).

For the Tannese, history began with the tragic, lasting war between the two political moieties sharing the island, the Numurkuen and the Koyometa. Tanna was torn asunder by that war, then torn again by Tanna Law and white contact. *Kastom* supporters spurn this time of misfortune. Their *kastom* is set against any political interpretation and, in their eyes, only the island's origins bear meaning.

The Paradigm of Space

The *kastom* people wished to go back to the starting point of history. This meant that history had to be completed and wrongs redressed, which would restore the unity of the island.

Restoring the time of the origins meant returning to the spatial organization of the boundless Great Space created by heroes and stones. The clans of origin needed to find their original places within Semo-Semo's ancient canoes. To do so, they had to abandon the places which they had often occupied at random in the course of history and, using traditional rituals, re-open the great dancing grounds and the places where their forebears had lived.

In customary fashion, traditional groups also endeavored to bring "dead lands" back to life. Those were the lands that had been abandoned following wars and epidemics of the nineteenth century. In the traditional view, de facto occupation and actual use do not necessarily establish land rights—neither does the act of conquest. Land is not a possession, it is a being; one can hold it only if one identifies with it. A right of origin represents a right of land tenure, and a man's customary name or title proves his identification with land. Therefore the "real man" or *man ples* is the individual who actually lives on the land of his ancestors from the era of magical stones, and who carries their real, or original, names.

If the "real" inhabitants have disappeared, the *napang niel* who were their closest allies—through blood and propinquity along the same road —keep the land in the name of the dead owners. They can bring the land back to life through ritual; they will then revive the former group's identity, take possession of its primordial sites, and use the same names. The *napang niel* resuscitate the vanished group. They become that group by "inhabiting" its territory, provided such right is acknowledged by all their nearest neighbors.

Accordingly, the Islanders' mystical vision of the world gave birth to a concrete spatial strategy, and in return this spatial strategy allowed them to found the original society of *kastom* anew, in other words, to re-create it as faithfully as possible. The goal of traditional groups was not so much to bring about an optimum population distribution throughout the island as it was to reconstruct the initial structure so that individuals could return to the places holding their identity. *Kastom* supporters wanted to restore the harmony that was alleged to exist between person and place at the time of the origins. To Tanna's "real places" the "real men" were meant to return. Only when the island's sacred space had been re-established and settled by its true inhabitants would the society of *kastom* find its identity, that is, its unity, its civil peace, and the whole array of its powers; only then would the *Shipimanwawa* definitely end and the issues of land tenure and placeless or "drifting men" be solved.

Stones and Canoes

Traditional thought holds that too much traveling or, rather, a lack of control over mobility entails misfortune. A man who is back in his place must stay there; only big men are entitled to have freedom and mobility to some extent. A Christian Islander from Lowtehl summed up the idea when he told me once: "*Kastom i talem: yu fala i stap, i stap. Sapos yu muv, yu spoilem graon blong fren blong yu* 'Kastom always says: stay in your place, because when you move out you throw the land of others out of balance'." *Kastom* partisans believe that conflicts and "land stealing" happen because men leave their places and wander from their roads. Uncontrolled mobility leads to warfare and disorder. By contrast, the society of *kastom* resembles a world of stones—or one of firmly rooted banyan trees. Men reach self-realization where they are and do so by rooting themselves deeply into the ground and pushing their foliage toward the sky. The tree or the stone is the metaphor for men, just as the bird is the metaphor for women (see Penoa's myth in chapter 9). Each small society on Tanna is a canoe made up of trees and birds, and represents a mobile structure with its roads, harbors, and networks. Men move inside their specific canoe, along the roads associated with it. Therefore, men are trees within canoes, exchanging birds from one canoe to another according to marriage rules. In the course of history, Tanna's network society grew dim and the order of *kastom* was shattered precisely because men lost their way and wandered onto other roads.

This tenet of *kastom* sheds light on the complex issue of war fugitives, outlaws, and migrants within the island. If such individuals are not adopted and do not receive names originating from the territory that welcomes them, they become "drifting men." Lacking depth, strength, and true identity, these people have neither places nor social status. The only solution for these uprooted individuals is to go back to the places from which their ancestors started, by way of the latter's original migration road. If this return journey is impossible, the fugitives must remain in a position of political insignificance and keep a humble profile. Removed from their own places and devoid of "roads," "drifting men" have no identity. They are shadows that can only exist in the name of the "real men" holding the territory. Hence, they have to ask the masters of that territory for the right to use the roads of ritual exchange and benefit from marriage alliances.[3]

Are *kastom* partisans under the yoke of a cold ideology that rules that people are forever bound by the dictatorship of territory? In that light, the despotism of the origins would replace the misfortunes of history. Some "fundamentalists" within *kastom* did perceive the issue in those terms, but most supporters of traditional thought had a purpose of a different order. Theirs was to re-create the sacred space of the *nepro* and thereby revive Tanna's political unity around its traditional chiefs as well as the equality of living conditions on the island. In the course of history, humankind had set internal limits to land tenure within the canoes. These limits had to disappear, to be replaced by an "agrarian communism" that implied a free sharing of land and goods within the community. Although traditional society may seem to be based on a rather aristocratic view, especially Tanna's "hawk society" (the society that created the *kweriya* and the *yremera*), its members are equal from the standpoint of material goods; within the undivided territory of the canoe, all people are entitled to behave freely, farm without constraints, and enjoy the same economic status. The cultural project of customary groups was far from being politically "reactionary." In fact, it carried the hope that modern contradictions could be bypassed through *kastom*.

Proponents of tradition also thought they could deal more easily with the problems brought about by modernity—including issues of an economic nature.

Kastom and Money

Currency is of limited importance in Tanna. Islanders possess little cash and appear remarkably detached in this respect. In general terms, Tanna's gift-giving and exchange-based economy plays a much larger role than its market economy. The small amounts of cash that do circulate within the island are rarely set aside for saving purposes, being instead continuously "given away." They go from hand to hand like a prestigious object imported from the outside and as fascinating as an exotic luxury good.

To illustrate, a German businessman by the name of Weiseman happened to visit the John Frum groups in White Grass. After touring the northwest section of the island with its broad, almost empty savannas, Weiseman decided to build a modern cattle ranch encompassing approximately two thousand hectares. A factory ship would come in regularly and be supplied with live cattle and pigs; it would transform these into canned goods on its return voyage to markets on the Pacific rim. Weiseman wore big hats, which he changed frequently; he smoked cigars and offered gifts. Remarkably plump, with a merry disposition, he appealed to the John Frum who felt he looked "American." For a token sum, the John Frum of Imanaka agreed to lease the White Grass lands—which were disputed by other groups. The John Frum would also supply a labor force. Along with one of his agents, Franz Bühler, the businessman sent equipment: one Land-Rover, two tractors, barbed wire, plows, and so forth. As they waited for the fabulous machines to arrive, the John Frum could believe the "cargo" had finally reached Tanna. The year was 1977.

The John Frum of White Grass had fantasies of riches for a time. For a time only, as the cattle ranch undertaking sunk rather quickly, like most other wonder projects set up in the group. But although Weiseman went bankrupt, Bühler carried on by himself. He was on good terms with the John Frum. Ever the adventurer, he cultivated large potato fields for two years then left for Brazil.

Despite this negative outcome, the John Frum had showed enthusiasm for the project and devoted some energy to it. The John Frum are far from being hostile to "progress." However, they must feel that a development project comes from "friendly territory" and, as Bühler understood, they must be given the liberty to organize themselves according to their own criteria.

Individual capitalistic entrepreneurs in Tanna generally rise from the ranks of Christian groups. By contrast, economic development schemes among *kastom* supporters can only succeed if they are carried out within the framework of community links and traditional alliances. That system is summed up in the Bislama word *kompani* 'company', which means the gathering of close, blood-related allies who share territory and land. Allies work as a team and on an equal basis, accumulating the profits from their work in a communal till.

Money represents a foreign, somewhat dangerous value. Money fascinates, of course, but as a "whim" that never reaches the essential core of *kastom*. To the proponents of tradition, money is part of the whites *"kastom."* Their own *kastom* is based on the values of land and magic, and European money cannot buy either. Accordingly, one should not attempt to define the values of traditional society in terms of economic motivations. Within *kastom* the sacred value, land-life, takes precedence over the secular value, money-profit. Such an attitude leads to a certain detachment among traditionalists as they deal repeatedly with the failure of development projects and the loss of their expectations.

When Bühler, discouraged, left White Grass for a more favorable environment, the John Frum realized the miraculous project had collapsed but forgave the businessman anyway. Imanaka villagers gave a big farewell party for Bühler who, in return, bequeathed them all his equipment, pickup truck, and Tyrolese records. With perfect equanimity, they left the two tractors and the plow to rust; the Land-Rover eventually disintegrated among the weeds.

Another example would be that of the Middle Bush cooperative[4] after independence, when the policy of aid to market gardening was suspended and the Agriculture Department focused on coffee production. The change in policy had a fatal impact on vegetable production. Yet this did not engender a feeling of disaster among *kastom* supporters even though they were made to lose a potential stream of cash benefits.

The attitude of the John Frum of Ipeukel toward tourism was revealing. The Australian Bob Paul, who had settled in Tanna in 1946, created the company Tanna Tours in the 1960s. The company organized tours to the volcano near Ipeukel and secondarily to the White Grass area, with its wild horses. By 1970, incidents involving local villagers had become increasingly frequent. Bob Paul set up a profit-sharing scheme whereby he would give the people of Ipeukel two Australian dollars per tourist, an appreciable amount of money at the time. However, the John Frum community around Sulphur Bay believed, probably wrongly, that Bob Paul was the unwavering political supporter of the Vanua'aku Pati. The John Frum reasoned as follows: Bob Paul's store, house, and tourist bungalows in Lenakel were located in the midst of a Christian, predominantly Vanua'aku, territory, therefore Bob Paul was the ally of vp partisans.

As a result, the John Frum closed off the volcano to tourists; following suit, their White Grass allies prevented visitors from having access to their own territory, with its savanna and wild horses. Violent incidents occurred while access to the volcano was closed for nine months in 1977–1978.[5] To explain their decision, Sulphur Bay residents sent a letter to the French district agent, a letter that ended with these words: "No tourist, no money, no problem." The best way to avoid money-related issues was (and still is) to have no money—a wise philosophy.

This controversy had political overtones as well. A Vila-based moderate leader had set up a tour company similar to Tanna Tours, which he called Yasur Company, with the aim of breaking the monopoly held by Bob Paul's organization. He failed in that endeavor—the John Frum were not motivated and gave him little help. "All this gets tiresome," they often said.

Mweles decided to prohibit access to the volcano because, in his own words, "the John Frum are said to want money or be jealous of what Bob Paul earns. But it is not true. I closed the volcano because I am weary of quarrels caused by money" (pers comm). People added: "*Kastom i no laikem mane* '*kastom* does not like money'," which implied that things of a different nature did not mix. Such a philosophy was not always easy to understand. Disenchanted, the trader Bob Paul stated: "My troubles began on the day I decided to share my profits and involve the John Frum in my business" (pers comm). In the same vein, the anthropologist Lindstrom (1982) tells of incidents that occurred in the course of a *toka* organized by Christians and *kastom* supporters in the White Sands region. Bob Paul offered a sum of money in exchange for inviting tourists from a cruise boat. The Christians accepted the money; *kastom* supporters did not. A violent quarrel followed.

Money Is a *Gras Sket*

As far as *kastom* and John Frum partisans are concerned, economic development, in and of itself, is less important than what it symbolizes. They have greeted various development measures in the same way they have a water supply project, accepting the pipes that originate from their allies' territories but rejecting those pipes that originate from springs or pipes located on their adversaries' territories. They follow the logic of the ritual exchange system whereby the meaning of a gift is based less on its intrinsic worth than on the characteristics of its origin. To a *kastom* partisan, a present from a friend or from an ally through the traditional road system, a *napang niel,* is always more valuable than a present from a stranger who does not belong to his network. Hence, development is perceived as a *niel,* an egalitarian exchange feast. It is a gift that refers to a system of alliance and takes a specific road. Further, contrary to what many Europeans believe or have believed, one does not necessarily become friends with a Tannese by offering a gift. Within traditional society, gift-giving only finds its meaning through either the personal bond or political alliance that precedes it. Along the same lines, development can deliver fascinating and impressive goods, but the interpretation varies according to the goods' specific meaning and the way they came (see Bonnemaison 1991*a*).

Among *kastom* partisans the individual entrepreneur is unknown—even though entrepreneurship is often the target of contemporary development. The idea that one man alone can succeed by making others work is still not readily accepted by a society based on equal exchange and the generalized distribution of goods. Money, when it comes, circulates through the chain of allies. It is said to be a *gras sket,* a mobile value that goes from hand to hand, in reference to the skirts made of multicolored fibers that women wear during rituals; along with other gifts, these skirts circulate in the course of alliance rituals.

A man who would keep the money he earns for his own use would not only be selfish but would turn his back on the values of his own society. Today, traditional Tannese companies set aside and accumulate the profits that would have otherwise gone to a single entrepreneur. This strategy prevents the traditional circulation of goods. While an individual may not keep an item of value for himself or for his own use—he is morally obliged to give it away—a company or a community may accumulate cash or goods, as these will eventually benefit all participants. Collective accumulation is allowed, but an individual must abide by the rules governing the circulation of goods.

According to tradition supporters, the white way of earning money is to sell everything, buy everything, and never give anything away. Melanesians have defined European *"kastom"* approximately in those terms and, by extension, their definition applies to the "customs" that reign in Vila, the capital of the archipelago. Yet they do not believe that capitalism (the "money-system") is inescapable. On the other hand, alliance with the whites who control the road of material well-being is a possibility, and even an imperative. This may be one of the essential meanings of the vision of the John Frum. They have sought alliances with mythical peers on the other side of the sea because, in their eyes, true power and therefore prosperity will result from having this kind of friends. By the same token, the John Frum do not consider development projects productive activities as such. Modern goods are only the symbols of the satisfaction that will be found at the end of the road. Used as ornaments or status symbols, such goods are not inherent to the island's social system, and neither are they seen as genuine outputs from a production cycle.

Although *kastom* partisans may want the objects that symbolize the whites' well-being, they do not wish to jeopardize the security of their own lifeways to get such objects. As *kastom* supporters often say: "Whites have money, we have *kastom.*" These are indeed two different value systems and modes of representation. *Kastom* partisans realize that the values of the market economy are at variance with the values of the economy of exchange among allies. Modernity intrigues them; its objects, its technology fill them with wonder, but the type of society associated with modernity does not really tempt them. In brief, the *kastom* people want modernity without being modern.

Nation and Canoe

Tannese society has yet to find within itself the strength to unite again. As long as this is the case, the current divisions will stifle any action or project. Thus, anglophone Christian groups greeted the idea of an independent nation with much enthusiasm. To *kastom* partisans the same idea seemed like a mask. Behind the mask, they believed, was the hegemony that Christian groups were once again trying to impose over Tanna. *Kastom* proponents also felt that the new state power might become more oppressive than the former colonial power. Further, they did not accept the very idea of a nation-state managed from an island other than their own. In *kastom* partisans' eyes, a nation is not the classic territorial system of a *pré carré*[6] organized by a state and marked out by frontiers. A nation is a network with flexible links held together by alliance and set within a great relational space. Therefore Tanna's *kastom* partisans see their nation as a freely moving canoe, a canoe that seeks out and opens up roads among its allies dispersed throughout the world.

The traditional nation thus defined is not closed off by a boundary. All those who, in one capacity or another, share the same vision or else some form of solidarity or fellowship belong to such a nation. In spatial terms, the nation of *kastom* is a reticular space, a network of places based on brotherhood and fellowship which can extend very far, even to the end of the known world, or stop at the door of the nearest neighbor.

A *kastom* canoe moves freely insofar as equal groups link up with each other along the road of alliance. To circulate, the canoe must obtain the goodwill of all equal points located along the journey. If such is not the case, space is split apart—other canoes stand still, exchanges are no longer possible, journeying comes to a stop, the whole society disintegrates. On the eve of independence, the Tannese felt they were in such a situation of fragmented space and generalized conflict.

Within the political space of *kastom,* each founding place is an absolute place holding within itself a material and spiritual principle. By extension, each of Tanna's canoes is a primordial place, even though it may in some cases derive its power and existence from another which was founded earlier. Hence, Tanna's traditional groups are unconstrained. Among them, there are no allegiances but only precedences, as dictated by their order of appearance. Clustered along the road of alliance, canoes have a free hand in carrying out their multiple interactions with each other. No canoe is entitled to enact laws for the others; no group may hold the center—or the periphery; all groups are complementary, necessary, and equal.

This configuration of apparent anarchy is set within space parameters that do not easily match those of the modern nation-state. Modern political space functions thanks to the force operated by the center over the periphery, be it of a democratic nature—with majority rule—or of a dictatorial nature—with party or "Big Brother" rule. Within traditional Melanesia, political space is egalitarian or even anarchical.[7] Rather than a central place, it has origin places. If the members of the social group decide to regroup on a larger scale and undertake great communal projects, they must gather within alliances where full consensus is the rule. This solution does not necessarily make society more peaceful, but it enlivens it prodigiously.

Because the Melanesian social contract involves a road of alliance through which participants demonstrate their consensus, this presupposes that all participants are alike to some extent. Such an egalitarian society is, by necessity, fairly homogeneous.

Kastom partisans, when they were part of the political opposition, did not feel at ease with the concept of a modern state supported by the nationalist camp. They also felt dominated and, accordingly, tried to pull out. Although aware of their opponents' logic, Vanua'aku Pati leaders came to the conclusion that *kastom* supporters were "rebels." Until its final outcome, Tanna's revolt was therefore seen and experienced along cultural as well as political lines.

Big Men and Political Commissars

In 1978, when *kastom* groups proclaimed their sovereignty and raised the flag of what they called Tanna's Nation, the existing conflict grew increasingly violent. Big men now faced not colonial masters but new adversaries, the Vanua'aku Pati's "political commissars." By affirming their nationhood, *kastom* supporters were going a long way, considerably further than if they had simply returned to traditional ways. Indeed, the *kastom*-based "paths of alliance" had organized a hard-core political movement that was contending with the Vanua'aku Pati network for power in the island. As they vied for political leadership, the two camps tried to answer one overriding question, each to their own advantage: Who has the right to lay down the law in Tanna?—the timeless question of all island societies. In Tanna's case, should it be the representatives of the new central government or the masters of the place from which the world of *kastom* originated?

Based, for the most part, on the network of Presbyterian villages, the VP organization covered the entire island. In each center, the party had named a "political commissar" who, besides organizing militants, was in charge of the district. The local Presbyterian minister and the political commissar were often one and the same. After its nationwide success at the polls, the Vanua'aku Pati had set up a government in early 1980: four ministers out of ten, including the prime minister, were Presbyterian pastors or Anglican priests. The national motto was now "*Long God yumi stanap* 'In God we progress'." This religious orientation went together with a progressive stance. The nationalism of the Vanua'aku Pati was "democratic," "popular," and allied with that of other Third World peoples. Like most progressive leaders in new Third World nations, VP leaders emphasized unity, national pride, and the need for economic development. They supported the liberation struggles of other peoples and refused any form of dependency or alignment, not only with former colonial powers but vis-à-vis political blocs in the Northern and Southern Hemispheres.

In the eyes of VP leaders, the word *kastom* initially represented the historical and cultural heritage of the nation they wished to shape. Vanuatu was now entering the concert of world nations. Vanua'aku Pati leaders aimed at building a modern country while keeping its Melanesian roots, returning not to the letter of tradition but at least to its spirit. Accordingly, they reclaimed their nation's precontact history; *kastom,* being the cultural reflection of that past, became the symbol of Melanesian identity (Tonkinson 1982*a*). This symbol, however, was powerful, ambiguous, and charged with emotion. It could be interpreted in numerous ways and be used as both a rallying cry and a call to discord (Lindstrom 1982).

What was meant by *kastom?* Was it a collective memory of the Melanesian past, a cultural heritage, a set of values, or—as Tanna's *kastom* groups emphasized—a system to organize both space and society? For the Tannese, *kastom* meant even more; it represented the "nation," that is to say, a specific space of alliance—a canoe with roads and without frontiers. Vanua'aku Pati leaders were satisfied as long as *kastom* was a vague identity-related concept, but they believed *kastom* would become a dangerous principle if it were to involve a political organization that could facilitate secession movements. Conversely, some moderate leaders made use of a *kastom*-based ideology to reject the very existence of a central power, all the more because this power was in the hands of their adversaries. For instance, Jean-Marie Leye, president of both the Federal party and the Tan Union, stated in an interview published in the weekly news magazine *Nasiko:* "We hold our power from *kastom* and from our ancestors. The people from one island do not want to be led by those from another island. It was so before the Europeans came, and it will be so after they leave. We want to return to the previous state of affairs. For we shall be free if we respect *kastom.* We used to follow *kastom* before independence, we shall do likewise after independence" (28 Feb 1980).

Vanua'aku Pati leaders became increasingly distrustful of *kastom.* Father Walter Lini, Anglican priest and chief minister, summed up the situation as it appeared to nationalist leaders: "People have used the idea of 'custom' to totally contradict the idea of development and democracy in this country. On Santo and Tanna custom has been carried to extreme by people who incorrectly claim their respect of traditional ways. It has become a political weapon and this has made it into something that is not Melanesian at all" (1980, 42).

In Tanna, *kastom* was far from being just a theory, however. Here, it was a vision, a worldview, a set of beliefs, and a reticulated space of roads and places; further, it was being shaped into a political weapon by historical forces. In their own way, the island's big men were trying to solve the internal issues set in motion by the disastrous *Shipimanwawa* and further compounded by the resentments born during the Tanna Law era. They were now contending with vp commissars on a daily basis, and a compromise was not at hand.

In the eyes of Tannese Vanua'aku Pati militants, *kastom* increasingly appeared as a dangerous symbol manipulated by a few with a view to establishing their personal power and preventing the legitimate national-ist movement from achieving its purpose. No longer a cultural symbol, *kastom* became a mark of obscurantism accounted for by its supporters' lack of education. A very old cliché was back, the cliché separating *skul* Christians and *kastom* pagans, in other words, those who had received the "light" of instruction as opposed to those who delighted in the "dark-ness" of illiteracy.

In March 1979, just before the events, the government, intent on putting an end to disturbances on the island, sent a commission of enquiry to Tanna. The commission tried to understand what the appar-ently quite explosive word *kastom* meant to the Tannese but was not able to get a definitive explanation. Reverend Korisa, then political commis-sar of the Vanua'aku Pati in Lowkatai, told the commission: "I think *kas-tom* is a big word. I don't know what you mean by *kastom*, . . . it is impossible to define *kastom*. Today many people don't know what's meant by *kastom*, it has different meanings to different people. It is a very large subject which concerns our daily life. With this word *kastom*, it seems we are digging up things we have already buried. Some groups here use *kastom* to maintain order" (COE 1979, 16).

To which Charley Nako, *kastom* leader of the Kapiel movement and Tan Union representative, retorted:

> The trouble in Tanna is of two kinds: one kind is the European one and the other one is the local kind. One kind is the church which fights *kas-tom*. If the church leaves the politics alone, it is alright, but they have gone into politics. The ones who went to church too much, or school, don't understand the correct meaning of *kastom*. . . . The real church of the villages is *kastom*, which wants peace and unity. . . . There [was] trouble when [the] Presbyterian church tried to fix it up, so [it] forced the people to go to church when they didn't want to. Now we have
> Tanna Law. We are living in the *kastom* way, not the Tanna Law way

resulting from the interference of the church. . . . Originally *kastom* was a kind of administration. . . . No one has the right to choose chiefs, except *kastom*. (COE 1979, 25–26)

His half-brother Tom Kasso added: "There was not any peace with Pastor Korisa's party and our *kastom* party; we made food for them but they never came" (COE 1979, 27).[8]

A Melanesian VP supporter from Ambrym, who was then acting British district agent, stated his opinion even more bluntly: "It is true that Tanna has very strong *kastom*. To most Tannese *kastom* means being able to drink kava, remain uneducated and not to be a member of any religion. For example, the people in Middle Bush, when they see a pastor from any church, they say, he is not a *kastom* man" (COE 1979, 56).

As the previous quotations illustrate, the two sides hardly listened to one another. They had not been on speaking terms for a long time, and each denied the other any shred of truth. Vanua'aku Pati supporters believed that returning to *kastom* meant going backward and even taking the road to hell. *Kastom* partisans feared a born-again "Christian power" that would reinstate a sort of dictatorship, a second Tanna Law. In Tanna—a rebellious island, but full of logical minds—one could find both the strongest champions of nationalism and the most eager supporters of a restoration of *kastom*. In very skillful ways, the two camps placed the strife in the light of their own history, thereby exacerbating the passions behind it.

When the *kastom* people were denied their right to a genuine *kastom,* they reacted by raising the stakes; likewise for the Christians, who were refused their right to a genuine, modern nation. The two movements spiraled on their own until they collided in the midst of the arena. That day, the island went mad.

Kastom supporters from Middle Bush and the southwestern part of the island watching traditional dances on 14 July 1979—Tanna's last Bastille Day before Vanuatu's independence. The festival included farewell dances in honor of French District Agent Roger Payen, who had been called back to Vila by the government of internal autonomy.

A Tannese member of the French police force (*milice*, left) with one of his counterparts from the British force. Between the two police forces the "dialogue" was as difficult as between the two Residencies.

The US flag was first raised in Tanna on 15 February 1978. About two thousand sympathizers watched one hundred young men parade in honor of the flag around the Ipeukel paddock.

John Frum soldiers practicing the US military drill, which they have rehearsed for months in secret. Their guns are bamboo sticks with their ends painted red. In the eyes of the John Frum, the American drill is like the *toka* of *kastom* groups: a show followed by a gigantic *niel*. On 15 February 1978 the John Frum of Ipeukel slaughtered forty head of cattle to feed their guests.

The American flag flies over Ipeukel for the first time. Over the John Frum soldiers' bare chests, the letters USA are inscribed in red, a color that represents human blood and symbolizes the John Frum movement.

Tom Mweles, historical and charismatic leader of the John Frum movement, surrounded by two John Frum guards of honor.

Aligned as for a parade, the historical leaders of the John Frum movement realize their dream: the US flag is now floating over Ipeukel (15 February 1978).

Willy Kuai (left), one of the thinkers within the *kastom* movement, with other *kastom* supporters. He was Tony Fornelli's assistant and, as one of the Four Corner (Forcona) leaders, was jailed by Condominium authorities in 1974.

Tanna's elders carry the memory of the island and hold customary power. Here, two wise men from the John Frum movement at the Ipeukel festival on 15 February 1978.

Youngster from Lenatuan, Middle Bush, 1979.

19 Conclusion:
The Men Ples

In a magnificent text, philosopher Michel Serres, while investigating the roots of his identity, carries on a dialogue with the landscape of the great Chinese plain. A Gascon peasant from the plain surrounding the Garonne River, Serres likens his experience to that of a seaman. In the plain, landscapes are oceanscapes and space is a sea; the problem is to find the way out, as if one were on an island. The sky, Serres adds, is the only possible escape route from a plain: "Through the highest part, to the highest part. Everybody runs upward to the highest part, as we do in the plain. . . . Total suffocation. [Chinese farmers] might as well reside very high up. . . . To soar straight up is the only possible direction" (1983, 28–29).[1]

Melanesian Islanders, and perhaps all islanders, do not look at the sky but at the earth, and their gaze does not so much soar as dig and plunge.

Metaphors of Identity

Four or five millennia and perhaps even longer ago, a navigating people discovered the islands of the archipelago by canoe and turned each of these high islands, with their volcanic, often jagged relief plunging into the water, into so many territories. Here, the navigators settled. Out of these splintered lands, which seemed outside time and where space was scarce, they carved their collective destiny.

The identity of Melanesian islands plunges into the bowels of the earth. Soaring toward the infinity of the sky only because it is also rooted beneath the surface of the earth, the tree became the metaphor for man—whom another metaphor had already designated as stone. Thus, the man who lives within his place and who stands straight will take root along

320

with the tree. Within his place, a man must, according to the ethics of *kastom,* carry out his destiny and exercise his power. As he becomes older, he then turns into a big man, that is, a "real man" who acknowledges and takes responsibility for his group. De facto, the individual who leaves his place and wanders from the roads of his ancestors loses his power and his status—at least until he returns.

Earth is a womb; her sons are men. By contrast, space is a sea, a "floating" value that has no depth and no duration. What a man considers valuable is the quality of his roots, in other words, his places of origin, like fixed points in the moving pattern of waves.

If a man is a place, what about society? The canoe, or *niko,* is the metaphor for the community. Much as an unconstrained, mobile value, society is a flexible spatial network evolving from and building itself by means of roads. A place provides a man with his roots; a canoe traveling on a road grants him the allies necessary for his survival and reproduction. The canoe's destiny is to circulate, to go beyond the tree, to move from place to place and island to island, wherever its roads lead it. That is the ultimate significance of the canoe of the John Frum people, who have been searching in their imagination for a road that can lead them out of the island—to the Big Land and the most powerful of allies very far away.

Each spiritual community in Tanna has its own roads and canoes. Like the John Frum, pagan *kastom* supporters built a canoe. Created after another founding trip, theirs was based on the recollection of a road: the one Ya'uto followed on the open sea to find out whether the truth of missionaries was universal. As for Christians, their society and systems of alliance are based on the same question, but they have given an answer opposite to that of pagans. Their road is the mission road.

Such fascination for the metaphors of road and canoe helps explain why Tannese society is not a mosaic of groups but a network of groups that see space—the space of their island and that of the world—primarily as a nexus of places and connecting roads. Each territory of *kastom* represents a fragment of road and a nexus of places or, in metaphorical terms, an alliance of stones and canoes. As for the expanse of the island, one does not possess it but one navigates it as if it were a sea. Places are like clusters of islands scattered along the roads of the canoe, and each territory is part of an archipelago surrounded by foreign land and open sea.

Tanna's spatial organization preserves the image of an island that one reaches by canoe. Through the force of this vision, the man of the canoe can live on the island as if the initial connection with the rest of the world had never been broken and the harmony of the origins had been attained once again. To balance the limited space around him, the

Islander journeys, digs, and plunges: the infinite number of his roads and the rootedness of his places make him forget that he is surrounded by finite space.

Tannese society is therefore just as rooted as it is peripatetic. It has also tried to mitigate the feeling of spatial confinement by diversifying the space of the island, by enriching it with as many symbols and magic places as it could possibly create, and by maintaining a form of connectedness with the outside world.

For this reason, Tannese society is set in a many-layered, open-ended relational space. Through culture, this society has attempted to give itself the linkages that nature did not offer, in an effort to build continuity in a world of discontinuity. Perhaps the paradigm of traditional Pacific Island culture is essentially this search for greater harmony and space beyond the uncertainties and bounds of nature. Melanesian Islanders seem to have never entirely accepted physical insularity; they have always had the dream of another space. As a result, they have developed the widest possible communication network, both concretely and through their imagination. From their origins, these islands have been ports of call for wandering canoes willing to sail with the winds of the world and search for another land, or even another continent. Without the open sea and the space beyond, which captivate it, Tannese society might not exist.

Kastom Re-created

Tanna may also be considered a microcosm of the world at large. In the dual conflict that took place on the island, an exemplary type of network-based society clashed with a centralized state in the process of being built and, just as symbolically, the organizing principles of *kastom* challenged state-focused modernity. Concurrently, the myth of the origins held by tradition supporters opposed the modern myth of progress. This conflict between "rooted men" and "drifting men" came as a shock to the Tannese. Yet, it reflected a universal conflict of ideas, which itself underscored two issues of particular relevance in Vanuatu: How can a modern nation-state be built in an archipelago where tradition co-exists with intense local particularisms? And how can the concept of a unitary state be reconciled with that of *kastom,* which implies both the independence of all members of the society, be they individuals or groups, and their consensus—a balance sometimes difficult to achieve?

Customary groups on Tanna have a political ideal, according to which they do not wish to construct so much as reconstruct the island's original society. That ideal goes beyond a mere wish: it is anchored in an archetypal space which, in the Islanders' view, need only be reactivated to give life and significance anew to the whole social construction. As men inhabit their places again, as they find their roads of alliance, they revive the functions and resurrect the powers associated with these places and roads. The cultural strength of Tannese society derives from this vital connection between space and humans. If their social fabric were destroyed, the Tannese would lose none of their heritage—provided they kept the memory of their places. By returning to the island's original space, they would recover the power to reconstruct their society along identical lines.

As a "spatial" or "geographical" society within which the process of history goes backward, cancels itself, and circles onward, Tannese society is timeless in a way; it wants to be outside the flow of history. In the island, time reduced to movement within space describes a closed circle. Tanna's timeless places thus become places of the absolute—they forge a Dreamspace.[2] In its most consummate expression, a society of this kind could only be created in a context of insularity, where discontinuity and spatial confinement reign.

The previous statement does not imply a sort of island-related environmental determinism whereby natural conditions would be the determining factor in the making of Tannese culture: in general terms, this type of explanation is of little relevance today. On the other hand, culture could hardly blossom if it were not closely connected with nature. Surrounding humans, nature exists on its own; however, culture makes it significant to them because it integrates the attributes of the natural environment through the representations elaborated by the community. This dynamic—or mesological (Berque 1986)—relationship between culture and natural environment helps fashion local identities.[3]

Underlying the cultural creativity of the people of Tanna is their representation of the geographical constraints affecting their island, along with the weight of a local history rich in symbols and replete with conflicts of ideas. This singular society built a space not only enchanted and prodigiously alive but, to use Dumézil's words about hierophanes quoted earlier, "clothe[d by] a discourse of much depth." In this respect, I thought it important to understand Tanna's spatio-cultural construction from the inside rather than "deconstruct" it from the outside. Steeped in memory and magic, that space makes the Islanders' lives both meaningful and empowered.

At first sight, the technology-driven, state-focused thrust of modernity seems to pass a sentence of death on this type of society, yet one may argue that the new world emerging in the late twentieth century could facilitate its revival, perhaps in another guise. In our so-called postmodern age, man shows nostalgic interest in societies organized on a more human scale. The current malaise in "advanced societies" is another factor that, along with the extraordinary growth of communications technology, could ease the renaissance of network-based communities. Indeed, new spatial structures are being shaped. Space—now seen as one "lump," made up of strictly demarcated parcels, delineated on the basis of rigid frontiers, and organized along the compact state-based model of centers and peripheries—seems to be evolving toward a reticulated space with multiple and interdependent nodes linked by a spiritually or ethno-culturally based principle of alliance, not unlike the Tannese case. From this perspective, Tanna's *kastom* represents much more than the formal model of a traditional society; paradoxically, it may foreshadow a novel type of sociospatial configuration.

In the final analysis, several aspects of Tanna's *kastom* seem remarkably contemporary: nostalgia for the past, the quest for a deeper relationship with nature, awareness of spatial and ecological limitations, the trend toward reticulated spaces, the birth of new forms of shamanism, a mistrust of politicized religions, the receding of the concept of statehood, and even the "war by consent" . . . under the eyes of all—that is, on television, where politicians may die, if only in a certain respect.

The cultural construction of Tanna's traditional society is thus not as anachronistic as it may first appear. Much of its discourse bears on the most current aspects of the age. This is not the least of the Tannese paradoxes. Fundamentally Tanna's *kastom* did not err when it chose the United States of America as its privileged partner to carry on a dialogue about the future of the world and the significance of modernity.

Living on an Island

Tanna's *kastom* created a spatial organization that allowed Melanesians to live in harmony with their environment. Through a prodigious network of sacred places, *kastom* also set up a territory of emotions, rich in meanings, sensations, and symbols. Finally, it helped forge Tanna's identity—an irrepressible and resilient identity to this day.

How can one live on an island? was perhaps *kastom*'s basic question. The question referred back to its premises: Melanesian identity emerged in an insular world where society's first problem was to survive, less in ecological than in cultural terms. In a confined world, fertile but closed and fragmented, Melanesians attempted to offset geographical exiguity with intense cultural creativeness.

Today, however, the onslaught of modernity may lead to the extinction of island culture, as is already the case in some regions of the group and other islands of Oceania. The ensuing situation would be a predicament for all concerned. Forsaking *kastom*, Islanders would find themselves cloistered in a world devoid of meaning, a world that they would probably abandon. Nothing would stand in the way of the fascination of *les lumières de la ville* 'city lights', the city being the only place where *kastom* loses its raison d'être. If such were the case, the end of Oceanic culture would mean the demise of the only cultural force that can still counter migration toward urban centers, whether inside the Pacific or at the periphery.

Most politicians and economic planners have not really understood that living on an island cannot be reduced to living there comfortably. In a closed space, isolated and easily marginalized, people need—more compellingly than elsewhere—not only a way of life but, more essentially, a reason to live. Islanders, cut off from the world, have to reinvent that world within their own space. By definition, they are creators of culture and their space stands as culture's repository. Current circumstances in many Pacific islands indicate that when traditional culture and social frames of reference disintegrate, space loses its enchantment, and vice versa. Made more "productive" by commercial plantations, suddenly the landscape is no longer attractive. Migration to urban centers and, whenever feasible, to cities on the rim becomes a standard practice: in islands almost devoid of inhabitants, transient tourists now stroll.

Modern sociocultural frames of reference have proved fragile. The destruction of Oceanian culture "killed" the spatial organization that went with it; and the death of a place implies the demise of its inhabitants.

Le Sentiment Géographique

Contemporary anthropology commonly states that, given political choices and historical situations, both tradition and views of the past are continuously re-created to answer present needs (see Keesing and Tonkinson 1982). Accordingly, on Tanna, there would be, within what is called *kastom*, change and constant innovation rather than conservation and continuity in cultural terms. Tannese culture probably follows this general rule. Yet, it is also endowed with a singular power of re-creation, in accordance with its own criteria and in harmony with the most ancient memory of the island.

Perhaps, as mentioned throughout this book, the secret behind Tanna's ability to "rebuild" itself from the core is the magic link between space and myths. Together, magical powers, representations, and the history of old wars and, more recently, of white contact, are held in a web of places, paths, and boundaries—a web that keeps these events strangely alive and imparts to them the intense force of signs incarnated by land. The island's geosymbolic space not only preserves *kastom* but also allows it to be replicated. That space makes up a system of signs, just as a language or kinship system does. Here space does not prevent the flow of history from taking place, but influences it in such a way that the spirit of conservation wins over that of rupture.

Thanks to its relation with the Great Space of the origins, Tannese society can live in a culture characterized by continuity; that relation is also at the core of the Islanders' *sentiment géographique* 'geographical feeling'. As a form of emotional and spiritual attachment to a landscape, *le sentiment géographique* anchors the inner, self-perceived identity of groups and conveys the feeling that one belongs less to a social order than to a place. This link helps maintain the essence of *kastom* in the island. Insofar as Tanna's space embodies the Islanders' beliefs, it represents a matrix of their culture: a close communion, rich in feelings and musings, is established between people and place. Thanks to this intense relation, the re-creation of the society of the origins remains at the heart of the island's cultural process. Islanders have chosen to live within the space of their places rather than by the consciousness of time; therefore Tanna's *kastom* stands not as a dream of change but as one of permanence.

Epilogue: A Return to Tanna

Will fighting on the island resume? In 1985, five years after my last stay, I went back to Tanna. The island was quiet and unusually peaceful. The members of customary groups who had been at the forefront of the revolt were silent, embarrassed to see me again, embarrassed mostly because they had lost, at least temporarily. As I spoke with the villagers, I understood that they wished to forget the events surrounding the revolt. *Kastom,* they told me, was still in their hearts, but they seemed to balk at actually saying the word.

The John Frum are on the fringe of society once again. Some have joined the Baha'i Church but continue to be "half John Frum, half Baha'i." Ipeukel villagers remain proudly isolated. Mweles, somber and aged, does not speak in public. On Friday nights, dances in honor of John are still performed under the Ipeukel banyan tree, but the audience is sparse.

Yet *kastom* is alive on the island today and seems to stand as a symbol of unity once again. In the evenings, men flock to dancing places to drink kava. The beauty of yam gardens sparkles. Postcircumcision festivals, exchange ceremonies, and *toka* rituals are being prepared for or are taking place at the four corners of the island territory. Less spoken of as a political model or a possible resurgence, *kastom* still lives in the dancing places of the original canoes; even former enemies seem to meet there occasionally. Although the people of *kastom* lost their bet over politics in the short run, they may have won it in terms of more fundamental cultural choices in the long run.

Perhaps Tanna's great silence portends a new awakening.

Notes

PREFACE TO THE ENGLISH EDITION

1 Institut Français de Recherche Scientifique pour le Développement en Coopération, or Scientific Research Institute for Development in Cooperation. Tropical areas are ORSTOM's main sphere of activity.

2 The major part of the information presented here is based on my *thèse d'Etat*, a more comprehensive work published by Editions de l'ORSTOM in two volumes of 540 and 680 pages respectively (Bonnemaison 1986a, 1987), and on my fieldwork in Tanna. When I rely on or take into account the work of another researcher, the reference is indicated in the text.

ACKNOWLEDGMENTS

1 A forerunner of all researchers on Tanna, Jean Guiart is the author of two texts about the island (1956a, 1956b). See also Tonkinson (1968), Wilkinson (1979), Bastin (1981), Brunton (1981, 1989), MacClancy (1983), Adams (1984), Van Trease (1984), Brunton (1989), and Lindstrom (1990).

PART ONE   THE INVADED ARCHIPELAGO

Forster 1777, 258.

1 On the Path to Myth: Quiros's Great Voyage

Quiros in Tostain n.d.

1 Terra Australis Incognita, the southern continent conjectured since antiquity.

2 Several sources tell the story of the expedition. Quiros dictated a narrative of the trip and on his return to Spain wrote a series of memoirs extolling his discoveries. Luis Vaez de Torres, "admiral" of the expedition and captain of the second ship, sent a detailed report to his sovereign. Accounts were also given by Brother Torquemada, Juan de Iturbe *(El Sumario Breve),* and Don Diego de Prado *(La Relation Sumaria).* For the most part, our knowledge of the relations between the Spaniards and the inhabitants of the newly discovered islands is

327

based on two shipboard journals. The first, by the Portuguese pilot Gonzales de Leza, mirrors rather well the state of mind of the officers and crew around Quiros. The original document was translated into French by Maurice Tostain (n.d.) and, unless otherwise indicated, is the source of the quotes throughout this chapter; where possible the date of the journal entry is given. The second document is the diary of Brother Martín de Munilla, a Franciscan and chaplain of the expedition. Munilla's interest in the peoples of these "heathen" islands was tinged with some mistrust.

3 Like most of these Polynesian islands, Hao is a ring-shaped atoll with an elevation of a few meters only.

4 All these islands were later identified. It is commonly assumed that Manicolo designated the east coast of the island of Vanua Levu (Fiji Islands), in the Wainikoro district which lies in the path of sea routes from Santa Cruz (Spate 1979).

5 Near Tikopia, the third captive "Indian" jumped into the water and swam vigorously toward the island, which was one or two leagues from the boat. "He made fun of us," de Leza wrote, "he was the best and the one who showed some promise."

6 Today it is known as Big Bay on the island of Espiritu Santo.

7 The Ora in Melanesian languages. The Spaniards called it the Jordan, a name still found on maps of the area.

8 The sound of horns is that of marine conches, used everywhere in the Pacific. They give out a long and gloomy note. Drums for dancing, also quite widespread, are made from a hollowed trunk. Finally, the sounds of small bells—familiar to the Spaniards—emanate from empty nuts, which dancers from the northern part of the archipelago fasten in bundles to their ankles during rituals.

9 It is the present site of the village of Matantas.

10 Munilla, ever practical, reported that this land, although rich and fertile, did not have any gold. Besides, he doubted it was a continent (Kelly 1966, 208).

11 Rather than "Terra Australis," the name of "Terra Austrialis" was chosen because of the Austrian links of the family that then reigned over the kingdom of Spain (Beaglehole 1968). Since that day, the big island discovered by the Spaniards has been called Espiritu Santo.

12 *"Que era cosa maravillosa ver tanta diversidad de caballeros que cierto no se visto quanto aquél mundo es mundo cosa semejante porque aquí avia caballeros marineros y caballeros grumetes y caballeros pajes de nao y caballeros mulatos y negros y indios y caballeros caballeros."*

13 "The new order is dedicated, in Prado's words, 'to defend the Indians from their enemies and from the others who might wish to injure them and other absurdities' " (Spate 1979, 136).

14 *Ichthyosarcotoxism* or fish poisoning [ciguatera—Trans.] is frequent in tropical waters of the Pacific Ocean. It is transmitted by fish that have ingested certain microscopic algae. The Spaniards described the fish responsible for it, which they named *pardos*. According to de Leza, "The disease was such that there was not a single body part that did not suffer" (29 May 1606).

15 Quiros raised an issue in his eighth petition: "My mission was to look for a great land and I succeeded in this endeavor: actually, my health and some inci-

dents about which I wish to keep silent prevented me from seeing all that I wanted to see." Such "incidents" probably implied a sort of informal mutiny, which is alluded to in other narratives of the voyage.

16 The Torres Strait separates Australia and Papua New Guinea.

17 Lying between the Matantas and the Jordan rivers, the region visited by the Spaniards is a two- to three-kilometer-long shoreline opening onto the great plain of the Ora.

18 By underlining and overestimating the geographical extent of his discovery, Quiros was trying to make his sovereign pay attention. However, this petition, like the others, received no answer.

19 The population that lived in Big Bay at the time of the Spaniards' arrival and that apparently had "neither king nor laws" has vanished almost entirely since then. Today, the great bay "with mild sky and well-ordered nature" is practically empty, with the exception of a few coastal villages, most of which were created when inland groups moved there recently. The loss is due to large-scale epidemics in the nineteenth century. Part of the population migrated to the east coast of the island where their offspring make up the present-day Port Olry community. According to all indications, this population that today is extinct or dispersed had developed an original culture by the time of the Spaniards' arrival; we can only know fragments of it. Likewise, the Melanesians of Big Bay would have handed down a now unknown version of the navigators' visit.

2 Happy "Savages"?

Forster 1777, 350.

1 The high judicial court.

2 *"L'état de l'homme naturel, né essentiellement bon, exempt de tout préjugé et suivant, sans défiance comme sans remords, les douces impulsions d'un instinct toujours sûr parce qu'il n'a pas encore dégénéré en raison."*

3 Bougainville was wrong on this count: the marks he observed on the Islanders' skin were not caused by leprosy but were probably ritual scars, puffed up by healing, or more simply common leucodermia, a type of harmless mycosis prevalent in the islands.

4 Common in the whole group are two great ritual decorations, the pig tooth curved into an ivory ring and the tortoiseshell. The two animals, one from the land, the other from the sea, play major roles throughout Melanesian mythology.

5 Variants, if any, are included in the quotations by Cook and Forster in this chapter. Original spelling has been respected.—Trans.

6 The Austronesian root for the name of the island is *tan* 'land'.

7 "[T]hese people are yet in a rude state, and if we can judge from circumstances and appearances, are frequently at war not only with their neighbours, but amongst themselves" (variant in Beaglehole 1961, 493).

8 A sign of the local aristocracy (see Part Two).

9 Such stones do not originate from the island's geological strata: to Aubert de la Rüe (1938), they are nephrite from New Caledonia, Ouen Island in particular. Nephrite, or greenstone, is also found in New Zealand and New Guinea. The

stones may have reached Tanna via an ancient connection, probably through New Caledonia. The memory of it is now lost; today, people think jade has a magic origin, the source of which lies in the eastern part of the island, in the area close to the volcano.

10 A ceremony of complete exchange among North American Indians: two groups trade, then destroy, all their goods.

3 *Wild Contact*

Fletcher 1986, 138–139.

1 For J.-M. Charpentier (1979), Bislama is the extension, in a novel form, of a vernacular tongue originally used in the Indo-Malay world by merchants who traveled by sea. The Portuguese played a major part in its diffusion.

2 In 1851, Paddon became one of the early settlers on Nou Island (New Caledonia); he died there in 1861 (O'Reilly 1957, 171–174).

3 Today, Melanesians themselves accept the term *Kanak,* whereas in the early part of the twentieth century it was regarded as disparaging.

4 Some have recently gone to Vanuatu to search for their villages and family roots. On this topic, see *Wacvie* by Faith Bandler, Brisbane, 1977. The author, who lives in Australia, tells the story of her grandfather who was kidnapped from Ambrym.

5 In the islands of northern Vanuatu, leadership is acquired through grades. The candidate undergoes a ritual test that grants him a specific grade within the traditional hierarchy. The test must be "paid for" by the candidate: numerous tusked pigs are sacrificed to that effect. Their number and value increase in step with the grade being reached. See Bonnemaison (1986*a*), Rodman (1973), and Vienne (1984).

6 Mathieu Ferray was killed on Ambae (Aoba) in 1883. Rossi met the same fate a few years later during a recruiting tour on Espiritu Santo (Port Olry). The luckier La Chaise, a half-caste from the island of La Réunion and former sailor on a recruiting ship, became thoroughly involved with Malo customs, killing pigs and reaching high grades within the traditional hierarchy. He wore a calico in the fashion of the people from his island. La Chaise, who was married to an Ambae woman, enjoyed genuine prestige on Malo and in western Ambae, playing as all big men do a central part in pig transactions. Because of his light skin, people from these two islands used to call him "Futuna." (Futuna, in the south of the group, is peopled by Polynesian speakers probably originating from Samoa or Tonga. Its residents are considered light-skinned people.)

7 Quoted in the text of an illustrated pamphlet (France, Sous-Secrétariat aux Colonies, 1889).

8 Higginson used this phrase, coined by Sir Charles Dilke, in a letter dated 3 June 1885 to the Ministry of Foreign Affairs (Deschanel 1888, 372).

9 Letter by Navy Captain Buchard to the French Ministry of Marine Affairs, 5 August 1908 (FRA).

10 (Miss Gruishens, *Sydney Morning Herald,* 25 November 1905, cited in *Le Néo-Hébridais* 1910). Translated from the French.

4 The Gospel and the Kingdom

Presbyterian missionary John Geddie, writing in 1848, quoted in Harrison 1937, 156.

1 Christian churches are also called *skul* in Bislama. To be *skul* is to be Christian.

2 Lieutenant Docteur, letter dated 1899, JNCA.

3 For an explanation of secret societies, see Codrington (1891) or the more recent Vienne (1984).

4 The last traditional pagan leader in Ambae, in the Lossori area, was converted in 1940; one last small group above Anbanga embraced Catholicism in the early 1970s.

5 Catholic Peasant Missionaries and Marginal Churches

"Aujourd'hui, plus de doute parmi les païens. Ils savent que se faire chrétien, c'est tarir la source de tout ce qui était leur vitalité, c'est-à-dire leurs fêtes païennes. Le village païen semble plein de vie, mais au village chrétien, c'est la mort. Ne sommes-nous pas trop sévères?" Father Loubière, writing from Namaram, Pentecost Island, quoted in Monnier n.d.*b*, 24.

1 *"La présence de vos missionnaires dans cet archipel serait pour moi une garantie que les missionnaires presbytériens, grâce à leurs intrigues, ne prendraient pas un ascendant exclusif sur les indigènes et ne pourraient pas ainsi contrarier la prise de possession des Nouvelles-Hébrides par la France. . . . C'est à vous maintenant de m'aider à faire une terre française de ces îles malgré tous les errements de la mère patrie"* (SFNH).

2 French navy officers, who were generally Catholic, did give discreet and useful help, but only in their own names.

3 "Malakula men do not like French missionaries: they have no boat, they have no wife, they have no children, they have nothing."

4 "It is the preserve of—and an avenue for—Protestantism."

5 Unless otherwise noted, all letters and diary entries quoted in this chapter are in the Catholic Mission Archives in Vila.

6 Among the first generation of Catholic missionaries, Father Vidil and Father Suas were known for their strong personalities. A resolute foe of the Presbyterian mission, Father Vidil eventually came in direct conflict with great customary leaders, in particular regarding the debt system that supported their authority. According to contemporary witnesses, these leaders caused his death by food poisoning in April 1898.

7 "All these people died of fright, grief, and the loss of their daily routine," wrote Father Salomon.

8 Father Emmanuel Rougier's life story is extraordinary. He was very enterprising; on his Fiji station he took in a Frenchman who had escaped from the New Caledonia penal colony. The man was heir to a rich metropolitan family and bequeathed all his fortune to the priest. In trouble with his hierarchy, Father Rougier left the order and undertook, on his own account, to colonize the Christ-

mas Islands, which are remote, uninhabited atolls in the central Pacific. The money earned by the former missionary to Fiji supported the endeavors of his brother, a missionary in Mexico (as related to the author by Father Joseph Allais, historian and Marist missionary in Western Samoa).

9 The distinctive sign of the Roman Catholics was that they carried a medal and a rosary. To "obtain one's medal" meant to embrace the Catholic faith and prepare oneself for baptism.

10 Melsisi people related that the British deported Father Louis Guillaume —in irons—to Noumea where, they said, he died from grief. In his letters, he stated that he had armed the Christians only because the latter were being "murdered with impunity by inland pagans" without anyone, especially not Condominium authorities, being willing or able to help them (Melsisi people, Tansip village, pers comm).

11 Namaram parishioners (pers comm). According to the missionaries, a woman settler by the name of Théodorine Fullet, originally from New Caledonia, used to give cartridges to the pagans who kept raiding the Namaram mission. She lived with a Kanak and operated a store on the west coast of the island, slightly to the south of the mission.

12 On the eve of World War II, there was still no public schooling in the New Hebrides, with the exception of a small French elementary school in Vila, mainly for the children of settlers and civil servants.

6 "Gone with the Wind"

The letters that Fletcher wrote during his stay in the archipelago from 1912 to 1920 are probably the best literary document and personal account in existence regarding that era. With his cultured mind and free thinking, Fletcher held unconventional views about the settlers' small world to which he belonged.

1 Such convicts had not completed their time in prison. They had been freed but had to reside in New Caledonia until the expiration of their sentences.

2 New Guinea was then the subject of a feud between German and British imperialistic interests. To prevent annexation by Germany, already present in the north, the Colony of Queensland took independent possession of southern New Guinea, thus presenting the two European nations with a fait accompli. It was feared that Queensland would proceed in like fashion in the New Hebrides.

3 The *Conseil régional* represented the official organ of the young colony.

4 The "Franceville" township was an entity from an administrative and legal standpoint: it celebrated weddings, had opened a population registry, and had created an optional mediation board. This experimental township initiated urban planning for Vila and built the Tagabe coastal road, or *Route des colons* (Brunet 1908; O'Reilly 1957).

5 The last European was killed by the Big Nambas in 1937 aboard his schooner, in connection with a case concerning the recruiting of women. The murderers released the Melanesian crew with these words: "Take the white man back to his Capman and tell [the Capman] why we killed him" (Mr Jacquier, Malo settler, pers comm).

6 In the northern islands of the archipelago, the *nakamal* is the "men's house." Men congregate there at the end of the day to drink kava. Some *tabu fires* are for the sole use of big men who have reached a high grade and become sacred men.

7 Most foreign settlers opted for French status.

8 In the United States: district attorney.—Trans.

9 The principle of land registration was inspired by Australia's Torrens Act. Each land plot was deemed to be a single entity whose title was proof of registration. Before the title was granted, one needed to petition the court, which had to complete an inquiry and a topographical survey. One year had to elapse before the judgment was carried out so that disagreements could surface. Subsequently, the judgment deed could be used in lieu of an ownership deed: a land title was delivered "removing from the property all rights or previous easements that had not been registered" (Grignon-Dumoulin 1928). The newly created Joint Court received nearly nine hundred registration requests. The topographical surveys were based on triangulation, a very difficult process to carry out in the field.

10 T. Wright, quotation from a speech given at a banquet for the Indochinese labor force, Vila (*Le Néo-Hébridais,* 1924).

11 "Franceville," "Tagabe," "Faureville," and "Courbetville," in addition to the abandoned center of Port Havannah, on the northern side of the island.

12 This was the term the British used to parody the Condominium.

13 *Vanua'aku* means "my country" in the languages of the northern part of the archipelago. The name of the nation of Vanuatu is derived from the term.

14 Most settlers and expatriates joined the moderate parties and some played a major political role in them, notably in Espiritu Santo where they were associated with the Nagriamel "religious-political" movement dominated by Jimmy Stevens (Hours 1974).

15 The "francophones" were the groups whose children attended French schools and the "anglophones" were those whose children attended British schools. However, neither group spoke a European language with the exception of some members of the elite who, for the most part, had been schooled outside the archipelago (see also Charpentier 1982*b*).

PART TWO TANNA: STONES WITHIN CANOES

Bong of Bunlap is quoted in Jolly 1982, 338.

7 Isle of Resilience

"L'île, c'est l'absolu par définition, la rupture du lien . . ." Michel Tournier, a French novelist, is the author of *Vendredi ou les limbes du Pacifique,* a reinterpretation of the life of Robinson Crusoe on a desert island.—Trans.

1 *"L'île n'est plus liée que par l'harmonie préétablie."*

8 Enchanted Space

"Ces hiérophanies cosmiques . . . sont le vêtement d'un profond discours" (Dumézil 1975, 7).

1 The term *Dreamtime* refers to the mythological world of the beginnings of Australia's Aboriginal society. Although they did not create the world, "great

ancestors," who are both men and animals, did shape its space. They have been living in sacred spots ever since: stones, mountains, trees, and water holes (see Eliade 1972). This vision is not unlike that of the Tannese.

2 The storytellers were Nemisa of Ipai and Niluan of Loanatom, Naporio tribe.

3 From the outset, the land's house *(numapten)* is thus compared with a canoe *(niko)*, in other words, a place linked by roads. The first Tannese canoe is an undivided territory with no inner boundaries.

4 Today's coastal road follows the *kwoteren*'s path in part.

5 This story and all others herein (such as the Semo-Semo myth, chapter 9) were recorded in Bislama, a language which could not capture all the nuances of the original version in one of Tanna's languages.

6 Kooman is "voice of the canoe" for one of the White Grass groups.

7 Islanders who do not belong to Kooman's alliance network do not know the myth, even though it is not secret.

8 The first stones were given names. So were the first magical trees and, in particular, the banyan trees (for instance, Nesis).

9 In the White Grass language, *penoa* means "pigeon."

10 In the White Grass language, *naunum* means "food" (*kakai* in Bislama).

11 Melanesians eat island cabbage *(hibiscus manihot)* after cooking the leaves.—Trans.

12 The literal meaning of *niel* is a pile of gifts heaped up in the middle of a dancing place: to make a *niel* means "to offer." The *niel* festival on Tanna is thus an exchange festival. The term also designates a hardwood tree that grows in coastal areas and is used for charcoal and house timber—*Casuarina equisetifolia,* ironwood or *oak tree* in Bislama (Pierre Cabalion, pers comm).

13 *Nemei* means "breadfruit" in the languages of Tanna (Darrell Tryon, pers comm).

14 This is why breadfruit trees produce larger fruit in eastern Tanna.

15 An insult is a very serious offense. The one who insults loses all credibility and the one who is insulted has the right to kill. Many wars are caused by an insult: verbal abuse is never forgotten and must be paid for. Penoa's behavior is consistent with Tanna's rules.

16 He is still there: Kooman's stone is located on the White Grass shoreline, while Noburbunemel lies further out as a submerged stone.

17 With the exception of the first moment of contact, when Cook was mistakenly given a pig and a few yams; the gesture was not repeated (chapter 2). Similarly for Quiros on Santo (chapter 1).

18 For example, the clan watching over the Tangalua area, in the northeast quadrant of Middle Bush, was exterminated when other clans decided on a raid of revenge following a particularly disastrous farming cycle. Allies from Lowkatai performed the deed, which neighboring clans could not carry out by reason of their blood ties with the designated victims. Tangalua has had no live keeper since then, but its evil powers are still present, rooted in the territory. That territory has been abandoned and the original names of its inhabitants are no longer in use. As the Tannese say, "the land is dead" *(tet land).*

9 Society of the Stones

Eliade 1972, 54.

1 The term *nepro* (or *niprow* depending on the linguistic area) is also associated with the tree *Bleasdalea lutea* (see Cabalion 1984a). In the White Grass region, this palm tree, whose heart is edible, is called *nip*. It was among the first to grow after the appearance of the banyan tree.

2 This mixture of tubers and coconut milk is steam-cooked under a pile of heated stones. *Lap-lap* is the archipelago's traditional dish and is served wrapped in leaves of island cabbage and other odorous herbs and leaves.

3 The Tannese believe that, ideally, the abdomen of a pregnant woman should stay small. Traditional "medicine" is used to reduce the belly of pregnant women.

4 The complete version of the myth is more detailed. It describes specific gestures for these traditional activities, along with various magical powers and the names of the places from which they originate.

5 When women participate in ritual night dances, they adorn themselves with the traditional grass skirt (*gras sket* in Bislama). The *gras sket* "is made up of strands originating from the back of banana leaves or from the bark of burao (*Cordia subcordata*). [The strands] are steeped. When they are dry, these thread-like fibers are rolled two at a time on the thigh to make a stronger and stiffer string which is used in the making of skirts." (Charpentier 1979, 173).

6 The liver is still here, in the guise of a black rock at Lenakel. This spot holds hidden powers that are unknown to Ipai residents. The liver is seen as a war-related symbol of strength and power.

7 In doing so, Kasasow and Kaniapnin were involved in a *niel:* they were sharing the body of their dead enemy to give it to the future men of Tanna, who were just birds at the time.

8 Within Tanna's traditional society, the hairless pig has the highest ritual value. In the northern part of the group, pigs are raised to grow curved tusks. In the south, the animal's worth is based on its weight and, curiously, on its lack of hair.

10 Society of the Hawk

"L'espace . . . apparaît comme une sorte de clairière défrichée et organisée par les mythes communautaires au sein de l'immensité d'un monde hostile et inconnu" (Gusdorf 1984, 103).

1 Tanna's artistic genius centers on the choreographed rituals of alliance. James Cook did note that Tannese chants were the most beautiful he had heard in Oceania. He discovered no other form of artistic endeavor such as sculptures or painted objects, which are commonly found in other islands of the group.

2 Although the *toka* festival is far from being orgiastic and any activity behind the scenes is carried out very discreetly, Presbyterian missionaries used that aspect as a pretext to ban the *nekowiar* and forbid night dances entirely. The ritual was reinstated on Tanna in the 1950s. Today, Christians take part in

it provided guards carrying oil lamps patrol the surroundings of the dancing grounds. The guards prevent illegitimate sexual encounters—with more or less effectiveness.

3 Ipai claims that in Semo-Semo's body it found the first *kweriya* (hawk)— which subsequently appeared in Ipeukel (see chapter 9)—an unfounded affirmation as far as inhabitants from the eastern part of the island are concerned.

4 Tanna's political moieties are inherited patrilineally: they are phratries. A man always belongs to his father's phratry, from which he receives name, status, and land rights, and also a title of power in some cases.

5 See chapter 11.

11 At War

1 According to Tannese lore, the islet of Mataso in the Shepherd Islands has been called Masaka ever since. The northernmost island known to Tanna's *kastom* followers is Tongoa. Oral traditions state that inhabitants of the Shepherd Islands have distant family links with the Tannese.

2 See Bonnemaison 1987, chapters 12 and 13, for a discussion of horticulture and mobility. See also Bonnemaison 1991*b*.

3 These stones are made from a mixture of unadulterated volcanic ashes and sap from milktrees *(Antiaris toxicaria);* the mixture turns into a type of plaster that can be modified in the required shapes and sizes. This plaster is set inside bamboo pieces and slowly heated. The end product is a small hard cementlike cylinder of homogeneous size and shape—a formidable projectile when expertly thrown from a sling.

4 For that reason, not a single *nekowiar* has been organized in Middle Bush or western Tanna in the last few years. Along the Napanaklai road especially, opposing viewpoints have been too strong. Intermediary links have refused to transfer messages originating from groups to which they are politically hostile.

5 The eastern part of the island, from White Sands to the southern tip, became nearly entirely populated by Numurkuen. So did the area around Lenakel, and northern Tanna in its entirety. The Koyometa fell back onto several enclaves in the southern part of Middle Bush (Lamlu) and in Tanna's southwestern quadrant.

6 It was the war of *manshipi* 'merchant ships' against *manwawa* 'warships'. These were the Numurkuen and Koyometa, respectively (see chapter 10).

12 The Return of Magic

Lévi-Strauss 1966, 21.

1 The symbolic split between hot and cold is widespread in Melanesian culture. For example, the ethnobotanist Dominique Bourret wrote about healing practices in New Caledonia: "Certain types of bark that are gathered on the east coast must be obtained when the light of the rising sun reaches them; likewise bark on the west coast must be gathered at the time of the setting sun. Such trees are called hot in the east and cold in the west; their bark is to be used for illnesses of an opposite nature, in other words, hot or cold illnesses. For instance, hot, dry, male plants will heal cold, humid, female illnesses, and vice versa" (1982, 506).

2 If the agrarian magicians did participate in a war expedition and if they struck or aimed at an enemy, they had to give the name of their *yani niko* beforehand, to announce that they were acting in the name of a war leader.

3 Here I am describing only magical practices known to all. Some cannot be told.

4 In particular, this practice was carried out in the clans that had the shark as one of their totems.

PART THREE   FIGHTING ON THE ISLAND

A John Frum supporter from southern Tanna, at a meeting in Middle Bush. See page 291.

13 The Pagans' Resistance

1 On the basis of their less than favorable report, the Belgian government decided to take no further interest in the New Hebridean archipelago; an "Anglo-Franco-Belgian tridominium" might otherwise have seen the light of day!

2 Probably one of the Bell brothers who had settled in Ipak. They were murdered by inland people (Wawn 1973, 24).

3 The whites left, keeping their "ownership rights" which they sold to others. Burns Philp thus acquired all its properties on Tanna, and Ballande its Black Beach plot. No settler ever directly exploited any of these properties, with one exception: the Australian Bob Paul converted his White Grass coastal plots into a livestock-raising station.

4 A Bislama word for "men of the bush" or inland men. The *manbus* are the opposite of the *mansolwora,* the men of the coast or "men of salt water."

5 With the exception of the *kawur* (a post-circumcision ceremony).

6 In other words, in the traditional style. Tanna Law prohibited such "useless" fancy; the new Christians had to keep their hair naturally frizzy, although they could be full-bearded in the likeness of the missionaries of that era.

7 The assessors acted as local advisors to the representatives of the joint administration wherever these dispensed justice. There was one assessor per large village or major population group.

8 On behalf of a New Caledonia company and with the opposite purpose in mind, Higginson had attempted the same operation at the level of the whole archipelago (1882).

9 Yaris Ya'uto, a Koyometa magician and the messenger's grandson and namesake, narrated the myth.

10 Here the history of the Presbyterian mission is told in the traditional fashion through a sequence of places connected with each other.

11 After this brief history of the mission, the main enemy is designated: not so much the European Presbyterian pastors, but the "Christian party" that developed around them.

12 Ipeukel was then a Christian village actively involved with Tanna Law; it claims to be the first village that was converted to Christianity.

13 Following internecine wars, the Tenlhyaone from Le'uluk had to flee from their territory. They took refuge in Lownhim, two kilometers northeast of Lamlu (see chapter 10).

14 The Lenemtehin headland is situated in a very remote area of the east coast. The pagans felt safe there because the coast was under the control of Middle Bush inhabitants. Lenemtehin was a major sacred site connected with the cult of the dead and numerous forms of magic.

15 One of the Loyalty Islands (New Caledonia).

16 The firearm Misis bears the symbolic name of Mission.

17 At this time the story reveals the traditional identity of the groups that led the pagan resistance. Most were Koyometa belonging to the alliance that had lost the *Shipimanwawa*.

18 The vessels symbolize the arrival of the Condominium; therefore there are two, one French, the other British.

19 The myth refers to the visit of a French ship in November 1912 (Guiart 1956b, 139–145) and the coming of the joint powers to Tanna. King was the name of the British Resident Commissioner who lived in Vila at the time. The name given to the French boat, *Makriko,* seems harder to explain. Its actual name was *Kersaint*.

20 This first French district agent reached Tanna in 1925. He was a navy physician who set up a hospital but was not very active as a Condominium agent. Nevertheless, his presence, even entirely symbolic, was enough to counteract the influence of the Presbyterian mission; among other things, it allowed for the coming of the Catholic mission.

21 A French ship called at Tanna, bringing in the building materials for the district agent's house, but the Lenakel Presbyterian party prohibited any beach landing and refused to help. The ship's crew was then quite surprised to see the pagan party come down from Middle Bush. With much enthusiasm, in the midst of chants and dances, the pagans helped to bring the cargo ashore and build the house, turning down offers of payment.

22 Southeast of Lifou in the Loyalty Islands.

23 Natuka from Itonga helped in the translation.

24 "Gidi" or Geddie was the first Presbyterian missionary in the group; he settled in Anatom. The *kastom* men see him as the "root" of all other missionaries and this is why they refer to him here. His name symbolizes the Tanna Law era even though he did not take part in any Tanna Law–related event.

25 In other words, he intercepts the message and prevents it from reaching the person for whom it was intended.

26 Nulak, the man from White Sands who authored the letter, speaks directly to the two nations making up the Condominium so that they start paying attention to the situation in Tanna.

27 This verse alludes to the capmen's positive response to the call from the pagan camp.

28 The verse refers to the Lenemtehin gathering. Sios—or George—is Sios Natingen. He lit the fire on the beach as a signal to the recruiters so they would take Ya'uto onto their ship.

29 Other Lenakel groups made a similar request to the Adventist Church, which settled in Tanna in 1932. Their request was related to a land tenure issue involving the Presbyterian mission (Guiart 1956b).

30 Loaneai was a stronghold of the Presbyterian mission located near the insurgent village of Loanatom.

31 Willingly or not, the Presbyterian missionary misunderstands the issue of the ownership of the Loanatom "station." It did not belong to France, but to the Catholic mission that had bought it from its previous owners. The missionary is chiding the physician for his role as an intermediary between the people of Loanatom and the Catholic mission, a role the French delegate played.

32 For their own edification, the French missionaries translated this letter and the following one. [The text given here was translated from the French.—Trans.]

33 The people of Loanatom have good memories of Father Bochu, who was their first missionary.

34 That of the family of the Ipai catechist Pierre Yamak, father of Alexis Yolou. Yolou was Tanna's francophone political representative.

35 This passage refers to the famous Lenemtehin meeting, the birthplace of the compact of resistance to Tanna Law. John Frum supporters from the west coast thereby acknowledge the primacy of Middle Bush within the *kastom* resistance movement—for good reason, since they were supposed to be Christians at the time.

36 Around 1920, Yopat lived in the small Christian village of Loaneai, north of Loanatom Bay. He later founded the village of Imanaka.

37 I was not able to find any information on a local trader called Jack Sapet, or the like. However, not all names of traders and copra makers are known; some only stayed on the island for a short time, especially those who were not involved with the mission. Jack Sapet may have been the individual who forwarded the message to a German settler in Erromango, who brought it to the French Residency in Vila (as mentioned in various documents, FRA).

38 Yopat's village, Imanaka, is situated above Loanpakel Bay. The bay is not a good anchorage.

39 In Bislama, the question is *"Hu ia em i rili man long Tanna?"* literally, "Who is the true man?" that is, "Who is the first man?"

40 Karapanemum plays a major part in the John Frum cosmology. He is the last of Tanna's heroes, the one whom founding myths credit with the introduction of pigs, black magic, and political "moieties." Karapanemum has been living on Mt Tukosmera—at 1084 meters one of the two highest elevations in Tanna (see chapter 10).

41 A dwelling place.

42 A hill in Imaneuhne country, north of White Grass, is actually dedicated to Karapanemum. During the Tanna Law era, Christians broke the taboos surrounding the place. The story has another connotation: viewed here as an offense to Karapanemum is the conversion to Christianity of a majority of Tanna's northern inhabitants, notably those of Green Hill and Imafin, a major magical place in northern Tanna.

43 A reference to John Frum's second appearance in Ipeukel, in 1940 (see chapter 14).

44 William Stober is president of the organization British Friends of Vanuatu.

45 At the time Hubert Goron, originally from Pontorson in Normandy (France), was a private surveyor in the island of Espiritu Santo. Somewhat tired of surveying land to be registered by European standards, he joined me in Tanna,

where he spent several months surveying the customary lands of the Tannese. We were able to make the first maps of the island showing the customary territories of the traditional canoes.

46 Since their defeat in traditional warfare, most Middle Bush pagans are Koyometa entrenched in their stronghold-like territories (see chapter 10). The ancient divisions of *kastom* are less clear-cut than before by reason of the large-scale population movements and epidemics that took place at the end of the nineteenth century.

14 *John Frum People*

The John Frum song was recorded in Imanaka in February 1978. The first verse means that a great message is coming, while the third verse refers to the weekly John Frum festivals in Imanaka. Jocteur's letter is in the archives of the French district agency in Tanna.

1 Here I refer to the "John Frum people" in the same way one might refer to the "*kastom* people" or to a "Christian people." Such a people is not a nation in the political sense of the term; it is made up of several autonomous groups which transcend their local divisions by adhering to a set of beliefs. Their cultural unity underlies a political alliance.

2 Because the first events at Green Point occurred before the intervention of British District Agent Nicol, written evidence is not available. Father Sacco was Loanatom's Catholic priest and lived on the island for nearly twenty-five years; he gave me an account of this early phase. His version is generally similar to the Ipeukel revelations, according to which John was in seclusion for two years before his message was divulged.

3 "*Les hommes de Tanna devaient se préparer à cette parousie.*" The word *parousie,* meaning advent in this context, comes from the Greek *parousia*—presence, being present.—Trans.

4 Teachers and catechists, respectively, had equivalent roles within Presbyterian and Catholic ranks. Teachers taught church doctrine and were the missionaries' representatives in the field. At the time they wielded much power locally.

5 James Nicol died alone in December 1944, run over by his jeep on an island trail: the vehicle had started moving by itself while he was closing a cattle fence on a steep hill. The Islanders remember Nicol as a controversial figure. Yet they do show some respect for him, to the extent of calling him a "strong man."

6 The image means he cannot sleep.

7 When ordering a song from a poet, one gives a basket filled with leaves.

8 Isula is a place name. The Isula canoe is the group made up of all clans associated with the Ehniu and Imafin dancing places. Gathering around Nelawiyang, these clans of magicians became the core of his movement.

9 The fight with Nicol's police force took place in Lamanspin Assim, in northern Tanna.

10 The word *nation* is used locally to designate Tanna's "canoes" and groups.

11 A reference to the Ipeukel leaders—Nambas, Nikiau, Nakomaha, and Mweles—who had been expelled by Nicol after the "sons of John Frum" affair and who were expelled a second time in December 1943.

12 According to John Frum leaders, US soldiers gave the flags directly to their Tannese friends. The flags were made of red-colored material.

13 Imanaka's martial ambience included something distinctive: the drill, followed by the customary meal, occurred to the sound of Tyrolese folksongs. After a two-year stay in White Grass, a German had left his record collection and battery-operated player to the villagers (see chapter 18). Tyrolese tunes were heard during the greater part of the ceremony—an unequaled case of "cultural plurality" at work.

15 The Bible Revisited

Kierkegaard's definition is from Gusdorf (1984, 359).

1 This myth was told to me in the Bislama language and I translated it into French using the words that seemed the most appropriate. By contrast with traditional myths, which lose their texture when they are not translated directly from the vernacular language, the John Frum myth "sounds good" in Bislama, undoubtedly because it was conceived directly in that language.

2 Noa, who is the Noah of the Bible, is obviously not included in pagan myths. Karapanemum and Kalpapen are the central figures of Tanna's "second society," that born of the east coast, at the foot of Yasur volcano, between Yaneumwakel and Ipeukel.

3 The Embuitoka dancing place is situated on the mountain behind the volcano. It represents the actual founding place of the Yenkahi "canoe." Ipeukel is the name of the coastal village to which mountain residents moved when they became Christian.

4 The Bislama word *finis* rhymes with *Paris*.

5 According to the myth, Ham is the ancestor of black Americans (the first syllable of their names is nearly identical). Perhaps because of James Nicol, James is deemed to be the progenitor of the English and by extension the forebear of all other white peoples. Set is the ancestor of the various peoples of intermediate color, the best known being the Polynesians. In the Ipeukel myth, America is the only country inhabited by whites and blacks together.

6 *Hammer* is the English word and *iken* means 'the place' in Tannese language. *Hammer Iken* rhymes with "Americans."

7 John Frum partisans see no contradiction when they state they are "half-and-half," that is, equally involved in Christianity and *kastom*. In their own words, "We have not left the *skul*, the Christians threw us out." Julia Wilkinson conveys the same idea in her excellent doctoral dissertation (1979).

8 Lenatuan, a village near Laonasis in northern Middle Bush, disappeared during the 1979–1980 political turmoil when its inhabitants relocated to other villages.

9 Traditional grounds near Imafin.

10 Here the myth enumerates all those whom Yapum Kassol entrusted with the mission to preserve *kastom* so that it could resurface one day.

11 Besides the star metaphor, the made-for-television film, called *The Return of Cargo,* also showed the marching with bamboo guns and the raising of the American flag on the Ipeukel dancing place on 15 February 1979. The John Frum leaders who agreed to participate in this TF1 project secretly hoped that the

film would carry their message to America. [TF1 is one of the French television networks.—Trans.]

16 Kastom *and Nation*

John Champion was the British Resident Commissioner in the New Hebrides from 1975 to 1978. His letter to *The Times* (London) was reprinted in *Nabanga,* a weekly newspaper published by the French Residency in Vila.

1 The New Hebrides National party was created in the early 1970s. It later changed its name to Vanua'aku Pati.

2 A monthly magazine, *Le Chasseur Français* has long been famous for its classified announcements.—Trans.

3 Europeans set up the *Union des Populations des Nouvelles-Hébrides* in Vila in the early 1970s. Francophone Melanesians also belonged to the union, which militated in favor of multi-ethnic and gradual independence. It gave birth to the *Union de Communautés des Nouvelles-Hébrides,* the foundation of the moderate alliance parties.

4 From a letter to the French Resident Commissioner written by Fornelli after his arrest (FDA).

5 The Church also condemned the French nuclear program in the Pacific.

6 He was the other "white king" on the island (a term coined by journalists from Australia and New Zealand).

7 The John Frum who lived in Ipeukel still refused schooling for their children. They wanted an American school or possibly a French school with an American teacher. As they were told that it was not easy to find one among the corps of French educators, they said they wished for a teacher from Quebec.

8 Since there was no registry office, the setting up of electoral rolls gave rise to numerous fraud allegations.

9 On this topic, see Hours 1974.

10 Letter dated 11 November 1976. Like all letters sent by the new generation of *kastom* supporters, it was written in Bislama. I translated it into French, as well as the other documents mentioned later (FDA). [As shown here, all these documents were translated from the French.—Trans.]

11 The White Sands–based Presbyterian missionaries were New Zealanders. The Tannese believed that New Zealand was the country most in favor of the Vanua'aku Pati's action.

17 *The Revolt*

"Hit them now, now . . ." (see note 27).

1 As mentioned previously, Isakwan is "Isaac the First," one of John Frum's "sons" born during the repression in the 1940s.

2 Tom Kasso, a teacher within the French education system, had the title of *délégué de la Coutume 'kastom* delegate'. The representative of the French resident commissioner in Tanna was called a *délégué* 'district agent'.

3 Niluan, *yani niko* 'voice of the canoe', holds Loanatom land in the name of the Koyometa Naporio group, a group exterminated by Numurkuen Ipai resi-

dents in the course of nineteenth-century warfare. Today, this land is at the core of a very serious land tenure and territory-related problem, which pits Niluan against all his neighbors.

4 The "magicians" who stated they had confessed under coercion went back to their village when the political situation changed.

5 Letter translated from the French.—Trans.

6 The votes cast for the Vanua'aku Pati amounted to 62.3 percent of the total, versus 37.7 percent for the moderates.

7 In 1978, the archipelago's various moderate political groups set up the Tan Union 'Union of the land', which later became the Federal party.

8 Tan Union representatives were Alexis Yolou for the John Frum and Charley Nako for the Kapiel, which stood for the *kastom* people of Middle Bush.

9 The Kastom movement joined the alliance of moderate parties in 1979. Headed by Tuk Nao, chief of Yapilmai, the movement included John Frum supporters and pagans from the southern part of the island.

10 Roger Payen.

11 Here the authors allude to the Regional Council that was to be set up on the island; the Vanua'aku Pati had obtained the majority of seats, again thanks to a few extra votes in its favor. The moderates believed that the elections had been rigged and demanded that they be repeated.

12 Corsica is an obvious reference to Fornelli.

13 The Condominium was set up in 1906. Here it is made to begin in 1910, the year when the first district agent, Wilkes, reached the island.

14 The participants spoke in Bislama. The translation is my own.

15 An allusion to the famous £100 fine that all John Frum still remember.

16 The rumor in Ipeukel was that John Frum himself would return to Tanna at the time of independence, in 1980.

17 This theme recurs in the speeches by *kastom* partisans: "After independence, we shall once again be what we used to be, unless our French ally agrees to help us, but this is not an obligation for that ally or for us."

18 The Vanua'aku Pati slogan. *Seli Hoo* is the call of Pentecost Islanders when they steer a canoe.

19 The last sentence means that French aid should not wander into the government camp but should, first and foremost, support the camp of *kastom*. More generally still, Thomas N. means that the French should help *kastom* partisans obtain their independence.

20 The parable is drawn from the John Frum's understanding of the Bible. The lion, an animal from the outside world, represents the Presbyterians who are devouring the children of *kastom*. Someone will kill the lion and become Tanna's king. He will then marry the daughter of the queen, in other words, the daughter of *kastom*.

21 Jean-Jacques Robert was the last French resident commissioner in the New Hebrides.

22 Andrew Stuart was Robert's colleague and the last British resident commissioner in the New Hebrides.

23 To offset the departure of the district agent, the French Resident Com-

missioner offered a Japanese "land cruiser" to the John Frum of Ipeukel. They turned down the offer, stating that they would rather see the district agent stay.

24 *Kastom* supporters had returned the key to Robert.

25 The Tan Union had become the Federal party. Its platform called for a broad decentralization of powers and for internal autonomy in each major island of the group.

26 This type of public prayer takes place on dancing grounds at kava-drinking time and is addressed to ancestors.

27 The Bislama word *kilim* has several meanings: to strike, hit, beat up, stop. *Kilim i tet finis* means to kill (Guy 1974).

28 In other words, "they have gone mad."

29 When Alexis died, his fourth child had just been born and his wife was still in the British hospital in Lenakel.

18 *The Meaning of Tanna's* Kastom

Mehl's statement originally appeared in his *"Raison, mythe et histoire"* in *Le Monde non-chrétien* (1948) and is quoted by Servier (1978, 14).

1 Thalweg: a line following the lowest part of a valley.—Trans.

2 "The indefinable grandeur of beginnings."

3 These principles may be modified in practice. "Drifting men" may settle in another place or hold a specific status in the name of another—provided the "real men" of that place or status find the shift advantageous or at least do not object to it.

4 Created with help from French District Agent André Pouillet, the GAM (Agriculture and Vegetable Production Group) was unquestionably a success from an economic and social viewpoint. Middle Bush residents farmed several hectares of common agricultural land; teams cultivated the land in turn. The sale of potatoes, in particular, brought some prosperity to Middle Bush.

5 On one occasion, Bob Paul and the French *gendarme* Willy Urben almost came to blows on the slopes of the volcano. Tourists who wanted to go up were stoned, and their Melanesian drivers punched. There were also numerous pitched battles between the villages closest to the volcano, Ipeukel and Yaneumwakel.

6 In French *pré carré* means both the bastion-like core of a territory and a battlefield.—Trans.

7 Here the author also suggested *libertaire,* which does not have the same connotation as the word *libertarian* in the United States. In France a *libertaire* opposes the social order and is situated to the left of the political spectrum.—Trans.

8 Kasso meant that the people of the Vanua'aku Pati had never tried to discuss matters with them or even met them, but that they had simply come to Tanna to dominate *kastom* partisans.

19 *Conclusion*

1 *"Par le haut, par en haut. Tous filent par en haut, comme nous, en plaine. . . . L'étouffement total. Autant habiter le très haut. . . . Planer vers le vertical reste la seule direction possible."*

2 They are also *lieux du coeur,* defined by a sense of space that is subjective and non-Cartesian. For more about these "heartfelt places," see Bonnemaison (1989).—Trans.

3 French geographer Augustin Berque coined the term *mésologie* or milieu to define the link between society on the one hand and space and nature on the other. Milieu represents a combination of places and areas both natural and culture-bound, collective and individual, subjective and objective, physical and phenomenological, material and ideological. *Médiance* is that which gives meaning to milieu in a descriptive and prescriptive sense (Berque 1986, 162).

Glossary

ika ussim	sacred area; stones with multiple powers
kapiel	sacred stone; Middle Bush political party (1978–1980)
kapiel assim	sacred place; stone with specific power
karipen	road of the great canoes
Koyometa	moiety; Numurkuen's rival
kweriya	hawk; emblem of the *yremera* aristocracy
kwoteren	Tanna's coastal road
nahwuto	companies
nakamal	dancing place and meeting place for kava drinkers
naotupunus	female and food stones; by extension, agrarian magicians who own these stones
napang niel	literally, the "*niel*'s hole," the one who takes precedence over others when given a *niel;* closest political ally along the road of alliance, a second self from whom one can request everything
nepro	Tanna's society of the origins
nepuk	banyan tree
nekowiar	exchange ritual in second society
niel	food exchange ritual; pile of gifts offered in the course of exchange rituals; ally with whom one exchanges presents and whom one calls upon to obtain a spouse; actual or potential brother-in-law
niko	canoe; group
nikokaplalao	road that encircles the island
noanuotuan	offshore road at reef's edge

347

numapten   the land's house (metaphor for Tanna)

Numurkuen   moiety; Koyometa's rival

Shipimanwawa last great war on Tanna; pitted *manshipi* 'merchant ship' against *manwawa* 'man-of-war'

stamba   place of the origins in Bislama (from the English "stump")

suatu   roads

tut   ritual belt

yani niko   voices of the canoe; male stones; masters of the canoe's land; speak and act in the names of the *yremera* lords; keeping in the back of the canoe, the *yani niko* steers it

yao   sea turtle

yarimus   spirit

yatamassim   taboo man; magician of a group

yremera   local aristocracy carrying the *kweriya* feather; customary nobility with precedence over the "voices of the canoe"; keeping at the front of the canoe, the *yremera* is the canoe's living emblem

References

Adams, Ron
1984 *In the Land of Strangers: A Century of European Contact with Tanna, 1774–1874.* Pacific History Monograph 9. Canberra: Australian National University Press.
1986 Indentured Labour and the Development of Plantations in Vanuatu 1867–1922. *Journal de la Société des Océanistes* 82–83: 41–63.

Armstrong, E. S.
1900 *The History of the Melanesian Mission.* London: Isbister.

Aubert de la Rüe, Edgar
1938 Sur la nature et l'origine probable des pierres portées en pendentifs dans l'île de Tanna. *L'Anthropologie* 48:249–260.

Bandler, Faith
1977 *Wacvie.* Brisbane: Rigby.

Barrow, George
1951 The Story of Jonfrum. *Corona* 3(10):379–382.

Bastin, Ronald
1981 Economic Enterprise in a Tannese Village. In *Vanuatu: Politics, Economics and Rituals in Island Melanesia,* edited by M. Allen, 337–355. Studies in Anthropology. Sydney: Academic Press.

Beaglehole, John C.
1968 *The Exploration of the Pacific.* 3d ed. Stanford: Stanford University Press.

Beaglehole, John C., ed
1961 *The Journals of Captain James Cook on His Voyages of Discovery,* vol. 2: *The Voyage of the Resolution and Adventure 1772–1775.* Hakluyt Society Extra Series no. 35. Cambridge: Cambridge University Press.

Bedford, Richard
1973 *New Hebridean Mobility: A Study of Circular Migration.* Human Geography Department Publication 9. Canberra: Australian National University.

Benoist, Hubert
1972 *Le Condominium des Nouvelles-Hébrides et la société mélanésienne.*
Paris: Pedone.
Berque, Augustin
1986 *Le sauvage et l'artifice: Les Japonais devant la nature.* Paris: Gallimard.
BN, *British Newsletter,*
1955–1973 Vila: Information Department, British Residency.
Bonnemaison, Joël
1986a *Les fondements d'une identité. Territoire, histoire et société dans
l'archipel de Vanuatu (Mélanésie),* vol. 1: *L'arbre et la pirogue.* Travaux et
Documents 201. Paris: ORSTOM.
1986b Passions et misères d'une société coloniale: Les plantations au Vanuatu
entre 1920 et 1980. *Journal de la Société des Océanistes* 82–83:65–84.
Special issue on plantations in the Pacific Islands.
1987 *Les fondements d'une identité* . . . , vol. 2: *Tanna: Les hommes lieux.*
1989 L'espace réticulé: Commentaires sur l'idéologie géographique. In *Tropi-
ques. Lieux et liens: Florilège offert à Paul Pelissier et Gilles Sautter,* edited
by B. Antheaume et al, 500–510. Paris: ORSTOM.
1991a Le développement est un exotisme. *Ethnies (Survival International)* 13:
12–17. Issue on *"La fiction et la feinte, développement et peuples autochtones."*
1991b Magic Gardens in Tanna. *Pacific Studies* 14 (4): 71–89.
Bougainville, Louis-Antoine de
1966 *Voyage autour du monde par la frégate La Boudeuse et la flûte L'Etoile.*
Paris: Les libraires associés, Club des Libraires de France et Union Générale
d'Editions. Reprint of first edition, 1771.
Bouge, Georges
1906 *Les Nouvelles-Hébrides de 1606 à 1906.* Paris: Augustin Challamel,
Librairie maritime et coloniale.
Bourret, Dominique
1982 *Les raisons du corps: Eléments de la médecine traditionnelle autochtone
en Nouvelle-Calédonie.* Cahiers ORSTOM, série Sciences Humaines 18 (4):
487–508. Paris: ORSTOM.
BRA, British Residency Archives
1940–1956 John Frum: Diary of Events.
BRF, *Bulletin d'Information de la Résidence de France aux Nouvelles-Hébrides*
1962–1975 Monthly. Vila: Service d'Information.
Brunet, Auguste
1908 *Le régime international des Nouvelles-Hébrides.* Paris: Augustin Challamel.
Brunton, Ron
1981 The Origins of the John Frum Movement: A Sociological Explanation.
In *Vanuatu: Politics, Economics and Rituals in Island Melanesia,* edited by
M. Allen, 357–377. Studies in Anthropology. Sydney: Academic Press.
1989 *The Abandoned Narcotic: Kava and Cultural Instability in Melanesia.*
Cambridge Studies in Social Anthropology 69. Cambridge: Cambridge University Press.

Cabalion, Pierre

   1984a Les noms des plantes en bichlamar: Origines, formations et déterminations botaniques. *Journal de la Société des Océanistes* 40 (78): 107–120.

   1984b Médecine traditionnelle et soins de santé primaire: Association ou développement séparé. Paper presented at Segundo Congresso Internacional de Medicina Tradicional y Folklorica, Mexico.

Calvert, Ken

   1978 Cargo Cult Mentality and Development in the New Hebrides Today. In *Paradise Postponed: Essays on Research and Development in the South Pacific,* edited by A. Mamak and G. McCall, 209–224. Sydney: Pergamon Press.

Chapman, Murray, and R. Mansell Prothero, eds

   1985 *Circulation in Population Movement: Substance and Concepts from the Melanesian Case.* London: Routledge & Kegan Paul.

Charpentier, Jean-Michel

   1979 *Le pidgin bislama et le multilinguisme aux Nouvelles-Hébrides.* Paris: Société d'études linguistiques et anthropologiques de France (CNRS).

   1982a *Atlas linguistique du Sud-Malakula.* Paris: Société d'études linguistiques et anthropologiques de France (CNRS)/ACCT. 2 vols.

   1982b La francophonie en Mélanésie: Extension et avenir. *Anthropologie et Sociétés* 6 (2): 107–126. Quebec: Laval University.

CMA, Catholic Mission Archives, Vila.

Codrington, R. H.

   1891 *The Melanesians: Studies in Their Anthropology and Folk-lore.* Oxford: Oxford University Press. Reprinted 1972 (New York: Dover Publications).

Crowley, Frank

   1980 *Colonial Australia: A Documentary History of Australia.* Sydney: Nelson.

Davillé, Ernest

   1895 *La colonisation française aux Nouvelles-Hébrides.* Paris: Librairie africaine et coloniale.

Daws, Gavan

   1980 *A Dream of Islands: Voyages of Self-Discovery in the South Seas.* Sydney: Jacaranda Press.

Deacon, Arthur B.

   1934 *Malekula: A Vanishing People in the New Hebrides.* London: Routledge & Kegan Paul. Reprinted 1970 (Oosterhout NB, The Netherlands: Anthropological Publications).

Deschanel, Pierre

   1888 *Les intérêts français dans le Pacifique.* Paris: Berger Levrault.

Descola, Jean

   1954 *Les Conquistadors.* Paris: Fayard.

de Tolna, Festetics

   1903 *Chez les cannibales: Huit ans de croisière dans l'Océan Pacifique.* Paris: Plon.

Docker, E.-W.

   1970 *The Blackbirders: The Recruiting of South Seas Labour for Queensland 1863–1907.* Sydney: Angus & Robertson.

DOM-TOM, Ministry of Overseas Departments and Territories, Paris.

Douceré, Victor
1934 *La mission catholique aux Nouvelles-Hébrides, d'après des documents écrits et les vieux souvenirs de l'auteur.* Paris: E. Vitte.

Dumézil, Georges
1975 Foreword. In *Traité d'histoire des religions,* by M. Eliade, 3–8. Paris: Payot.

Dunmore, John
1978 *Les explorateurs français dans le Pacifique.* Pape'ete, Tahiti: Les Editions du Pacifique. Translation by G. Pisier of *French Explorers in the Pacific,* vol. 1: *The Eighteenth Century.* Oxford: Oxford University Press, 1965.

Eliade, Mircea
1969 *Le mythe de l'éternel retour. Archétypes et répétitions.* Rev. ed. Paris: Gallimard.
1972 *Religions australiennes.* Paris: Payot.

FDA, French District Agency
1940–1980 Archives. Originally in Tanna, now in Aix-en-Provence, France.

Fletcher, Robert J. [Asterisk, pseud.]
1986 *Isles of Illusion: Letters from the South Seas,* edited by Bohun Lynch. London: Century. Reprint of first edition (1923, Constable).

Forster, Georg
1777 *A Voyage Round the World in His Britannic Majesty's Sloop, Resolution, Commanded by Capt. James Cook, During the Years 1772, 1773, 1774, and 1775.* 2 vols. London: B. White, Robson, Elmsly, Robinson.

FSSC, France, Sous-Secrétariat aux Colonies
1889 *Les colonies françaises: Les Nouvelles-Hébrides.* Paris: Ministère des Affaires Etrangères.

FRA, French Residency Archives
?–1980 Vila, now in Aix-en-Provence, France.

Geslin, Yves
1948 La colonisation française aux Nouvelles-Hébrides. *Cahiers d'Outre-Mer* 1 (3): 245–274.

Girard, René
1978 *Des choses cachées depuis la fondation du monde.* Paris: Grasset.

Grignon-Dumoulin, Pierre
1928 *Le Condominium et la mise en valeur des Nouvelles-Hébrides.* Paris: Presses Universitaires de France.

Guiart, Jean
1956a Culture Contact and the "John Frum" Movement on Tanna, New Hebrides. *Southwestern Journal of Anthropology* 12:105–116.
1956b *Un siècle et demi de contacts culturels à Tanna (Nouvelles-Hébrides).* Publications de la Société des Océanistes 5. Paris: Musée de l'Homme.
1986 La conquête et le déclin: Les plantations, cadre des relations sociales et économiques au Vanuatu. *Journal de la Société des Océanistes* 82–83:7–40.

Gusdorf, Georges
1984 *Mythe et métaphysique: Introduction à la philosophie.* Paris: Flammarion. Reprint of 1953 edition.

Guy, Jacques
1974 *Bichelamar Handbook*. Pacific Linguistics 34. Canberra: Australian National University.

Hagen, A.
1893 Voyage aux Nouvelles-Hébrides et aux îles Salomon. *Le Tour du Monde* (Paris) 22:337–384.

Harrisson, Tom
1937 *Savage Civilization*. London: Victor Gollancz.

Higginson, John
1926 *Le Mémoire de John Higginson: Les Nouvelles-Hébrides*. Coutances, France: Dr Auvray.

Hilder, Bernard
1976 The Voyage of Torres. MA thesis, Macquarie University, Sydney.

Hours, Bernard
1974 *Un mouvement politico-religieux néo-hébridais: Le Nagriamel*. Cahiers ORSTOM, série Sciences Humaines 2 (3–4): 227–242. Paris: ORSTOM.

Howe, K. R.
1984 *Where the Waves Fall: A New South Sea Islands History from First Settlement to Colonial Rule*. Sydney: George Allen & Unwin; Pacific Islands Monograph Series no. 2, Honolulu: University of Hawaii Press.

Imhaus, E. N.
1890 *Les Nouvelles-Hébrides*. Paris: Berger-Levrault.

JM, *Jeune Mélanésie*
1980 Newsletter, three times a month, 12 April to September. Vila.

JNCA, Joint Naval Commission Archives
1887–1906 Vila, now in Aix-en-Provence.

Jolly, Margaret
1982 Birds and Banyans of South Pentecost: *Kastom* in Anti-colonial Struggle. *Mankind* 13 (4, special issue): 338–356.

Keesing, Roger, and Robert Tonkinson, eds
1982 *Reinventing Traditional Culture: The Politics of* Kastom *in Island Melanesia*. *Mankind* 13 (4, special issue).

Kelly, Celsus, trans & ed
1966 *La Austrialia del Espíritu Santo: Documents on the Voyages of Quiros to the South Sea, 1605–1606*, vol. 1. Cambridge: Cambridge University Press.

Lambotin, Joseph
1891 Letter from Port Sandwich [1888?]. *Annales des missions de l'Océanie* (Lyon) 8:64–80.

Lebot, Vincent, and Pierre Cabalion
1986 *Les kava de Vanuatu*. Travaux et Documents 205. Paris: ORSTOM.

Lévi-Strauss, Claude
1966 *The Savage Mind*. Chicago: University of Chicago Press. Translation of *La Pensée sauvage* (Paris: Plon, 1962).

Lindstrom, Lamont
1980 Spitting on Tanna. *Oceania* 3:228–234.
1982 *Leftamap Kastom:* The Political History of Tradition on Tanna (Vanuatu). *Mankind* 13 (4, special issue): 316–329.

1987 Drunkenness and Gender on Tanna, Vanuatu. In *Drugs in Western Pacific Societies: Relation of Substance,* edited by L. Lindstrom, 98–118. Monograph 11, Association for Social Anthropology in Oceania. Lanham, MD: University Press of America.

1990 *Knowledge and Power in a South Pacific Society.* Smithsonian Series in Ethnographic Inquiry. Washington, DC: Smithsonian Institution Press.

Lini, Father Walter

1980 *Beyond Pandemonium: From the New Hebrides to Vanuatu.* Suva: University of the South Pacific.

LNH, Le Néo-Hébridais: Journal Français Indépendant, Politique, Agricole et Commercial

1909–1942 Vila, monthly; frequency varied.

LTO, Land Tenure Office

var. Archives, Vila.

Lynch, John

1977 *Lenakel Dictionary.* Pacific Linguistics 55. Canberra: Australian National University.

1978 Olgeta Langwis Blong Saot. In *Man, Langwis Mo Kastom Long Niu Hebrides,* edited by Ron Brunton et al, 55–60. Development Studies Center. Canberra: Australian National University.

McArthur, Norma, and John Yaxley

1967 *Condominium of the New Hebrides: Report on the First Population Census.* Port Vila: Government Printer.

MacClancy, Jeremy

1980 *To Kill a Bird with Two Stones.* Port Vila: Cultural Centre.

1983 Vanuatu and Kastom: A Study of Cultural Symbols in the Inception of a National State in the South Pacific. PhD dissertation, Department of Anthropology, Oxford University.

McKay, Graeme

1981 Bulletin de presse (Press Report). Mimeograph.

Markham, Albert

1873 *The Cruise of the Rosario.* London: Sampson Low.

Markham, Clement

1904 *The Voyages of Pedro Fernandez de Quiros.* Series 2, vols 14 and 15. London: Hakluyt Society.

MMA, Melanesian Mission Archives

var. Correspondence, diaries, and other writings. Honiara, Solomon Islands (on loan from Bernard Vienne).

Michel, Emile

1948 La tentative de colonisation belge aux Nouvelles-Hébrides et aux îles Fidji et Salomon (Mission Michel-Eloin, 1861). *Bulletin des Séances* 1:138–157. Brussels: Institut royal colonial belge.

Miller, Graham

n.d. *Live: A History of Church Planting in the New Hebrides.* Sydney: Presbyterian Church.

Miller, R.

1975 *Misi Gete: John Geddie, Pioneer Missionary to the New Hebrides.* Launceston: Presbyterian Church of Tasmania.

Molisa, Grace, et al
1982 Vanuatu: Overcoming Pandemonium. In *Politics in Melanesia,* edited by Peter Larmour, 84–114. Suva and Vila: University of the South Pacific.

Monnier, Paul
n.d.*a* Cent ans de mission: L'église catholique au Vanuatu. Histoire de l'église catholique dans l'île de Tanna, Vanuatu. Mimeograph. Marist Mission, Vila.
n.d.*b* One Hundred Years of Mission: The Catholic Church in the New Hebrides–Vanuatu 1887–1987. Translation of Cent ans de mission: L'église catholique au Vanuatu 1887–1987. Mimeograph. Marist Mission, Vila.

Morrell, W. P.
1966 *Britain in the Pacific Islands.* 2d ed. Oxford: Oxford University Press.

Nabanga
1975– Weekly, in French and Bislama, with occasional English. Vila: French Residency.

NHBR, *New Hebrides Biennial Report*
1949–50 to 1971–72 London: HMSO.

NHCE, New Hebrides Commission of Enquiry
1979 Report. Mimeograph.

O'Reilly, Patrick
1949 Prophétisme aux Nouvelles-Hébrides: Le mouvement John Frum à Tanna 1940–1947. *Le Monde non-chrétien* (Paris) 10:192–208.
1957 *Hébridais.* Publication 6. Paris: Société des Océanistes.

Parnaby, Owen
1972 The Labour Trade. In *Man in the Pacific,* edited by R. G. Ward, 124–144. London: Oxford University Press.

Parsonson, G. S.
1956 La mission presbytérienne des Nouvelles-Hébrides: Son histoire et son rôle politique et social. *Journal de la Société des Océanistes* 12:107–138.

Philibert, Jean-Marc
1976 La bonne vie: Le rêve et la réalité. PhD dissertation, University of British Columbia, Vancouver.
1981 Living under Two Flags: Selective Modernization in Erakor Village, Efate. In *Vanuatu: Politics, Economics and Rituals in Island Melanesia,* edited by M. Allen, 315–336. Studies in Anthropology. Sydney: Academic Press.
1982 Vers une symbolique de la modernisation au Vanuatu. *Anthropologie et Sociétés* 6 (1): 69–98. Quebec: Laval University.

Picanon, Ernest
1902 Rapport de tournées aux Nouvelles-Hébrides. FRA, Vila.

PIM, Pacific Islands Monthly
1930– Sydney: Pacific Publications (to July 1988). Currently, Suva: Fiji Times.

Rallu, Jean-Louis
1991 *Les populations océaniennes aux 19e et 20e siècles.* Paris: INED & PUF.

Regenwanu, Sethy
1981 *The Land in Vanuatu: Twenty Ting Ting Long Taem Long Independens.* Suva & Vila: University of the South Pacific.

Rentoul, Alexander
1949 "John Frum: Origin of New Hebrides Movement." *Pacific Islands Monthly* 19 (6):31.
RMO, Revue des Missions d'Océanie, Paris.
Rodman, Margaret
1981 Customary Illusions: Land and Copra in Vanuatu. PhD dissertation, McMaster University, Hamilton, Ontario.
1984 Masters of Tradition: Customary Land Tenure and New Forms of Social Inequality in a Vanuatu Peasantry. *American Ethnologist* 11 (1): 61–80.
Rodman, William
1973 Men of Influence, Men of Rank: Leadership and the Graded Society on Aoba. PhD dissertation, University of Chicago.
Russier, Henri
1905 *Le partage de l'Océanie.* Paris: Vuibert & Nony.
Sautter, Gilles
1979 Le paysage comme connivence. *Hérodote* 16:40–67.
Scarr, Deryck
1967 *Fragments of Empire: A History of the Western Pacific High Commission, 1877–1914.* Canberra: Australian National University Press.
Serres, Michel
1983 *Détachements.* Paris: Flammarion.
Servier, Jean
1978 Signification du mythe dans les civilisations traditionnelles. *Problème du mythe et de son interprétation.* Actes du Colloque de Chantilly. Les Belles Lettres. Paris: Jean Hani.
sfnh, Société Française des Nouvelles-Hébrides
var. Archives, Vila. Now in Aix-en-Provence.
Shineberg, Dorothy
1967 *They Came for Sandalwood: A Study of the Sandalwood Trade in the Southwest Pacific, 1830–1865.* Melbourne: Melbourne University Press.
Sope, Barak
1974 *Land and Politics in the New Hebrides.* Suva: South Pacific Sciences Association.
Spate, O. H. K.
1979 *The Spanish Lake.* Canberra: Australian National University Press.
Speiser, Felix
1913 *Two Years with the Natives of the South Pacific.* London: Mills & Boon.
Tam-Tam
1980–1984 Monthly, Vila.
Thompson, Gabrielle
1981 Natives and Settlers on the New Hebrides Frontier 1870–1900. *Pacific Studies* 1:1–18.
Thurston, J. B.
1957 Carnets de voyage. *Journal de la Société des Océanistes* 13:69–90.

Tonkinson, Robert
  1968 Maat Village, Efate: A Relocated Community in the New Hebrides. PhD
    dissertation, Department of Anthropology, University of Oregon, Eugene.
  1982*a* *Kastom* in Melanesia: Introduction. *Mankind* 13 (4, special issue):
    302–305.
  1982*b* National Identity and the Problem of *Kastom* in Vanuatu. *Mankind* 13
    (4, special issue): 306–315.
Tostain, Maurice, trans.
  n.d. Récit par Gaspar Gabriel de Leza . . . 1606; requête no 8 du capitaine
    . . . Quiros . . . ; copie de quelques avis . . . 1609 par . . . Quiros. Partial
    translation of: *Historia del Descubrimiento de los Regiones Austriales*,
    edited by Don Justo Zaragoza, Madrid: Biblioteca Hispano-Ultramarino,
    1880. Translated from Spanish to French. Mimeograph.
Tournier, Michel
  1979 Entretien avec D. Bougnaux et A. Clavel. *Silex* (Grenoble) 14:12–16.
    Special issue about islands.
Tryon, Darrell
  1976 *New Hebrides Languages: An Internal Classification*. Pacific Linguistics
    series C, no. 50. Canberra: Australian National University.
  1987 *Bislama: An Introduction to the National Language of Vanuatu*. Pacific
    Linguistics series D, no. 72. Canberra: Australian National University.
Tuan, Yi-Fu
  1989 *Morality and Imagination: Paradoxes of Progress*. Madison: University
    of Wisconsin Press.
Van Trease, Howard
  1984 The History of Land Alienation. In *Land Tenure in Vanuatu*, edited by
    Peter Larmour, 17–30. Suva: University of the South Pacific.
Vienne, Bernard
  1984 *Gens de Mota Lava*. Paris: ORSTOM & Société des Océanistes.
Vo V, *Voice of Vanuatu*
  1980–1983 Weekly, Vila. (Began as *Voice of New Hebrides*, 1979–1980.)
V V, *Vanua'aku Viewpoints*
  1977– Monthly, Vila. (Began as *New Hebridean Viewpoints*, 1971 to March
    1977.)
Walter, Annie
  In press Prestige et savoirs des femmes: Un aspect de la médecine populaire à
    Vanuatu. Paris: ORSTOM [1993]. (Doctoral dissertation, Université de droit,
    d'économie et des sciences d'Aix-Marseille.)
Ward, R. Gerard
  1972 The Pacific Bêche-de-mer Trade with Special Reference to Fiji. In *Man
    in the Pacific Islands*, edited by R. G. Ward, 91–123. Oxford: Oxford Uni-
    versity Press.
Watt, Agnes
  1896 *Twenty-five Years' Mission Life on Tanna, New Hebrides*. London:
    J. Paisley & R. Parlane.
Wawn, William
  1973 *The South Sea Islanders and the Queensland Labour Trade*. Edited by

Peter Corris. Pacific History Series. Canberra: Australian National University Press; Honolulu: University of Hawaii Press.

Weightman, Barry
1989 *Agriculture in Vanuatu: A Historical Review.* Portsmouth, UK: British Friends of Vanuatu.

Wilkinson, Julia
1979 A Study of a Political and Religious Division on Tanna. PhD dissertation, Department of Anthropology, Cambridge University.

Worsley, Peter
1968 *The Trumpet Shall Sound.* 2d augmented ed. New York: Schocken Books.

Selected Works by
Joël Bonnemaison

1974 Espaces et paysages agraires dans le nord des Nouvelles-Hébrides: L'exemple des îles d'Aoba et de Maewo. *Journal de la Société des Océanistes* 44: 163–232, 45:259–281.

1976a Circular Migration and Wild Migration in the New Hebrides. *South Pacific Bulletin* 26 (4): 7–13.

1976b *Tsarahonenana: Des riziculteurs de montagne dans l'Ankaratra (Madagascar).* Atlas des structures agraires à Madagascar, no. 2. Paris: ORSTOM.

1977a The Impact of Population Patterns and Cash Cropping in Urban Migrations in the New Hebrides. *Pacific Viewpoint* 18 (2): 119–132.

1977b *Système de migration et croissance urbaine à Port-Vila et Luganville (Nouvelles-Hébrides).* Travaux et Documents 60. Paris: ORSTOM.

1978 Custom and Money: Integration or Breakdown in Melanesian Systems of Production. In *The Adaptation of Traditional Agriculture: Socio-Economic Problems of Urbanization,* edited by E. K. Fisk, 25–45. Development Studies Centre Monograph 11. Canberra: Australian National University.

1980 Moving Food in Rural Areas: A Case Study of Central Pentecost. In *New Hebridean Systems of Food Distribution,* edited by R. G. Ward, T. McGee, and D. Drakakis-Smith, 150–178. Development Studies Centre Monograph 25. Canberra: Australian National University.

1981 Voyage autour du territoire. *L'Espace Géographique* 10 (4): 249–262. Special issue on cultural geography.

1984 Social and Cultural Aspects of Land Tenure. In *Land Tenure in Vanuatu,* edited by Peter Larmour, 1–5. Suva: University of the South Pacific.

1985a Territorial Control and Mobility within Vanuatu Societies. In *Circulation in Population Movement: Substance and Concepts from the Melanesian Case,* edited by Murray Chapman and R. Mansell Prothero, 57–79. London: Routledge & Kegan Paul.

1985b The Tree and the Canoe: Roots and Mobility in Vanuatu Societies. *Pacific Viewpoint* 25 (2): 117–151. Reprinted in *Pacific Viewpoint* 26 (1, 1986): 30–62, special issue: *Mobility and Identity in the Island Pacific,* edited by Murray Chapman.

1985*c* Un certain refus de l'Etat: Autopsie d'une tentative de sécession en Mélanésie. *International Political Science Review* (Los Angeles) 6 (2): 230–247.

1985*d* Vanuatu: La Coutume et l'indépendance. *Hérodote* 37–38: 145–161.

1986*a* A propos de l'affaire Greenpeace. Là-bas, à l'ouest de l'Occident: L'Australie et la Nouvelle-Zélande. *Hérodote* 40:126–139.

1986*b* *La dernière île.* Paris: Arléa/ORSTOM.

1991*a* Le taro-roi: Une horticulture d'abondance dans l'archipel du Vanuatu (Mélanésie). In *Aspects du monde tropical et asiatique,* collective work, 305–315. Paris: Presses de la Sorbonne.

1991*b* Vivre dans l'île: Une approche de l'îléité océanienne. *L'Espace Géographique* 2:119–125.

1992 Le territoire enchanté: Croyances et territorialités en Mélanésie. *Géographie et Cultures* 3:71–88.

With B. Antheaume
  1988 *Atlas des Iles et Etats du Pacifique Sud.* Montpellier: GIP Reclus & Paris: Publisud.

With B. Hermann
  1980 *Vanuatu.* 2d ed. Noumea: Les Editions du Pacifique. First published as *Les Nouvelles-Hébrides,* 1975.

With J. H. Powell
  1988 L'expérience de la frontière: La nature et la société en Australie. In *L'Australie 88: bi-centenaire ou naissance,* edited by G. Ordonnaud et A. Syriex, 25–50. Paris: France-Empire.

Index